The Arms Trade and Europe

CHATHAM HOUSE PAPERS

An International Security Programme Publication
Programme Director: Professor Sir Laurence Martin

The Royal Institute of International Affairs, at Chatham House in London, has provided an impartial forum for discussion and debate on current international issues for 75 years. Its resident research fellows, specialized information resources, and range of publications, conferences, and meetings span the fields of international politics, economics, and security. The Institute is independent of government.

Chatham House Papers are short monographs on current policy problems which have been commissioned by the RIIA. In preparing the papers, authors are advised by a study group of experts convened by the RIIA, and publication of a paper indicates that the Institute regards it as an authoritative contribution to the public debate. The Institute does not, however, hold opinions of its own; the views expressed in this publication are the responsibility of the author.

CHATHAM HOUSE PAPERS

The Arms Trade and Europe

Paul Cornish

THE ROYAL INSTITUTE
OF INTERNATIONAL
AFFAIRS

Pinter
A Cassell Imprint
Wellington House, 125 Strand, London WC2R 0BB, United Kingdom

First published in 1995

© Royal Institute of International Affairs, 1995

British Library Cataloguing in Publication Data
A CIP catalogue record for this book is available from the British Library

ISBN 1-85567-285-5 (Paperback)
     1-85567-284-7 (Hardback)

Typeset by Koinonia Limited
Printed and bound in Great Britain by
Biddles Limited, Guildford and King's Lynn

Contents

Acknowledgments

I am grateful to colleagues at Chatham House for their guidance and help in the course of my research, in particular Professor Sir Laurence Martin, Professor Jack Spence and Professor Trevor Taylor. The Chatham House study group which followed this project from its inception was a vital source of criticism, ideas and information. I am grateful to all who attended the meetings, or who provided comments in writing, for giving so generously of their time and energy. I should also like to thank those politicians and officials in Britain, Europe and the Far East who agreed to be interviewed. My participation in the Cameron Commission of Inquiry in Cape Town in June 1995 was an unexpected opportunity to review some of the issues which I address here, in a particularly open and refreshing environment, and I am grateful to the Commissioners and their staff. My collaborator in this project has been Dr Joachim Krause of the Deutsche Gesellschaft für Auswärtige Politik in Bonn, and I am grateful to him and the DGAP for their congenial and constructive approach to the project. Without the efforts of Dr Peter van Ham and the Western European Union Institute for Security Studies, the conference which was held in Paris towards the end of this project would not have been the success it was. In Chatham House, Margaret May, Emma Matanle, Hannah Doe, Tom Lee and the staff of the library have all helped in the production and publication of this paper. Lastly, special thanks are due to the Volkswagen Stiftung for so generously supporting this project.

Plenty of thanks, but no blame; any errors of fact, logic or judgment are, of course, entirely my own.

September 1995   Paul Cornish

Abbreviations and acronyms

ACA	Agency for the Control of Armaments (WEU)
ACDA	Arms Control and Disarmament Agency (US)
AG	Australia Group
CAT	Conventional Arms Transfer
CBW	chemical, biological weapons
CCP	Common Commercial Policy (EC)
CFSP	Common Foreign and Security Policy
CoCom	Coordinating Committee for Multilateral Export Controls
CRL	Common Reference List
CSCE	Conference on Security and Cooperation in Europe
EC/U	European Community/Union
EDEM	European Defence Equipment Market
EEC	European Economic Community
EP	European Parliament
EPC	European Political Cooperation
EPCI	Enhanced Proliferation Control Initiative
FCO	Foreign and Commonwealth Office (UK)
GATT	General Agreement on Tariffs and Trade
GPS	global positioning satellite
IAEL	International Atomic Energy List (CoCom)
IEPG	Independent European Programme Group
IGC(PU)	Intergovernmental Conference (Political Union)
IIL	International Industrial List (CoCom)
IML	International Munitions List (CoCom)
MAP	Military Assistance Program
MBT	main battle tank
MTCR	Missile Technology Control Regime

NATO	North Atlantic Treaty Organization
NBC	nuclear, biological, chemical
NSG	Nuclear Suppliers Group
QMV	qualified majority voting
SEA	Single European Act
SEM	Single European Market
SIPRI	Stockholm International Peace Research Institute
TEU	Treaty on European Union ('Maastricht Treaty')
WEAG	Western European Armaments Group
WEU	Western European Union
WMD	weapons of mass destruction

For me there is only one true morality; but it might not fit you, as you do not manufacture aerial battleships. There is only one true morality for every man; but every man has not the same true morality.

ANDREW UNDERSHAFT, ARMS MANUFACTURER, IN ACT I OF G.B. SHAW'S *MAJOR BARBARA* (1906)

A Westerner who wants to grapple with this subject must try, for a few minutes, to slip out of his native Western skin and look at the encounter between the world and the West through the eyes of the great non-Western majority of mankind.

ARNOLD TOYNBEE, DIRECTOR OF STUDIES, CHATHAM HOUSE, BBC REITH LECTURES (1952)

If you have scruples, don't sell arms at all.

MAHATHIR MOHAMAD, PRIME MINISTER OF MALAYSIA (MARCH 1995)

Chapter 1

Introduction

This study addresses recent efforts by the member states of the European Union (EU) to devise common procedures by which to supervise and regulate their involvement in the international trade in weapons and related technology. The study is concerned with the trade in 'conventional' weapons and weapons platforms, such as armoured fighting vehicles, artillery, combat aircraft and warships, and associated technology. It does not examine the illegal or covert international trade in conventional and other weapons, nor does it address the proliferation of nuclear, biological and chemical weapons of mass destruction.

As the Cold War drew to a close from the mid-1980s, military spending around the world began to fall. Domestic arms markets contracted and the size of the global trade in weapons, military equipment and related technology began a steep decline. The international arms market not only shrank, but its character and dynamics also began to change dramatically. With mounting public pressure for a 'peace dividend', and the acceptance by governments that Cold War levels of military spending and deployment were no longer necessary or justifiable, the Cold War protagonists soon found themselves with large excesses in defence manufacturing capacity. Defence industries and governments identified a number of possible courses of action, including defence conversion, diversification out of defence manufacturing, industrial consolidation and restructuring within the defence sector, and weapons exports. Conversion of manufacturing plants from military to civilian production was widely discussed but was soon perceived to be something less than the cure-all for which many had hoped. In the West, the claims for defence conversion were met with a sceptical response, particularly from those governments which took a free-market approach to defence industrial restructuring after the Cold War. In the former Soviet Union and among its allies, it was realized that the only marketable, hard-currency-earning commodity was weapons – good, relatively cheap swords, rather than badly marketed, over-engineered ploughshares. Diversification, whereby defence industries, conglomerates and multinationals expand and acquire non-military sectors, met with a more favourable response in industry, especially in the West. But diversification proved to be difficult, and many firms found that expertise and knowledge accumulated in the defence sector did not travel well. The third option was received rather more favourably. A great deal of effort has been devoted to national and international restructuring and consolidation in the defence sector, and some firms have even shaken off non-military interests altogether.

In spite of narrowing prospects for overseas sales, the export option was also seized upon by the defence industry. At a time of global recession, governments, too, were interested in a course which could enable 'vital' or 'strategic' national industries to be sustained, unit production costs to be reduced and further research and development to be funded. The scene was thus set for a 'new age of export driven proliferation'.[1] With similar conclusions being reached throughout the defence manufacturing world, it appeared that the 'peaceful' post-Cold War world would have an arms market which, although considerably smaller, would in many respects be more diverse, vigorous and competitive than its Cold War predecessor. With huge excesses in supply combined with declining demand, it would also be a market in which much of the initiative had shifted to the buyer. As this shift took place, so the struggle for market share became increasingly competitive. Defence export decisions became ever more responsive to commercial considerations and contracts became increasingly complex, often involving the transfer of manufacturing plants, 'know-how' and key, sensitive technologies through offset and countertrade arrangements. The development of the buyer's market also inhibited efforts to control defence-related trade. At the national level, no matter how rigorous their export-control policies and practices, individual governments saw that the glut of old and new suppliers meant that any decision to deny a given export might simply result in the buyer going elsewhere; the complaint that 'if we don't export, others will' was heard increasingly. Competition for market share also diminished the chance for wider supply-side consensus on the control of exports of certain weapons or technologies to certain destinations, making multilateral supply-side regulation of the defence trade increasingly difficult.

The end of the Cold War not only saw the advantage, in market terms, passing to the buyer; it also saw the buyer becoming rather more self-assured. During the Cold War, non-aligned or Third World states felt themselves to be in a struggle to achieve the dignity and respect due to them as full members of the international system of states. Nowhere was the sense of dissatisfaction more plain than in the United Nations. As the membership of the UN expanded rapidly during the 1950s and 1960s, so discrepancies were perceived between the Charter's promises regarding the sovereign equality of states, and the *Realpolitik* of a world dominated by the superpower confrontation. But with the passing of the Cold War, the promises made in the UN Charter are now expected to be honoured. Aware of their increasing importance in the international economic system, Third World states have become far less willing to accept second-class status. For these states, the end of the Cold War is the triumph of nationhood and state sovereignty, and the end of the decades-long struggle for decolonization and full membership of the international system. Their sense of frustration has been apparent for many years, but what distinguishes the current mood is that many governments and leaders feel able to add substance to the rhetoric. Technological, economic and even military advantages are still enjoyed by the West/ North, and there is no doubt that these advantages confer a certain authority and bargaining strength over Third World customers. But as these states assume an increasingly important role in the global economy, the West's potential for 'leverage' is likely to become more limited.

With manufacturers anxious to sell, particularly in the 'boom' market of the Asia-Pacific region, and with an increasingly assertive and self-confident clientele, the international trade in conventional weapons and related technology is changing in two important ways. First, with so much more now being heard of a state's right, under Article 51 of the UN Charter, to defend itself and, by extension, to decide for itself what, and from whom, to buy in the arms market, the manufacture of weapons and the trade in them are increasingly seen in national terms. The ownership of modern conventional weapons, and the ability to manufacture them, are now widely held to be normal, inalienable and even essential attributes of a modern, sovereign nation-state. The international arms trade is best described and understood in 'systemic' terms, as an elaborate network of relationships between various national interest groups on the one hand, and internationally between suppliers and recipients on the other.[2] But what is becoming clear is that the dynamic behind the modern arms trade – and the main obstacle to its regulation – is the new, self-confident nationalism of the post-Cold War era. The second important feature of the contemporary arms trade is the absence of an internationally accepted, central organizing principle. Many of the conditions which underpinned the hegemonic arms trade relationships of the Cold War have now been undermined. It is no longer possible to describe the international arms trade primarily as an extension of East–West power politics, or even as the manifestation of the foreign policy of the world's weapon manufacturers and suppliers. But if it is clear that the trade is no longer organized along the relatively simple lines of Cold War power politics, it is much less obvious what, if anything, could provide a new organizational core. The international arms market is more commercially oriented than at any time during the Cold War, but it seems unlikely that the market alone will be able to provide the political and moral principles and procedures by which the trade should, arguably, be regulated. With the 'new world order' offering very little in the way of controlling mechanisms, even at the most basic level of Cold-War-style spheres of influence, something approaching political and economic free trade in arms may have arrived.

In August 1990 Iraq invaded Kuwait and the ostensibly revitalized UN and the 'international community' faced their first major challenge. Following Iraq's defeat, information about the ease with which Saddam Hussein had played the international arms market, and the embarrassing provenance of much of Iraq's weaponry, suggested to many that an unregulated or poorly regulated international arms market was not acceptable. A rush of declarations and initiatives then followed: the declarations of June 1991 and January 1992 by the Conference on Security and Cooperation in Europe (CSCE) and the subsequent publication in November 1993 of 'Principles and Guidelines governing Conventional Arms Transfers'; the Group of Seven's 'Declaration on Conventional Arms Transfers and NBC Non-Proliferation' in July 1991; the 'Guidelines for Conventional Arms Transfers' issued by the Permanent Five members of the Security Council in October 1991; and the UN's Conventional Arms Register launched in December 1991. By mid-1995, however, none of these initiatives had achieved much of note, if achievement is measured in terms of restraining the eagerness with which established arms suppliers exploit the international export market.

The member states of the European Union occupy a very large share of the international arms market. In 1993, according to the US Arms Control and Disarmament Agency, the fifteen states that are now members of the EU together exported conventional weapons and military equipment worth US$6,950 million – some 32 per cent of the world total.[3] Using different counting methods, the US Congressional Research Service described France as the leading weapons supplier to the developing world in 1994.[4] The governments concerned, and the institutions of the EU, have sought to bring a degree of organization to these activities. The object of this book is to describe EU involvement in various aspects of the international arms trade, and to assess the potential for a common EU system or code by which to manage that involvement. Is there anything about the politics, organization and structure of the EU which suggests that this important group of supplier states will succeed where others have so far been unable or unwilling to practise self-restraint?

One signal lesson of the Iraqi arms build-up was that the transfer of weapon manufacturing technology, and dual-use technology, can over time prove to be as significant as transfers of completed weapons. The modern 'arms' trade has to be understood as involving weapons of varying sophistication, tangible technology of both military and civil origin, and intangible 'know-how'. Yet the peculiarities of EU treaty law, and the preferences and prejudices of several member governments, require distinctions to be drawn between the transfer of completed weapons and military equipment on one hand, and manufacturing technology on the other. Accordingly, Chapter 2 reviews west European involvement in the arms trade and its regulation since 1945, leaving the trade in certain types of technology to be discussed in Chapter 3. The scene having been set, the next three chapters make a more analytical contribution. Chapter 4 examines the commercial and industrial obstacles to effective EU regulation. Turning to the politics of European integration, Chapter 5 assesses the scope for cooperation in foreign, security and defence policies in the EU, and gauges the likely effect on multilateral export regulation. Chapter 6 completes the discussion by looking outside the confines of the EU at the conceptual side of arms-trade regulation, and particularly at the problem of defining and sustaining a central, universal code of practice. Chapter 7 summarizes the discussion and offers some concluding comments.

Chapter 2

Weapons

Introduction

There could be no better site than western Europe for a laboratory dedicated to the research of the modern (post-1945) arms trade. Here, most aspects and functions of the arms trade have been experienced and discussed: import; research and development; sole, collaborative and licensed manufacture; export; and unilateral and multilateral export regulation and management. Conspicuously absent from the list is the use of weapons in a major international war in Europe. The Cold War confrontation did, nevertheless, make great enough demands on western Europe's defence industrial base. And although it proved unnecessary to test the products of Europe's defence industries on home territory, there have been many armed conflicts around the world since 1945 in which weapons of European origin have been used, by European and other forces. At the time of writing this study, events in former Yugoslavia also warn against any complacency in this regard. This chapter begins by explaining how west European states became involved in the import, manufacture and export of major conventional weapons after 1945. The second part of the chapter shows how, during the Cold War, these same states were drawn into various initiatives to regulate the trade in which they had developed such expertise. This chapter stops short of examining the effect on arms export regulation of the Maastricht Treaty and the Common Foreign and Security Policy, which are discussed in Chapter 5.

Import, manufacture and export of major weapons systems

Large-scale imports of arms into western Europe began during the Second World War. Under its March 1941 Lend-Lease Act the US government supplied great quantities of naval, military and air-force weapons and equipment to Britain to support the war against Germany. During its four-and-a-half years of operation the Lend-Lease scheme provided Britain with some $27 billion of military and other goods.[1] Lend-Lease came to an abrupt end in the summer of 1945, but it was not long before the exigencies of the emerging Cold War, combined with large surpluses of military equipment lying idle in the United States, led to the supply chains being restored. Shortly after the enunciation of the Truman Doctrine, in May 1947, the US Congress passed the Greek and Turkish Aid Act by which supplies of US weapons and equipment were passed to those two countries. The year 1949 saw the passage through Congress of the Mutual Defense Assistance Act, designed to assist the allies of the United States in the newly formed North Atlantic Treaty Organization (NATO).

The supply of US arms and equipment became a vital issue again after June 1950, following North Korea's invasion of the South. Convinced that the action in the Far East was the precursor to Soviet aggression in western Europe, a programme of rapid and comprehensive rearmament began, a great proportion of which involved assistance from the United States under the Military Assistance Program (MAP). MAP aid increased dramatically in the mid-1950s.[2] Although the Korean war ended in 1953, the quality and availability of US equipment were such that western Europe was to remain an important outlet for US arms for many years. The economic and industrial recovery of Europe meant that dependency on US arms and military equipment would not last for ever, yet it was not until the early 1970s that arms exports from 'NATO Europe' began to outstrip arms imports, the majority of which had come from the United States.[3]

The recovery and expansion of Europe's defence industries after the war were not uniform. In France, for example, it was not until the early 1960s that defence industries were able to enter the export market in a convincing way. The Italian and West German defence industries were both restricted by postwar controls, although in the Italian case these were largely removed by about 1951.[4] The Italian industry then expanded rapidly, while remaining closely connected to US defence development and production. West Germany remained under close military occupation until the late 1940s. Key issues such as West German rearmament and the reconstruction of the defence industry were not, however, resolved until October 1954 with the signature of the Modified Brussels Treaty. Protocols III and IV to the Modified Treaty placed quantitative and qualitative restrictions on German arms production, and created a regime under which any agreed production could be closely supervised. Among the many weapons listed were weapons of mass destruction (WMD), artillery, tanks, missiles, warships and military aircraft. By 1984 the controls on the production of conventional weapons had been abolished, although prohibitions on the development of WMD were maintained.[5] The British defence industry had survived the war well, and emerged in a strong position to claim a sizeable market share. With clients in the Middle East, Africa, South and Southeast Asia, Britain enjoyed a prominent role in the world arms market. But British success was not to continue unchallenged for long: 'During the fifties, Britain accounted for 21 per cent of total major weapon exports to developing countries. During the sixties, this share had fallen to 11 per cent.'[6]

The rapid growth of defence industries throughout western Europe also persuaded the United States to seek more sophisticated relationships with European partners. As 'buying off the shelf' from the United States was viewed ever less favourably, it had to turn to licensed production agreements, with the attendant transfer of technology. Aircraft such as the F-104 *Starfighter*, the *Hawk* and the *Bullpup*, and the *Sidewinder* missile are all examples of early agreements for the licensed production of sophisticated military equipment.[7] All this meant that from the 1960s onwards, a 'second tier'[8] of west European manufacturers was able to compete increasingly effectively in the world market. These manufacturers were often somewhat less concerned about East–West politics than the United States, but nevertheless generally remained within the broad parameters of Cold War politics.[9] During the late 1960s the leading west European arms exporters (France, the Federal Republic of Germany, Italy, the Netherlands and the UK) secured approximately 10 per cent of the global conventional arms market.[10] In the early 1970s, the picture was complicated by OPEC oil-price rises and the huge demand for weapons in the Middle East. By now the global arms market was also seeing the 'indigenization' of weapons production and export among previous re-cipients such as Israel, India, Brazil and South Africa, largely as a result of licensed production and other offset arrangements. Nevertheless, the same west European exporters took an increasing share of the growing world arms market. From less than 8 per cent in 1971, the European share had almost doubled by 1975 and subsequently rose to over one-quarter of the world total by 1980.[11] By the early 1980s arms exports had become a vital source of income for Europe's defence industries, with some 70 per cent of Italian conventional arms production being exported, 50 per cent for France, 42 per cent for the UK and 20 per cent for the FRG.[12] In some cases, these exports were to prove controversial; between 1987 and the imposition of the arms embargo in 1991, France alone supplied over 16 per cent of Iraq's weapons imports.[13]

Regulation of arms exports during the Cold War

The period between 1945 and the end of the Cold War not only saw European defence industries achieve and maintain a convincing role in world arms trade, it also saw European governments follow a 'trend towards government control of arms exports' which had been developing in the interwar years.[14] In the 1990s it may seem axiomatic that governments should wish to supervise and regulate the arms trade, and in historical terms it has been the norm for governments to do so.[15] Europe has, however, dallied with *laissez-faire* approaches to the arms trade, particularly in the late nineteenth century and in the years before the First World War,[16] and there are still occasional voices arguing that the arms trade is like any other commercial sector and should therefore not be subject to peculiar intervention by governments. Regulatory efforts were both formal and informal, ranging from arms trade embargoes to transparency initiatives. Activity also took place on many levels, from the UN down to *ad hoc* cooperation among governments. At the bottom of this pyramid of activity is the development of humble national export controls, without which, arguably, none of the larger multilateral initiatives could have been attempted.

Unilateral arms export controls
Several European governments, such as those of France, Italy and Britain, had begun to develop formal national export control systems during the 1930s. The concept of national control was therefore well established by the time the war ended in 1945 and other west European governments began to introduce their own systems. These national systems often shared certain features, including some or all of the following:

- a list of weapons and goods, the export of which required a special licence;
- a list of 'target' countries, either proscribed or preferred;
- a list of criteria or standards against which applications to export might be judged;

9

- a licence-application procedure and a bureaucracy to enable interdepartmental consultation;
- a method by which licence grants and denials could be verified and policed nationally, a customs service at frontiers and ports, and a set of penalties and the means to impose them;
- a method to guarantee the 'end-use', or non-re-export of the licensed and exported consignment to a destination which would otherwise not have been licensed.

There were, however, important differences across the range of national systems, reflecting different legal and constitutional practices and foreign policy expectations. The pursuit of rigorous national export control policies was sometimes more declaratory than real, particularly among governments which promoted arms exports through special governmental offices and provided 'soft loans' and export credit guarantees. Differences in the scope and quality of national export controls became firmly established; in 1991 the European Commission carried out a survey of national export control systems throughout the EC and discovered that, more than four decades after the supposed renaissance of west European export controls, systems were far from uniform and in some cases standards were extremely low.[17] In spite of the development of elaborate national systems, and in spite of the growing public debate, the export of arms from western Europe since 1945 has been characterized less by restraint than by commercial opportunity-seeking – an observation which begs obvious questions about the sincerity and/or effectiveness of arms export control systems. In some cases, national controls have been simply inadequate for the task. In most other cases, the system has been framed in such a way as to leave the government concerned with the maximum flexibility and the minimum of binding, legislative commitment. The current policy of the British government, for example, is to judge export applications 'on a case by case basis in the light of established criteria'.[18] The FRG, often cited as having the most restrictive approach to arms exports, recently relaxed its rules for weapons exports in order to 'fall in line with emerging European standards for arms exports'.[19]

International regulation

What can be said of national export controls is that they made it possible for west European governments to participate in some sort of structured, multilateral approach to arms trade control. The most obvious structure lay in the Cold War itself. Although west Europeans are often accused of having had the most pragmatic and commercially oriented approach to arms trading during the Cold War, from the point in the 1960s when European defence industries began to take a global market share through to the end of the Cold War, western arms export practices generally corresponded to the bipolar division of the world. West European arms producers and exporters also subscribed to the Coordinating Committee for Multilateral Export Controls (CoCom). CoCom was established in 1949 as a semi-formal, non-treaty embargo-type arrangement to prevent the export of key technologies and weapons to the Soviet Union and the communist bloc.

But it was not only the Cold War which drove efforts to structure and regulate the postwar international arms trade. European governments participated in mandatory and voluntary UN arms embargoes, such as those against South Africa in the 1960s and 1970s. Several European governments were also involved in early attempts by the UN to bring about an international arms-transfer registration system, an idea which was more or less achieved in December 1991 with the establishment of the UN Conventional Arms Register. European governments also helped to devise normative codes of practice for arms exports. The first attempt, the Tripartite Declaration of May 1950, grew out of concerns about a possible arms race in the Palestine area following the 1947–9 war. Britain, France and the United States agreed to provide Israel and the Arab states with only those arms necessary for internal security, for 'legitimate self-defence' and for the 'defence of the area as a whole'. The declaration was worded against the 'aggressive' use of imported weapons and against the use of such weapons to alter territorial boundaries.[20] If any one of the three parties objected to a given arms order then the order would not be met. The declaration resulted in the establishment of the Near East Arms Coordinating Committee which proved to be 'quite effective in controlling the transfer of arms until 1955 when the Soviet Union negotiated the Czech arms deal with Egypt'.[21]

A rather less positive contribution was made by European states to the US-Soviet Conventional Arms Transfer (CAT) talks held in 1977–8. The CAT talks began as an attempt by the Carter administration to expand upon the strict arms-transfer policies which had been developed in Presidential Directive 13 (PD13) of 17 May 1977. PD13 proposed an imaginative set of ideas and criteria to which US arms export decisions should conform, but it also called for the definition of 'norms of supplier restraint' – the bedrock of what promised to be a sophisticated, effective, multilateral regime aimed at control of the global arms trade by the main suppliers acting in conjunction with the recipients. The talks collapsed in December 1978, partly as a result of disagreements within the Carter administration over the broad character of the initiative, and partly because of superpower sensitivity regarding certain key regions. But west European governments also had some responsibility for the failure. Although the prime aim of the talks was to reach agreement between the United States and the Soviet Union, if the resulting vacuums in the arms trade were not simply to be filled by avaricious Europeans, it made sense to include Europe's arms exporters in the process. The reactions of European governments, when asked whether they could support the US-Soviet initiative, ranged from deep scepticism to inertia; Europe would not join the initiative until it was clear that the Soviet Union was willing to be involved. To some extent, this reflected reasonable caution on the part of the Europeans, whose defence industries would be disproportionately affected by any multilateral restraint agreement.[22] European motives may, however, have been more machiavellian; by directing the United States at the highest fence first, the idea may have been to bring the whole enterprise crashing down.[23] Whatever the real motives of the Europeans, the talks collapsed and the initiative, denied the broad support it needed, became no more than a bilateral arrangement doomed to failure; 'it was a mistake to concentrate so heavily on bilateral talks with the Soviet Union, without a greater involvement on the part of West European suppliers'.[24]

West European regulation

While broader international schemes were being discussed, west European governments were also examining the prospects for more local export-control collaboration. With differing standards and systems of national export controls across western Europe, any multilateral export-control initiative by these countries was bound to encounter difficulties from the outset. Nevertheless, several attempts have been made to set up a multilateral arms export control system within western Europe, with four institutions playing a leading role: the Western European Union (WEU), the European Parliament, the European Commission and the European Political Cooperation process (EPC). At the simplest level, some degree of information exchange and transparency, and even commonality in arms export control policies, was considered essential if the WEU's arms stockpile management schemes were to be achieved. It was also thought necessary to create a general sense of confidence in the efficacy of national and international arms embargoes, confidence which would be eroded if European neighbours simply overlooked or were unable to enforce the embargo. Since the 1960s concern had been mounting over the effect of arms exports on the stability of Third World recipients and on the growth of Third World debt, and so it was also thought prudent to ensure that self-denial would not simply open a market opportunity for a less scrupulous European competitor. More recently, there have been calls for tighter, even supranational, west European arms export control policies. The Single European Market with its customs-free trading area prompted demands for a common policy on exports within the EC, and a Community-wide policy on exports of arms outside it.

West European embargoes were imposed against Argentina following the invasion of the Falkland Islands in 1982, against Israel after the invasion of Lebanon in 1982, and against Syria in 1986, after allegations that Syria had been involved in attempting to place explosives on board an Israeli passenger aircraft at a London airport. Europeans have also participated in *ad hoc* multilateral embargoes with non-European partners, such as that imposed by Italy, Belgium, the Netherlands and the United States during the 1967–70 Nigerian civil war. There have also been attempts to make European arms export policies more anticipatory or normative, as in the Modified Brussels Treaty of 1955. The Treaty tried to go far beyond the mere restriction of German arms manufacturing and exports. Protocol IV established the Agency [of the WEU] for the Control of Armaments (ACA). The role of the ACA was not only to police the restrictions on manufacturing set out in Protocol III, but also to control the stocks of key armaments held by each WEU signatory. In order to make the control of such stocks 'effective', it was made clear that the ACA would require control over the production and import of weapons in Europe. Although the activities of the ACA were to be 'confined to the mainland of Europe', and although it was never intended that it should become a central export regulatory body, the preoccupation with stocks of armaments meant that there would have to be some intrusion into member states' export activities, as Article XXII of Protocol IV made clear:

> Each member of the [WEU] shall keep the Agency informed of the quantities of armaments of the types mentioned in Annex IV to Protocol No. III, which are to be exported from its territory on the mainland of Europe. The Agency shall be entitled to satisfy itself that the armaments concerned are in fact exported. If the level of stocks of any item subject to control appears abnormal, the Agency shall further be entitled to enquire into the orders for export.[25]

Although the ACA developed into an elaborate reporting and verification system, the effect on national arms export policies was negligible and it never approximated to a central arms export decision-making body for western Europe. By the mid-1980s the ACA had become more an advisory than a regulatory body.

The ACA initiative did, however, set the scene for a subsequent, rather more ambitious WEU initiative. With growing concern over destabilizing arms sales to the Third World, and with the West seen in some quarters to be capitalizing on the tensions emerging from the process of decolonization, in December 1969 the WEU Committee on Defence Questions and Armaments adopted a draft proposal on the regulation and supervision of the international arms trade.[26] The proposal discussed several ways in which WEU member states could make their arms export decisions more responsible and become involved in international efforts to control the arms trade. Under the WEU initiative, states manufacturing 'major armaments', such as aircraft, missiles, tanks, warships, heavy artillery and radar, would be enjoined not to export such weapons if such exports were judged 'likely to increase the risk of war in any region of the world'. The initiative was, however, inherently discriminatory, in that it did not address the arms traffic 'within the great military alliances'. Although the proposal was adopted by the WEU Assembly, the WEU Council – representing WEU governments – was far less enthusiastic. Providing a foretaste of the European position during the CAT talks of the 1970s, the Council argued that the arrangement could work only with 'the active support of all major supplying countries', and that the views of the recipients would be 'a key factor'.[27] In 1978 another WEU study, the Dankert *Report on Arms Procurement*, claimed that arms exports to the Third World would not be necessary if a fully integrated, self-sustaining European defence market could be created. The Dankert Report thus pointed to a key influence on European defence industries after 1945: the reluctance of governments to surrender their independence in matters of defence and the defence industry. This view, symbolized by governments' continued attachment to Article 223 of the 1958 Treaty of Rome, is discussed more fully below.

The issue of common European defence manufacturing and procurement also brought another parliamentary assembly into the debating arena, but with barely more convincing results. The European Parliament (EP) took an approach similar to the argument for defence industrial rationalization which had already been made by the WEU.[28] The EP argued that a more efficient European market would not only save money and contribute to the European share of the NATO burden, but would also reduce the pressure on European manufacturers to export arms. The EP's first major attempt to address arms sales policies came in 1983 with the Fergusson Report of the Political Affairs Committee.[29] Like the 1978 WEU study, the Fergusson Report looked at the creation of a common European defence market and manufacturing base. But the report also addressed the issue of arms exports more directly. The report noted that although any 'international system of guidelines' on arms exports would need the support of the United States and the Soviet Union, efforts by the EC would nevertheless be an 'important step'. It recommended a return to the CAT talks of the 1970s, with European participation, and supplier/ recipient talks in 'precarious' regions. The report called upon governments to 'establish rules governing the export of arms from Member States to third countries', called for restrictions on the export of certain types of weapons (to be specified), and recommended a continual review process.[30]

Commenting on the Fergusson Report, the EP Committee on External and Economic Affairs went further and called for a 'European Convention against arms exports' which would have to be developed under the auspices of the intergovernmental EPC process, noting that 'it is scarcely conceivable that the Community could be given responsibility for matters relating to arms exports, which are closely linked with the foreign policies of individual countries, until a common foreign policy has been formulated'.[31] The Committee proposed an export control system based on an exclusive 'standard list' of preferred countries, and a 'European arms exports control agency which would supply information on arms exports'.[32] The Committee made three recommendations to the EP. The first of these, the rather anodyne recommendation that arms exports to the Third World be reduced, was carried in plenary. The EP did not, however, support the second and third recommendations: that an EC policy on arms exports should be adopted and that a European arms exports control agency should be established. Issues such as these were debated heatedly at Strasbourg, with a vigour which reflected a basic lack of consensus among European governments, resulting in 'little subsequent implementation'.[33]

In 1986, with the passage of the Single European Act (SEA), it appeared that the major obstruction noted in the Fergusson Report was weakening. The main purpose of the SEA was, in the words of Article 8A of the EEC Treaty, to programme the development of 'an internal market comprising an area without internal frontiers in which the free movement of goods, persons, services and capital is ensured'. The removal of intra-EC customs barriers would have an immediate effect on national arms export controls. It was also realized that the Single European Market (SEM) could have a more general effect on the defence industry, particularly if national practices in the defence sector threatened to undermine the overall aim of common industrial policies and practices. However, while the timetable for the SEM was new, the underlying principles were familiar; arguments for extending Community competence into defence manufacturing and procurement had been made in the late 1970s and early 1980s, when the Fergusson Report was being prepared.[34] The distinguishing feature of the SEA, as far as arms export policies were concerned, was that it seemed to offer greater integration in foreign and security policies, the absence of which had been noted as a major drawback by the Fergusson Report. This inspired the EP's next major review of the arms trade. In February 1987 the Political Affairs Committee commissioned another study which was eventually tabled at the EP on 22 February 1989 as the Ford Report.[35]

The Ford Report argued that the SEM would provide 'an opportunity to move towards common weapons procurement and to reduce the dependence of Community manufacturers on the export trade'.[36] An efficient and 'effective' common European defence market would enable manufacturers to amortize research and development costs and achieve economies of scale without exporting weapons: 'the rationalisation of the European armaments sector by means of armaments cooperation will reduce the necessity to export arms'.[37] But the report recognized that there could be no certainty that a more efficient European defence sector would lose its interest in arms exports, particularly since the Independent European Programme Group (IEPG) clearly viewed increased efficiency as the precursor to more successful export bids.[38] In order to prevent a more efficient European industry simply competing for a larger share of the world market, and in order to hedge against the use of other arguments – such as defence-industry unemployment – to justify arms exports, the report saw that a political consensus would be required. The newly institutionalized EPC seemed to offer the opportunity to achieve just such a consensus. The report claimed that the SEA 'prevent[ed] member states from taking any action which would endanger the security of the countries of the [EC]' and inferred that since arms exports 'could endanger European security' they could 'legitimately be regulated by the Community'.[39] The report called for a 'common arms sales policy' to be developed through EPC based on the following principles:

- the security interests of the [EC];
- the state of democracy of a potential recipient country;
- its real need and the potential purpose of the purchase of armaments;
- its respect of human and civil rights;
- its ability to pay without damaging the internal economy too much;
- the need to limit countertrade because of its distorting effect on world trade.[40]

But the stumbling block was the question of how any Community competence in defence-related matters could be allocated and controlled. The report called on the Commission to 'clarify the interpretation of Article 223 of the Treaty of Rome and Title III of the Single Act as regards the development of a Common Arms Market in Europe'.[41]

Since the 1958 Treaty of Rome (EEC), the pursuit of integrated policies in arms manufacturing, procurement and export has been impeded by the reluctance of the main European arms producers to accept a central EC role in matters of defence. The 'high politics' of national security were the special preserve of sovereign national governments and were not to be subsumed into any civil commercial and industrial integration taking place in the 'common market'. NATO was the central defence alliance and any collaboration in the European context was to take place within the limited, intergovernmental confines of EPC. Since the SEA implicitly denied the possibility of collaboration in the 'military' aspects of security, the point at issue was whether European defence industrial policy and procurement, and by extension certain aspects of arms exports, could come under the rubric 'political and economic'. By allowing member states to derogate from EC competition rules on the grounds of national security, Article 223 has been a major obstacle in the way of the extension of Community competence into defence-related areas: 'The Single Market notwithstanding, as long as Article 223 ... remains unchanged, the EC Commission cannot hope to gain full control over the European arms market.'[42] Article 223 reads as follows:

1. The provisions of this Treaty shall not preclude the application of the following rules:
   (a) No Member State shall be obliged to supply information the disclosure of which it considers contrary to the essential interests of its security;
   (b) Any Member State may take such measures as it considers

necessary for the protection of the essential interests of its security which are connected with the production of or trade in arms, munitions and war material; such measures shall not adversely affect the conditions of competition in the common market regarding products which are not intended for specifically military purposes.

2. During the first year after the entry into force of this Treaty, the Council shall, acting unanimously, draw up a list of products to which the provisions of paragraph 1(b) shall apply.

3. The Council may, acting unanimously on a proposal from the Commission, make changes in this list.

In a sense, therefore, the Ford Report issued a challenge to the Commission and member governments to clarify precisely where EC supranational authority ended and national sovereignty began. Previously, the Commission had 'tended to hold back' on questions related to arms exports.[43] But in March 1989, possibly emboldened by the recent publication of the Ford Report, the new Internal Market Commissioner, Martin Bangemann, called for a Commission role in directing not just arms production, but also trade, indicating a shift in the terms of debate.[44] The Commission has continued to argue against the segregation of the defence sector and has been especially keen to see the suppression, or at least restrictive application, of Article 223. The development of the dual-use technology export regulation, a good example of a clash between cautious governments and an ambitious Commission, is discussed in Chapter 3, while Chapter 5 reviews the current controversy surrounding the extension of Community competence into defence-related areas.

Europe after the Cold War

From autumn 1989, the context in which thinking about European defence industry and arms exports had so far taken place did not so much alter as disappear. The ending of the Cold War set the agenda for change. But it was the Gulf War of 1990–91 which prompted the members of the EC to seek new ways to control arms transfers. Some of Iraq's major arms suppliers were EC members, and in some cases European troops in the US-led coalition faced Iraqis wielding high-specification weaponry which had been exported from Europe. After the war, as the UN organized a series of inspections of Iraqi weapons research and manufacturing facilities, it also became clear that several EC states had supplied, knowingly or otherwise, weapons-related technology to Iraq. The handling of the Iraq/Kuwait crisis was portrayed in some quarters as proof of the inadequacy of EC foreign policy cooperation in the more loosely ordered post-Cold War world. This perception contributed to the review of EC foreign and security policy-making which had been under way since December 1990 in the Intergovernmental Conference on Political Union (IGC[PU]). With Europe's defence industries increasingly reliant on weapons exports, with some sense of responsibility for having allowed Saddam Hussein to build up what the UN and others considered to be a 'destabilizing and excessive' collection of weapons and technology, and with calls to review and tighten foreign and security policy cooperation, the debate in western Europe developed rapidly.

The main participants in the EC debate remained the Commission, the Parliament and the member states through the EPC process. The Commission continued its campaign to scrap Article 223, particularly in the context of the dual-use regulation. The EP moved quickly to join and influence the debate. On the day the Berlin Wall was breached, 9 November 1989, the EP's Political Affairs Committee asked permission to report on the development of a European security policy. The report was drafted during 1990 and published in April 1991 as the *Report on the Outlook for a European Security Policy*, also known as the Poettering Report.[45] Noting that the SEA stipulated that the EP should be 'associated with the development of a common foreign and security policy', the Poettering Report addressed the European security debate in broad terms and advocated the introduction of an integrated CFSP which would improve upon and 'overcome' the 'intergovernmental character of EPC'.[46] As far as defence industrial cooperation and arms transfers were concerned, the report supported the immediate deletion of Article 223 from the EEC Treaty, called upon the Commission to consider creating a 'special independent agency', the purpose of which would be to 'monitor and control the production and sale of arms in the Member States, among themselves and to third countries',[47] and called for a 'common policy on controlling arms exports' encompassing 'common standards', 'effective monitoring' and 'reduced dependence on exports to third countries'.[48]

The outcome of the IGC(PU) fell somewhat short of the expectations of the Poettering Report, both generally and in terms of arms exports. Undeterred, the EP returned to the debate in September 1992 with a much firmer resolution on arms exports.[49] The EP threatened 'utmost disapproval if new arms markets are sought in Third World countries in order to offset arms cuts in Europe' and called for 'matters pertaining to armaments production and the arms trade' to be 'brought within the Community ambit in anticipation of European Union'. Reflecting a sentiment shared in some capitals, the resolution also argued that extension of the Community's competence in these fields would be 'the first plank in the Common Foreign Security Policy (CFSP)'. The resolution insisted that a 'strict common arms production policy' and a 'common market in arms' would 'help save costs and reduce arms exports to Third World countries'.[50] Arms exports should take account of the 'sufficiency principle': 'Member States should undertake coordinated steps with a view to cutting off supplies of war material to third countries whose military capability is sufficient for their own defence'.[51] The September 1992 resolution was particularly ambitious regarding arms transfer controls and the role of the EP in decision-making. Among informal official reactions to the resolution, the view that it was 'a good job we can afford to ignore the EP' was not untypical, and the impression given by newspaper headlines such as 'EC nations vote for controls on weapons exports' proved to be exaggerated.[52]

The main forum for action on conventional arms exports remained the EPC process, up to the entry into force of the Maastricht Treaty in 1993. Interest did not simply begin with the commencement of the IGC(PU) in December 1990, however. In the summer of 1989, a Political Committee working group was convened to examine the problems which the SEM might pose for national arms export controls. The Dutch floated the idea of using a Benelux-style system, where the original supplier's export policies and licences would be honoured throughout the Community. Little real progress was made, however, until spring 1991, following the expulsion of Iraqi forces from Kuwait.

In March 1991 the Political Committee agreed that another *ad hoc* group of experts should meet to consider coordination of national policies on conventional arms exports and definitions of arms embargoes. The first meeting of this new body – the Ad Hoc Working Group on Conventional Arms Exports – took place on 16 April 1991. The group's first tasks were to compare national positions and investigate the possibility of further action. Already, differences were emerging between those member states such as Britain and France which sought to limit the process to a comparison of national lists of controlled military goods, drawn up in addition to CoCom's munitions list, and those such as Germany which sought to integrate national policies, seeing such a process as a 'springboard' to an eventual CFSP. The first fruits of the comparison of national practices was the statement made in June 1991 after the Luxembourg European Council, listing seven criteria for conventional arms exports found to be common to the member states. These criteria, along with the eighth which was agreed at the Lisbon European Council twelve months later, are reproduced in the Appendix. At Luxembourg, rather than use the language of 'common policy' and integration, the Council was merely hopeful that a 'common approach' based on 'criteria of this nature' might lead to 'a harmonization of national policies'.[53] It was stressed at the time, and repeatedly since, that several governments did not consider the criteria to be the first steps towards a common policy on arms exports, nor was there a commitment that all criteria would be 'applied' in all cases.

Technical experts also met during summer 1991 to discuss a 'Common Reference List' (CRL) of weapons and military items, to the export or transfer of which the common criteria might be applied. Other meetings addressed arms embargo policies and practice, and a comparison was made of export licensing procedures to see where they could be aligned. The 'Review of Existing EC and UN Embargoes with a View to Joint Action on Implementation' was concluded on 8 July 1991 when the Political Committee endorsed the group's proposal for a four-level 'menu of options' for arms embargoes:

- Level 1: weapons designed to kill and their ammunition;
- Level 2: weapons platforms;
- Level 3: non-weapons platforms;
- Level 4: ancillary equipment.

Over the following months the *ad hoc* group worked on four main areas: comparison of the lists of goods to which partners applied their conventional arms export policies, and the development of the CRL; comparison of the employment of end-use certificates and non-re-exportation clauses; a survey of national procedures for the revocation of export licences; and a comparison of practices concerning commercial and industrial negotiations, the signature of conventional arms export contracts, and the control of production, storage and transport of conventional arms prior to their export. Fine-tuning has continued ever since. There was also, within the *ad hoc* group, some discussion about the effect of the SEM, in particular whether the internal market would result in less effective ex-Union export controls. But the problem was essentially procedural rather than legal or in terms of competence, since Article 223 was still very clearly in force. This seemed to be of particular concern in mid-December 1992, when the group agreed on a system of interim documentation to deal with intra-Union arms exports while a 'Standardised Accompanying Document' was being devised.

While the EPC was examining the coordination of conventional arms export policies, the IGC(PU) continued its work, culminating in the Treaty on European Union (TEU), or Maastricht Treaty, in December 1991. The TEU entered into force in November 1993 and the 'three-pillared' European Union came into being. The EPC process was replaced by the Common Foreign and Security Policy. CFSP remained, however, an intergovernmental affair, differing from EPC principally in the sense that foreign and security policy cooperation was given a more formal base in the Union Treaty, and in the sense that CFSP went beyond the 'political and economic' aspects of security policy claimed by the SEA to embrace 'all questions related to the security of the Union, including the eventual framing of a common defence policy, which might in time lead to a common defence'.[54] The continued preference for intergovernmentalism was seen both in the retention of Article 223 and in the carefully crafted CFSP voting process known as 'joint action'. CFSP, and the joint-action process, are examined in more detail in Chapter 5, but it is appropriate at this point to examine the manner in which arms exports came to be a candidate for the process, not least because the outcome may have been the result of bureaucratic confusion.

The TEU makes plain, in Article J.1.1, that CFSP is to cover 'all areas of foreign and security policy'. Although security policy logically embraces questions of defence policy and the creation of a 'common defence', an impression supported by the wording of Article J.4.1,[55] Article J.4.3 indicates that issues with 'defence implications' would not be appropriate for the closer forms of cooperation being made available under CFSP. In effect, CFSP and the joint-action process were to be confined to non-defence security issues and foreign policy issues, with the latter being thought to offer the best possibilities for developing more intimate intergovernmental cooperation through joint action. Ultimately, however, various *security* issues were listed as potential candidates for joint action, rather than 'softer' foreign policy-type issues. In the approach to the Maastricht European Council, governments had been attempting to draw up two lists, one of security issues which might be appropriate for CFSP, and another of foreign policy issues which might be suitable for joint action. In the end, the foreign policy issues were thought too sensitive for joint actions and were deleted. This left a list of security issues known as the 'Asolo List' which, although more sensitive than the foreign policy issues, were then listed as candidates for joint action.[56] The mistake was soon realized and resulted in the 'Declaration on Areas which could be the Subject of Joint Action' not being published with other Treaty documentation. Instead, governments were invited to spend more time discussing subjects for the joint-action process. In June 1992 the Lisbon European Council created an Ad Hoc Working Group on Security under the auspices of the Political Committee, with a mandate to prepare a report on possible areas for joint action for the Edinburgh European Council. The working group held its first meeting on 23 September 1992 in London during the UK Presidency and eventually forwarded its report to the Political Committee in Brussels at the beginning of December. The handling and publication of the report caused some disagreement. Those member states which had yet to ratify the Union Treaty were sensitive to anything which might interrupt ratification. Others were more aggressive and demanded that the report and its conclusions be published. In the end, after threats to leak the report to the media if it were not published, it was agreed to publish the report in full with the conclusions of the Edinburgh European Council, 7–8 December 1992. The Ad Hoc Group had examined the subject in three broad categories:

- 'Areas suitable for joint action by the Union as from the entry into force of the Union Treaty';
- 'Wider issues which the Union will need to address in the course of developing common policies in the security field';
- 'Adjustments to the structure of working groups under the Political Committee which will enable the work under [the two categories] above to be taken forward'.

The object of the report was to build upon the results of EPC and to develop those areas where member states were already working together. In an attempt to water down the commitment to use the joint-action process in security-related areas, the list of issues consisted 'largely of areas in which the Community and its member states are adopting a common approach, or which, based on the experience of [EPC], seem to have the potential for such action'. The report listed four sets of issues which might be suitable for joint action: the CSCE process, disarmament and arms control in Europe, non-proliferation of WMD and economic aspects of security. The CSCE process offered little scope for joint action on arms exports, except insofar as the CSCE's Forum for Security Cooperation was developing a position on conventional arms exports, to which the Union might contribute. The second and third areas offered no additional grounds for joint action on conventional arms exports, but under 'economic aspects of security' there were various transparency and cooperation measures which appeared to offer the possibility of tighter cooperation in matters related to arms exports.

Other than the continuing harmonization of national commodity lists, the development of a standardized accompanying document for intra-EU arms exports and the resolution of certain legal problems regarding the application of the four-level embargo, little further work has been done on the development of integrated arms export policies within the institutions of the EU. The eight criteria have not been adopted or implemented in any formal sense by the EU or the member governments. This is not surprising, given that the criteria were the result of a comparative rather than a policy-making exercise. There have, nevertheless, been two developments which will serve to conclude this chronology of west European involvement in the defence trade, and its regulation. Since late 1992, prompted by the Saferworld organization, the EP has been pressing for the implementation of a 'Code of Conduct' in conventional arms exports based on the eight criteria. A Saferworld report called for the EC to 'act quickly and achieve a high degree of harmonization', particularly in view of the imminence of the SEM. The report recommended that the eight criteria be applied on a sliding scale from the most serious level of an 'international crime of state', to a 'violation of international obligations', to situations where 'arms export restraints might be politically prudent or morally desirable, but where their adoption would clearly be in excess of what is demanded in international law'. In addition, Saferworld recommended a four-level categorization of arms destinations, with exports to those countries listed in 'Group 4' being 'completely banned'.[57]

As well as inspiring the UN General Assembly to call for a worldwide Code of Conduct, the report contributed to a revival of EP interest in arms exports. In January 1995 a 'Resolution on the Need for European Controls on the Export or Transfer of Arms' called for a 'coherent and comprehensive arms control policy on the Union level'. With the 1996 IGC on the horizon, the EP called for the new policy to be included in the CFSP and for Article 223 to be abolished. A 'European Agency for the control of arms exports' was to be investigated and member states were asked to work towards establishing an 'international code of conduct on the control of arms transfers and exports'.[58] A 'European Code of Conduct', based on work by Saferworld and endorsed by 40 European non-governmental organizations, was launched in Brussels on 11 May 1995 with the endorsement of the EP. Finally, the fact that on 1 January 1995 the European Union accepted three more members has also affected the terms of debate. The addition of Swedish, Finnish and Austrian arms exporters will result in no more than a negligible increase in the EU share of the world arms market. These countries may, however, make their presence felt more clearly in the political debate surrounding the development of common arms export policies. Although not regarded as having loose export policies, Sweden in particular is known to have a robust view of the place of defence industry in national security and would be reluctant to see the removal of Article 223.

Chapter 3

Technology

Introduction

National arms export control systems began to be developed during the 1930s, and many west European countries had some form of supervisory and regulatory mechanism in place by the end of the Second World War. Following the war, these relatively new ideas of export control were applied to technology as well as to weapons. The war had demonstrated on several occasions the strategic benefits to be gained from exploiting new technology, and the risks of allowing an adversary to gain the technological upper hand. Ever since a premium had been placed on straight branches of yew from which bows could be made, and for as long as armourers have had a marketable vocation, both the materials and the 'know-how' for weapon design and manufacture have been prized assets. But the Second World War also showed that strategic advantage was no longer solely a matter of bigger and better weapons. To be sure, Second World War technology had produced guided cruise and ballistic missiles and, of course, the atomic bomb. But radar surveillance and tracking, radio jamming, secure communications systems and rudimentary 'code-cracking' computers were all important examples of the strategic significance of 'harmless' technology. In addition to operations on land and sea, the Second World War also confirmed the strategic value of air power. And by the middle of the twentieth century, the strategic potential of outer space, the deepest oceans and the invisible electromagnetic spectrum were also being investigated. In all this, the microchip was to become for the Cold War what the machine-gun and tank had been for the trench warfare of 1914–18. A 'silent revolution' in warfare had begun, whereby 'superiority over the enemy' would be obtained 'by *qualitative* means'.[1]

With the concept of governmental export control but a few years old, the challenge of the postwar years was to control the traffic not just in weapons but also in related technology. In time, 'related technology' came to mean three different things: the technology used to make weapons; the technology used to make militarily useful equipment such as radars; and the technology which could have both military and innocent civilian applications and which became known as 'dual-use'. As the Cold War progressed, it was dual-use technology which was to cause the biggest political, organizational and commercial difficulties: 'One of the key features of machine tools is versatility. A lathe or a milling machine can be configured to produce parts for a car or a military personnel carrier, parts for a domestic appliance or a rifle ... any competent engineer could [make] the adjustments necessary to turn out military products.'[2]

This chapter is concerned with the development of technology export control systems by the members of the EU. As with the control of arms exports, the foundation of any multilateral technology export control initiative must be effective national instruments. The first part of this chapter therefore looks briefly at the character of national technology export control mechanisms and compares US and west European systems. For most of the period since 1945, most west European governments have practised multilateral export controls not through one of the institutions of the European Community/Union, but in CoCom, the origins, procedures and prospects of which are summarized in the second part of this chapter. The final part of the chapter turns to the development of the EU dual-use regulation.

National export controls

A number of surveys, commercial and academic, have been made of national export control systems, including those of established and new member states of the EU.[3] At an official level, the individual member states of the EU and the European Commission have all been involved in comparisons of national practices and in attempts to 'harmonize' those practices around a mutually acceptable character and standard of control. The various surveys show that all members of the EU now have an elaborate national control structure. In many cases, particularly rapid improvements have been made in the past four or five years, often in response to arms and technology trade scandals exposed during the 1980s. Allegations of improper behaviour by governments and individuals continued to be made into the 1990s, causing significant political instability for a number of EU governments. As a Commission survey made clear in 1991, complex multilateral export control regimes can only be as good as the national systems on which they depend.

The essential features of an export control system were summarized in Chapter 2: a list of controlled commodities; a list of proscribed (or preferred) destinations; a set of export criteria or guidelines; a licensing process and bureaucracy; an enforcement system; and, finally, some provision to prevent re-export or unauthorized 'end-use'. The surveys mentioned above show that the outlines of a common approach had already been adopted by EU members in all these key areas, some time before the formal implementation of the EU dual-use regulation on 1 July 1995. Most sets of national export criteria, for example, referred to the supplier's international obligations, including the enforcement of embargoes, the question of tension, conflict and even war in the country or region of destination, and the customer's record in terms of human rights. As far as controlling the export of weapon-related and dual-use sensitive technology was concerned, most national systems within the EU enforced the lists of technologies already agreed in the Nuclear Suppliers Group (NSG), the Australia Group (AG) and the Missile Technology Control Regime (MTCR). On the industrial dual-use side, most systems either replicated or followed closely the lists of goods set out in CoCom's Industrial List. But even decades of cooperation in CoCom failed to ensure complete uniformity, particularly in the important areas of implementation and enforcement.[4] Some EU members had a preferred country list, while others identified proscribed destinations. Some admitted to having a list of proscribed destinations, but refused to make the list public. Some included among their criteria the economic health of the client and its 'defensive sufficiency'. These proved, however, to be minor differences relative to the high degree of commonality which obtained, at least in organizational terms, and which made possible the development of the EU's multilateral technology export control initiative.

For the purposes of this study four features of European national export control systems, illustrated in the various surveys, merit particular attention. First, parliamentary involvement in export controls is very limited, where it exists at all. At most, national legislatures can expect notification of export decisions and deliveries after the event. In general, policies and decisions regarding sensitive exports remain the preserve of the executive branch of government. National executives may, with some reluctance, be willing to surrender certain of these functions to a central European organization, and may be willing to share their export decision-making process with other EU partners. But in the current climate it seems unlikely that involvement could be extended to the EU's own democratic organ – the European Parliament – when it has not yet been extended to national parliaments. The second feature is that the recently expanded EU now has four members (Austria, Finland, Ireland and Sweden) which have traditions of non-alignment during peace and neutrality during war. This could have two implications for the development of common European policies in defence-related manufacturing and export. Particularly in Austria and Sweden, the policies of non-alignment and neutrality have implied independence of foreign suppliers of defence equipment. This in turn has led to the development of strong national defence industries. With a national mind-set that supports the development and maintenance of a national defence sector, it might be expected that defence exports, without which any national defence industry would be in difficulties, would be viewed through the same prism. These same countries might also, for historical and cultural reasons, balk at attempts to ally European defence exports with common European foreign, security and, particularly, defence policies.

The third feature to note is the variation in attitudes to Article 223 of the 1958 EEC Treaty. Article 223 remains, for some, the final obstacle to full-scale EU cooperation in all matters relating to defence manufacturing and export, although some new member states such as Finland appear to have little interest in the fate of Article 223; Finland is, after all, a minor manufacturer and exporter of weaponry. Germany, a rather more significant exporter of military equipment and sensitive technology, favours the abandonment of Article 223 in favour of a fully harmonized, EU-wide 'single policy' in arms exports, one which would be less restrictive than current national policies. On the other hand, Britain and France, both large-scale exporters of defence-related equipment and weapons, would not be willing to abandon the protection, as they view it, which Article 223 offers against over-restrictive and intrusive central EU policies. To complicate the picture, Sweden – a significant exporter but with a tradition of neutrality – shares the British and French view that Article 223 should be retained, but only in order to prevent the EU applying common export control standards which could be lower than those currently applied by Sweden.

The final feature is the relationship between government and industry. Industry generally has little if any formal involvement in the development of national export control policies. In many EU member states, little effort is made to include industry even on an information-only basis, although some governments do go to great lengths to communicate policies and changes to industry. Some member states, though not all, require exporters to nominate a company board member or executive to administer export control compliance and to accept responsibility for breaches. Differences across the EU in the government/industry relationship can also be seen in the extent to which industry is expected to police itself. The 'catch-all' clause of the EU regulation is discussed more fully below; what might be said at this point is that the notion that industry can be made to have an open-ended responsibility for the failure of export controls can present legal and constitutional difficulties for several member states and may create legal conflicts within the EU. Britain and Germany, for example, both employ catch-all provisions, although the precise understanding and meaning of the expression differs in each case; in Germany, catch-all clauses come into effect if the exporter has 'positive knowledge' of intended misuse, but in Britain the catch-all or 'end-use' clause operates not only when an exporter 'knows', but also when he has 'grounds for suspecting' that a given export might be misused.[5] In the British official view, the exporter carries a high degree of responsibility:

> generally the initial responsibility for determining the need for a licence under the 'end-use' control will rest with you [the exporter]. You know the capabilities of your products, your customers and potential customers and the circumstances of any particular order far better than Government officials.[6]

The British approach does not, however, find unqualified support around the EU; an official of one of the newest member governments described the catch-all as 'totalitarian'.

Germany in fact operates two catch-all clauses; one relating to conventional weapons production and one to nuclear matters. Germany's policy is exceptional in that many other national catch-all clauses, as well as the appropriate clause of the EU regulation, refer only to weapons of mass destruction.[7] Although WMD non-proliferation is not covered in this study, the catch-all is relevant in that it represents an attempt to employ export control practices which originate in, and are appropriate for, the United States, but which are alien to government/industry relationships in Europe. The catch-all appeared in US legislation in December 1990 in the form of the 'Enhanced Proliferation Control Initiative' (EPCI). The EPCI imposed new licensing requirements in order to prevent the proliferation of chemical and biological weaponry and related technology and materials. The initiative stated that a licence would henceforth be required in a number of circumstances, including 'If a US person knows that a proposed export or other assistance is destined for CBW or missile activities in listed regions, countries, or projects.'[8] The EPCI is in keeping with a long tradition in the US of export controls, a tradition in which the executive branch of government has accrued immense, almost absolute authority to limit trade – both general and military-related – for reasons of national security or foreign policy, even to the extent of conducting general 'economic warfare'. The US International Traffic in Arms Regulations, for example, allow the Office of Defense Trade Controls of the State Department to suspend, revoke or deny any licence without prior notice. The general character of postwar US export controls dates from the 1949 Export Control Act, passed in the context of rapidly deteriorating East-West relations:

> Two important principles were embodied in the 1949 legislation and have survived virtually intact through multiple revisions. First, the executive branch was to enjoy broad authority to determine what products or technical data should be subject to export licensing, to administer the licensing system, and to impose penalties for violations. Second, the rule-making process, including the composition of the control list, was (and continues to be) largely exempt from the usual process of public comment and virtually immune from judicial review.[9]

Thus, the export from the United States of almost any good, from tanks to toys, along with the relevant hard, soft and intangible technology, requires official approval. For the vast majority of exports, the good concerned has no strategic value whatsoever. Nevertheless, the export has still to be approved, usually in the form of a licence which is termed 'open' or 'general', but which is no less a licence. Where the export of weapons or sensitive technology is concerned, even a relaxation of controls can be made only by issuing a new licence; when, in April 1994, the Clinton administration sought to allow US exporters to supply low-level dual-use technology to the former Soviet Union and the People's Republic of China, without first seeking government approval, the method chosen was to issue a new, general licence. At the time, this concession was described as a 'key change in US export licensing procedures',[10] but the incident also illustrates the importance placed in the United States on licensing and government control. Although the Clinton administration has sought to reduce the burden of individual licensing, especially with regard to civilian telecommunications equipment and certain computers, the US export control system is still largely 'commodity-based' rather than 'destination-based', and in these circumstances there remains a blanket presumption that exports should be regulated.[11] Tight government control of exports from the US means that trade restrictions and embargoes can be switched on and off rapidly and relatively simply and, as noted above, with little or no opportunity for redress offered to industry and the public. The EPCI catch-all, and the fact that US commodity control lists often contain a so-called 'bucket entry' designed to spread the coverage of the lists as widely as possible, are symptomatic of this culture of control. Exports from the United States are in effect a matter of privilege rather than right. In mid-1995 it was proposed that the US export control system be 'entirely reorganized and streamlined' and that licensing requirements be made much more specific.[12] One result of the proposed changes will be to make government-industry relationships more flexible and reasonable. But for the present, US government continues to err on the side of regulation. US industry therefore remains committed to defensive self-regulation and to understanding and complying with government thinking in order to avoid wasting time, effort and money.

In Europe, and in Japan, a different view prevails. Although commodity control lists appear to be very similar to those used in the United States, the underlying presumption in these countries is that export is a right. The right to export is not unlimited, but the burden lies on governments to identify and list sensitive commodities and destinations and it is only within these parameters that industry can be expected to act responsibly and conform. If a proposed export falls outside the listed prohibitions then the responsibility or otherwise of the exporter should not come into question, and the export should proceed. In Europe, the expectation is that export controls should be kept to the minimum necessary. If industry can be expected to be self-policing, in the sense of the catch-all idea, then the reasons for export prohibitions must be reasonable and clearly stated. If the reasons given are imprecise or open-ended, the right to export might be impinged upon unnecessarily and unfairly. The majority of exports from Europe take place without any form of licensing whatsoever, unlike in the United States. General and open licences are used in Europe, but only in order to moderate a licensing system which is regarded as exceptional, rather than as a means to extend nominal control over all exports, as in the United States. Arguably, the introduction into Europe of a tight, US-style regulatory system, along with the catch-all idea which readily follows from it, could help to improve national licensing systems and might then become the basis for a uniform, EU-wide system. But such a step would present fundamental constitutional challenges and would require significant change in the cultural and legal character of industry-government relations in western Europe. In any case, Europe would be importing a model of licensing which its origina-tor was in the process of revising or even abandoning.

Multilateral technology export controls: CoCom and its successor

Postwar attempts at multilateral export control began with the Coordinat-ing Committee for Multilateral Export Controls (CoCom). CoCom was founded in 1949, at the height of the Cold War. Britain and other western states saw that the export of machine tools and other technology to the Soviet Union, while it might be commercially beneficial, could have adverse strategic consequences.[13] CoCom was not a treaty-based ar-rangement, and its proceedings were not held in the public eye. The organization was based in the US Embassy in Paris, where regular meetings took place and where a permanent Coordinating Group carried out its work.

Sometimes described as the 'economic arm of NATO', CoCom's aim was to restrict the supply of key technology and commodities to Cold War adversaries. The Soviet Union and its satellites, China and other countries all appeared on a 'Country List' of proscribed destinations. In order to prevent diversion of key technology via third countries, CoCom partners also initiated a 'Third Country Cooperation Initiative'. The partners (NATO members less Iceland, plus Japan and, since 1989, Australia) agreed to national enforcement of agreed controls on goods and technologies contained in three commodity lists which were updated every four years. The 'International Munitions List' (IML) covered conventional arms, munitions and items which were unequivocally mili-tary, and subsequently formed the basis of the exclusions under Article 223 of the EEC Treaty. The 'International Atomic Energy List' (IAEL) dealt with technology needed for nuclear-weapon design and testing. Finally, the 'International Industrial List' (IIL) included items with dual civil/military use. The IIL covered a huge range of products and techno-logy, including advanced materials such as carbon fibre (which might be used in aircraft production), computer-controlled machine tools and the appropriate software, silicon-based micro-circuitry, high-grade digital and laser telecommunications equipment, optical and sensor systems, navigation technology and other types of marine equipment. From the point of view of Western national and multilateral control of technology transfers, the importance of CoCom cannot be overstated; by one account CoCom was nothing less than 'the principal forum for the Western allies to agree upon and implement restrictions on trade in weapons and dual-use goods and technologies with Soviet-bloc and other Communist countries'.[14] National export controls were heavily influenced by CoCom, and the EU dual-use regulation developed in its shadow.

CoCom was both a tool of economic warfare and a general strategic embargo. It was always a difficult matter of good intelligence and sound judgment to know which goods and technologies contributed to Soviet military capability, and which western industries should therefore suffer restrictions.[15] It was generally accepted that the most CoCom could do was delay the acquisition of leading technologies by the communist bloc, thereby ensuring that the West maintained the technological upper hand. But, in spite of the perceived presence of an overwhelming, unifying military threat to the West, CoCom was never free of controversy and misunderstanding among its partners. Having agreed unanimously on the content of the destination and commodity lists and any amendments, CoCom partners had to seek a 'general exception' if they wished to export a listed good to a proscribed destination. Since an exception could also only be agreed unanimously, this process, known as 'consensus licensing', effectively meant that each partner had a 'right to veto the sales of others'.[16] However, since CoCom was a voluntary organization, the use of the veto was always a delicate matter and had to be balanced 'against the possibility that members may withdraw from the group at any moment without notice'.[17] The key criterion was whether the proposed export would improve the recipient's military capabilities; commodities which appeared on the IAEL or the IML were therefore never approved for export, although those on the IIL were often the cause of dispute. Some partners made use of 'administrative exception notes' by which they stated that certain items would be subjected to national control and would not be made subject to collective review in CoCom and hence vulnerable to a veto.[18]

Although the end of the Cold War brought the rationale for CoCom into question, many continued to argue for a multilateral forum to control the export of sensitive technologies. Partly in response to the expansion of WMD non-proliferation regimes into the dual-use area, and partly to present a more accommodating face to the technology-starved former Soviet Union and its allies, in 1990 CoCom began to reduce its IIL to a 'Core List' of especially sensitive technology.[19] This list was finalized in February 1992, although disagreements remained over controls on certain technologies such as computers and telecommunications.[20] May 1992 saw the creation of an informal CoCom Cooperation Forum, acknowledging that many former Warsaw Treaty states not only needed western technology for their economic stability and could be removed from CoCom's Country List, as was Hungary in February 1992, but also that 'the new strategic threats were the dangers of the spread of weapons of mass destruction to Third World countries'[21] and to terrorist groups.[22] Thus, the idea was born of using CoCom as a general export control mechanism, rather than a more focused, East–West technology embargo or weapon of economic warfare.

At a meeting of CoCom partners at The Hague on 16 November 1993 it was agreed that the forum was now defunct, and that CoCom controls should be phased out by 31 March 1994. On the eve of the organization's demise, however, the partners agreed that a replacement forum should be in place by the end of 1994. For the interim period, partners agreed to maintain the commodity lists – the 'Core List' residue of the IIL became known as the 'Interim List' – while accepting more flexibility and national discretion in the granting of export licences.[23] CoCom was duly wound up on 31 March 1994, while negotiations continued to find an appropriate successor regime. The question of the membership of any new body provoked controversy. Those who saw in the new body a means to manage global dual-use technology and conventional weapons transfers argued that Russia must be made a member of the new organization from the outset, with the PRC and other states also joining eventually. Britain and France, in particular, argued that the new body would have little meaning without Russian membership. Russia's arms sales to Iran became a sticking point. Russia's pledge in September 1994 that it would halt future arms sales to Iran ignored existing contracts to supply top-grade MiG-29 and SU-24 combat aircraft, T-72 main battle tanks and infantry combat vehicles, and failed to convince the United States. It was not until 29 June 1995 that Russia and the United States finally reached a firm agreement. As a result, by midsummer 1995 it was expected that Russia, Poland, Hungary and the Czech Republic would all be invited to join the seventeen original partners and the six cooperating partners (Austria, Finland, Ireland, New Zealand, Sweden and Switzerland) for high-level discussions on CoCom's successor in September 1995.[24]

Even with the membership issue approaching resolution, and having agreed on a provisional title for the new organization (New Forum), there remained deep uncertainty about the basic rationale for the new body. There was general agreement that the new body should cover the export of military and dual-use technologies, but some doubts as to how – or whether – the arrangement could also cover conventional weapons exports. The problem of how to replace CoCom's Country List also led to disagreements. The United States was eager to name the four so-called 'pariah' states (Iran, Iraq, Libya and North Korea) as the main targets of the new regime, but European partners were 'steadfastly against this'.[25] The British Foreign Office described the difficulty facing the negotiators in the following way:

> instead of looking simply at trade with countries that formerly made up the Warsaw Pact, we are now looking at trade with the whole world. In the area of dual use technology where a lot of the members of COCOM are big traders, we have in the negotiations the difficulty of striking a balance between the security desiderata which point to something ... close to the old COCOM system and which gives as much chance to restrict trade as possible and at the other extreme the wish to promote legitimate trade in dual use goods which argues for controls which are focused ... on end users and end uses on which we have concerns, and does not any longer have a kind of blanket effect. What is proving difficult in the negotiations so far is to strike that balance.[26]

Problems also arose in the selection of criteria or guidelines by which partners would judge potential arms and military-equipment exports. According to one British source, by March 1995 there had been 'virtually no progress' in agreeing such guidelines.[27] Discussion of the new regime's consultation process has also revealed deep divisions. The United States has consistently argued for prior notification of impending sales among the partners. But some states felt that this practice would expose their defence companies to price-cutting manoeuvres,[28] and one senior British official described the idea as 'anathema'. What seems more likely is that the national veto will be abandoned, bringing the old 'consensus licensing' process to an end, and that the new regime will, instead, be a looser and more informal arrangement in which national discretion, known as 'administrative exceptions' in CoCom, will predominate. While the emphasis on national judgment and implementation may be a realistic response to political and commercial pressures, it is difficult to see how an effective multilateral control regime could be built upon such unsteady foundations; the stress on national discretion could prove to be a fatal flaw.[29] The pressure to ease export regulations and promote exports is great, particularly in the United States, and could overwhelm the new regime. If the outcome of the post-CoCom negotiations is no more than a loose, toothless 'transparency' agreement among suppliers, this could prove damaging to European manufacturers and exporters of sensitive conventional weapons-related technology. Some European industrialists worry that if the only multilateral regime governing US exports is the post-CoCom arrangement, this could give US industry competitive advantage over European competitors governed by a far more restrictive EU dual-use regulation.

The EU dual-use export regulation

With so many EU members involved both in CoCom and the various WMD technology-control initiatives, there is a great deal of experience of multilateral technology export control within the EU. Nevertheless, it has so far proved difficult to harness that experience in one or other of the Union institutions. From the earliest days, some member states have been particularly sensitive to the issue of Community competence in areas which, although clearly matters of trade and competition, also touch on national foreign, defence and security policies. This situation is partly explained by Article 223 of the 1958 EEC Treaty, discussed in Chapter 2. The list of goods to be covered by Article 223, derived from the CoCom IML, was agreed soon after the EEC Treaty was signed. The list includes conventional weapons such as artillery, tanks, missiles and warships, as well as the ammunition for such weapons, and also mentions nuclear, biological and chemical weapons. Military computers and electronic equipment are included, as well as other military equipment such as parachute fabric and water-purification plants. The final paragraph concerns manufacturing technology which is exclusively military, rather than dual-use: 'Machines, equipment and items exclusively designed for the study, manufacture, testing and control of arms, munitions and apparatus of an exclusively military nature included in this list'.[30]

The list has not been updated since 1958. Many of the weapons have been superseded, and a good deal of modern military equipment is not included. The failure to modernize the list may have suggested to some governments that the principle of exception matters more than the content of the list, with each government being free to decide for itself which commodities are covered by the Article. Some critics have suspected governments of applying Article 223 as loosely as possible to dual-use technology as well as arms and military technology, in order to maintain national competitive advantage within the European market.[31] In fact, the legal ground has long been established that members cannot derogate from Community commercial and industrial policies by citing the military side of dual-use goods. If a good has a civilian use, then the Community has competence, even where dual-use goods are managed by other regimes such as CoCom, the NSG, the AG and the MTCR. In other words, exemption from Article 223 is to be limited as far as possible to the list of military goods and technologies appended to it. Checks against cynical misinterpretation of Article 223 can be found in Articles 224 and 225 of the EEC Treaty, and in Article 223 itself, paragraph 1(b) of which states that any exclusions under the Article 'shall not adversely affect the conditions of competition in the common market regarding products which are not intended for specifically military purposes'. The principle of restricted derogation was reiterated by the Commission after the adoption of the Single European Act.[32] It follows that Community competence extends into all areas not explicitly reserved for national prerogative, including the dual-use goods listed in the CoCom IIL. Article 223 was not amended by the Single European Act, was not scrapped in accordance with Commission proposals,[33] was not rescinded by the Maastricht Treaty in December 1991, and remains a source of controversy.

The Commission first began to examine the issue of export controls on sensitive and dual-use goods in the 1980s. When the Single European Act of 1986 set the date for the beginning of the single market, the export control issue loomed still larger. Given EC members' commitments to the various dual-use export control bodies, especially CoCom, it became apparent that a single market with no internal customs barriers would require a Community-wide policy for the export of sensitive or strategic goods which could not be exempted under Article 223 and which were therefore vulnerable to EC industrial, commercial and competition policies. Unless all EC members had comparable export policies and standards of implementation, licence-free trade in dual-use technology within the single market area could enable unscrupulous exporters to evade controls in their home state by exporting first to a customer in another EC state with more lax controls before re-exporting to the final, perhaps otherwise proscribed, destination. In the longer term, it could also be that states with more lax controls could, unfairly, attract additional investment for the manufacture of dual-use goods. The winding-down of CoCom posed another problem, since those EC members which were also CoCom partici-pants had introduced simplified licensing systems for exports of sensitive goods to other CoCom partners and CoCom cooperation countries.

It was not only the effect of the single market on sensitive export policies which had to be considered, however, but also how such policies might affect the internal management of the single market, where as much as 5 per cent of internal trade is in goods which could be classified as dual-use.[34] The single market requires there to be no internal barriers or idiosyncratic export control systems which might divide the market. However much they agreed with EC common commercial policy, if member states were adamant in their wish to control exports of dual-use technology on grounds of national security, the result could only be anti-competitive practices where the civilian use of the technology or com-modity was concerned. Unless controlled dual-use items are traded freely within the EC, without the delays and costs associated with the obtaining of licences, there could be significant barriers to civil trade.

For all these reasons, along with the perception that transnational indus-trial cooperation could offer less scrupulous companies a means to evade the strongest national restrictions, the long-drawn-out attempt began to fashion a compromise between Community competence in trade matters, and national prerogative in the areas of foreign, security and defence policies. While respecting the Community's competition policies and the aims of the single market, the object of the exercise was to ensure that free and flexible intra-EC trade did not make possible the diversion of sensitive goods to third countries via the weakest link in the EC 'fence'. The first step in the development of an EC/EU dual-use policy was a fact-finding survey of national practices carried out by the Commission in 1991. In a 'communication' to the Council and Parliament, the Commission, referring to the need 'to ensure that export-type controls on intra-EC trade do not hinder the completion of the internal market',[35] listed 'key elements' for 'an operational and effective system at Community level':

- 'a common list of dual-use goods and technologies which are subject to control';
- 'a common list of destinations, although the nature of this list, i.e. whether it should be a list of "proscribed" or of "special facilities" destinations will require further reflexion';
- 'common criteria for the issuing of licences for exports from the EC';

39

- 'a forum or mechanism in which to coordinate licensing and enforcement policies and procedures';
- administrative cooperation.

The Council of Ministers set up an Ad Hoc High Level Working Party to examine the issue and in August 1992 the Commission made a formal proposal for an EC-wide regulation system.[36]

Negotiation of the dual-use regulation proved to be a protracted affair. Among many issues of concern was whether the regulation should adopt the CoCom consultative model, or whether some central licensing body should be created. Member states examined in microscopic detail the various legal, timetable and voting questions raised by the proposed regulation. One concern was whether licences issued by one member state would be valid throughout the Community, or whether member states should have a *droit de regard* over exports from their ports under licences issued by another member state. Some members called for a catch-all clause, and others for a 'safeguard' clause which could operate when national security was considered to be at stake, even in the case of exports to other EC states. Reflecting deep misgivings about the integrity of the boundary between Community competence and national prerogative, the most difficult issue was the content and purpose of the lists which would support the regulation. Some members argued that lists of sensitive technologies, of favoured or proscribed destinations and of guidelines for making export decisions came too close to foreign and security policy-making to be placed under Community competence and could not therefore form part of a Commission-based regulation system. In late 1992 the Commission accepted that these three key lists should be a matter for governments.

The issue then became one of deciding how to draw up and implement the lists, in such a way that national sensitivities could be respected. While the regulation drew its authority from Article 113 of the EEC Treaty and was therefore a matter for qualified majority voting (QMV), several governments argued that QMV would not be an appropriate way to draw up and implement the lists, given their foreign and security policy implications. Late in 1993 the Belgian government offered a compromise which was subsequently adopted. The compromise was to seek agreement on the content of the lists through the 'joint action' process of the CFSP pillar of the TEU, and to publish the lists as annexures to an intergovernmental CFSP decision rather than include them in the Commission regulation. Use of the joint-action process, which is examined more closely in Chapter 5, broke the deadlock and on 14 June 1994 ten of the then twelve Council members agreed to the adoption of the regula- tion. Danish and Belgian reservations were waived in the following weeks, but it was not until late December 1994 that final agreement was reached on the form and content of both the regulation[37] and the joint- action decision.[38] By now the proposed implementation date of 1 January 1995 had slipped to 1 March 1995. However, translation and administra- tive difficulties delayed the formal publication and implementation of the regulation, and the 1 March 1995 deadline was also postponed. This caused a certain amount of inconvenience for those governments and industries which had prepared the legal and administrative ground for the regulation and had, at the last minute, to revert to old practices. Finally, on 1 July 1995, almost three years after the Commission's original proposal, the regulation and the joint action both came into force, creat- ing a 'Community regime for the control of exports of dual-use goods' and constituting 'an integrated system involving, in accordance with their own powers, the Council, the Commission and the Member states'.[39]

The basic aim of the regulation is to ensure that the export from 'the customs territory of the Community' of certain dual-use goods (listed in Annex I to the joint-action decision) does not take place without authori- zation. Intra-EU trade in these goods and in other unlisted dual-use goods is not covered by the regulation, although there is scope for governments to impose licensing requirements on such trade in certain circumstances. A central element of the regulation is the catch-all clause, a feature which aroused some controversy during negotiations. Article 4 states that the export even of unlisted goods must be licensed if the exporter is informed by his national authorities, or is simply 'aware', that the goods are intended for use in WMD or missile manufacture. It is left to member governments to decide how – or whether – to legislate in the potentially controversial matter of establishing an exporter's knowledge, or mere 'grounds for suspecting', that a given export is intended to be misused. Article 5, the 'safeguard clause', allows governments to prohibit the export of any other, unlisted dual-use goods, provided any prohibitions are notified to the Commission and other governments. Article 6 lays down the requirement to license any export of goods subject to the regulation, unless 'simplified formalities' are to be used, for example when the recipient is one of the countries listed in Annex II to the joint-action decision. Once issued, however, any individual, general or global authorization is to be valid throughout the EU. Article 7 states that export authorization is a matter for 'the competent authorities of the [member state] in which the exporter is established'. But if the goods to be exported are located elsewhere in the EU, the relevant government is granted a brief period in which to object to the export. Indeed, a member state may object to any export from the EU if it perceives its 'national interests' to be at stake, but in these cases the licensing government is required merely to 'immediately engage in consultations of a non-binding nature' with the government raising the objection. Article 8 requires member states to 'take into consideration' the 'common guidelines' annexed to the joint-action decision when deciding upon an export authorization. Article 10 permits each member state temporarily to interrupt the export of goods from its territory, even though the export has been licensed elsewhere in the EU, if there are grounds to suspect that the licence was issued incorrectly, or if circumstances have changed. In 'exceptional circumstances', otherwise entirely valid and proper exports can be prevented if a member state decides that the export 'would be contrary to its essential foreign policy or security interests or to the fulfilment of its international obligations or commitments'. As far as penalties are concerned, Article 17 leaves enforcement and punishment to national authorities, merely calling for any penalties to be 'effective, proportionate and dissuasive'. Remaining articles deal with administrative and record-keeping matters, coordination between the member states, legal arrangements and procedures to cover a 'transitional period', the duration of which is left unclear. Article 22 states, *inter alia*, that the regulation does not affect 'the application of Article 223 of the Treaty establishing the European Community'.

The joint-action decision is, by comparison, a concise and straightforward document, the object of which is to introduce the five lists referred to in the regulation. Annex I to the joint action lists licensable dual-use equipment in ten categories:

- nuclear materials, facilities and equipment;
- materials, chemicals, 'microorganisms' and 'toxins';
- materials processing;
- electronics;
- computers;
- telecommunications and 'information security';
- sensors and lasers;
- navigation and avionics;
- marine;
- propulsion systems, space systems and related equipment.

The export outside the EU of goods in these categories is to be specifically authorized, unless the destination appears in Annex II to the joint action, a list of destinations for which 'simplified formalities may be applicable'. With Austria, Finland and Sweden having now joined the EU, Annex II lists no more than six countries: Australia, Canada, Japan, Norway, Switzerland and the United States. The omission of a list of sensitive or proscribed destinations could prove to be a grave weakness in the overall regulation, by giving governments 'significant discretion in deciding whether the proliferation risk associated with a prospective recipient country is outweighed by the benefits of exporting controlled items to that country. Such discretion could limit the effectiveness of an agreement among EU Member States on a common list of controlled goods and technologies.'[40] Annex III to the joint action lists the 'factors' which authorities will 'take into account' when deciding whether export applications should be authorized. These include commitments to international non-proliferation agreements, internationally agreed embargoes, 'considerations of national foreign and security policy' including the Luxembourg and Lisbon conventional arms export criteria, and finally, 'considerations about intended end-use and the risk of diversion'. Annex IV lists goods such as nuclear reprocessing plants, stealth technology and rocket-propulsion systems which, although already listed in Annex I, are considered by some member states to be so sensitive that for the duration of the 'transitional period', all intra-EU exports will require national authorization. Annex V lists those goods which some member states continue to define as military, rather than dual-use, and which are therefore excluded from the regulation under Article 223. Annexes III and IV, it would seem, provide a counterweight to the Commission's earlier insistence that Article 223 should be applied restrictively.

There remains, clearly, a great deal of national discretion with regard to the application of the dual-use regulation. Given that some member states are very sensitive to perceived challenges to national prerogative in the key areas of foreign policy, security and defence, a careful compromise of this sort was perhaps inevitable. In such circumstances, the combination of the Article 113/QMV regulation with a set of CFSP/ unanimous lists is a notable achievement, but it remains to be seen whether the 'linked system' will be a simple and successful formula or a hopeless attempt to juxtapose two very different approaches to European cooperation.

Chapter 4

Industry

Introduction

The term 'European defence industry' is a useful shorthand expression for the purposes of this study, but may suggest more homogeneity than actually exists. Within the EU there are many national defence sectors, organized and oriented according to different national preferences and industrial practices. There is a vast array of prime and sub-contractors, and a complex set of intra- and extra-European cooperative ventures. Some sectors of defence industry have weathered the end of the Cold War better than others, but all are in a state of flux, and are experiencing or anticipating major structural change. Several different political and industrial strategies are being considered. It is nevertheless possible to identify the main arguments surrounding the future of European defence industry, and the main industrial and political challenges being faced, and on this basis to discuss the potential of the EU as a multilateral arms and technology export regulatory forum.

The various national defence sectors have three general features in common. The first is that defence industry and government are in a close relationship. This results in part from a 'national security' mentality which sees defence industry as a vital national resource, a strategic asset rather like standing armed forces. Another explanation is that governments are the sole or main customer for the products of Europe's defence industries. But if the relationship is generally close, it is not uniform. Britain, for example, has traditionally adopted a *laissez-faire* approach to defence industry and declared against adopting an interventionist defence industrial policy. The French government, on the other hand, has historically had a much closer relationship with French defence industry, as owner, manager and customer. But at both extremes the industry/

government relationship is changing. During 1995 the British government moved in the direction of a 'defence technology strategy', with talk of the need for a 'much improved relationship' between government and industry,[1] and away from the 'rigid competitive policy' of the late 1980s.[2] At roughly the same time, the French government began to warn French defence industry that the comfortable and dependable relationship of the past was coming to an end.[3] Even so, the relationship between government and defence industry in Europe generally is likely to remain very close. In these circumstances any restructuring of national defence sectors will be highly charged politically. And at the regional level, any plan or policy for the future of Europe's defence industries must satisfy, perhaps more than any other industrial sector, deeply held national commercial and political preferences. The result is likely to be political and economic distortions in the European defence sector as a whole; where the 'final customers' are solely or mainly governments, 'the problems of eliminating scope for preferential deals are especially difficult'.[4]

The second feature occurs with rather more consistency. Defence industries in Europe have a manufacturing capacity far in excess of what their customers might require, nationally or regionally. Following the end of the Cold War, domestic defence equipment markets have contracted dramatically. Table 4.1 illustrates the reduction in defence expenditure, both in real terms and as a percentage of GDP, among the current members of the EU between 1985 and 1993.

In total, the current members of the EU spent US$15,764 million (constant 1993) less on defence in 1993 than in 1985 – a reduction of 8.2 per cent. Yet, although the economic environment in which European defence industry operates has clearly become harsher over the past decade, there remains an excess in manufacturing capacity over conceivable European demand. The problem can be illustrated by main battle tank (MBT) manufacturing. By the end of 1994 the current fifteen members of the EU owned a total of about 12,500 MBTs, of various types and vintages. As all fifteen governments look to reduce their defence spending, and with Cold War armoured-warfare scenarios slipping out of fashion, the demand for new MBTs is sure to fall. Even if all European MBT manufacturers had full and equal access to this dwindling market, the competition for any remaining orders would be stiff among the three manufacturers struggling to survive: one in Britain, one in Germany and one in France. Similar duplication of resources can be found in many other European defence equipment sectors, such as warships and combat aircraft. Furthermore, with no clear sense of the level at

Table 4.1 Defence expenditure, 1985–93

	$m (constant 1993)		%GDP	
	1985	1993	1985	1993
Austria	1,696	1,650	1.2	0.9
Belgium	5,409	3,805	3.0	1.8
Denmark	2,747	2,701	2.2	2.0
Finland	1,974	2,100	2.8	2.0
France	42,918	42,898	4.0	3.4
Germany	46,330	36,654	3.2	2.1
Greece	3,060	4,074	7.0	5.5
Ireland	420	560	1.8	1.1
Italy	22,576	24,400	2.3	2.0
Luxembourg	84	117	0.9	1.0
Netherlands	7,814	7,070	3.1	2.2
Portugal	1,610	2,360	3.1	2.8
Spain	9,900	7,870	2.4	1.5
Sweden	4,194	5,500	3.3	2.3
UK	41,891	35,100	5.2	3.6

Source: 'International comparison of defence expenditure and military manpower in 1985, 1992 and 1993', tables prepared for but not printed in *The Military Balance 1994–95* (London: IISS, 1994).

which defence spending will 'bottom out', surplus manufacturing capability could prove to be a permanent feature; 'continuous disarmament creates permanent overcapacity'.[5] The problem of overcapacity is compounded by the fact that defence industry continues to be viewed predominantly through a national prism. The result is that manufacturing overcapacities do not automatically translate into market-led restructuring of the overall European supply base, as they might in a more straightforward market. And for as long as governments resist the discipline of a Europe-wide market for the sake of national protectionism, distortions in Europe's defence industrial base will persist and will make the overall reduction and rationalization of manufacturing capacity slow and difficult.

The situation in Europe stands in marked contrast to that in the United States, and this introduces the final general feature of European defence industry: the fact of extra-European competition, mainly but not exclusively from the United States. A useful, simple comparator is the market for MBTs. With a 1994 stockpile of some 15,000 MBTs, the size of the MBT market in the United States is not very much greater than that in the EU. More significant is the fact that the United States has one defence market, rather than fifteen, and one defence budget which, in 1993, stood at over US\$297 billion; more than \$1 billion greater than the defence budgets of all current EU members combined. The United States also has one defence policy, one style of government-industry dealings and, above all, one MBT manufacturer. The US defence industry is able to achieve standards of efficiency and economies of scale that European manufacturers cannot at present match. With higher production costs and lower production volumes, European defence manufacturers face stiff competition for any international export orders.[6] To make matters worse, the price and quality of US defence equipment often undermines attempts to pursue a 'buy European' policy, as the Dutch and British decisions in 1995 to buy the McDonnell Douglas AH-64 *Apache* attack helicopter illustrate.

Restructuring the market

In the face of straitening national defence budgets and inadequate national procurement shopping lists, one response is to seek to broaden the scope of the market in which Europe's defence industries sell their products. Market expansion could occur in three ways. First, Europe's manufacturers could be given open access to the whole of a European defence equipment market. Open access would have to be awarded equally, across the EU. But since there are known to be overcapacities in all defence manufacturing sectors, even when the maximum size of any Europe-wide market is taken into account, it would seem that open access could only be efficient and ensure the survival of some manufacturers in certain member states, if it were accepted that other manufacturers, in other member states, would face closure. The underlying sources of national defence industrial protectionism would therefore have to be addressed at some point, and it seems unlikely that these issues could be resolved as a happy consequence of an open EU defence market. A second option might be described as the 'transatlantic' solution. The idea that NATO's defence manufacturers should all have equal access to defence equipment markets on both sides of the Atlantic has received a good deal of attention, both during and after the Cold War. In 1989 and 1990 some impetus was given to the creation of a 'two-way street' in transatlantic defence trade. But subsequent attempts to create a more productive atmosphere, such as the efforts of NATO's Conference of National Armaments Directors to agree a politically binding 'Code of Conduct' for intra-alliance defence trade, were described in late 1994 as developing 'slowly' and 'cantankerously'.[7] The politics of the pork barrel operate on both sides of the Atlantic. And even if enlightened self-interest did prevail, and a genuinely open transatlantic market did come about, Europe's defence manufacturers would still have to compete against US giants, such as Lockheed Martin, producing high-quality, well-priced and often battle-proven equipment.

The third and final market-expansion option sees Europe's defence manufacturers venturing into the international export market and fighting for a global market share. The export option is attractive, and a standard response to defence industrial overcapacity.[8] European defence industries would undoubtedly offer keen competition in many areas. But at a time of global recession in defence spending, resulting in a contracting global defence market, Europe's industries face extremely stiff competition for export orders. Competition comes not only from US manufacturers but also from 'second tier' producers, particularly those in Southeast Asia and the Asia-Pacific region. And the long-awaited Russian arms export drive might also intrude upon the scene.

The reality is that attempts to modify and broaden the market for European defence equipment do not in themselves offer a solution to manufacturing overcapacity in Europe. The problem is not simply one of market access and vigorous marketing. The three options discussed above all point in one direction: restructuring of the manufacturing side. Market expansion has to take place, but 'streamlining of what is left of the European defence industrial base takes precedence'.[9] Only then will it be possible for overcapacities to be reduced and for European industry to compete on something approaching an equal footing with its US counterparts.

Restructuring the manufacturers

The key questions now become how and where might such restructuring take place, and when; and what might the effect be upon efforts to establish in the EU a multilateral regulatory system? Since the 1980s European defence industry has tried to follow two, not obviously compatible, paths to restructuring.[10] The first path involves consolidation at the national level, and the creation of monopoly suppliers. The second path amounts to the 'Europeanization' and 'internationalization' of the European defence industry through the development of transnational ties. The second path presents two broad possibilities, one of which is the 'project-led' restructuring of the sort currently favoured by the British government. As far as the British government is concerned, project-led restructuring is defined more by the dynamics of the market than the politics of European integration. The second transnational restructuring option would involve a European defence industrial 'big bang', with full-scale reorganization and rationalization of the region's defence industries. This option can barely be examined or understood outside the context of European political integration and will accordingly be defined here as 'supranational restructuring'.

National restructuring

Restructuring or concentration at the national level reflects the determination to sustain national self-sufficiency in defence manufacturing. In order to mitigate the effect of manufacturing surpluses and other inefficiencies, government and industry might embark upon a policy of 'vertical integration', whereby certain manufacturers would receive special status in government procurement competitions, enabling the company to absorb its national competitors and persuading it to specialize in that manufacturing area. This 'national-champion' approach could result in one or very few national defence giants providing all manufacturing and prime contractor services for government. Although the general trend is for national consolidation to be sought in parallel with internationalization, some supporters of the national-champion approach reject the latter idea; the chairman of Britain's GEC has described the idea of 'cross-border rationalisation in the European defence industry as naive, since all main European countries will ... want to maintain a strong element of self-sufficiency'.[11] Some Swedish industrialists apparently share similar views, as do some in France. In spite of changes in the government-industry relationship in France, the national-champion approach remains popular in French industry and government, where it is also viewed as a possible basis for supranational restructuring.

There are several questions to be asked about the national-champion approach, not least whether governments as customers could any longer receive the benefits and value for money which they would expect in a more openly competitive environment. It is also difficult to accept that any national defence budget alone could sustain one or a small number of such national champions, however well restructured and efficient they may be. And if the post-Cold War requirement for military equipment is unable to match the political determination to sustain a national defence industrial base, the result might be that governments are forced to prop up uncompetitive industries with increased subsidies. Defence companies protected in such a way would certainly be able to produce good defence equipment, but might find it more difficult to produce equipment of the highest quality within a reasonable budget. Foreign customers might therefore prove hard to come by, especially as the global 'buyer's market' continues to contract. But whatever the difficulties, government and industry would simply have to expand foreign sales. Not only would governments in this position be tempted to assist industry through export credit guarantees and further subsidies, they would also be unlikely to accept any collective export regulation system which might restrain sales. Of all the options available, the 'national-champion' approach is therefore least compatible with the development of an effective EU export control regime.

Project-led restructuring
Between national consolidation and supranational restructuring lies the 'project-led' option, championed by the British government and popular with industry. The project-led approach seeks to satisfy two demands: the economic and political imperatives of European defence industrial consolidation on one hand, and commercial competitiveness on the other. Governments and industry have already developed a range of cooperative and collaborative arrangements: project consortia such as the Anglo-French-Italian 'Project Horizon' air-defence frigate programme, joint-stock venture companies such as the 1993 initiative between GEC-Marconi (UK) and Thomson-CSF (France) to study the feasibility of new radar equipment, equity swaps, cross-border mergers and acquisitions and co-marketing agreements. Where the project-led approach departs from past practice is in its rejection of IEPG-style work-sharing arrangements known as *juste retour*, whereby collaborative projects were divided proportionately between participating countries, often with little account taken of the skill and efficiency of the various national defence sectors. *Juste retour* was a political response to the need for defence industrial collaboration, but fostered national and Europe-wide inefficiencies. In the name of competitiveness, the project-led approach rejects both *juste retour* and the 'Euro-champion' idea discussed below.

The main argument against project-led consolidation is that European defence industry can be both collaborative and competitive, and therefore efficient, only to the extent that the whole edifice is held together with the glue of political commitment to European integration in areas of high politics. Yet Britain's adherence to competitive defence procurement has so far prevented such a leap of faith. While calling for greater efficiency in Europe's defence industrial base, Britain has nevertheless repeatedly rejected calls for European preference and often bought US equipment 'off the shelf'. The interim purchase of C-130J transport aircraft and the AH-64 attack-helicopter contract are but two examples of a practice which has exasperated integration-minded defence industrialists and politicians throughout Europe. Many of Europe's defence industrialists view competition with their US counterparts as inherently unfair. By this view, British procurement of US equipment not only impedes the essential process of integration in Europe, it also makes it easier for US government and industry to sabotage the consolidation of European defence industry and thereby retain competitive advantage.[12] At the *Eurosatory '94* defence exhibition in June 1994, eleven European defence manufacturing associations signed an agreement which 'essentially circled the wagons against the United States' by calling for 'an internal defense market to ensure that European equipment is competitive', and for 'buy European' procurement policies in Europe.[13]

Supranational restructuring
Supranational restructuring involves a combination of vertical and horizontal integration, and is the most highly charged option politically. The basic principle is that Europe's defence equipment requirements would be provided by 'Euro-champions': defence industrial 'clusters' offering one MBT manufacturer, one combat-aircraft manufacturer, one warship manufacturer, and so forth. These clusters would be big, and fit enough to compete on the world stage.[14] Euro-champions could be organized in one of two ways. Assuming that EC anti-trust legislation and commercial policies could be waived or ignored, in each manufacturing sector transnational monopolies could be allowed to consolidate. Alternatively, each sector could be served by national specialists: Germany as Europe's MBT manufacturer, Britain for warships and France for combat aircraft, for example. France and Italy are among EU members which have expressed an interest in such an approach, and some European defence industrialists have taken a similar position.[15]

A division of labour along the lines of a 'defence industrial Yalta' is, however, unlikely without a wholly new political climate in Europe; 'such a scenario implies a willingness to give up a wide range of capabilities and to accept dependence on others'.[16] Even if the political climate were to become more suitable, there would still be difficult decisions to make as to the allocation of specializations and the sharing of benefits;

responsibility for Europe's MBTs would be considered less generally beneficial for a national economic and industrial base than responsibility for combat-aircraft manufacturing. And there would still have to be some means of ensuring that the overall system remained internally competitive, with national governments receiving value for money.

Implications for export regulation

Deeply entrenched ideological positions, and the apparent willingness in some quarters to accept inefficiency and overcapacity as the inevitable costs of national defence industrial protectionism, suggest that any re-structuring will be slow, if progress is made at all.[17] Whatever the outcome, defence exports are sure to have a central role in any national, project-led or supranational approach to restructuring. It was suggested earlier that national consolidation alone would have the most destructive effect on attempts to create an EU-wide export regulatory system. For the most part, however, national consolidation is seen as a complement, rather than an alternative, to some form of international cooperation.[18] The most immediate difficulty with the project-led approach is the problem of ownership of the transnational venture, and the question of responsibility for compliance with export control guidelines.

Ownership and responsibility

If the 'market-led' restructuring option continues to be pursued, with more cross-border joint-venture companies and project consortia being established, questions arise as to the ownership and legal status of such industrial bodies; who – or what – is responsible to whom for compliance with export controls and guidelines? At what level of political authority should such controls and guidelines be issued? Transatlantic and global collaborative ventures could also present similar problems, as could Euro-champion transnational conglomerates. Could such bodies make it possible to avoid national and multilateral export policies and restric-tions? Or could they simply make the task of export control, nationally and regionally, more difficult than it would otherwise be? Since defence consolidation is in part driven by the desire to compete more vigorously and effectively in what remains of the European and world defence markets, attempts to regulate trade in weapons and technology might be unwelcome. There is already some evidence to suggest that the export of multinationally produced defence equipment causes difficulty for na-tional and multilateral export control systems, even for relatively anodyne international initiatives such as the United Nations Register of Conventional Arms.

There could be basic inconsistencies between an export control system which operates as a collective effort by fifteen governments, and a pattern of defence consolidation which produces new, cross-border industrial and political entities. By one account, governmental influence upon European defence industry is already diminishing, with defence companies 'following the directives of the authorities less and less'.[19] But other analysts argue that large multinational defence companies are not inherently more difficult to control than smaller companies. After all, every trading company has to be registered somewhere, and when it does so it comes under a national jurisdiction. Larger firms may, in addition, be more anxious to understand and comply with all relevant export control regulations, simply because they have more to lose in the event of misunderstandings or wilful non-compliance.[20] Most legitimate exporters of weapons and sensitive technology appear to accept that the international defence market is not a free-for-all and that exports should conform to national practices and to nationally implemented multilateral agreements. In any case, the gradual assumption of extra-territorial powers by European governments should tighten the regulatory grip.

If the various modes of project-led transnational consolidation cause difficulties, these should not be overstated. Provided sufficient regulation can be achieved at some level, project-led consolidation does not present a *prima facie* case for an export control authority at a commensurate – i.e. supranational – level in Europe. This may be a complacent view, too accepting of a situation which is, arguably, commercially inefficient and unstable. But it is a view which corresponds to the current parameters of the defence industrial consolidation debate. The question is, can these parameters, and the possibilities and expectations which follow, be altered? Is the project-led approach merely the least bad course while the political commitment to trans-European defence industrial consolidation is lacking? Any regulatory challenges posed by project-led, *ad hoc* consolidation clearly have to be addressed. But a more serious, structural problem may be that governments' unwillingness to make concessions to collective organization and discipline in these areas of high politics will always prevent the development of common export policies and practices. Furthermore, without a common regulatory framework, industry may be prevented from achieving the standards of efficiency and competitiveness which are required, never aspiring to anything more than *ad hoc* project-led arrangements; one prominent German defence industrialist has called for 'common rules and guidelines for exports' as a necessary precondition for a 'truly European arms industry'.[21] Questions of 'political restructuring' form a persistent sub-text to the defence industrial consolidation debate, and cannot for long be excluded from the discussion.

Political restructuring

Any discussion of trans- or supranational authority in the defence field soon turns to Article 223 of the EEC Treaty, frequently cited as the main stumbling block to Commission regulation of an ill-organized and inefficient European defence sector. By one view, Article 223 is an anomaly which 'hinders the market-driven restructuring that government and industry leaders say is vital for European defence contractors to compete in the international market. And as long as Article 223 remains in force, governments will find it difficult to resist the urge to micromanage industry's restructuring.'[22] It could equally be argued that Article 223 enables governments to avoid altogether the difficult task of restructuring.

As with the question of industrial ownership, it is possible to overstate, or at least misconstrue, the problem of Article 223. Too often, Article 223 is described as if it were an external imposition, a foreign body the simple excision of which would make way for harmonious and efficient industrial restructuring. Of course, if Article 223 were to be deleted by the 1996 IGC, or at some subsequent time, the effect on multilateral export controls in the EU would be dramatic. National and cross-border mergers and acquisitions would all have to run the gauntlet of EC competition policy. National subsidies such as export credit guarantees could all be challenged. Elaborate compromises between Community competence and national prerogative, as in the dual-use regulation, would no longer be necessary. Defence-related exports would, arguably, be as much a matter for EC competence as for the CFSP pillar of the EU, and a fully centralized decision-making authority for the regulation of defence exports could result. But Article 223 is a home-grown political device, and its excision is likely to be much less neat. What is at issue is not merely a clause in a treaty, but fundamental concerns over the scope and direction of political integration in the EU. There are signs, even in France, that governments are increasingly willing to relax their special interest in defence industry and accept some form of cross-border industrial rationalization. All this suggests that uncompromising protectionism, of which Article 223 is a symbol, is considered by governments to be less suitable and realistic for post-Cold War Europe. This is not, of course, tantamount to saying that national preference has been or will be abandoned altogether. But if the pattern of change in the politico-industrial relationship is a matter of evolution rather than revolution, it could be that the precise requirements for common export licensing and regulation will only be revealed gradually. These functions could of course be served by the Commission, but this would require a more abrupt departure from past practice than governments seem able or willing to contemplate at present. Alternatively, if major changes in the political make-up of the EU are unlikely in the short term, it could be more productive to ask how far governments are willing to 'pool' their authority and what sort of intergovernmental organization they would be willing to accept, rather than remain trapped in the rhetoric surrounding Article 223.

The main difficulty is that there is a logic to European defence industrial rationalization which outstrips the pace at which political integration is taking place in the sensitive areas of foreign, security and defence policies. It can persuasively be argued that one part of the solution to the EU's arms manufacturing overcapacity is to allow defence firms to compete freely, across the EU, in a 'European Defence Equipment Market' (EDEM). An EDEM, like its commercial cousin, would require some form of organization and regulation, and a legal framework. Given that the manufacture and purchase of defence equipment is driven by the requirements of a small number of governments, it is clear that the organization running an EDEM would be no more or less than an EU common procurement agency. Regulation of defence procurement caught the eye of the Commission some time ago,[23] and the Commission 'has gradually increased its authority in the defence industry field, by adopting a position on joint ventures and on acquisitions in the defence industry that have been based on the existing paragraphs on competition policy in the Treaty of Rome'.[24] But the Commission's authority over activities in the defence sector is heavily circumscribed, as is suggested by the British decision in October 1994 to cite 'essential security interests' and invoke Article 223 in order to exclude the Commission from involvement in the British Aerospace bid for Vickers Shipbuilding and Engineering Ltd.[25] The more established route to cooperation in defence procurement has, instead, so far been intergovernmental. The WEU Declaration published with the Maastricht Treaty called for 'enhanced cooperation in the field of armaments with the aim of creating a European armaments agency'.[26] The WEU duly set up a new agency: the Western European Armaments Group (WEAG). In December 1992 the WEAG took over from the IEPG, and set its sights on the creation of a European defence procurement system of the sort which the IEPG had called for in its December 1990 Copenhagen document.

At some point, however, a relatively straightforward question must be asked: on behalf of whom, or what, would a common procurement agency act? If the motive is simply efficiency and the avoidance of waste, something like the British 'project-led' model of restructuring could apply. When EU governments identify a common need for, say, a combat aircraft or warship, it would make sense to manage the competition among competing consortia and perhaps then, on behalf of the customer-governments, manage relations with prime contractors up to the point at which the equipment is delivered. But for others, viewing defence procurement and industrial restructuring as an element of European political integration, the attraction of a common procurement agency is that it may lead to a common European defence system. There is, however, some uncertainty about the ordering of the relationship between common procurement and common defence. A survey of European national armaments directors in June 1994 found that some EU members such as the Netherlands saw that highly integrated procurement policies could promote a common defence policy. Other EU members, however, saw a common defence policy as the necessary precursor.[27]

The difference in approaches can be seen most readily in contrasting views of the role and expansion of the bilateral Franco-German armaments agency. The agency was created in December 1993, to be responsible for joint procurement and research and development, and to assist in the creation of the Franco-German 'Eurocorps'. From the outset there were fears that the bilateral body would challenge and undermine the agency called for in the 1991 WEU Declaration, just as there were fears that the 'Eurocorps' itself would undermine the European 'pillar' of NATO. Partly to allay these concerns, during 1994 the French and German governments allowed their agency to move closer to the WEU. By the end of the same year the WEU had postponed its own plans to establish a European armaments agency. But the goal of a European armaments agency was not abandoned altogether; with no rival, the Franco-German body was increasingly seen as a nucleus of the wider organization.[28] In late 1994 and 1995, with more WEAG members applying for membership of the expanding Franco-German body, the two founders saw their idea being overcome by the political wrangling which had already bedevilled the WEU's efforts in this field. Disagreements developed over the purpose and future of the agency. Britain, willing to join the club only if the rules could first be changed to its satisfaction, argued for no more than a 'joint projects office' and appeared, particularly to France, to be obstructing attempts to turn common procurement into deeper political and strategic cooperation. Disagreement also grew over whether a commitment to European preference was a reasonable condition for membership of the agency.

Discussion of the relationship between common procurement and common defence is unavoidably circular; it is not yet clear whether an EU procurement system will be the cause or the consequence of political integration in defence and security policies. It is not even clear that common procurement, however it comes about, will be the best solution industrially and commercially: 'The risk exists that joint procurement – which may be years away – could end up just coddling local arms makers.'[29] But what can be said is that before the process can go much further, a degree of political commitment will have to be made. If one object of common EU procurement is to supply standard equipment made by European defence firms to European forces, then there must at some point be agreement to create those forces, agree their missions, and agree their operational military requirements. Without such agreements, any EU system of defence procurement, and defence restructuring as a whole, will lack a vital rationale. Similar things might be said of calls for a common export control agency. Defence industrial restructuring in Europe is aimed not only at the European market, but also at international exports. If an EDEM would create the need for some form of EU procurement agency, so activity in the export market by 'Euro-industries' would require management by a common export agency. Once again, defence industry appears broadly in favour of such an agency,[30] although industry's concern is more to clarify and harmonize EU export arrangements, and make them more efficient, than to contribute to the debate over political integration.[31] In the end, however, the political dimension cannot be avoided. No discussion of defence industrial restructuring, defence procurement, arms export policies and Article 223 can continue for long before the questions of common foreign, security and defence policies arise. Before examining these issues in Chapter 5, the present chapter turns finally to the internationalization of defence manufacturing and global technology transfer.

Internationalization of defence industry

The pursuit of foreign partners and subsidiaries is not unique to Europe's defence industries. It is normal practice for all firms, not just those in the defence sector, to seek foreign connections in order to share costs and reduce risks, gain access to foreign innovation, achieve economies of scale and penetrate foreign markets. When domestic economic conditions are unfavourable and risks are at their highest, pressure to seek international partners can be strong. Accordingly, internationalization has become especially popular with Europe's defence sector.[32] Joint ventures and international mergers can be global as well as European. In some cases, defence companies have been tempted to shift whole sectors of their production cycle to developing regions in order to take advantage of cheaper labour and production costs and unrivalled expertise in the manufacture of certain key sub-components such as semi-conductors. This process, known as 'off-shoring', has been especially noticeable in the 1990s. Often, the chosen site has been the Asia-Pacific region and Southeast Asia, with Taiwan, Indonesia, South Korea and Singapore being highly favoured.[33] Internationalization inevitably involves the transfer of technology and manufacturing skills. Often though, technology transfers take place in a more deliberate way, as part of offset arrangements in arms-transfer deals. As the pursuit of foreign partners and the willingness to transfer technology through offsets become increasingly important for European defence manufacturing, so the task of multilateral export control becomes more complex and difficult.

The spread of arms manufacturing capability
Internationalization of defence industry inevitably leads to the diffusion of weapons-related manufacturing capability. In most cases, unavoidably export-oriented European defence industries do not have the luxury of choice; in exchange for market access most clients now demand the transfer of manufacturing technology in the form of direct technology transfers, sub-contracting deals, and licensed co-development and co-production. Although most production still takes place among the traditional 'first tier' of weapons suppliers, the result of internationalization is that a significant 'second tier' as well as a less important 'third tier' of weapon producers have now developed.[34] Often, states appear keen to acquire an arms manufacturing capability in the face of the harshest commercial and economic logic. This points to an important feature of the spread of arms manufacturing capabilities around the world; the spread is the result both of supplier industry 'push' and recipient 'pull'. The 'indigenization' of weapons production capability is partly a result of arms manufacturing being seen as an attribute of a sovereign and politically mature state. Rather than attempt to build up an arms industry

from nothing, a goal which would require decades of industrial and scientific development to be condensed into a few years, most states take advantage of offset agreements made in connection with arms purchases in order to ensure the acquisition of the necessary technology and skills.[35] Offsets commonly involve an agreement by the supplier to co-produce the weapon or its parts with the recipient country and, in time, even to license full production. Given the decline in domestic markets and the creation of a more open, worldwide 'buyer's market' for arms, offset demands are becoming increasingly difficult to resist. A good example of the spread of technology through offset deals is the South Korean purchase of General Dynamics F-16 fighters from the United States. Korea will purchase 12 planes direct, assemble 36 from production kits prepared in Fort Worth, and make the remaining 72 in Samsung Industries in Seoul.[36] But perhaps the best known are the arrangements made between Saudi Arabia and various arms and technology suppliers. In the 1980s Saudi Arabia signed deals with the United States, Britain and France which involved the transfer of technology and know-how. The 'primary goal' of Saudi Arabia's offset programme was described as 'self-sufficiency in the high technology civil and, where feasible, defence industrial sectors'.[37]

Self-sufficiency in arms manufacturing results not only from permissiveness in the transfer of technology through offsets, however. Perversely, inconsistent policies or over-zealous export controls and embargoes can have a similar effect. Israel's response to the fickle behaviour of suppliers was both to seek a variety of suppliers, in order to reduce dependence on any single one, and, from the mid-1950s, to develop its own defence sector. Israel never achieved self-sufficiency in its arms industry, but certainly became a considerable exporter during the 1980s. SIPRI ranked Israel as the twelfth largest arms exporter for the period 1981–90, and according to Israel's own estimates, arms and equipment worth some US$1,500 million were exported in 1989.[38] Defence industrial self-sufficiency was, however, achieved by South Africa. The November 1977 UN embargo banned the supply of defence equipment to South Africa and prevented UN members buying South African weapons. According to one assessment, 'The arms embargo ... obliged South Africa's defence industry to become largely self-sufficient in providing military equipment for the [South African Defence Force] ... By the late 1980s the domestic defence industry had acquired across-the-board production capabilities and was able to supply the SADF with the bulk of its equipment needs.' Clandestine measures were often used to acquire key technologies, and some firms evaded the embargo by using South African subsidiaries. South Africa's arms industry flourished and the country became a major arms exporter in its own right, especially to fellow 'pariah' states and regimes.[39] South Africa never had much respect for the embargo,[40] but when it was lifted on 25 May 1994 the way was open to expand into the world arms market.

The internationalization of conventional weapons production, and the arrival on the scene of a number of small but perfectly formed arms and technology suppliers, able to dominate niches in the international market and to supply to 'renegade regimes',[41] suggest that the management of the international arms trade may now have moved well beyond the control of any relatively small group of supplier governments, even where those governments agree to act completely in concert. When fully coordinated, supplier cartels might be able to manage their own sector of the international market but probably ought not to expect to manage the market as a whole. The difficulty is that, once this limitation is perceived, it feeds back to and undermines the very notion of limited supply-side coordination. In these circumstances, the best that might be expected is some form of 'transparency' confidence-building measure, of the sort offered by the UN Conventional Arms Register, if and when it is expanded to include domestic procurement and weapons production. More ambitiously, 'leading edge' weapons manufacturers and exporters may be able to identify and restrict access to new, strategically important technologies, but this too is becoming increasingly difficult.

Diffusion of technology
The strategic impact of new military technology is a subject of endless fascination. Recent accounts often refer to film footage taken of cruise missiles 'turning left' at road junctions in Baghdad during the 1991 bombardment, and precision-guided munitions disappearing down ventilation shafts; there can be no doubt that the technological sophistication of modern weaponry is increasing at a rapid rate. Among the projects currently running in western defence research laboratories, the possible development of micro-robot 'soldier ants' is particularly striking.[42] The thirst for sophisticated military equipment is spreading around the world; Malaysia, for example, is reportedly determined to produce its own precision-guided 'smart' munitions.[43] Advocates of the so-called 'Revolution in Military Affairs' see the current phase of military innovation as heralding a new era in military technology and strategy.[44] An alternative view is that the current 'revolution' is no more than the latest phase in a

period of continuous rapid development which began in the mid-nineteenth century and which looks set to continue.[45]

The origins, duration and strategic impact of modern military technological innovation are of less interest here than the implications for attempts to control the rate and scope of technological diffusion. Are export-control policies based upon the relatively simple premise that key technology can be 'owned', and denied to outsiders, any longer possible or wise? Is it possible for the most advanced industrial nations to maintain the leading edge in military technology? The first problem which industrialized governments confront in this regard is the increasing difficulty of distinguishing between civilian and military technological development and application. The notion of 'spin-off' has been familiar since the 1950s; military research laboratories consumed vast sums for research and development and, occasionally, an application emerged which could have innocent civilian use. But during the 1970s and 1980s the 'direction of dependence' began to change and innovation began to flow from the commercial to the military sector, 'a trajectory characterized by spin-on rather than spin-off'.[46] In some cases, leading-edge civilian firms have moved 'horizontally' into the defence sector, thus adding to the pressure on already beleaguered defence industries. The civilianization of leading-edge technological development is becoming so marked that the expression 'dual-use technology' is losing the precision it may once have had and is coming to mean nothing more than 'technology' itself. In some cases, the distinction between civil and military is deliberately blurred, as in the US 'Technology Reinvestment Project' which seeks out for special funding those military research projects which can have civilian applications.[47] The US programme has led, for example, to military global positioning satellite (GPS) locating devices being used in family cars, and combat-fighter software being used in the entertainment industry.[48] Other examples of civilian use of military-related technology and equipment include image-intensifying and infra-red night-vision and surveillance devices, data compression for rapid image and information transmission, lasers, mine detection, and obstacle-avoidance alarms for helicopter pilots. British promotion of 'dual-use technology centres' emulates the US policy.[49]

The commercialization of technological innovation implies a diminution of government control over strategically significant research and development. Particularly in liberal, free-market democracies, the scope for government control of commercial research is already limited. What is more, as technological capability spreads around the world, more states are becoming highly competent on or just behind the leading edge, even to the extent of dominating important niches such as semi-conductors. The commodities being traded are also changing. There is now much more interest in trading spare parts, components and upgrade packages,[50] to the extent that the transfer of technology is becoming a more important 'medium of exchange' than completed weapons plat-forms.[51] As trade becomes more technology-based, as technology in-creasingly has both civil and military applications, and as technological diffusion occurs by 'intangible' means, or in the mind of a scientist, so the trade is becoming 'almost impossible to control'.[52] If technology denial policies are becoming difficult, there are also arguments to sug-gest that they are unfair. Restricted access to those 'bronze medal technologies' which have become part of 'modern industrial and silicon society' could condemn some states to 'third class industrialization and a perpetually lower standard of living'.[53] Almost thirty years ago, D.S. Landes predicted the practical and political problems which would ob-struct policies of technology denial:

> The one ingredient of modernization that is just about indispensable
> is technological maturity and the industrialization that goes with it;
> otherwise one has the trappings without the substance, the pretence
> without the reality ... This world, which has never before been
> ready to universally accept any of the universal faiths offered for its
> salvation, is apparently prepared to embrace the religion of science
> and technology without reservation.[54]

For all these reasons, technology denial and export control policies face an uphill struggle. If technology denial is applied unwisely the effect could be to drive thwarted clients down the path of WMD development and deployment. One approach could be to focus upon those 'leveraging technologies' which could help to create 'military capabilities of strate-gic consequence',[55] but this may imply a model of deterrence, based on mutual respect for certain weapons, which may simply not be available in the conventional sphere. Furthermore, if it continues to be possible to fight wars with second- or third-rate weapons, and even with basic agricultural implements, then the obsession with leading-edge weaponry could prove dangerously misplaced. The developed world could find itself equipped more and more with 'baroque arsenals' but wholly ill-equipped to deal with low-level conflict breaking out around the world.[56] If, in spite of these reservations, technology denial and export control remain the preferred responses, there is another fundamental decision to be made. Should the focus of the denial policy be upon the 'end-use' (i.e. a commodity-list approach) or the 'end-user' (i.e. a country-list approach)? The British government has argued that the latter is the most reasonable and reliable course but, as the negotiations over the successor to CoCom have shown, others are more in favour of a 'shift away from a mind-set that focuses on lists of technology that countries deny either in general or to specific destinations', to an approach which places more emphasis on 'managing the uses to which that technology is put'.[57]

Chapter 5

Politics

Introduction

Chapters 2 and 3 have shown that, while willing to cooperate in the management of defence-related trade, some EU member governments have set strict limitations on the extent and character of any cooperation. And in Chapter 4 it became clear that defence industrial consolidation in the EU raises more than just practical difficulties and cannot be discussed as if taking place in a political vacuum. A *leitmotif* in the development of the EU has been the distinction – often more imagined than real – between the competence of central, supranational authority and that of national governments. In spite of the complex and highly integrated industrial, commercial and economic arrangements which have developed since the 1950s, dismissive expressions such as 'low politics' and 'common market' have been used to suggest a boundary, beyond which lies the 'high politics' of foreign, security and defence policies. The latter have been portrayed as the last bastion of state sovereignty and national prerogative, with member governments resisting the 'federalism' and 'creeping competence' of the supranational 'headquarters' in Brussels. Cooperation in high politics is not inconceivable, but when it has taken place the preference has generally been for intergovernmentalism, with the outcome less a single integrated policy than a compromise between various national policies. In 1996 the EU will conduct a full review of its founding document, the Maastricht Treaty on European Union. The remit of the Intergovernmental Conference is to review the Treaty and assess the implications of an expanded membership. Cooperation in foreign policy, security and defence is expected to occupy a large part of the agenda, with the detailed procedures and expectations of CFSP and the joint-action process receiving much attention. Since the manufacture, procurement and export of conventional arms and sensitive technologies all clearly have connotations of 'high policy', the planned review of cooperation in these areas is sure to have implications for the development of common export control policies. The aim of this chapter is to gauge how, or indeed whether, the political dimension of the export control debate might develop in the near term.

EU 'external policy'

If the common foreign, security and defence policies of the EU are never to be more than the cautious agreement of member governments to cooperate in certain, usually peripheral, areas without 'surrendering' national authority, then it would be unreasonable to expect the outcome to be different from similar attempts at cooperation in these policy areas by any other group of like-minded states. As for the management of defence-related trade, there would be little reason to expect the result to be any more integrated or effective than other past and current efforts at multilateral management. But this prognosis extends from a portrayal of the EU high-politics debate which is too stark. What is often obscured by the rhetoric is that the EU has become an important international actor in its own right and that, even in areas of high politics, the boundaries between national prerogative and Community competence have become difficult to define and sustain. With an 'external policy' rubric covering commercial and economic matters, the EU has been 'from its inception an international phenomenon'.[1] What is more, member governments have been willing to transfer 'most of their sovereignty in the field of foreign trade policy to the Community'.[2] For the convinced 'Euro-sceptic', pursuit of the Common Commercial Policy (CCP) and the part played by the EU as a unitary negotiator during the GATT negotiations, could all be dismissed as nothing more than the inevitable extra-EU dimensions of its low-politics functions. But even at this level, the boundary between 'high' and 'low' is often less clear than might be imagined. The dual-use regulation discussed in Chapter 3 is a good example of this overlap; the regulation itself (rather than the joint action and its annexes) is based on Article 113 of the 1958 EEC Treaty, the decision-making mechanism described as being 'central to the whole edifice' of the CCP.[3]

European political cooperation

The EU also has a more explicit tradition of cooperation in high politics. EPC sought to enable informal, *ad hoc* cooperation in certain foreign policy areas and it, too, contributed to the blurring of the boundaries between 'external' and 'foreign', 'low' and 'high'. As EPC developed during the 1970s the decision to exclude the Commission from its proceedings became untenable, particularly when foreign *economic* policy was clearly an integral part of foreign policy. The October 1981 London Report finally admitted the Commission to full association with EPC.[4] Until the 1986 Single European Act, EPC functioned outside the legal framework of the EC. Although the role of the Commission in foreign policy-making was not significantly enhanced,[5] Title III of the SEA gave EPC a basis in EC law, and attempted to bring the process closer to the objectives and procedures of the EC. Member governments were now to endeavour 'jointly to formulate and implement a European foreign policy' (SEA Article 30.1) and were to 'co-ordinate their positions more closely on the political and economic aspects of security' (SEA Art. 30.6.a). The Commission was to be 'fully associated with the proceedings' of EPC (SEA Art. 30.3.b), although the process was to remain essentially intergovernmental. This was the new mould in which member governments were able to reach agreement on a variety of arms export supervision and management matters: the list of eight criteria, the common reference list, the arms embargo framework and the comparison of national arms export administrative practices. In November 1993, with the ratification of the Treaty on European Union,[6] EPC was replaced by the CFSP. Whereas foreign policy cooperation had previously taken place in the shadow of the EC, in a relationship which, although intensifying, was still uneasy and cautious, it now became one of the three 'pillars' of the new European Union. In spite of the hope held by the Commission and some member governments that the TEU would result in a merger of EC and EPC and a fully integrated foreign and security policy-making machinery,[7] CFSP remained an intergovernmental process. The role of the Commission in foreign policy-making was enhanced, but cautiously so. The Commission's right of initiative, which it had previously enjoyed exclusively in EC-related areas, was extended into matters of foreign and security policy but was to be shared with member governments.[8] As for the European Parliament, although the TEU gave it the power to negotiate directly with the Council of Ministers, it remained largely on the periphery of any foreign policy-related activity.

By differentiating so firmly between intergovernmental and supra-national policy areas or 'pillars', the TEU might well be thought to have halted rather than encouraged progress towards more integrated foreign policy-making in the EU. EPC was hardly the embodiment of a fully mature supranational foreign policy, but its semi-formal nature did sug-gest a certain flexibility and even dynamism, and it might have been possible to devise more imaginative and integrated procedures as time went on. Yet the TEU did advance the debate in a number of important ways, and although CFSP is best understood as an aspiration, it cannot fairly be said that CFSP is merely EPC in another, more rigid guise. In the first place, the TEU prompted the Commission to embark upon a 'bicephalous' approach to external/foreign policy. In May 1993 a new Directorate General was established (DG1A) with responsibility for external political relations. The original DG1 retained its 'traditional agenda' of 'explicitly economic issues'.[9] The new directorate faced opposition both within the Commission and from member governments as it tried to establish its role, but it was nevertheless clear that the creation of DG1A represented a further blurring of the boundaries re-ferred to earlier, with the EU coming closer than ever before to having its own 'foreign ministry'. In October 1994 the new Commission President, Jacques Santer, reorganized the various external-relations portfolios within the Commission. For the five years from January 1995 the Com-mission is to be organized along more geographical than functional lines. There was, however, no suggestion of acquiescence in the Commission's outlook; in the horsetrading over portfolios, the responsibility for the conduct of CFSP was removed from Hans van den Broek and taken over by no less than the Commission President himself.

CFSP also has certain features which could take foreign policy coop-eration far beyond what was possible in EPC, and which could have important effects upon multilateral management of defence-related trade within the EU. Comprehension of the scope of the CFSP provisions is often made difficult by the use of obscure and ambiguous language, but the TEU provides for three levels of intergovernmental cooperation in foreign policy and related fields, ranging from 'systematic cooperation' and 'common position' (both offered by TEU Art. J.2), to 'joint action' (offered by TEU Art. J.3). The first amounts to no more than agreement among the governments to 'inform and consult one another within the Council on any matter of foreign and security policy of general interest in order to ensure that their combined influence is exerted as effectively as possible by means of concerted and convergent action' (TEU Art. J.2.1).

In some circumstances, the Council of Ministers might move to the next level and agree unanimously upon a 'common position' to which national governments will be 'politically' (rather than legally) bound to conform (TEU Art. J.2.2). The third level, 'joint action', attempts to move beyond reactive declarations of opinion or preference. Joint action provides for a more integrated decision-making process, one which could enable the EU to behave more like a national government by projecting a coherent foreign policy, rather than merely responding to foreign developments. Thus, on the basis of 'general guidelines' agreed unanimously and issued by the European Council concerning the scope of CFSP, the Council of Ministers can decide (also unanimously) that certain matters should be subject to joint action and (again unanimously) that certain aspects of the joint action should be implemented by majority voting (TEU Art. J.3.1-2). The joint-action voting and implementation provisions have with some justification been described as a 'clumsy compromise'.[10]

In December 1992 at Edinburgh the European Council published its first set of guidelines. Under the sub-heading 'Economic Aspects of Security', certain arms export-related matters were listed as possible candidates for joint action: transparency in conventional arms transfers; the 'transparency in armaments' item on the agenda of the UN Conference on Disarmament; the follow-up to the UN Register of Conventional Arms; the adoption by the CSCE of common arms export criteria similar to the EPC criteria; and common licence revocation procedures and review of existing UN and European arms embargoes. What is most striking about the European Council document is its emphasis on transparency in arms exports (three out of the five items listed), an exercise which has so far proved to be low-cost and low-impact in political terms. The CSCE item resulted in the adoption in November 1993 by the Forum for Security Cooperation of a list of 'Principles and Guidelines' concerning conventional arms transfers; a document which has also so far defied gravity. The final item hardly represented a great advance; discussion of common licence-revocation procedures and embargoes was a familiar aspect of EPC. In late October 1993, days before the TEU entered into force, the first five joint actions were listed: the promotion of peace and security in Europe; the Middle East; former Yugoslavia; elections in Russia; and South Africa. Subsequent joint actions concerned the provision of humanitarian aid to Bosnia, the definition of an EU position at the Nuclear Non-Proliferation Treaty Review and Extension Conference in spring 1995, and a May 1995 moratorium on the export of anti-personnel land mines. The joint-action procedure was also used to draw up and publish the control lists relating to the EU dual-use regulation.

By introducing majority voting onto the hallowed ground of foreign policy, the joint-action process could be an important, and possibly far-reaching, innovation; 'perhaps the overriding success of the [TEU] that compensates for a whole range of more disappointing factors'.[11] But whatever its potential, for a number of reasons it is an innovation which is unlikely to have immediate effect. For as long as CFSP remains essentially an intergovernmental forum, it is doubtful that the tradition of unanimity, 'bred through decades of EPC',[12] will give way easily, and it will therefore obstruct majority voting. Often though, rather than push disagreement to the point at which the only recourse would be to block EPC decision-making by use of a national veto or, under CFSP, to persuade other member governments to resort to the heavy hand of majority voting, governments have instead accepted the mood of the apparent majority in order to ensure a 'unanimous' decision.[13] If, in spite of ostensible adherence to unanimity, intergovernmental working practice favours consensus over confrontation, then it is still more unlikely that majority voting will be much used. This could have one of two effects. Governments might be persuaded to seek common ground and 'build' consensus in difficult areas or, conversely, the outcome could be that those areas where confrontation is most likely would remain untried by the joint-action/majority-voting process. In the latter case, the outcome would be that majority agreements could be achieved only at the level of the lowest common denominator. Governments might find it useful to have agreement in certain peripheral policy areas, but the main incentive would be the symbolic value of agreements made relatively easily, with minimal political cost and disharmony; 'the maintenance of unity can take precedence over policy content resulting in a common position that lacks effective substance'.[14] Furthermore, since joint actions 'commit the Member States in the positions they adopt and in the conduct of their activity' (TEU Art. J.3.4), deviation from which could face legal challenge from other member states, in some areas some member governments might be reluctant to be pushed into a corner politically and legally, with the result that those policy areas would once again not be considered suitable for the joint-action process. Finally, with such a wide variety of subjects potentially suitable for joint action, in different categories of political importance, experience and difficulty, the joint action process cannot be uniform in implementation. Some joint actions will be easier to identify and implement than others. The South Africa joint action, for example, was built upon a high level of consensus in national policies towards South Africa and was thus relatively easy to agree.[15]

With the impending IGC in mind, governments began preparing position papers in early summer 1995. A 'reflection group' of national experts met in Messina, Italy in early June 1995 to begin drawing up an agenda for the IGC. The developing debate embraces several fundamental issues such as the rate at which the EU will take on new members from central and eastern Europe, the timetable for monetary union, and the degree to which the EU can function as an *à la carte* organization in which member states can determine their own terms of membership. Sharply differing national positions on these and other issues suggest that the debate will be vigorous, both before and during the IGC. Some governments take the view that the object of the 1996 IGC should be less a major redraft of the treaty than delicate 'fine-tuning' of the EU and its already ambitious agenda.[16] But the institutions of the EU have also provided position papers and a steady input to the debate, and tend to take a more far-reaching approach. In a Commission paper published in early May 1995, Santer caused concern in some national governments when he demanded more majority voting in CFSP. Santer's approach, and the Commission's generally unfavourable view of intergovernmentalism in foreign policy coordination, built upon an earlier report on CFSP commissioned by Hans van den Broek, the Commissioner for external political relations. The report condemned the 'inertia and impotence of the CFSP and WEU' as the 'inward and outward reflection of a lack of capacity or will to act, particularly as regards the threat and/or use of force by the Union'. The report went on to recommend a 'central capacity for analysis and planning' in all matters relating to CFSP and defence, and commented on the 'twin perils of blinkered concentration on hastily conceived "joint actions" on the one hand and sterile bureaucratisation on the other'.[17] The EP's position paper published in May 1995 also caused some controversy with its call to abolish the national veto in virtually all EU policy-making and legislation, including foreign, security and defence matters.

Prospects for cooperation in the management of defence-related trade will be determined by the fate of CFSP at the IGC. A number of outcomes are conceivable. First, the CFSP 'pillar', and with it the joint-action process, could collapse completely, with foreign, security and defence policy-making being completely 'renationalized'. This outcome would see the abandonment of any attempt at systematic cooperation in export controls. The most that could then be expected would be a return to *ad hoc*, reactive intergovernmental cooperation. While no doubt favoured by those 'Euro-sceptics' most anxious to limit supranationalism in the EU generally, this outcome is extremely unlikely. CFSP may have uncertain foundations, but it has become an established feature of the EU, largely because member governments have seen fit to cooperate, at different levels of sophistication, in a widening array of areas related to foreign and security policy. 'Spill-over' from cooperation in the CCP also makes it difficult to isolate 'high politics'; as Britain's foreign secretary remarked in October 1994, 'The question is not the need for cooperation but its *form*.'[18] This leaves at least the possibility of continuing with some form of cooperation in defence-trade matters. The second hypothesis lies at the opposite end of the spectrum and would see the merging of the EC and the two intergovernmental 'pillars'. In a fully integrated Union, the Commission would have, more than simply a voice, the exclusive right of initiative in foreign, security and defence matters. With the expansion of the EU to a membership of twenty or more states from western, central and eastern Europe, the integrationist school also argues for genuine majority voting in such matters. A fully integrated EU would mean supranational control of defence-related trade going far beyond anything yet achieved, or even attempted, in Europe and elsewhere. But given the high level of scepticism regarding the EU's performance and potential in these areas, scepticism which is unlikely to diminish by late 1996, this option too can be ruled unlikely.

A more probable fate for foreign policy cooperation within the EU is the continuation, possibly with some adjustments, of the existing CFSP system. CFSP currently offers a form of intergovernmental cooperation which is more systematic and formal than that which obtains in the judicial and home affairs 'pillar', but which falls short of the centralism and supranational authority of the EC. This median position, which could be described as 'enhanced intergovernmentalism', might see defence and security matters being detached from foreign policy cooperation and placed in a fourth, more clearly intergovernmental 'pillar'. But even if the basic structure of CFSP were to remain unchanged, there would still be potential for effective cooperation in defence-related trade. The full range of current CFSP cooperation would be available: information exchange, common position and joint action. By this latter view, rather than expect the character of CFSP, or the EU itself, to change so radically that a new, fully integrated approach to supply-side defence trade management could be possible, it is more prudent to ask where, in the spectrum offered by 'enhanced intergovernmentalism', defence trade

71

management might find a home and whether it is reasonable to expect anything beyond peripheral, lowest-common-denominator agreements.

With CFSP and the joint-action process still in their infancy, it is too early to judge accurately where the political limits of export control cooperation in the EU might lie. The use of the joint-action process to clear the blockage over the dual-use regulation might in time prove to have been the first, cautious step towards closer integration. But for several reasons, more modest expectations are probably in order for the immediate future, with defence trade cooperation probably remaining at the less developed end of the range of CFSP options. It has already been shown that the agenda for joint action is very wide. The fact that joint actions have been possible in certain areas and functions does not indicate that the process will be applicable, to a uniform standard, across the whole agenda. Although there has clearly been a good deal of cooperation in matters associated with defence-related trade in the EU, the results of this cooperation have been limited and largely reactive. The ground may simply not be as fertile as that from which, for example, the South Africa joint action grew. To begin at a much lower level of cooperation, in an area of policy which has so far been fiercely guarded by governments, and to expect very much more than basic agreements, may therefore be too ambitious at present. In some respects, cooperation in defence-related trade has been so delicate and difficult that it was unwise to include it on the first joint-action agenda, giving credence to the claim discussed in Chapter 2 that the December 1992 Edinburgh European Council 'general guidelines' for joint actions only included arms export-related matters as a result of bureaucratic confusion over the 'Asolo List'.

That the joint-action process was never meant to be applied to defence-related matters, arguably including arms exports, is also suggested by Article J.4.3 of the TEU which states plainly that 'Issues having defence implications dealt with under this Article shall not be subject to the [joint-action] procedures set out in Article J.3.' Although the mandate for CFSP includes 'all questions related to the security of the Union, including the eventual framing of a common defence policy, which might in time lead to a common defence' (TEU Art. J.4.1), it would therefore appear that CFSP was not expected to be applied uniformly, in all relevant policy areas, from the outset. If defence industries could be described as vital strategic assets in terms of national defence and security, then it could be reasonable to extend the same logic to the arms exports which currently sustain those industries. This raises the intriguing possibility that the TEU contains within it something like an Article 223 limitation on the scope of CFSP, enabling member governments to cite 'defence implications' as a means to deflect the joint-action process away from defence-related areas. Article 223, it should be remembered, restricts EC involvement in 'the production of *or trade* in arms'. This apparent contradiction will be addressed at the 1996 IGC, until which point EU foreign ministers meeting in the the General Affairs Council have recommended that joint actions should not be 'explicitly' defence-related.

The broader question of the extension of EU cooperation into the fields of security and defence can never be far from the discussion of export control cooperation. Some of the long-standing prejudice against EU involvement in defence matters has given way recently. In the United States, the view that European defence cooperation could only under-mine NATO has softened, partly in the face of Congressional demands for Europe to shoulder more of the burden of its own defence and security affairs after the Cold War. A new mood is also indicated by France's gradual *rapprochement* with NATO's military structure since 1992,[19] and by Britain's 'change of tack' to support a 'European power bloc in Nato' in autumn 1994.[20] But whatever the possibilities for defence-related cooperation in the EU, several member governments are deter-mined that the process should remain unequivocally intergovernmental. During a speech in Brussels early in 1995, Britain's defence minister insisted that 'European defence and security should remain the preserve of EU governments alone – without any role for the Commission or the European Parliament.'[21] On a more emotional level, the possibility that armed forces might be asked to risk their lives for what might be described as a remote political process has also raised misgivings:

> More than any other policy field, security and defence strike at the heart of national sovereignty. For the foreseeable future none of the EC members can be expected to commit itself to majority decision-making or to accept the authority of a supranational body on questions of life and death.[22]

For as long as political, cultural and emotional considerations of this sort persist, 'enhanced intergovernmentalism' is the very most that might be expected, but even this may be too ambitious in certain policy areas. Ultimately, this inertia may only be overcome when member govern-ments decide that it is in their interests to do so. The history of the EU shows that governments have been willing to 'pool sovereignty' when analysis of the costs and benefits of cooperation point in that direction. But it is instructive to remember that at the beginning of EPC, the 'benefit' which governments sought was nothing more than 'a forum in which to exchange information and attempt to coordinate positions *without directly affecting their vested national interests*'.[23] Given the harshly competitive conditions of the international arms market and the lingering perception that defence manufacturing is above all a national asset which, for domestic political, industrial and strategic reasons, is best served by retaining a substantial degree of national control, it is not yet apparent that member governments will be willing to cooperate in defence-related trade in anything other than non-contentious and peripheral areas, and in a non-compulsory way. As Chapter 4 showed, although the 'national-champion' view of defence industry in Europe has many critics in government and industry, several key governments have yet to be convinced that the economic and industrial benefits of integrating arms exports and other defence industrial functions could offset the possible political costs of sharing political decision-making in these areas.

Chapter 6

Principles

Introduction

Previous chapters have shown that multilateral efforts to manage the international trade in conventional arms and technology have generally not been an unqualified success, particularly where west Europeans have been involved. It has proven difficult for arms supplier states to go much beyond relatively straightforward, reactive, punitive arms embargoes. Technological diffusion and the lack of cohesion among the suppliers help to explain this deficiency. But it is the possibility of a deeper, conceptual weakness in multilateral arms trade management which is the focus of this chapter. The first part of the chapter turns to fundamental questions; why should states in general wish to cooperate in the management of the arms market, and what types of cooperation are, or could be, available? The next step, in search of a central organizing principle, is to compare conventional arms export initiatives with more explicitly norm-driven WMD non-proliferation regimes. The third problem to address is whether conventional arms export policies can be directive and used as levers to modify the behaviour of clients, or indeed whether export decisions can be shaped at all by behavioural expectations assumed to be universally valid.

Cooperation in arms export controls: motives and means

To ask why states should wish to cooperate in regulating the arms trade begs a prior question; why is national regulation sought in the first place? Although it is true to say that many regulatory initiatives have been proposed on behalf of the international community, or humanity itself, it appears that a powerful sense of protecting or advancing national interest often lies at the heart of efforts to manage the arms trade multilaterally. National interest is an expression notoriously resistant to simple definition, but it is often in the name of this vague concept that governments cooperate and seek to achieve, or make more effective, their individual goals of management and supervision. These goals reflect various pragmatic, legal and ethical requirements and judgments.

The pragmatist might see that for as long as there has been a demand for weapons and military equipment there has also been interest in the conduct and consequences of any transactions, with regular intervention in the market place by those responsible for the production and supply of relevant goods and technology. Studies of the arms trade cite examples of intervention going as far back as the Middle Ages, with a brief phase of *laissez-faire* practice at the end of the nineteenth century seen as the exception to prove the general rule.[1] The essential quality of defence-related trade, which underpins most assessments of the economic, political, technological and strategic implications of a given transaction, and which drives governments to intervene, is that the trade involves the distribution of military power. By extension, the defence and even survival of governments, states and societies could be affected; 'trade in armaments ... [has] potential to affect a nation's security [assuring] its treatment as a phenomenon uniquely relevant to world politics'.[2] The pragmatist's perspective, therefore, amounts to the claim that it must be in the interest of governments to avoid possible adverse consequences of defence-related trade by controlling the trade and the market place.

As far as proliferation and arms exports are concerned, national governments are both the primary source and the agent of international law, and are required by that law to have the means to supervise and regulate the arms trade. In some circumstances, unregulated arms sales and transfers could amount to illegal intervention or even outright aggression. The international community of states having agreed, in the UN Charter and various Security Council and General Assembly resolutions, to join in preventing such transgressions, it follows that states have an obligation to cooperate in arms trade regulation.[3] Having agreed in Article 2.5 of the Charter to 'give the [UN] every assistance in any action it takes', all UN member states are committed to 'refrain from giving assistance to any state against which the [UN] is taking preventive or enforcement action' and to 'establish standing mechanisms for the national regulation of their arms exports in order to be in a position to enforce mandatory arms embargoes'.[4] Embargoes are not the only issue, however. States must meet a variety of obligations in international law, such as not supporting terrorist groups, and this requires all states to have the means to supervise and control any transfer of arms, ammunition and military equipment, whatever the circumstances of the transaction.[5] Some arms control and disarmament treaties have required states to manage the redistribution of military equipment. The 1990 Conventional Armed Forces in Europe Treaty (CFE), for example, was an elaborate agreement to reduce the numbers of conventional forces deployed in Europe by NATO and the Warsaw Pact.[6] With large amounts of high-quality military equipment about to be dismantled or destroyed, NATO's response was to implement an 'Equipment Transfer and Rationalization Programme'. The programme, also known as 'cascade', was designed to ensure that NATO allies could upgrade their arsenals with advanced, surplus stock while at the same meeting the overall reduction commitments made in the CFE treaty.[7] International humanitarian law, or the laws of war, can also require governments to cooperate in restricting the supply of certain weapons.

Mention of the laws of war introduces the moral dimension to the discussion. Humanitarian law stigmatizes certain military practices and weapons as inhumane, indiscriminate or disproportionate. As the recent campaign against anti-personnel landmines illustrates, arguments from this perspective can have a powerful influence on defence-related trade.[8] It is, of course, not just the conduct of war which raises ethical objections and questions: 'For the Christian non-pacifist, as for the pacifist, this is not an industry like any other. Selling weapons is not exclusively an economic issue.'[9] Discussion of the ethics of defence-related trade is often rather entrenched. At one extreme lies the argument that weapons are morally neutral, that 'weapons do not make war, people do'. The bitter conflict over the separation of India and Pakistan in 1947 is often cited as evidence of destruction, killing and cruelty on a vast scale achieved without the benefit of modern weaponry. Events in Rwanda in 1994 provide a more recent illustration of the same argument. By this argument, moral concern about the transfer or possession of certain types of weapons is a misplaced and self-indulgent obsession with technology; the only proper subject for moral examination is the intention of the maker, owner or buyer of the weapon. In any case, the argument might continue, it is difficult to define and sustain objective moral criteria. Important general principles, such as the need to enable states to defend against aggression, or even the need to deny arms to oppressive regimes, may prove to be less than universally and eternally valid and beg many secondary questions which can only be answered in context. There is, for example, no universal agreement on what makes an appropriate or 'legitimate' level of self-defence, and a convincing definition of 'aggression' has so far eluded the UN. Defence-related trade, the argument might conclude, therefore takes place in a moral vacuum; there may be reasons why governments should intervene in the arms trade, but morality is not one of them.

At the other extreme lies the proposition that defence-related trade is more causative than symptomatic of conflict and is therefore an ethical issue in its own right. Interwar reaction against the 'merchants of death' who, allegedly, fuelled the 1914–18 war, illustrates this thinking, as does the currently popular analogy between defence-related trade and the illegal trade in narcotics, with talk of tackling the 'arms pushers' who corrupt and manipulate their 'victims'.[10] The proposition extends into the notion that certain machines and technologies, far from being morally 'neutral', can be described as 'offensive' or 'destabilizing' and should therefore be banned or subject to special controls. As the basis for informed, balanced decisions on defence-related trade, each of these alternatives is as 'simplistic and inadequate' as the other.[11] The first approach suggests either that the international system is reducible to a Darwinian free-for-all, or that officials and policy-makers are just impotent ciphers, trapped in a 'Greek tragedy, the tragedy of necessity, where the feeling aroused in the spectator is "What a pity it had to be this way"'.[12] However, even the most convinced adherent of *Realpolitik* will at some point be drawn into making ethical judgments: 'The notion of "national interest" is based upon the values of the national community, values which can be regarded as the product of its culture and as the expression of its sense of cohesion, values which define for men what they believe to be right or just.'[13] Yet the alternative suggestion that mankind is being obstructed, by arms traders and even some machines, from achieving a natural state of global harmony seems to go too far at a time when aggressors, dictators and other unsavoury characters plainly exist. The ethical debate on defence-related trade may be doomed to vacillate fruitlessly between these irreconcilable positions, and may as a result offer little in terms of policy advice. What is certain, however, is that much of the pressure exerted on Western governments by their electorates will stem from general, ethically motivated disquiet about the conduct and consequences of defence-related trade.

For a variety of pragmatic, legal and moral reasons, therefore, governments on the supply side of defence-related trade are motivated or pressurized to manage their involvement in the market. All states involved in the trade have developed some sort of management system, and it is at this unilateral level that most management of defence-related trade has taken place.[14] Some analysts argue that the trend towards multi-lateralism is misplaced, and that efforts at the unilateral level offer the only real possibility of control.[15] But governments, aware of the diversity of the global market and of the spread of manufacturing capability, and conscious that the internationalization of defence industry, notably in western Europe, implies the need for some form of multilateral management, are nevertheless drawn to multilateral cooperation in managing defence-related trade. Yet as the number of manufacturers, suppliers and purchasers increases, so it becomes necessary to involve more and more governments in any regulatory initiative if success is to be achieved, and the practical and political obstacles to effective cooperation accordingly become higher. Particularly when certain of the vigorous new arms exporters have acquired their capability in spite of the best efforts of the original suppliers, then, for as long as they retain their 'pariah' status, it is unlikely that they would be willing to cooperate in regulating the arms trade. In other words, as the need to cooperate becomes more pronounced, so the scope for effective cooperation can diminish.

When governments decide, for whatever reason, that the management of defence-related trade could best be achieved in concert, a number of options present themselves. The simplest conceivable form of export control cooperation would be that which takes place on an *ad hoc* basis, as circumstances required, and which results in jointly implemented arms or technology embargoes. With no attempt to organize the cooperation in any formal or institutional way, and no attempt to justify the cooperation through an appeal to a higher political or moral authority, initiatives of this sort might best be described as reactive, concerted, militant diplomacy. Such agreements, made at short notice and for a short period, might be relatively easy to make and could have a rapid effect, both on domestic public opinion and on the 'target' state. But *ad hoc* initiatives involving just a few like-minded states might also prove easy for the participants to leave, and equally easy for the targets to evade. Governments are accordingly persuaded both that cooperation should have some form of organization, and that the initiative should include as many of the relevant suppliers and recipients as possible or appropriate. Another consideration might be that governments which appeared too willing to implement unilateral, *ad hoc* embargoes might become known to the demand side as politically and commercially unreliable. The relationship between supply and demand can never be guaranteed. This applies in all areas of industry and commerce, including the trade in arms and technology, particularly when 'buyer's market' conditions prevail. In these circumstances, governments might wish to legitimize their action by, say, a UN Security Council Resolution or by appealing to universalist ideals such as the advancement of human rights. What is more, with research, development and training times often lasting well over a decade, it is generally thought necessary to take a long view when considering how, and for how long, to restrict the arms and technology trade. Cooperation in the management of defence-related trade therefore suggests three desiderata. First, the initiative will seek to be organized and institutionalized, rather than appear merely a casual arrangement between governments. Second, the participants will draw upon a higher authority rather than appear to be driven by mere *Realpolitik* and national interest. Legal and political authority might come from the UN, while moral authority might come from religious conviction or from adherence to other universalist ideals. Finally, the initiative is likely to take place over time rather than appear spontaneous and short-lived.

When cooperation between states becomes deliberate and prescriptive, and where a formal or semi-formal organization is sought, so it becomes appropriate to think in terms of 'regimes'. The creation, maintenance and consequences of regimes have received a great deal of attention in academic writing on international relations. By one popular definition, international regimes amount to 'principles, norms, rules and decision-making procedures around which actor expectations converge in a given issue-area'.[16] Casual, *ad hoc* cooperation in the management of defence-related trade, of the sort referred to earlier, would be described as 'short-term calculations of interest', and would therefore not qualify as regimes. Instead, regimes involve 'some sense of general obligation',[17] and this must be manifested over time. Where the object of the regime is to manage defence-related trade, the 'sense of general obligation' could, but need not necessarily, exclude the state or states which are or which become the target of the regime. By one account, regimes are quintessentially 'hegemonic structures ... in which the rules are clear and obeyed' and are therefore best seen as a legacy of the Cold War.[18] Although too much can be expected from elegant theorizing, regime theory does nevertheless help to explain the modes of formal cooperation open to governments.

Cooperation in the control of defence-related trade might be achieved in one of two ways. The key to the first, the enforced or hegemonic trade-management regime, is that the norm or 'sense of general obligation' is agreed by the suppliers but not accepted by the recipients or targets. There are two variants of this type of initiative. The first variant is a relatively straightforward matter of denial and domination, the best example of which would be the conditions imposed on a defeated state. Rather more subtle, and much more complex, enforcement can also be a matter of drawn-out, systematic trade restrictions such as the CoCom initiative of 1949–94 and, more recently, the various WMD technology-transfer control regimes such as the NSG and the MTCR. The second variant could be described as 'hegemony by stealth', where access to arms or technology becomes, more than a matter of foreign policy or commerce, a process of *de facto* hegemony through 'leadership and the manipulation of incentives'.[19] Clients might be required to accept certain conditions regarding their overall military expenditure, their relations with neighbouring states, their support for arms control initiatives and even the character of their society and government in exchange for access to the market. Generally, aid conditionality is not a novel concept and features regularly in current debates on foreign aid and demilitarization. In their July 1991 'Declaration on Conventional Arms Transfers and NBC Non-Proliferation', the Group of Seven industrialized democracies agreed that donor countries should 'take account of military expenditure where it is disproportionate when setting up aid programmes'.[20] Making foreign aid and investment conditional on the behaviour of the recipients is a controversial subject. Yet when conditionality tactics are employed in the arms and sensitive-technology trade, not only does the familiar contradiction emerge between market opportunism and market regulation, but the idea also appears to assume a degree of consensus, both among suppliers and between suppliers and recipients, which is unlikely given post-Cold War market conditions.[21]

The second broad approach is to seek the 'consensual regime', one which is genuinely multilateral, involving suppliers as well as recipients, and which is based upon a universal or at least widely held set of norms and values. The various initiatives to prevent the proliferation of nuclear, biological and chemical weapons would fall into this category although, as suggested earlier, some features of these regimes (such as the export control arrangements) appear to have more in common with supply-side exclusivity. The presumption against horizontal proliferation of WMD transcended the Cold War confrontation and still has a considerable international constituency. Complacency in this regard may, however, be increasingly misplaced. Since the end of the Cold War there have been

several instances of acquisition and even use of WMD in obvious contra-
vention of the various regimes. But maverick WMD research and development programmes are hardly a new phenomenon and to some extent
serve to emphasize the general non-proliferation norm. What may prove
far more hazardous is the possible erosion of this general norm among
more responsible states and governments. The difficulties in negotiating
the review and extension of the Nuclear Non-Proliferation Treaty and the
unhurried ratification of the Chemical Weapons Convention may indicate a loss of faith in the blanket presumption against WMD proliferation.

However vulnerable the WMD non-proliferation regimes are becoming, they are still considerably more solid and durable than anything
which might be called a norm against conventional proliferation. It is not
easy to transfer WMD non-proliferation ideas and practices to the conventional area; while there are 'unambiguous ethical, pragmatic and
power-political' reasons to prevent nuclear proliferation, and 'considerable international acceptance' of those reasons, 'in the area of conventional arms there are no such unambiguous answers.'[22] By this view, the
best that might be hoped for is a global regime to ban the production and
trade in particularly inhumane or brutal weapons. To the extent that the
law of war, and even international law in general, is but the sum of the
will of the international community of states, then humanitarian and legal
restraints upon the international arms trade could themselves be described as a 'consensual regime'.

In pursuit of an international conventional arms trade norm

There is wide agreement in the literature as to the difficulty of establishing and maintaining a set of general norms or values which might govern
the transfer of conventional weapons and related technology. Some hope
has been expressed that the December 1991 UN Register of Conventional Arms might be the first step towards the creation of a globally
respected body of values,[23] but international support for the Register has
been slow to develop. Governments are pushed, for a variety of reasons,
towards some form of multilateral regulation of the arms trade. Yet this
impulse has so far had limited effect. The complex task of balancing
commercial, political and moral considerations would doubtless be
facilitated by the identification of a principle or code by which to shape
difficult decisions nationally and multilaterally. It may equally be that no
such value exists or could ever be identified, or that the norm being
sought is no less than one which could deal with aggression, conflict and

war itself. In any case, the search for such a code has so far been of more interest to analysts of the international arms trade than to participants in it. This is in part attributable to the character of the post-Cold War arms market, which emphasizes a competitive, non-cooperative commercial logic and which makes it difficult even for like-minded suppliers to define common goals and rules by which to regulate their participation in the arms trade.

Beyond commercial considerations, other explanations might be offered for this dilemma. The end of the Cold War adversarial relationship has removed one important source of structure and control. The hegemonic, or 'spheres of influence', character of Cold War arms trading has been replaced by what might be termed the 'Article 51 argument', one which seems singularly unlikely to produce the elusive norm. Article 51 of the UN Charter guarantees each state's 'inherent right of individual or collective self-defence'. As the British government and others have argued, Article 51 implies that states have 'the right to acquire the means with which to defend themselves.'[24] Comments to this effect were included in several of the post-Cold War regulatory initiatives launched in 1991. If self-defence is a key attribute of sovereignty, the argument might continue, then any interference in the right to self-defence, for example by instituting an arms embargo, undermines the notion of national sovereignty, one of the key features of the international system. Since national sovereignty is an attribute which the 'interferers' also enjoy and would be unwilling to surrender, and since their 'interfering' is usually done in the name of an international system built upon the concept of national sovereignty, it can be seen that the 'Article 51 argument' does some damage to the search for a central organizing value. It is also possible that governments have become conditioned to see conventional arms transfers as a peripheral issue, if not normal or even preferred practice. This conditioning could be seen as a legacy of the Cold War, when WMD arms control and non-proliferation tended to capture the greater part of government and public imagination. Given East-West tension, this bias was reasonable but it had the effect of relegating conventional arms transfer controls to the second order and even meant that conventional arms transfers became a 'release valve', or a means to continue the Cold War struggle by other, non-WMD means. The WMD/conventional substitution issue remains relevant today, in that an over-restrictive arms trade regime which had the effect of pushing the 'target' state down the path of WMD acquisition would probably be seen as counterproductive.

The diffuse post-Cold War international order, combined with a legacy of relative indifference to the spread of conventional weapons, seems to offer three choices, none of them especially convincing as a guiding principle. First, the 'Article 51 argument' could be taken to mean that the international arms trade can only be judged in relative or regional terms; an overarching or absolute set of values is logically, politically and morally unattainable. A second choice could be to apply the Cold War 'release valve' idea and argue that the international arms trade ought still, in certain circumstances, to be encouraged. The priority would be to ensure that states are not persuaded that their goals could be realized through the acquisition of WMD. This argument could also extend into the idea that states have a moral obligation to sell arms to those engaged in self-defence against an aggressor. There is a compelling simplicity to both the 'Article 51' and the 'release valve' arguments, but since both entail a presumption of access to the arms market rather than restraint of it, it appears that the pragmatic, legal and moral considerations which prompt states to wish to control the market would have to be compromised in some way. A third option could be to argue that while self-defence is indeed a right of states, it is a right which must be enjoyed within the rule-based international legal and political system. More importantly, one state's right to self-defence should not entail an unqualified moral and legal obligation on other states to export weapons, except where there is a treaty requirement to assist or defend allies.[25] But if the best that can be said is that 'decisions must be made', then the third option is hardly more than a restatement of the problem, rather than a solution to it.

Trade in conventional arms and technology differs from WMD proliferation in three other respects. First, although the risks which may accompany the acquisition of a large conventional arsenal ought not to be underestimated, these risks are best understood in local or at most regional terms. This same complacency could, however, prove to be wholly misplaced with regard to the acquisition by some states of WMD. Nuclear, biological and chemical weaponry, and ballistic missiles, have been described as 'catastrophic weaponry', weapons which would, if used, 'necessarily devastate civilian populations with catastrophic consequences'.[26] Simply put: 'the global threat from states acquiring more conventional arms is qualitatively different from that of the same states acquiring nuclear armaments'.[27]

The second distinction lies in the character of the weapons. WMD are often perceived and described in absolute terms, strategically, politically, legally and morally. These perceptions have so far exerted a powerful influence upon decisions regarding the development, possession and possible use of WMD. But the same might not be said of conventional weapons. The manufacture, ownership and deployment of conventional weapons are more readily understood to be a function of a given political and military context, rather than directive of it.[28] Although it must be correct to say that in some circumstances, certain weapons can be 'destabilizing' or offer an 'offensive' capability, it is particularly difficult to apply such judgments in a categorical way where conventional weapons are concerned. The technical capabilities of a given conventional weapon system are available to the possessor to exploit, in aggression as in defence; 'destabilizing' and 'offensive' are therefore judgments which can only be made in context. For a military commander in a defensive position, the vital task is to steal the initiative from the aggressor, and 'offensive' weapons such as tanks could be used legitimately for this purpose. A conventional confrontation is often as much about the initiative and ability of the military commander as it is about the quantity and quality of the weapons being deployed. On many occasions, being on equal terms in armaments, or even being the underdog, has had little bearing on military decisions. Indeed, some military commanders appear to view qualitative and quantitative disadvantage as a challenge to be met, and rather relish acting the role of David outsmarting Goliath. The performance of the Israeli armed forces on the Golan Heights in 1973 is often cited in this respect, but a more recent example of the triumph of self-confidence over military capability might be the Chechen rebels' struggle against Russian armour and air power in late 1994 and 1995. It is also relevant to note that US and NATO military doctrine underwent a 'revolution' in the 1980s and early 1990s, the result of which is a deliberate blurring of offensive and defensive in military planning and operations.[29]

The final distinction between the conventional arms trade and WMD proliferation is one which recalls the precepts of academic international regime theory on the one hand, and the facts of a diffuse and possibly uncontrollable worldwide conventional arms and technology production base on the other. As the production base broadens so it must become more difficult to control: 'multilateral efforts at controls can be effective only when the objects of controls are wholly within the influence orbit of those seeking to implement them'.[30] On a more theoretical level, diffusion also undermines one of the principles of effective non-proliferation; that 'deviants' should be kept 'small in number, isolated, and manageable'.[31]

These practical and theoretical stipulations might be relevant in the field of WMD proliferation, but they are largely inappropriate for the post-Cold War conventional arms market.

Cultural relativism

If there are practical and logical difficulties in establishing regimes by which the conventional arms and technology trade might be controlled, and if the norms and values upon which such regimes might be based appear particularly hard to identify, a related problem lies in the way such attempts at regime-building are viewed by both non-participants in, and targets of, the regime. The problem becomes most pronounced when the arms and technology recipients with the most awkward questions are at the same time enjoying the benefits of a buyer's market.

It has been suggested earlier in this chapter that a basic tension exists between the goal of arms trade regulation on one hand, and the principles of state sovereignty and non-intervention on the other. This tension might be caricatured in the following way. If self-defence and, by extension, the arms trade are attributes of sovereignty then a state should expect to be treated by its peers as 'innocent until proven guilty'; that is, to be allowed to exercise its self-defence and arms purchasing rights until good reason emerges why it should not. The tension mounts when the machinery of regulation is linked in some way to what is perceived to be the furtherance of the regulators' interests and values, which may be described by the regulators as universal values, but not accepted as such by the recipients or by other supplier governments. The tension is greatest when the linkage becomes prescriptive, and the regulators' values are presented as norms and standards to which all states should aspire. Of the various post-Cold War attempts to supervise or control the conventional arms trade, the UN Register of Conventional Arms emerges as the most neutral and even-handed, and the least judgmental. But the UN Register is more a supervisory than a regulatory initiative and has not yet, in any case, achieved general international support. The 'Permanent Five' and Group of Seven initiatives of 1991, however, went beyond the goal of restricting aggression and breaches of international peace and security to use such expressions as 'legitimate self-defence' when referring to potential recipients. From the recipient's point of view, expressions of this nature could imply that the right of self-defence has become less an attribute of state sovereignty, one which could be described as absolute and inalienable within the parameters of international law, than a quality which can be defined, awarded or denied by a group of states in the international system. The CSCE's November 1993 'Principles Governing Conventional Arms Transfers' went one step further and mentioned 'the respect for human rights and fundamental freedoms in the recipient country', as well as 'legitimate security and defence needs', as criteria against which potential conventional arms purchasers should be judged. The European Union's eight 'criteria', listed in the Appendix, present some of the same thinking. And in 1995, in a similar vein, the International Committee of the Red Cross began to investigate the possibility of linking arms transfer decisions to a potential recipient's compliance with the international humanitarian law of armed conflict.

With relatively clear and convincing sets of norms having been developed to accompany the various WMD non-proliferation initiatives, there is a strong temptation to assume that something similar ought to be available in the sphere of conventional arms and technology transfers. Yet the search for such a code is invariably contentious, and begs fundamental questions. Which is the main, organizing principle in the international system – the supposed universality of interests and values perceived by many to be characteristically Western, or the sovereign authority of individual states? Are ideas such as human rights and democracy universal, and universally applicable, values? The facts of the buyer's market, and the logic of the 'Article 51 argument', make it possible for recipient states to challenge the practice of 'hegemony by stealth', as they might perceive it. But there is a growing school of thought which argues that the imposition of conditions regarding human rights, democracy, and so forth are unacceptable because these are essentially Western, Judaeo-Christian values and concerns, rather than any universal standard. Even if they were acceptable as universal values, some would argue that they are ideals rather than policy prescriptions and that some states will require much more time to work towards these ideals while remaining stable and secure. In early 1995 a US Institute for National Security Studies report noted that while 'the global advancement of democracy and respect for human rights' had made 'notable strides' in the 1980s, the experience of the 1990s and the immediate prospects were less encouraging.[32] Although conditions were generally improving around the world, the report noted that 'democratic ideals' were in some cases being observed only perfunctorily. Since the end of the Cold War, these ideals had come under 'severe pressure' in many of the 'new democracies'. In some cases, the explanation was to be found in a clash of priorities:

Many new democracies have discovered problems in reconciling group rights and individual freedom with political stability. Severe contractions of national economies have frequently turned public opinion against democratic reformers who were raised to leadership in the wake of the Soviet Union's disintegration, most notably in Russia itself.

Other explanations offered in the report for the uneven application of democratic principles include the surge in nationalist feeling, awakened by improvements in communications and education, the close connection in some areas between political and religious movements, and the belief that religion, ethnicity and 'group consensus' are values which matter more than democratic ambitions. But the report also argued that the spread of democracy had in some senses been too successful, that democratic values had been spread too thin, and that 'with the global diffusion of democracy, it has become clear that what is meant by "democracy" varies from state to state as a result of differing cultural influences.'

The authors of the *Strategic Assessment* may have been influenced by two publications which appeared in 1993 and which received a great deal of attention thereafter. In the first, an article by Samuel Huntington, broadly similar assumptions of cultural relativism were explored, but on a global scale.[33] Huntington argued that the bases of future conflict would be primarily cultural, rather than ideological. He presented an image of a non-Western world whose peoples and governments were no longer willing to be 'the objects of history as the targets of Western colonialism' but would join the West as 'movers and shapers of history'.[34] Huntington found that the West had made use of ill-defined notions such as 'world community' and 'universal civilization' to legitimize the spread of Western values and preferences, political, economic and moral. Not only was the idea of a universal civilization at odds with 'the particularism of most Asian societies', but the values being presented also differed 'fundamentally' from those found in other civilizations: 'Western ideas of individualism, liberalism, constitutionalism, human rights, equality, liberty, the rule of law, democracy, free markets, the separation of church and state, often have little resonance in Islamic, Confucian, Japanese, Hindu, Buddhist or Orthodox cultures'.[35] Huntington also applied his 'clashing civilizations' thesis to the spread of conventional arms and technology. While most Western countries were reducing military spending and military power, many in the Middle East and Asia-Pacific regions were increasing theirs and asserting their 'right to acquire and to deploy whatever weapons they think necessary for their security'. In response to this loss of control, Huntington saw the West attempting to use arms control – 'a Western concept and a Western goal' – along with political and economic pressure to prevent the development of 'military capabilities that could threaten Western interests'. For their part, the states of the Middle East and the Asia-Pacific rim were developing a 'Confucian-Islamic military connection ... designed to promote acquisition by its members of the weapons and weapons technologies needed to counter the military power of the West.'[36]

If, in Huntington's view, cultural differences are the new determinants of international politics and an important explanation of the character of the post-Cold War arms trade, broadly similar things might be said of warfare itself, as in John Keegan's *A History of Warfare*, also published in 1993. Keegan found that warfare could only be understood in relative terms, as an expression of cultural structures and preferences. He found the resort to war, and conduct in war, to be a subject rather more complex and diffuse than the Clausewitzian model so popular in the West:

> Culture is ... a prime determinant of the nature of warfare, as the
> history of its development in Asia clearly demonstrates. Oriental
> warmaking, if we may so identify and denominate it as something
> different and apart from European warfare, is characterised by traits
> peculiar to itself ... Future peacekeepers and peacemakers have
> much to learn from alternative military cultures, not only that of the
> Orient, but of the primitive world also.[37]

A sense of cultural relativism might therefore be useful for those seeking to describe and understand the modern, post-Cold War world, and might help to explain some of the shortfalls noted in the *Strategic Assessment* report. At the simplest level, cultural relativism suggests that Western values and practices cannot after all be considered universal, but have to be placed alongside other, equally respectable and valid systems. Cultural relativism also, self-evidently, undermines the very notion of universalism itself. The tensions and contradictions which follow from this observation can be seen in the realm of international law. To the extent that the primary element of the international political system is the sovereign state, admitting of no superior secular authority or 'world government', then the system could be described as anarchic. But, in the sense conveyed by the expression 'anarchical society', the relations between the primary elements of the system conform to predictable patterns and are governed by rules.[38] Some international lawyers see themselves, therefore, not as practitioners of a supervening rule of law in the domestic sense, but as advocates of a cooperative, contractual law between states. In this sense, international law has been defined as 'the record of restrictions on sovereignty accepted by states', with its 'principle function' being to 'overcome the initial presumption of sovereignty and nonintervention'.[39]

But the fact that states are willing to enter into contractual relationships with each other − a minimalist definition of international law − should not be taken as evidence that all international or universal concepts will be treated with the same respect or in the same way. Nowhere is this more apparent than when concepts such as human rights, individual freedoms and democracy come into discussion. It might be thought that the Western origins of these ideas would wholly prejudice their wider acceptance, but the reality is more complex. Although human rights is by definition a universalist idea, and might therefore be rejected from the outset in some quarters, most states have accepted international definitions of the term, and have even agreed to be bound in international treaty law. This suggests that in certain cases universalism is not necessarily unacceptable. The distinction to be drawn is that whereas international law is to a large extent an expression of state sovereignty, concepts such as human rights and democracy are more clearly perceived to cut across and intrude upon that sovereignty because they are perceived to be more normative. The untidy outcome is that although states may have agreed upon definitions of human rights, some reserve the right, as sovereign members of the international community, to decide where, when and by whom these political goals should be realized. Unlike international law which is, in some respects, the servant of sovereignty, 'The universality of human rights fits uncomfortably in a political order structured around sovereign states.'[40]

In response to this dilemma, it may be necessary to adopt a compromise offered by such expressions as 'weak cultural relativism' and 'relative universality'.[41] It may also prove necessary to embark upon the abstract exercise of distinguishing between *absolute* and *universal*:

> we must reject the absurd test the Enlightenment imposed on religious and moral beliefs, namely that only if they were *universal* could they be *true*. As anthropologists began to uncover the full diversity of human behaviour, philosophers drew the conclusion that since

many of our deepest convictions about humanity were not universal, they must be false. This is a fallacy and deserves to be challenged.[42]

But as far as the international market for arms and related technology is concerned, the awkward reality which cannot be avoided is that many non-Western countries now feel themselves in a position to decide, on their own terms and for their own applications, what is meant by human rights, freedom and good government. Thus, in May 1993, at about the time Huntington's article appeared, Asian nations assembled in Bangkok to issue a new definition of human rights, one which stressed social stability and economic development over individual freedoms. Ideas of this sort continue to be heard, particularly in the Asia-Pacific region and in Southeast Asia. Malaysia's prime minister, Mahathir Mohamad, has become an especially outspoken critic of Western attempts to proselytize:

No one, no country, no people and no civilisation has a right to claim it has a monopoly of wisdom as to what constitute human rights ... [Western liberals] have no right at all to talk of human rights, much less judge others on this issue ... The record of the democratic governments of the West is not very inspiring. Unless their own interests are at stake, as in Kuwait, they would not risk anything in the cause of democracy. Is it any wonder that many countries are leery of the liberal system propounded by the Western democrats?[43]

Mahathir earlier gained notoriety for his angry response to British media accusations regarding the Pergau Dam 'trade and aid' scandal. In a letter to the *Financial Times*, Mahathir declared that 'Malaysians are not concerned about British scruples over selling arms ... If you have scruples, don't sell arms at all.'[44] In July 1995 Malaysia was one of the leading Organization of Islamic Conference states to declare the UN arms embargo on Bosnia invalid, and to offer military supplies to aid the Bosnian Muslims.[45] Malaysia's close neighbour Singapore, also with close ties with the West, has been similarly critical. Outcry following the legal case in which the *International Herald Tribune* was found guilty of contempt of court prompted Singapore's High Commissioner in London to publish his view that 'democracy is a long process and, in the short term, it is better perhaps to have more prosperity than democracy', and to note that 'Dogmatic assertions that Western democracy will inevitably triumph over Asian values only reminds Asians of the fervour with which Communists once proclaimed the inevitable triumph of Communism.'[46] And following the collapse of a British merchant bank in March 1995, the same High Commissioner chastised *The Economist* for assuming that 'London bankers are the only people who have the integrity and ability to regulate and operate foreign exchanges. When a vulnerable British bank collapses it is not wise to blame it on regulatory failure on the part of your former colonial subjects – and their institutions – without checking the facts. Hubris indeed.'[47] The PRC has long argued along these lines. For the PRC, sovereignty and non-intervention have always been declared to be the basis of relations between states. Thus, in January 1995, following a US report on human rights abuses in the PRC, the Chinese response was to argue that 'The human rights issue is within the scope of the sovereignty of a country. Every country has the right to protect and promote human rights in accordance with its own situation.'[48] By one account, even the PRC's radical intellectuals had come to accept that the military crackdown in June 1989 was necessary and were supportive of Deng Xiaoping's view that the Soviet Union's attempt to achieve economic liberalization and political liberalism simultaneously was not an example which the PRC should attempt to follow.[49]

If, as is apparent from arguments of the sort advanced by Malaysia, Singapore and the PRC, the universal and unconditional acceptance of predominantly Western standards cannot be assumed, then it follows that political arrangements which draw upon – or merely make reference to – these standards could also be open to challenge. In these circumstances, discussion of the universality of human rights and democratic values could become an abstract and possibly counterproductive preoccupation. If the arrangement is one which simply and explicitly requires states to meet Western preferred standards of behaviour before, for example, commercial relationships can develop, then it is open for non-Western states to choose whether to comply with or reject that requirement, just as it is open for Western states to make such stipulations in the first instance. But these same standards assume a more rigid, prescriptive and controversial air when they are presented as universal values. At best, the outcome might be reduced scope for successful commercial relationships between states with different cultural systems. At worst, the outcome could be a perception of Western proselytizing and 'hegemony by stealth'; a tacit attempt to undermine national sovereign authority.

The West/North still has some means to compel Third World and developing countries to behave in certain ways, usually by attaching conditions to aid and investment provisions. And for the most egregious offences against Western opinion and standards of behaviour there are various types of embargo and economic sanction, and even military action. But arms transfer controls have not been a great success as a tool of coercive diplomacy,[50] and coercion hardly seems the stuff of which a global arms trade ethic and code of conduct could be made. Furthermore, as the Asia-Pacific region and Southeast Asia become ever more technologically and commercially dynamic and wealthy, and therefore attractive to Western investors, so it seems increasingly unwise for the West to insist upon the transcendence of values and standards which its potential commercial partners evidently do not share. Western self-confidence is least appropriate in the case of conventional-arms and technology transfers. Networks of arms sales and weapons development projects already stretch from the Middle East to the Asia-Pacific rim. With the inauguration in January 1995 of the Malaysia-Singapore Defence Forum, one object of which will be to enhance defence industrial collaboration between the two countries, and with Singapore also apparently offering defence industrial management expertise to the PRC,[51] it would appear that something similar to Huntington's 'Islamic-Confucian' connection could indeed be developing. In these circumstances, attempts by the West, or by the so-called 'supply side', to make conventional arms and technology transfers conditional could be viewed as culturally and morally arrogant and could prove to be commercially counterproductive. The eight EU arms export criteria appear to run precisely this risk. Adopting a wilfully contrary position, it could be argued that all but one of the criteria either assume the universality of standards and practices which may simply not be accepted, or assume for the EU the right to make judgments on the behaviour and concerns of other states. Only the fifth criterion, which refers to the national security demands of EU member states, could be said to make neither implicit nor explicit demands on the behaviour of the EU's conventional arms and technology clients.

Chapter 7

Conclusion

This study has focused on attempts by a group of arms- and technology-exporting states to cooperate in regulating their international trading activities. Historically, international efforts to reduce – or merely manage – the global trade in conventional weapons, equipment and related technology have had a patchy record and have proved difficult to sustain. Multilateral arms and technology embargoes, or restricted access regimes, have been used frequently, sometimes to great effect. But conventional arms embargoes and the like have been seen to be contingent phenomena, shaped more by changing political and strategic circumstances than by the possibly more durable, but rather less tangible, notion of the disinterested will of the 'international community'. For 45 years after the end of the Second World War, the international arms trade was dominated by the East-West confrontation, and the trade expanded dramatically during these years. As far as regulation is concerned, the best that might be said of the Cold War is that it imposed some sense of order on the international arms market. The 1990s have seen rapid contraction in the global market from the postwar peak in the late 1980s. But in the absence even of the rudimentary discipline of the Cold War, with the spread of arms manufacturing and technological capability, and with the arrival of a buyer's market for conventional military equipment and related technology, the shrinking market of the 1990s has become less ordered and predictable. Accordingly, recent initiatives to bring the arms trade under some form of international control look set to share the fate of similar attempts made earlier this century. Against this unpromising background, this study assesses the potential of the members and institutions of the European Union as managers of a sizeable share of the international arms trade, and asks

94

whether the patchy record of multilateral regulation might now be improved.

The unique political and legal structure of the EU requires different approaches to be taken to controlling the export of conventional weapons on the one hand, and related technology on the other. Chapters 2 and 3 show how these different problems have been addressed since 1945. In both cases the key to effective multilateral cooperation has been the existence of functioning national export control systems. All current members of the EU have developed complex national arrangements in recent years, although standards are not yet uniform across the EU and even the most elaborate systems remain vulnerable to deception. Furthermore, as far as the trade in conventional weapons is concerned, the development of rigorous national export control systems has, in the major west European arms exporting countries, been offset by commercial opportunity-seeking. This tension was apparent during the Cold War but has come to the fore during the 1990s. The pursuit of commercial opportunity does not sit easily with the development of multilateral – or even national – arms export self-restraint regimes. But if EU governments have so far been wary of a disciplined, centralized export control regime, they have nevertheless made important progress in the 'harmonization' of national definitions, policies and practices. The institutions of the EU – particularly the Commission and the Parliament – have also developed impressive knowledge, if not direct experience, of multilateral arms export regulation. Although a tight, formal regime has not yet come about, and may never, what can at least be said is that the knowledge and practical experience of multilateral arms export regulation in the EU is more advanced than in other, similar initiatives, as is the quality of the debate surrounding these issues.

Much closer cooperation has been achieved in the field of sensitive-technology export control. Pending a full comparison with the successor organization to CoCom, the EU dual-use regulation is unrivalled as a formal, legally based, comprehensive system of technology export control by a group of states. The closeness of this cooperation can be attributed in part to the participation by many EU members in the CoCom exercise. Another contributing factor is the manner in which the European Commission has nurtured common economic, commercial and industrial policies and advanced the cause of the Single European Market. In so doing, the Commission has enabled, or required, governments to cooperate more closely in technology exports. It may also be, finally, that badly regulated technology exports are perceived to be potentially more hazardous in the long term than weapons exports. The reasons for and against weapons exports are relatively easy to discern. Much more demanding is the task of assessing the rationale behind the acquisition of technology and know-how, particularly when the technology in question is dual-use, with both civil and military applications, and especially when militarily useful technology is dual-capable for both conventional weapon and WMD purposes.

To have come this far in the joint regulation of conventional weapon and technology exports is impressive, particularly when set against the more modest achievements of other supply-side export control initiatives. But it is not clear that the EU has yet produced something fundamentally different to, and possibly more durable than, these other initiatives. Will the potential of the EU as an export control regulator be determined by the perceptions of self-interest which drive reactive, contingent, embargo-type initiatives, or will there be agreement upon a set of objective, disinterested values and standards against which exports can be judged? Will there be a convincing rationale for self-restraint? Without such a rationale, and without the discipline of the Cold War or something like it, it is difficult to envisage the international arms trade – and the EU's part in it – being ordered by anything more edifying than national commercial and strategic priorities. Chapters 2 and 3 show that national prerogative is still predominant, even, to a large degree, in the operation of the dual-use regulation. Export control cooperation or 'harmonization' of this nature is more a coincidence of perceptions of national self-interest than a disciplined regime of self-restraint, and the two should not be confused. Agreements can always be made at the lowest common denominator, even in the most difficult policy areas, but they may prove to be more rhetoric than substance. And commitments made in fair weather may be jettisoned when conditions deteriorate. To assess whether the EU has – or could – come up with a new rationale, Chapters 4 and 5 examined European defence industrial consolidation, and European foreign and security cooperation, respectively.

Chapter 4 explored various schemes for restructuring west European defence industry; a necessary task given manufacturing overcapacities and vigorous competition, particularly from the United States. Two points stand out. First, any industrial restructuring or rationalization is likely to involve extra-European exports. The notion that the region's defence industries could be reconfigured in such a way that exports would not be sought or necessary is far-fetched. It is not certain that even the EU defence market would be rich enough to sustain leading-edge defence research, development and manufacturing. What is more, it would require a very courageous – or very foolish – politician to deny a lean, reconstructed and vigorous industrial sector the opportunity to compete in a world market from which other countries were plainly benefiting.

The second key observation is that defence industrial restructuring in the EU is likely to continue to be a slow, incremental and above all inter–governmental (rather than supranational) process. This prediction stems from an analysis of European integration in foreign, security and defence policies made in Chapter 5. Although the EU's Common Foreign and Security Policy will be reviewed in 1996, fundamental change to the consensus-based, intergovernmental structure of CFSP is considered here to be unlikely. The process could certainly be tightened in some areas, but the most that should be expected is 'enhanced intergovernmentalism'.

The lessons to be drawn from these observations – the continued need for exports on the one hand and the preference for cautious intergovernmentalism on the other – are twofold. First, it is important to resist the beguiling, mechanistic logic which moves relatively easily and rapidly from calls for a common European defence equipment market to a need for a common procurement agency, and culminates in a case for a central European export control agency. This logic is attractive, but specious, simply because it assumes that the much slower, more cautious process of political integration can somehow be ignored or outstripped. The same misconception frequently intrudes upon discussion of Article 223 of the EEC Treaty, when arguments for its removal often ignore the reasons for its creation and the case for its retention. The relationship between industrial restructuring and central export control on one hand, and the process of political integration on the other, presents a 'chicken or egg' dilemma of precedence. The sense of this study, however, is that the political will to integrate in areas of 'high politics' will determine the scope and vitality of any institutional arrangements, rather than vice versa. The second lesson to be drawn, implied by the first, is that if cooperation in the management of defence-related trade by the govern-ments and institutions of the EU is to continue, it will in the main take place in less contentious areas and in a non-compulsory, non-binding manner. The political will for an extensive revision of CFSP is uncertain, and as presently constituted neither CFSP itself nor even the joint-action process seem likely to produce centralized policy-making machinery in areas of high politics, including defence-related trade.

This study has also tried to demonstrate that it is not only internal conditions which will determine the EU's effectiveness as a multilateral export control body, but also that there are external factors – practical and conceptual – which limit the potential of the EU. On the practical side, the diffusion of defence manufacturing capability and technological expertise around the world indicates that a significant and growing part of the international trade in these goods is already well beyond the control of the EU. This suggests two things. First, the EU might wish to control its own part in the international arms market, but cannot reasonably expect to be able to regulate the international market as a whole. Second, self-regulation by a limited group of suppliers will encounter the difficulties implied by the argument that 'if we don't export, others will', referred to above and earlier in the study. This argument may not be particularly sophisticated, but its basic political force cannot be overlooked.

Chapter 6 looked at some of the conceptual issues surrounding export controls. For pragmatic, legal and moral reasons, governments are prompted to intervene in defence-related trade. But the perception that 'a unilateral defence sales embargo ... would amount to little more than counter productive gesture politics',[1] persuades these same governments that their national goals might best – or only – be achieved in some multilateral framework. There are two broad types of multilateral regime: hegemonic/denial and cooperative. The political and strategic circumstances of the post-Cold War world push governments towards the second course, and in so doing create a demand for a central organizing principle. There are a number of explanations for this wish to establish a universal code or standard. If, as the diffusion of arms manufacturing capability suggests, control of the international arms trade can no longer be merely a matter of denial, and if the effectiveness of any control regime is proportionate to the number of existing and new weapons exporters participating in it, then there is a requirement to find a new rationale which can both replace military and technological hegemony, and have sufficiently wide appeal. Another explanation could be that when arms exporters have awkward decisions to make, they find it easier to do so in the name of some detached, objective standard for which they cannot be held responsible. Finally, and most simply, international cooperation in any field presupposes some common ground between governments. As the cooperative venture broadens its membership, it becomes more difficult, but also more important, to establish this common ground.

Chapter 6, however, shows the common ground to be meagre. When 'buyer's market' conditions obtain, and when the post-Cold War world is witness to self-confident 'cultural relativism' among recipients and non-

Western suppliers alike, it is too easy for buyers to take the line of least resistance and make purchases of weapons, military equipment and technology unencumbered by the political, moral and cultural baggage of certain suppliers. The rather bleak vision offered by Chapter 6 presents two alternatives in policy terms. First, the notion that multilateral cooperation in defence-related trade should reflect some higher, objective set of values, ethical or otherwise, could be abandoned altogether. There could, arguably, still be scope for principled national decision-making, and for cooperation with like-minded states, but the international arms trade would be understood as a global phenomenon without a global explanation. It might then be, however, that the idea of regulation, either national or multilateral, would prove unsustainable in the face of the 'if we don't export, others will' argument. This in turn would undermine the basic pragmatic, legal and moral considerations which initially persuaded governments that the arms trade should be regulated, and which then drew them into seeking some form of multilateral cooperation. If there is a need for multilateral regulation, there is also a need to find some means by which the initiative can be bound together. Since hegemonic or denial-type approaches are either unfashionable or inappropriate, the discussion returns to the quest for a generally acceptable set of values.

The second, rather less pessimistic position is that objective values can be defined, but only if it is accepted that these values might not be applicable universally. Thus, a group of suppliers might decide to apply conditions regarding human rights, democratic process and government spending to any defence exports, but would do so out of their own conviction. Conditionality of this sort, wherever the source of inspiration, would still be unlikely to appeal to many potential buyers and would present an opportunity for other suppliers. The 'if we don't export, others will' argument would still have force, but then the facts of a buyer's market and feelings of cultural relativism suggest that it always will. What this approach would do is make it easier for a limited number of suppliers, such as the members of the EU, to act in concert and achieve some if not all of the benefits of multilateral cooperation, and may also enable other suppliers and recipients to understand the motives of the collaborating governments and decide on a more informed basis whether or not to cooperate themselves. If standards of behaviour are to be convincing, without being portrayed as universal, they should express the cultural and moral preferences of the political organization from which they spring. What this means is that whatever the political level at

which strategic, commercial and foreign policy decisions are made regarding the arms trade, should also be the level from which the values
and standards are derived. By this argument, the 'conceptual weakness',
referred to at the beginning of Chapter 6, lies not in attempting to apply
objective standards to the arms trade, but in applying those standards at
an inappropriate political level. For the arms trade to be value-driven
requires inquiry not only into the rightness or otherwise of a given export
decision, but also into where, when and by whom that decision is made.
One widely argued method to achieve a more balanced appraisal of the
arms trade involves increasing parliamentary 'oversight' of the decision-
making process; it is not that parliamentary involvement would necessarily make any decision more moral, but that open discussion would enable
moral arguments to be heard and evaluated, itself an advancement ethically. The least acceptable position, from this perspective, is the one in
which the member states and institutions of the EU currently find themselves. At the level of national government, where arms export decisions
are made, there is little or no parliamentary oversight, and a tendency to
argue that moral considerations can only be admitted once universally
acceptable values are identified. Among the institutions, there is similar
appeal to universal values, some oversight from the European Parliament, but practically no executive authority. Even in the dual-use regulation, the Commission's authority appears to have been balanced by the
retention of sufficient national prerogative. By denying the EU – for
whatever reason – the necessary decision-making authority, the unhappy
result is that a structurally inadequate political mechanism is tied to
universalist ideals, in a formula which fails to convince much of the
world. In these circumstances, it is debatable that 'a co-ordinated EC
approach would command much greater international credibility than an
initiative by a single Member State'.[2]

The EU, its institutions and member governments, and critics of its
role as an arms and technology export regulator, are left with two choices.
First, it could be argued that national, rather than multilateral, decisions
and standards are all that could be expected. For standards to be applied
nationally, and to be seen to be applied, would require parliamentary
oversight to be increased. This could result in an individual exporter setting
an example of good behaviour and helping to limit weapons proliferation
through the 'social proof' idea.[3] There would be scope for effective
intergovernmental cooperation of the sort achieved in the AG, CoCom
and MTCR, although these initiatives depended to a large extent either
on the discipline of the Cold War or on the existence of widely held

WMD non-proliferation norms. Governments could seek further 'harmonization' of standards and practices, and in so doing ease some of the difficulties raised by the export of joint-venture weapon systems, develop intelligence-exchange mechanisms, and find ways to involve Europe's defence industries more effectively. Governments could also, finally, promote transparency initiatives such as the UN Register of Conventional Arms – possibly the only international initiative which does not fall foul of the 'Article 51' argument – with the aim of 'exporting' confidence as well as arms. By these means, EU governments might enhance the security of the EU by restricting the spread of key technologies, and would be in a position to deepen their cooperation if and when they decided to give more substance to CFSP. But the drawbacks to this minimalist approach to multilateral defence trade regulation are that the national benefits of multilateral cooperation would be forgone, that it would prove difficult for the expanding EU to accept new partners with possibly sub-standard national export control systems, and that there would still be political and administrative difficulties caused by 'Europeanized' defence industries.

The alternative is to put the EU in such a position that it can devise and project its own standards, and match those standards with an appropriate and effective arms and technology export decision-making process. This view, however, suggests a model of foreign and security policy-making in the EU which is unlikely to develop in the near future. The more likely outcome is that neither option will be selected, and that governments will retain their prerogatives as export controllers while arguing, perhaps disingenuously, that one role of the EU is to define the elusive common ground upon which an effective international code of conduct can be built. In this case, the EU will already have fulfilled its limited potential as a multilateral regulator and will be unable to change the pattern of poor achievement which has so far attended efforts at multilateral regulation of the international arms trade.

Appendix

The European Union Arms Export Criteria

The Luxembourg criteria, June 1991

- Respect for the international commitments of the member States of the Community, in particular the sanctions decreed by the Security Council of the [UN] and those decreed by the Community, agreements on non-proliferation and other subjects, as well as other international obligations;
- the respect of human rights in the country of final destination;
- the internal situation in the country of final destination, as a function of the existence of tensions or internal armed conflicts;
- the preservation of regional peace, security and stability;
- the national security of the member States and of territories whose external relations are the responsibility of a member State, as well as that of friendly and allied countries;
- the behaviour of the buyer country with regard to the international community, as regards in particular its attitude to terrorism, the nature of its alliances, and respect for international law;
- the existence of a risk that the equipment will be diverted within the buyer country or re-exported under undesirable conditions.

Source: European Council, *Declaration on Non-Proliferation and Arms Exports*, Luxembourg, 29 June 1991.

The Lisbon criterion, June 1992

● The compatibility of the arms exports with the technical and economic capacity of the recipient country, taking into account the desirability that States should achieve their legitimate needs of security and defence with the least diversion for armaments of human and economic resources.

Source: European Council, Lisbon, June 1992.
Note: The original French proposal was to consider the technical and economic capacity of the recipient country, with which Britain, Belgium and Germany were broadly in agreement. Italy, however, wanted to focus on 'legitimate' levels of defence. The final product reflects both approaches.

Notes

Chapter 1: Introduction

1 S. Willett, 'Dragon's fire and tiger's claws: arms trade and production in Far East Asia', *Contemporary Security Policy*, 15/2 (August 1994), p. 114.
2 K. Krause, *Arms and the State: Patterns of Military Production and Trade* (Cambridge: Cambridge University Press, 1992), p. 5.
3 US Arms Control and Disarmament Agency (ACDA), *World Military Expenditures and Armaments Transfers 1993–1994* (Washington, DC, 1995), Table II, p. 91ff.
4 'France overtakes US in arms sales to Third World', *The Times*, 9 August 1995.

Chapter 2: Weapons

1 H. Pelling, *Britain and the Marshall Plan* (London: Macmillan, 1988), p. 4.
2 K. Krause, *Arms and the State: Patterns of Military Production and Trade* (Cambridge: Cambridge University Press, 1992), p. 100.
3 Arms Control and Disarmament Agency (ACDA), *World Military Expenditures and Armaments Transfers (WMEAT)*, 1966–75 (Washington, DC), p. 56.
4 Prohibitions on the postwar Italian defence industry are set out in Articles 51–54, 59, 61 64 and 70 of the Italian Peace Treaty of 10 February 1947; F. Tanner (ed.), *From Versailles to Baghdad: Post-War Armament Control of Defeated States* (New York: United Nations, 1992), pp. 184–7.
5 D. Gerhold, 'Armaments control of Germany: Protocol III of the Modified Brussels Treaty', in Tanner (ed.), *From Versailles to Baghdad*.
6 Stockholm International Peace Research Institute (SIPRI), *The Arms Trade with the Third World* (London: Paul Elek, 1971), p. 216.

7 J. Stanley and M. Pearton, *The International Trade in Arms* (London: Chatto & Windus/IISS, 1972), p. 87.

8 The three-tiered structure is described in Krause, *Arms and the State*, p. 31.

9 R. Harkavy, 'The changing international system and the arms trade', *The Annals of the American Academy of Political and Social Science*, vol. 535 (September 1994), p. 20.

10 ACDA, *WMEAT*, 1965–74, Tables III and IV.

11 ACDA, *WMEAT*, 1971–80, Table II.

12 F. Pearson, 'Problems and prospects of arms transfer limitations among second-tier suppliers: the cases of France, the [UK] and the [FRG]', in T. Ohlson (ed.), *Arms Transfer Limitations and Third World Security* (Oxford: Oxford University Press for SIPRI, 1988), p. 141.

13 ACDA, *WMEAT*, 1991–92, Table III, p. 133.

14 Krause, *Arms and the State*, p. 73.

15 Ibid., p. 73.

16 Ibid., p. 61.

17 H. Mueller, 'The export controls debate in the "new" European Community', *Arms Control Today*, 23/2 (March 1993), pp. 11–12.

18 House of Commons Foreign Affairs Committee, *UK Policy on Weapons Proliferation and Arms Control in the Post-Cold War Era,* vol. II (London: HMSO, March 1995), FCO memorandum dated 6 July 1994, para. 26.

19 'Germany eases rules for weapons exports', *Defense News*, 12 December 1994.

20 See T. Taylor, 'A discussion of techniques for arms transfer controls', in J. Simpson (ed.), *The Control of Arms Transfers* (FCO/BISA Seminar Report, 23 September 1977), pp. 35–6.

21 A.J. Pierre, *The Global Politics of Arms Sales* (Princeton: Princeton University Press, 1982), p. 203.

22 J.M. Lamb and J.L. Moher, *Conventional Arms Transfers: Approaches to Multilateral Control in the 1990s* (Ottawa: CCACD, Aurora Papers no. 13, September 1992), pp. 12–13.

23 See Pearson, 'Problems and prospects', p. 126.

24 Pierre, *Global Politics*, pp. 286, 290.

25 See Tanner, *From Versailles to Baghdad*, p. 212.

26 Assembly of the WEU, Document 500, 4 December 1969; see SIPRI, *Arms Trade*, pp. 108–9.

27 Reply of the WEU Council to the WEU Assembly, 25 March 1970, quoted in SIPRI, *Arms Trade*, p. 109.

28 See Pearson, 'Problems and prospects', p. 147/note 67 for a reference to the Klepsch Report of the EP Political Affairs Committee, 1978.

29 *Report on Arms Procurement within a Common Industrial Policy and Arms Sales*, European Parliament Working Document 1-455/83, 27 June 1983 [Fergusson Report].

30 Fergusson Report, p. 8.
31 European Parliament Working Documents, PE 78.344/fin., 27 June 1983, p. 61.
32 Ibid., p. 62.
33 Pearson, 'Problems and prospects', p. 147.
34 H. Bauer, 'Institutional frameworks for integration of arms production in Western Europe', in M. Brzoska and P. Lock (eds), *Restructuring of Arms Production in Western Europe* (Oxford: Oxford University Press for SIPRI, 1992), p. 38.
35 *Report on European Arms Exports*, European Parliament Session Documents, Series A, Document A2-0398/88, PE 118.374/fin., 22 February 1989 [Ford Report].
36 Ford Report, p. 6, preambular paragraph C.
37 Ford Report, p. 7, preambular paragraphs K and L.
38 Ford Report, p. 23. This had already been recognized by the Committee on External and Economic Affairs (CEEA) in their opinion on the Fergusson Report. The CEEA also noted the argument that a more efficient European defence sector might feel inclined 'to step up rather than reduce overall exports'; CEEA on Fergusson Report, PE 78.344/fin., p. 61.
39 Ford Report, p. 30.
40 Ibid., p. 9.
41 Ibid., p. 8, para. 1.
42 Bauer, 'Institutional frameworks', p. 42.
43 Pearson, 'Problems and prospects', p. 147.
44 Bauer, 'Institutional frameworks', p. 39.
45 *Report on the Outlook for a European Security Policy: The Significance of a European Security Policy and its Implications for European Political Union*, European Parliament Session Documents, A3-0107/91, PE 146.269/fin., 29 April 1991 [Poettering Report].
46 Ibid., p. 8.
47 Ibid., p. 9.
48 Ibid., p. 10.
49 'Resolution on the Community's Role in the Supervision of Arms Exports and the Armaments Industry', European Parliament Resolutions, A3-0260/92, PE 161.873, 17 September 1992.
50 Ibid., p. 64.
51 Ibid., p. 65.
52 'EC nations vote for controls on weapons exports', *The Independent*, 19 September 1992.
53 European Council, *Declaration on Non-Proliferation and Arms Exports*, Luxembourg, 29 June 1991.
54 *Treaty on European Union* [TEU], Title V, Article J.4(1), European Communities No.3 (1992), (London: HMSO, May 1992).

55 TEU Article J.4.1: 'The [CFSP] shall include all questions related to the security of the Union, including the eventual framing of a common defence policy, which might in time lead to a common defence'.
56 See T. Taylor, 'European cooperation on conventional arms exports', ISA Annual Conference, March 1994 (unpublished paper).
57 Saferworld, *Arms and Dual-Use Exports from the EC: A Common Policy for Regulation and Control* (Bristol: Saferworld, 1992).
58 European Parliament Minutes, PE 186.411, Thursday, 19 January 1995 (Provisional Edition).

Chapter 3: Technology

1 G. Hartcup, *The Silent Revolution: Development of Conventional Weapons, 1945–85* (London: Brassey's, 1993), p. xxiii.
2 P. Henderson, *The Unlikely Spy* (London: Bloomsbury, 1993), p. 9.
3 See I. Anthony (ed.), *Arms Export Regulations* (Oxford: Oxford University Press for SIPRI, 1991); Saferworld, *Arms and Dual-Use Exports from the EC* (Bristol, 1992); Export Control Publications, *Worldwide Guide to Export Controls* (Deltac Ltd, 1993 and annually); American Bar Association, *Beyond CoCom – A Comparative Study of Export Controls* (Washington, DC, 1994); and Deltac/Saferworld, *Proliferation and Export Controls: An Analysis of Sensitive Technologies and Countries of Concern* (Deltac, 1995).
4 American Bar Association, *Beyond CoCom*, p. 4.
5 *The Dual-Use and Related Goods (Export Control) Regulations 1995 [DUEC]* (London: HMSO, 1995, SI No. 271), para. 3(2).
6 Export Control Organization, Department of Trade and Industry, *A Guide to Export Controls [Pre-Publication Version]* (London, February 1995), para. 3.3.
7 American Bar Association, *Beyond CoCom*, pp. 22, 109.
8 I. Anthony, 'The United States', in Anthony (ed.), *Arms Export Regulations*, p. 187.
9 M.B. Wallerstein and W.W. Snyder, 'The evolution of U.S. export control policy: 1949–1989', in National Academy of Sciences, *Finding Common Ground: U.S. Export Controls in a Changed Global Environment* (Washington, DC: National Academy Press, 1991), p. 310.
10 'New US licence is key to export ban review', *Jane's Defence Weekly*, 16 April 1994.
11 American Bar Association, *Beyond CoCom*, pp. 11–13.
12 *Federal Register*, 60/91 (11 May 1995), p. 25268.
13 See P. Cornish, *British Military Planning for the Defence of Germany, 1945–50* (London: Macmillan, 1995), Chapter 1.
14 American Bar Association, *Beyond CoCom*, p. 3.

15 C. Hofhansel, 'From containment of communism to Saddam: the evolution of export control regimes', *Arms Control*, 14/3 (December 1993), p. 378.

16 B. Roberts, 'From Non-Proliferation to Anti-Proliferation', *International Security*, 18/1, Summer 1993, p. 165.

17 I. Anthony, 'The co-ordinating committee on multilateral export controls', in Anthony (ed.), *Arms Export Regulations*, p. 209.

18 'The U.S. and multilateral export control regimes', in National Academy of Sciences, *Finding Common Ground*, p. 65.

19 Anthony, 'The Co-ordinating Committee on Multilateral Export Controls', pp. 207–11.

20 T.W. Galdi, 'Advanced weapons technology: export controls before and after the Cold War' (CRS Report for Congress, 93-22 F, 6 January 1993), pp. 7–8.

21 Ibid., p. 8.

22 'Accord near on Cocom successor', *The Financial Times*, 8 November 1993.

23 'Cocom sets stage for successor', *The Financial Times*, 31 March 1994.

24 'Russia can join arms control pact', *Defense News*, 10 July 1995.

25 'Moving towards the New Forum', *BASIC Reports*, No. 46 (20 July 1995).

26 House of Commons Foreign Affairs Committee, *UK Policy on Weapons Proliferation and Arms Control*, vol. II, p. 43.

27 Unnamed British official quoted in 'The successor to CoCom', *BASIC Reports*, No. 43 (15 March 1995).

28 'Dispute delays export control regime', *Defense News*, 14 November 1994.

29 American Bar Association, *Beyond CoCom*, p. 4.

30 For a copy of Order 255/58 of 12 April 1958, the list of products referred to in Article 223(2), see A.C. Allebeck, 'The European Community: from the EC to the European Union', in H. Wulf (ed.), *Arms Industry Limited* (Oxford: Oxford University Press for SIPRI, 1993), pp. 214–16.

31 H. Mueller, 'The export controls debate in the "new" European Community', *Arms Control Today*, 23/2 (March 1993), pp. 10–11.

32 Mueller, 'The export controls debate', pp. 10, 11, and Allebeck, 'The European Community', pp. 193, 194, 207. See also N. Prouvez, 'Implementation and enforcement of an EC arms and dual-use goods export policy', in Saferworld, *Arms and Dual-Use Exports*, p. 88.

33 H. Bauer, 'Institutional frameworks for integration of arms production in Western Europe', in M. Brzoska and P. Lock (eds), *Restructuring of Arms Production in Western Europe* (Oxford: Oxford University Press for SIPRI, 1992), p. 40.

34 *The Financial Times*, 17 February 1992.

35 European Commission, *Export Controls on Dual-Use Goods and Technologies and the Completion of the Internal Market*, SEC (92) 85 (final), 31 January 1992.

36 *Proposal for a Council Regulation (EEC) on the Control of Exports of Certain Dual-Use Goods and Technologies and of Certain Nuclear Products and Technologies*, COM (92) 317 (Final), 31 August 1992.

37 'Council Regulation (EC) No. 3381/94 of 19 December 1994 setting up a Community regime for the control of exports of dual-use goods.'

38 'Council Decision No. 94/942/CFSP of 19 December 1994 on the joint action adopted by the Council on the basis of Article J.3 of the Treaty on European Union concerning the control of exports of dual-use goods.'

39 Council Decision No. 94/942/CFSP, Article 1.

40 American Bar Association, *Beyond CoCom*, p. 99.

Chapter 4: Industry

1 See R. Freeman, 'Opening Statement to HCDC/TISC Inquiry Into Defence Procurement and Industrial Policy', 23 May 1995 (London, Ministry of Defence press release).

2 'One on one' (interview with R. Freeman), *Defense News*, 12 June 1995.

3 'Juppé redefines defense industry in France', *Defense News*, 17 July 1995.

4 W. Walker and P. Gummett, 'Nationalism, internationalism and the European defence market', *Chaillot Papers*, no. 9 (September 1993), p. 45.

5 E. Feuchtmeyer, 'The European armament market – an industrialist's concern', *Military Technology*, 17/10 (1993), p. 45.

6 R. Smith, 'Is Europe pricing itself out of the market?', *Journal of the Royal United Services Institute*, February 1994, p. 48.

7 'A survey of military aerospace', *The Economist*, 3 September 1994, p. 18.

8 K. Krause, *Arms and the State: Patterns of Military Production and Trade* (Cambridge: Cambridge University Press, 1992), p. 58.

9 Feuchtmeyer, 'The European armament market', p. 42.

10 E. Sköns and H. Wulf, 'The internationalization of the arms industry', *The Annals of the American Academy of Political and Social Science*, September 1994, p. 47.

11 'A Eurogun is a tricky thing', *The Economist*, 8 April 1995, p. 84.

12 F. Tusa, 'Aerospace: recovering and fighting', *Armed Forces Journal International*, September 1994, pp. 47–51.

13 'Rebuild allied trade' (leader), *Defense News*, 4 July 1994.

14 For a comment on the incompatibility of the 'Euro-champion' with the Community's 'industrial strategy', see D. Dinan, *Ever Closer Union? An Introduction to the European Community* (London: Macmillan, 1994), p. 368. On the necessity of 'Euro-champions' for the sake of the European defence sector, see Feuchtmeyer, 'The European armament market', p. 45.

15 'Leotard: speed European restructuring', *Defense News*, 19 September 1994; 'Industry plans drift in EU's regulatory limbo', *Defense News*, 29

May 1995; 'Industry urges EU to coordinate defense base', *Defense News*, 3 July 1995.

16 Walker and Gummett, 'Nationalism, internationalism and the European defence market', p. 65.

17 For a pessimistic view of the prospects in the short term, see Smith, 'Is Europe pricing itself out of the market?', p. 50.

18 Sköns and Wulf, 'The internationalization of the arms industry', p. 47.

19 M. Sandström and C. Wilén, *A Changing European Defence Industry: The Trend Towards Internationalisation in the Defence Industry of Western Europe* (Stockholm: Swedish Defence Research Establishment, December 1993), pp. 66, 72. See also Sköns and Wulf, 'The internationalization of the arms industry', p. 56.

20 C. Hofhansel, 'From containment of communism to Saddam: the evolution of export control regimes', *Arms Control*, 14/3 (December 1993), p. 397.

21 T. Enders (DASA), quoted in Sköns and Wulf, 'The internationalization of the arms industry', p. 56.

22 'Industry plans drift in EU's regulatory limbo', *Defense News*, 29 May 1995.

23 See W. Walker and P. Gummett, 'Britain and the European armaments market', *International Affairs*, 65/3 (Summer 1989), pp. 431–2 on SEA Article 30.6(b) and on COM (88) 650 of 17 November 1988, in which the Commission claimed a need to examine defence procurement. Commission forays into this area have often provoked alarm, particularly in Britain; 'EC threat to arms industry', *Sunday Telegraph*, 29 March 1992.

24 Sandström and Wilén, *A Changing European Defence Industry*, p. 73.

25 'BAe instructed not to notify EU', *The Financial Times*, 20 October 1994.

26 Declaration on WEU, C.5.

27 'European defence cooperation', *Military Technology*, 18/6 (1994), pp. 23–33.

28 'British mull position in arms group', *Defense News*, 21 November 1994.

29 'Europe is losing the weapons shoot-out', *Business Week*, 12 June 1995.

30 I. Anthony (ed.), *Arms Export Regulations* (Oxford: Oxford University Press for SIPRI, 1991), p. 2; A.C. Allebeck, 'The European Community: from the EC to the European Union', in H. Wulf (ed.), *Arms Industry Limited* (Oxford: Oxford University Press for SIPRI, 1993), p. 209; Hofhansel, 'From containment of communism to Saddam', p. 395.

31 'Trans-Atlantic harmony faces many obstacles', *Defense News*, 29 May 1995.

32 R.A. Bitzinger, 'The globalization of the arms industry: the next proliferation challenge', *International Security*, 19/2 (Fall 1994), p. 183.

33 S. Willett, 'Dragon's fire and tiger's claws: arms trade and production in Far East Asia', *Contemporary Security Policy*, 15/2 (August 1994), p. 115.

34 I. Anthony, 'The "third tier" countries: production of major weapons', in

Wulf (ed.), *Arms Industry Limited*, p. 380. In *Arms and the State*, p. 141, Krause argues that the urge to export will be especially strong in the second tier.

35 T. Taylor, 'Conventional arms: the drives to export', in T. Taylor and R. Imai (eds), *The Defence Trade: Demand, Supply and Control* (London: RIIA/IIPS, 1994), p. 101.

36 *Defense News*, 13 September 1993.

37 'Offsets: taking a strategic view', *Jane's Defence Weekly*, 5 February 1994.

38 Anthony, *Arms Export Regulations*, p. 86.

39 P. Batchelor and S. Willett, 'To trade or not to trade? The costs and benefits of South Africa's arms trade', *Military Research Group Working Papers*, no. 9 (1995), pp. 5–6.

40 'Pretoria fired up to defy arms embargo', *Sunday Telegraph*, 10 January 1993.

41 B. Roberts, 'From non-proliferation to anti-proliferation', *International Security*, 18/1 (Summer 1993), p. 145.

42 D. Shukman, *The Sorcerer's Challenge: Fears and Hopes for the Weapons of the Next Millennium* (London: Hodder & Stoughton, 1995), p. 193.

43 Ibid., p. 152.

44 See D. Jablonsky, 'The Owl of Minerva flies at twilight: doctrinal change and continuity and the revolution in military affairs', *Professional Readings in Military Strategy*, No. 10 (US Army War College, May 1994).

45 B. Buzan, *An Introduction to Strategic Studies: Military Technology and International Relations* (London: Macmillan/IISS, 1987), p. 27.

46 Willett, 'Dragon's fire and tiger's claws', p. 116.

47 'US Army sees cost savings in dual-use technology', *Defense News*, 21 November 1994; 'Capitol Hill is dual-use battlefield', *Defense News*, 27 March 1995.

48 M. Tapscott, 'Firms putting defense skills to work on smart cars, roads', *Defense Electronics*, February 1994.

49 Freeman, HCDC/TISC statement, 23 May 1995.

50 S.G. Neuman, 'Controlling the arms trade: idealistic dream or realpolitik?', *Washington Quarterly*, 16/3 (Summer 1993), p. 64.

51 M. Moodie, 'Managing technology diffusion and non-proliferation in the post-Cold War era', *International Security Digest*, 2/1 (October 1994).

52 E.J. Laurance, *The International Arms Trade* (New York: Lexington, 1992), p. 167. See also W.H. Reinicke, 'No stopping now: high-tech trade in the new global environment', *Brookings Review*, Spring 1994.

53 P.D. Zimmerman, 'Proliferation: bronze medal technology is enough', *Orbis*, 38/1 (Winter 1994), p. 82. See also D. Mussington, 'Understanding contemporary arms transfers', *Adelphi Papers*, no. 291 (September 1994), p. 20.

54 D.S. Landes, *The Unbound Prometheus: Technological Change and Industrial Development in Western Europe from 1750 to the Present* (Cambridge: Cambridge University Press, 1969), pp. 7, 554.

55 Roberts, 'From non-proliferation to anti-proliferation', p. 148.

56 See M. Kaldor, *The Baroque Arsenal* (London: André Deutsch, 1982).

57 For the British government view, see FCO oral evidence 6 July 1994, in Foreign Affairs Committee Minutes of Evidence, vol. II, p. 43. For the contrasting opinion, see Moodie, 'Managing technology diffusion'.

Chapter 5: Politics

1 M. Smith, 'The Commission and external relations', in G. Edwards and D. Spence (eds), *The European Commission* (Harlow: Longman, 1994), p. 249.

2 B. Soetendorp, 'The evolution of the EC/EU as a single foreign policy actor', in W. Carlsnaes and S. Smith (eds), *European Foreign Policy: The EC and Changing Perspectives in Europe* (London: Sage, 1994), pp. 112–30.

3 Smith, 'The Commission and external relations', p. 251.

4 See S. Nuttall, 'The Commission and foreign policy-making', in Edwards and Spence (eds), *The European Commission*.

5 Ibid., p. 293.

6 *Treaty on European Union* [TEU], Cm 1934 (London: HMSO, 1992).

7 Nuttall, 'The Commission and foreign policy-making', p. 295.

8 M. Holland, *European Common Foreign Policy: From EPC to CFSP Joint Action and South Africa* (London: Macmillan, 1995), p. 12.

9 Smith, 'The Commission and external relations', p. 270.

10 D. Dinan, *Ever Closer Union?: An Introduction to the European Community* (London: Macmillan, 1994), p. 473.

11 Holland, *European Common Foreign Policy*, p. 25.

12 Ibid., p. 227.

13 Ibid., p. 78.

14 Ibid., p. 220.

15 Ibid., p. 225.

16 'Opportunity for fine-tuning', *The Financial Times*, 10 May 1995.

17 'High-level Group of Experts on the CFSP', *European Security Policy Towards 2000: Ways and Means to Establish Genuine Credibility*, Brussels, 19 December 1994.

18 'Pillars of the Community', *Independent*, 4 October 1994.

19 See A. Menon, 'From independence to cooperation: France, NATO and European security', *International Affairs*, 71/1 (January 1995).

20 See 'Britain changes tack to back European power bloc in Nato' and 'Charm offensive: the Foreign Secretary sees the future on French fields' [leader], *The Times*, 28 October 1994. See also P. Cornish, *The Five*

Years' Crisis? European Security after the Cold War, RIIA Briefing Paper, No. 19 (March 1995).

21 'Rifkind backs WEU as Europe's defence arm', *Guardian*, 31 January 1995.

22 A. van Staden, 'After Maastricht: explaining the movement towards a common European defence policy', in Carlsnaes and Smith (eds), *European Foreign Policy*, p. 153.

23 Dinan, *Ever Closer Union?*, p. 467 (emphasis added).

Chatper 6: Principles

1 R. Harkavy, *The Arms Trade and International Systems* (Cambridge, MA: Ballinger, 1975), p. 213; K. Krause, *Arms and the State: Patterns of Military Production and Trade* (Cambridge: Cambridge University Press, 1992), p. 61.

2 E.J. Laurance, *The International Arms Trade* (New York: Lexington, 1992), p. 4.

3 The legality of supplying arms is discussed in I.D. DeLupis, *The Law of War* (Cambridge: Cambridge University Press, 1987), p. 66 ff.

4 I. Anthony (ed.), *Arms Export Regulations* (Oxford: Oxford University Press for SIPRI, 1991), p. 1, and UN Charter Article 2.5.

5 L. Blom-Cooper, *Guns for Antigua* (London: Duckworth, 1990), p. 100.

6 *Treaty on Conventional Armed Forces in Europe and Declarations* (London: HMSO, March 1991, Cm. 1477).

7 See J. Dean and R.W. Forsberg, 'The future of conventional arms control', *International Security*, 17/1 (Summer 1992), and I. Anthony, 'The United States: arms exports and implications for arms production', in H. Wulf (ed.), *Arms Industry Limited* (Oxford: Oxford University Press for SIPRI, 1993), p. 77.

8 For a discussion of humanitarian law in respect of anti-personnel mines, see P. Cornish, *Anti-Personnel Mines: Controlling the Plague of 'Butterflies'* (London: RIIA, 1994).

9 B. Kent, 'A Christian unilateralism from a Christian background', in G. Goodwin (ed.), *Ethics and Nuclear Deterrence* (London: Croom Helm, 1982), p. 64. See also R. Williamson, *Profit Without Honour? Ethics and the Arms Trade* (London: CCADD, 1992): 'arms transfers need to be subordinated to clear moral and political goals'.

10 K. Subrahmanyam, 'Third World arms control in a hegemonistic world', in T. Ohlson (ed.), *Arms Transfer Limitations and Third World Security* (Oxford: Oxford University Press for SIPRI, 1988), p. 36.

11 Ohlson, 'Introduction', in *Arms Transfer Limitations*, p. 10.

12 J.G. Stoessinger, *Why Nations Go to War* (New York: St Martin's Press, 1993 [sixth edition]), p. 80.

13 J. Frankel, *International Relations in a Changing World* (Oxford: Oxford University Press, 1988), p. 95.

14 E.J. Laurance, S. T. Wezeman and H. Wulf, *Arms Watch: SIPRI Report on the First Year of the UN Register of Conventional Arms* (Oxford: Oxford University Press for SIPRI, 1993), p. 53.

15 E.J. Laurance, 'Reducing the negative consequences of arms transfers through unilateral arms control', in B. Ramberg (ed.), *Arms Control Without Negotiation* (London: Lynne Rienner, 1993), pp. 176–9.

16 S.D. Krasner, 'Structural causes and regime consequences: regimes as defining variables', in S. D. Krasner (ed.), *International Regimes* (London: Cornell University Press, 1983), p. 1.

17 Ibid., p. 3.

18 P. van Ham, *Managing Non-Proliferation Regimes in the 1990s: Power, Politics and Policies* (London:RIIA/Pinter, 1993), p. 48.

19 O. Young, 'Regime dynamics, the rise and fall of international regimes', in Krasner (ed.), *International Regimes*, p. 98 ff.

20 Group of Seven London Economic Summit, 'Declaration on Conventional Arms Transfers and NBC Non-Proliferation', July 1991, para. 6.

21 For a discussion of an 'incentives-based' approach to arms and dual-use technology transfer regulation, see D. Mussington, *Understanding Contemporary International Arms Transfers* (London, IISS, Adelphi Paper no. 291, September 1994), pp. 48–50.

22 J. Simpson, 'The nuclear non-proliferation regime as a model for conventional armament restraint', in Ohlson (ed.), *Arms Transfer Limitations*, p. 237. See also Laurance, *The International Arms Trade*, p. 55.

23 J.M. Lamb and J.L. Moher, *Conventional Arms Transfers: Approaches to Multilateral Control in the 1990s* (Ottawa: CCACD, Aurora Papers no. 13, September 1992), p. 20.

24 House of Commons, *UK Policy on Weapons Proliferation*, FCO memorandum, para. 24.

25 See S. Ellworthy and P. Ingram (eds), 'International control of the arms trade', *Current Decisions*, no. 8 (April 1992), p. 35, and CCADD, 'The sale and transfer of conventional arms, arms systems and related technology' (London, 1977), p. 9.

26 B. Kellman, 'Bridling the International Trade of Catastrophic Weaponry', *The American University Law Review*, 43/3 (Spring 1994), p. 757 (note 2).

27 Simpson, 'The nuclear non-proliferation regime', p. 231.

28 C.S. Gray, 'Arms control does not control arms', *Orbis*, 37/3 (Summer 1993), p. 333.

29 See A. and H. Toffler, *War and Anti-War: Making Sense of Today's Global Chaos* (London: Warner Books, 1995).

30 Harkavy, *The Arms Trade*, p. 220.

31 J. Keeley, quoted in G. Chafetz, 'The end of the Cold War and the future

of nuclear proliferation: an alternative to the neorealist perspective',
Security Studies (Summer 1993), p. 146.

32 Institute for National Strategic Studies, *Strategic Assessment 1995: U.S.
Security Challenges in Transition* (Washington, DC, 1995), pp. 187–8.

33 S.P. Huntington, 'The Clash of Civilizations?', *Foreign Affairs*, 72/3
(Summer 1993). Another exposition of the 'clashing civilizations' thesis
can be found in A. and H. Toffler, *War and Anti-War*, especially
pp. 19–28.

34 Huntington, 'Clash of civilizations?', p. 23.

35 Ibid., p. 40.

36 Ibid., p. 47.

37 J. Keegan, *A History of Warfare* (London: Hutchinson, 1993), pp. 387,
392.

38 H. Bull, *The Anarchical Society: A Study of Order in World Politics*
(London: Macmillan, 1977).

39 J. Donnelly, *International Human Rights* (Oxford: Westview Press, 1993),
p. 29.

40 Ibid., p. 30.

41 For these two expressions see, respectively, Donnelly, *International
Human Rights*, p. 35, and A. Cassese, *Human Rights in a Changing World*
(Cambridge: Polity Press, 1994 [transl]), p. 50.

42 J. Sachs, *Faith in the Future* (London: Darton, Longman and Todd, 1995),
p. 66.

43 Quoted in R. Sachi and G. Fikry, 'Dr Mahathir and Malaysia's diplomatic
agenda', *Asian Defence and Diplomacy*, 1/1 (January 1995), p. 7.

44 Letters, *The Financial Times*, 17 March 1994.

45 'Muslim world to arm Bosnians', *The Times*, 24 July 1995.

46 Letters, *Independent*, 26 January 1994.

47 Letters, *The Economist*, 25 March 1995.

48 'China tells US not to meddle', *The Times*, 3 February 1995.

49 'But the people of China have a stake in the status quo', *The Japan Times*,
11 January 1995.

50 I. Anthony, *The Arms Trade and Medium Powers: Case Studies of India
and Pakistan, 1947–90* (London: Harvester Wheatsheaf, 1992), p. 37.
See also M. Brzoska and F.S. Pearson, *Arms and Warfare: Escalation,
De-escalation and Negotiation* (Columbia: University of South Carolina
Press, 1994).

51 *Asian Defence and Diplomacy*, 1/1 (January 1995), p. 28.

Chapter 7: Conclusion

1 C. Masefield, 'Defence exports: the challenge ahead', *Journal of the Royal
United Services Institute*, 140/4 (August 1995), p. 15.

2 N. Prouvez, 'Arms and dual-use exports in the European Community', in J. Dahlitz (ed.), *Avoidance and Settlement of Arms Control Disputes* (New York and Geneva: United Nations, 1994), p. 30.
3 G. Chafetz, 'The end of the Cold War and the future of nuclear proliferation: an alternative to the neo-realist perspective', *Security Studies* (Summer 1993), p. 142.

also in this series ...

Michael Cox

US FOREIGN POLICY AFTER THE COLD WAR
Superpower Without a Mission?

Contents

• The constrained superpower?

• From geopolitics to geo-economics? Competing in a global economy

• Planning for the next war: restructuring defence

• Strategic alliance or cold peace? Managing post-Communist Russia

• Atlantic rift? The United States and Europe after the Cold War

• The United States meets the Pacific century

• Whatever happened to the Third World?

ISBN 1 85567 221 9 (pbk)

'... the most important book to date about post-Cold War American foreign policy ... required reading for anyone trying to understand the international role of the last remaining superpower at the close of the century.' – *Benjamin Schwarz, formerly RAND*

'A splendid account of recent US foreign policy ... shows both the surprising continuities after the Cold War as well as the dramatic shifts from geopolitics to geo-economics ... there is no better book to read on Clinton's foreign policies.' – *Professor Melvyn Leffler, University of Virginia*

'... a clear-headed and thoughtful assessment ... Cox has looked well beyond the headlines to produce the most comprehensive and far-sighted study of this confusing topic so far.' – *Martin Walker, US Bureau Chief, The Guardian*

'No one understands American foreign policy better than Michael Cox, as he demonstrates once again in this informed and stimulating study.' – *Ronald Steel, Professor of International Relations, University of Southern California*

Michael Cox is a member of the Department of International Politics at the University of Wales in Aberystwyth, and Associate Research Fellow at the Royal Institute of International Affairs.

November 1995   RIIA/Pinter   Price £11.99

HD9743 Hill APA 3453 5-1-96 S/O
E922C67
1995

Advance Praise for

Image and Education

"This is an exceptional book that will have a major impact on educational theory, classroom instruction, and teacher education. Applying notions of surveillance and spectacle to educational policy and practice, Vinson and Ross provide tools to examine critically—and transform—prevailing regimes of standardization and high-stakes schooling. A refreshing and much-needed work!"

> Teresa L. McCarty, Professor of Language, Reading and Culture
> and Interim Dean, College of Education, University of Arizona;
> Editor, Anthropology and Education Quarterly

"*Image and Education* is an excellent work, one that should contribute greatly to our understanding of the mechanisms and foundations of contemporary U.S. schooling. Vinson and Ross have succeeded in introducing educators to many unique, radical and important ideas, ideas that the current educational establishment can no longer afford to ignore."

> Marc Pruyn, Associate Professor of Curriculum and Instruction,
> New Mexico State University; Co-editor (with Luis Huerta-Charles)
> of Teaching Peter McLaren: Paths of Dissent *(Peter Lang, forthcoming)*

"Vinson and Ross bring a new and bold perspective to the practice of educational theory. Their work deserves a wide readership and should be very influential among not only current scholars, but among the wider community of educational practitioners and other stakeholders as well. Unquestionably, their views hold relevance for a wide range of fields, including curriculum theory, research on teaching, educational policy, assessment studies, and critical pedagogy."

> Lisa J. Cary, Assistant Professor of Curriculum and Instruction,
> The University of Texas at Austin

Image and Education

extreme teaching
rigorous texts for troubled times

Vol. 7

Joe L. Kincheloe and Danny Weil
General Editors

PETER LANG
New York • Washington, D.C./Baltimore • Bern
Frankfurt am Main • Berlin • Brussels • Vienna • Oxford

Kevin D. Vinson
and E. Wayne Ross

Image and Education

Teaching in the Face
of the New Disciplinarity

PETER LANG
New York • Washington, D.C./Baltimore • Bern
Frankfurt am Main • Berlin • Brussels • Vienna • Oxford

Library of Congress Cataloging-in-Publication Data

Vinson, Kevin D.
Image and education: teaching in the face of the new disciplinarity /
Kevin D. Vinson and E. Wayne Ross.
p. cm. — (Extreme teaching, rigorous texts for troubled times; 7)
Includes bibliographical references (p.) and index.
1. Teaching. 2. Mass media and education. 3. Critical pedagogy. I. Ross, E. Wayne.
II. Title. III. Extreme teaching: rigorous texts for troubled times; v.7.
LB1025.3 .V56   371.102—dc21   2002010419
ISBN 0-8204-6229-2
ISSN 1534-2808

Die Deutsche Bibliothek-CIP-Einheitsaufnahme

Vinson, Kevin D.:
Image and education: teaching in the face of the new disciplinarity /
Kevin D. Vinson; E. Wayne Ross.
–New York; Washington, D.C./Baltimore; Bern;
Frankfurt am Main; Berlin; Brussels; Vienna; Oxford: Lang.
(Extreme teaching; Vol. 7)
ISBN 0-8204-6229-2

Cover design by Joni Holst
Author photo by Steve Fleury

The paper in this book meets the guidelines for permanence and durability
of the Committee on Production Guidelines for Book Longevity
of the Council of Library Resources.

Printed in the United States of America

*To Olivia and Paula
and
to Mom and Dad*

—Kevin D. Vinson

To Sandra, Rachel, and Colin

—E. Wayne Ross

❊TABLE OF CONTENTS

❈ACKNOWLEDGMENTS

IT IS AN AWESOME task to think about all the people who have in some way influenced the creation and completion of this book. As authors, the debts we have amassed and will always owe, and the gratitude we feel toward the many friends, colleagues, and family members who have helped us so much, are humbling to even contemplate. Needless to say, we could not have done it alone.

We wish first to thank the staff of Peter Lang Publishing, especially Christopher Myers and Sophie Appel, for their creativity, their excellent work as editors, their inexhaustible patience, and their unwavering commitment to our work. We could not have asked for a better experience.

We also wish to acknowledge the series editors, Joe Kincheloe and Dan Weil, whose efforts have seen *eXtreme Teaching* through from its very conception. Their support and long-standing encouragement, as well as their own work as first-rate educational scholars, have been indispensable and always inspiring.

In many ways, three individuals made this book even possible: Joseph Cirrincione, Linda Valli, and Steven Selden. Here, words simply cannot suffice.

A number of professional friends and colleagues are due special recognition for their remarkable kindness, their endurance, their expertise, their willingness to challenge and contribute to some of our ways of thinking, their unselfishness with their time, and their continuing loyalty: Terri McCarty and Jane Erin (who commented on earlier drafts), Walter Doyle, Kathy Carter, Bruce Johnson, Robin Ward, Molly Romano, Richard Ruiz, Susan Ellis, Paul Robinson, Gary Rhoades, John Taylor, Bob Hendricks, Paula Baltes, Ken and Yetta Goodman, Shari Popen, Brad Erford, Don Reitz, Don Hofler, Beatrice Sarlos, Bill Amoriell, Kathleen Cornell, Sharon Ann Wall, Sharon Rhodes, Joe Procaccini, Bob Peters, Victor Delclos, Lee Richmond, Kathy Woods, Randy Wells, John Welsh, Rex Shepard, and George and Sharon Schmidt. From each of them we have learned and gained immensely.

We also, of course, appreciate the invaluable importance of our students, both undergraduate and graduate, at several universities. Our gratefulness for their contributions to the evolution of our commitments and perspectives, and their unselfishness in thinking with us through frequently challenging and difficult—sometimes even "out there"—viewpoints cannot be overstated. We especially acknowledge Cynthia Anhalt, a doctoral student at the University of Arizona, who was kind enough to read and comment on an earlier draft of the book in its entirety. We disparage only in knowing that many of our students may never know the extent or the results of their input.

We thank friends and fellow scholars Perry Marker, David Hursh, Steve Fleury, Rich Gibson, Marc Pruyn, Joe Bishop, Susan Noffke, Valerie Ooka Pang, Ceola Ross Baber, Jeff Cornett, Michael Peterson, Avner Segall, Michael Whelan, Gloria Ladson–Billings, Lisa Cary, Bill Stanley, Jane White, Cleo Cherryholmes, Larry Stedman, Ken Teitelbaum, Marc Bousquet, and Heather Julien, who have been with us through all the struggles, doubts, victories, and defeats. Their insights, advice, and leadership continue to be invaluable.

And, finally, we thank our families. To our parents, James B. and Helen M. Vinson and Bobby G. and Jean C. Ross, we owe everything. They are, indeed, the best. We thank, as well, Cindy and Vicki Vinson, for their undying love and support. To our partners, Paula Vinson and Sandra Mathison, and to our children, Olivia Michelle Vinson and Rachel Layne Ross and John Colin Mathison Ross, your love, your caring, and your faith in us—and your amazing knowledge of schooling—can never be repaid. Our eternal dedication, thanks, and love.

PART I

Image and Education

✿CHAPTER ONE

Image and Education: An Introduction

There is something soul-destroying about the manufacture of illusions....
    —Shulevitz (2001, p. 31)

The relation between what we see and what we know is never settled.
    —John Berger (cited in Goodheart, 2000, p. A27)

We are simulators, we are simulacra (not in the classical sense of "appearance"), we are concave mirrors radiated by the social, a radiation without light source, power without origin, without distance, and it is in this tactical universe of the simulacrum that one will need to fight—without hope, hope is a weak value, but in defiance and fascination.
    —Jean Baudrillard (1995, p. 152)

Without a doubt our epoch prefers the image to the real thing, the copy to the original, the representation to the reality, appearance to being. What is sacred for it is only illusion. More than that, the sacred grows in its eyes to the extent that truth diminishes and illusion increases, to such an extent that the peak of illusion is for it the peak of the sacred.
    —Ludwig Fuerbach (cited in *Spectacular Times*, n.d.)

Image is everything.
    —Tennis player Andre Agassi, TV commercial for Canon Inc.

No Child Left Behind
    —President George W. Bush (2001)

1994–1996: 79.3%
1997–1999: 79.2%
    —National Center for Education Statistics (2000), high school completion rates for Texas students from 1994 to 1999, the period during which President George W. Bush was governor of Texas, and during which approximately 20% of students were "left behind."

When I look at an image, it doesn't occur to me that it might ruin my composure, or alter the way I think, or change my mind about myself. There is no risk, no harm in looking.
    —Elkins (2001, p. B7)

... [I]t should be noted that if a picture is worth a thousand words, [then] in order to understand it, reflect on it, or explain it, we might need to use a thousand and one words. And, even then, there is nothing transparent or inherently truthful in the world of images.
    —Fischman (2001, p. 31)

The self within you is merely a mirror image, the reflection of flowers in water. You can neither enter the mirror nor can you scoop up anything, but looking at the image and becoming enamoured of it you no longer pity yourself.

To lose images is to lose space and to lose sound is to lose language. When moving the lips can't produce sounds what is being expressed is incomprehensible, although at the core of consciousness the fragment of the desire to express will remain. If this fragment of desire cannot be retained there will be a return to silence.

Xu Wei's couplet, "The world is a false illusion created by others, what is original and authentic is what I propose", seems to be more penetrating. However, if it is a false illusion why is it created by others? And whether or not it is false is irrelevant, but is it necessary to allow others to create it? Also, as for what is original and authentic, at issue is not its authenticity but whether or not it can be proposed.
    —Xingjian (2000, pp. 350, 351, & 448)

For years, people have been complaining about the media's invasions of privacy. But the flip side is equally disturbing—the incredible hunger that so many Americans have to have their privacy invaded by the media.
    —Dowd (2002a, p. 13)

I have a friend who is convinced that American daytime talk television—Ricki Lake, Jerry Springer and the rest—is a massive racist, sexist and classist conspiracy. I[t] offers up a cabinet of curiosities in which misshapen, inarticulate, dysfunctional grotesques are paraded before the gaze in order to provoke wonder and amusement. And the great majority of them are female, working-class and black.

The history of freak shows would make an unedifying subject for a book. It would show us that human nature has not changed very much since the time when the inmates of Bedlam were a public spectacle. Depressingly, we take pleasure in witnessing the extreme, the bizarre and the abnormal, presumably as a way of reassuring ourselves of our own normality.
    —Bate (2002, p. 24)

I am indebted to [my former student], who has made the connection between the lights and sounds of the casino and the shadows in Plato's cave. In [his] visual representation of the cave, he drew the inside as the casino where he works. His depic-

tion of a world that is experienced as an everyday reality but is nonetheless fake ac-
curately illustrates what Plato was emphasizing: All sense perception is a kind of
illusion.
> —Swift (2002, p. B5)

We are in science fiction now. Whoever controls the media—the images—controls
the culture.
> —Allen Ginsberg (quoted in Weil, in press; see also Weil, 2002)

While we look not at the things which are seen, but at the things which are not seen:
for the things which are seen are *temporal; but the things which are not seen* are
eternal.
> —II Corinthians, 4:18

...[T]here are no limits on the mind's demand for meaning once the perception and
representation of meaning have become the basis of life.

Within a cosmology, all things are related in special, storied, intentional ways. A
complexity of motive, perception, action, and belief builds on itself, deepens. A sense
of time emerges and becomes inseparable from the creation of an image, and the
way in which that must be seen and used. Nothing is random. There can be no such
thing as a [meaningless] doodle....

Here these archaic symbols embody no specific meaning...but symbolism as such:
the possibility that certain images, placed in certain contexts, can generate endless
meaning.
> —Marcus (1995/1997, pp. 183 & 190)

Applying the...guidelines [for choosing a name] will result in an effectively nick-
named operation, an outcome that can help win the war of images *[emphasis*
added]. In that war, the operation name is the first—and quite possibly the deci-
sive—bullet to be fired. Mold and aim it with care.
> —Sieminski (1995, no page number provided)

American imagination demands the real thing and, to attain it, must fabricate the
absolute fake.
> —Umberto Eco cited in Gabler (2002, Section 4, p. 1)

If you want to know all about Andy Warhol, just look at the surface.... There's noth-
ing behind it.

The reason I'm painting this way is that I want to be a machine.

I like boring things. I like things to be exactly the same over and over again.... Be-
cause the more you look at the same thing, the more the meaning goes away, and
the better and emptier you feel.
> —Andy Warhol, cited in Updike (2003, p. 112)

And remember, piglet. Two thirds of all the shadows you see are not real shadows at all.
      —Chabon (2002, p. 443)

FOR GOOD OR BAD, for better or worse, we live in an age of image. All around us, 24/7, we face a steady and unremitting bombardment of *purposeful* representations (e.g., Steinberg & Kincheloe, 1997)—advertisements, photographs, dolls, photocopies, television shows, movies, DVDs, Web pages, and so on—each designed to say something about, or to get us to say something about, who we are individually and as a society—how we should think and/or act and/or be. We can be digitalized, perhaps even cloned—reproduced, if not in the end altered by the "progress" of "biotechnology" (e.g., Fukuyama, 2002; McGinn, 2002). If we become unhappy with our (or others') images of ourselves, we can change them, "easily" enough through plastic surgery, graphics software, and public relations experts, but perhaps in the relatively (*very?*) near future also through the technologies of "genetic engineering" and real-time "virtual reality."

Such images, of course, do not appear in a vacuum, *ex nihilo*, but instead spring forth and persist (or not) and mutate (or not) *organically* as part and parcel of the larger society that manifests them, and that is necessarily manifested by them, and of this larger society's shifting and contested social, economic, cultural, political, scientific, technological, linguistic, and ideological characteristics, conditions, and circumstances. *Images are part of our everyday lives, and our everyday lives are lives of images.*

Yet these images, as is also the case with our everyday lives, are fundamentally power-laden, even capitalistic, and are therefore neither natural nor neutral. They do not simply *exist,* nor do they in fact exist *simply.* They are contested and struggled over and with and against and for, and endlessly, seemingly, at times, chaotically, mulled over and interrogated and interpreted and exhibited and viewed. For, like knowledge and culture, images subsist in a circular relationship with power: Images are, in part, the effects of power (and capital), and power is, in part, the effect of images. Images (re)produce power, and power (re)produces images. Thus "image/power" or "power/image" essentially parallels Foucault's (1980, 1993) famous notion of "power/knowledge" or "knowledge/power." Ultimately, it is this linking, deep down, of power and image that sustains our present and overall critical pedagogical project, our effort as presented in this work.

At heart, and on multiple and competing levels, images help us make sense of our identities, our lives, our positions, and our institutions, yet they do so within hierarchical and asymmetrical contingencies of power, ideology, and cultural politics, such that certain powerful images dominate. Our questions? Fundamentally, whose images dominate and with what conse-quences? Who benefits as a result of these images—of the political economy of images? What are the connections between image and power? And, lastly, if not most significantly, of what importance are *controlling images*—that is, both control *over* images (i.e., who has it, how, why, and to what ends?) and control *by* images (i.e., where "controlling images" mean *images that control*)?

Setting

Over the past several years, popular cultural/media-produced images of various aspects of schooling have become increasingly commonplace and, arguably, important relative to understanding contemporary education (if not also society itself; see Maeroff, 1998). Hollywood films, for example, that address, to varying degrees of validity, key elements of teaching and learning proliferated at a remarkable pace during the 1980s and 1990s, garnering critical praise and achieving some of the movie establishment's highest hon-ors (e.g., *Fast Times at Ridgemont High* [Heckerling & Crowe, 1982], *Mr. Holland's Opus* [Herek, 1995], *Stand and Deliver* [Menéndez, 1987], *Dangerous Minds* [Smith, 1995], *187* [Reynolds, 1997], *The Emperor's Club* [Hoffman, 2002], and *Dead Poets' Society* [Weir, 1989], among many oth-ers). Although such cinematic portrayals have a long history (e.g., *Goodbye, Mr. Chips* [Wood, 1939]; *The Prime of Miss Jean Brodie* [Neame, 1969]; *Blackboard Jungle* [Brooks, 1955]; and *To Sir, with Love* [Clavell, 1967], among others; for a more complete list, see Wells & Serman, 1998, p. 194), today it seems especially clear that producing films about teachers and/or teaching—that is, producing educational *images*—can be highly lucrative, enticing, and popular. (Arguably, there has been also a certain perhaps mu-tual movie-TV "spillover effect" as evidenced by recent TV attempts to ad-dress schools and schooling, to cash in as it were—e.g., *Boston Public*, the short-lived *Dangerous Minds*—a popular cultural phenomenon with its own uneven and peculiar history, e.g., *Our Miss Brooks; Room 222; Welcome Back, Kotter;* etc.) Likewise, news media portrayals—for example, of "school failure" and/or "ineffectiveness" based upon the (re)presentation of standardized test scores—whether indicative or not of any holistic and com-plex, authentic classroom realities at all—have multiplied and in many ways grown increasingly problematic (as have political policies such as "No Child Left Behind" and media images of school violence, to cite just two of any number of other possible and related examples).

What both cinematic and news media depictions of education, schooling, and teaching signal are the creation, propagation, reproduction, and consequences of "images." They simultaneously *contribute to* and *reflect the influence of* the popular (and potentially dominating) construction of powerful pedagogical conceptions, ideologies, worldviews, and social/cultural/political/economic perspectives.

Of course such images—their causes and consequences—are not *inherently* negative or evil (nor, of course, are they inherently positive or good). In fact, on some level, everyone with even the slightest awareness of schooling invents, responds to, and makes use of them for a range of shifting and multiple purposes. We do so, for instance, in reciprocal and fluid relationships not only with popular culture and the media, but also with such human characteristics as *memory* (e.g., "back when I was in school...") and through the very contingencies of *everyday lived experiences* (e.g., as parents, students, educators, etc.; see Maeroff, 1998, especially his "Introduction"). Images do, however, become troubling if and when they: (a) hyper-privilege the interests and statuses of particular (and predictable?) individuals, groups, and/or ideologies; (b) promote and/or work to (re)produce specific and power-laden injustices, inequalities, or modes of oppression; and (c) result in the perpetuation of anti-democratic modes of understanding, practice, and/or policymaking. The corporate-conglomerate environment responsible for the production of films and the dissemination of news and information encourages if not demands at the very least a critical attitude in response.

This proliferation of images—its corporatist leanings as well as its more general overall and evolving significance—makes clearer the importance of a second contextual characteristic of contemporary schools and society, namely the convergence or coexistence of *spectacle* and *surveillance*. As we discuss in chapter three, this merging in part provides the foundation within which the construction, perpetuation, interpretation, and utility of images, pedagogical and otherwise, take place. Its meanings and actualities, those of this merger, play out within further, and deeply interconnected, contextual underpinnings, including recent technological change (e.g., 24/7 television, DVD burners, Webcams, etc.); the expansion of global, information-based, state-sponsored, corporate capitalism; demographic diversity; the development of public education as a major *national* political issue; and the current tendency toward standards-based educational reform (SBER; see also here the Democratic-Republican "consensus" that we describe in chapter four) as *the* dominant and "official" US reform priority.

The starting point for this work is fourfold. First, echoing broadly constructivist orientations, we accept that we *all* (assuming at least *some* knowledge of public schooling) create unique pedagogical images as we seek to make sense of our daily lives, specifically vis-à-vis multiple, individual, various, shifting, and complex interactions among popular cultural/media representations, experiences, reminiscences, beliefs, philosophies, public issues, and formal educational policies and practices. Second, we assume that these images are at the same time both contextually positive *and* negative, and that they spring forth according to an array of critical contingencies, including those of hierarchical dominance and various forms of marginalization. Third, we suggest that they not only contribute to how we ascribe meaning to teaching and schooling, but that they are, in turn, *ultimately and reproductively exemplified*—sustained—in the works of those individuals and institutions responsible for and identified with their (images') production and their socio-political and socio-economic effects. And fourth, we understand that these images, as they influence how we comprehend schooling, subsequently and thus affect such critical conditions as (1) how teachers teach and actualize curriculum; (2) how parents and community members view and conceive of education; (3) how students make sense of their learning experiences; and (4) how policymakers and "educational leaders" both manufacture and evaluate policy.

Purpose

In *Image and Education: Teaching in the Face of the New Disciplinarity*, we seek to address the complexities of a singular yet difficult and evermore crucial piece of reality, namely that which connects image and education. We pursue understanding *and* action, theory *and* practice, and classrooms, schools, *and* society. We attempt to shed light on a number of issues and topics that we feel affect, or should affect, anyone with even a passing interest in schooling.

Given the possible significance of popular cultural/media (re)presented pedagogical images, we first and most basically raise and pursue the following question: How might we understand the creation, maintenance, reproduction, and consequences of cultural/media-produced and propagated pedagogical images (e.g., in terms of representations of and struggles over [in]effective teaching, appropriate content, instructional purpose, educational policy, and the relationships between both teachers and students and schools and society)? Accordingly, for schooling, how do such images influence and reflect what we know and how we know it?

More directly, we aim to:

1. Explore the potential importance of pedagogical images as indicated in, for example, the popular cinema and the various news media outlets;
2. Investigate and illustrate the relevance of several models by which pedagogical images might be interpreted and/or critically interrogated (e.g., those provided by cultural studies/popular culture [Storey, 1994, 1996, 1998], film studies [Hill & Gibson, 2000], media studies [Sardar & Van Loon, 2000], and visual culture [Mirzoeff, 1999], as well as via the works of Bakhtin [1981], Barthes [1977], Baudrillard [1995], Boorstin [1961/1992], and McLuhan [e.g., 1964/1994]);
3. Examine and critique the settings and circumstances surrounding educational images (e.g., surveillance, spectacle, technological change, the status of public education as a public issue, globalization, everyday life, SBER, and so on); and
4. Consider the plausible and practical implications of this inquiry for educational practice, policymaking, and theoretical and empirical scholarship.

Our overall aim is to explore ways in which educators can work to understand and to help others understand the creation, meaning, and consequences of popular pedagogical images, and to identify and interrogate practical strategies and tactics (e.g., *dérive* and *detournement*; see chapter seven) with which to resist their potentially dominant/dominating influences—particularly with respect to democracy, the collective good, authenticity, and anti-oppressive education.

Defining Image

There are, of course, many ways of defining the term "image," both as a noun—*an* image—and a verb—*to* image. According to the *Merriam Webster Collegiate Dictionary* (on-line version), *an* image is:

1. a reproduction or imitation of the form of a person or thing; especially: an imitation in solid form: STATUE
2. a: the optical counterpart of an object produced by an optical device (as a lens or mirror) or an electronic device; b: a likeness of an object produced on a photographic material
3. a: exact likeness: SEMBLANCE (God created man in his own [image]—Gen 1:27 [RSV]); b: a person strikingly like another person (she is the [image] of her mother)
4. a: a tangible or visible representation: INCARNATION (the [image] of filial devotion) b: archaic: an illusory form: APPARITION
5. a: (1): a mental picture of something not actually present: IMPRESSION; (2): a mental conception held in common by members of a group and symbolic of a basic attitude and orientation (a disorderly courtroom can seriously tarnish a community's [image] of justice—Herbert Brownell); b: IDEA, CONCEPT
6. a vivid or graphic representation or description

7. FIGURE OF SPEECH
8. a popular conception (as of a person, institution, or nation) projected esp. through the mass media (promoting a corporate [image] of brotherly love and concern—R. C. Buck) [and/or]
9. a set of values given by a mathematical function (as a homomorphism) that corresponds to a particular subset of the domain

And according to *The New Oxford Dictionary of English* (on-line version) an image is "a representation of the external form of a person or thing in sculpture, painting, etc." It is, moreover,

1. a visible impression obtained by a camera, telescope, microscope, or other device, or displayed on a video screen
2. an optical appearance or counterpart produced by light or other radiation from an object reflected in a mirror or refracted through a lens
3. MATHEMATICS a point or set formed by mapping from another point or set
4. a mental representation or idea: *he had an image of Uncle Walter throwing his crutches away*
5. a simile or metaphor: *he uses the image of a hole to describe emotional emptiness*
6. the general impression that a person, organization, or product presents to the public: *she strives to project an image of youth*
7. [in SING.] a person or thing that closely resembles another: *he's **the image of** his father*
8. [in SING.] semblance or likeness: made **in the image of** God [and/or]
9. (in biblical use) an idol

Both sources trace the origins of "image" through Middle English and Old French and relate "image" etymologically to the Latin *imago* or *imitari*, meaning "to imitate." The *Merriam Webster Thesaurus* (on-line version) includes the following as synonyms, related words, and/or idioms:

1. double
2. picture
3. portrait
4. ringer
5. simulacrum
6. spit
7. spitting image
8. counterpart
9. equal
10. equivalent
11. match
12. chip off the old block
13. dead ringer
14. speaking likeness

15. spit and image
16. IDEA
17. apprehension
18. conceit
19. concept
20. conception
21. impression
22. intellection
23. notion
24. perception [and]
25. thought

To paraphrase our own previous work (e.g., Vinson, 2001a), we have defined *image* as:

> a *picture* or *representation* [or *copy*] of some thing, event, or situation that exists materially and/or spiritually in *some* situated reality.... (p. 367)

Taken together, these definitions suggest a number of plausible patterns or themes, as well as an array of theoretical classification schemes (i.e., ways to address the relatively large number of meanings formally attributable to the term image). For our purposes perhaps one reasonable set of distinctions can be drawn according to the complex interplay among "intent," "accuracy," and "understanding."

Regarding *intent*, and considering the various definitions and synonyms, clearly some approaches to image aim to present an *exact replica*, that is to capture "perfectly" the *essence* if not entirety of some thing, object, person, idea, or event (etc.). Here, the "perfect" image would be either a literal duplicate or a reproduction entirely indistinguishable from the original. The image itself would signify or mean, then, precisely what was signified or meant by the thing itself. In effect, the image would *be* the original. Metaphorically, think *photocopy* or, perhaps, still life *photography*, if and when the goal is to "capture" or "mirror" something absolutely and precisely, and when the *ideal* image is one that approximates "nature" as closely and accurately as possible (see, e.g., "dead ringer," mentioned earlier).

On the other hand, some images (and their producers) seek a representation that *intentionally* "distorts" a given target or focal point. In these instances, interpretation and subjectivity outweigh any effort at genuine replication, for good or bad. Often such images strive for some larger, thematic or aesthetic "message," such as, for instance, purposefully making reality appear either better or worse than it is. In some cases, a negative image is presented so that its "real" article seems relatively good, while in others a positive image allows some object reality to appear relatively bad (e.g., "the general impression," mentioned earlier), most notably, perhaps, in terms of whole-part relationships (e.g., between school and district) or relationships between differentially positioned yet parallel entities (e.g., between two high schools within the same school district).

A second characteristic involves *accuracy* and the degree to which some given image faithfully adheres to its target and/or the extent to which its claimed or supposed likeness is either *selective* or instead in some way "merely" *representative*. Take, for example, a newspaper photograph of a fight between two high school boys under the headline "School Violence Increasing." Well? First, consider the *selectivity* of the image. Of the near infinite number of photographic possibilities inherent in any given school setting, this exemplifies only one. School violence may or may not be increasing, but in the context of that particular photograph we know, and *can* know, very little. Did the photographer select that particular fight to capture out of the many simultaneously occurring? In every other concurring circumstance, was the school a paragon of placidness and calm? Does the photograph represent an everyday happening, or was this the first such fight in several years? Is the headline an overgeneralization? Is the given setting a microcosm of some larger and emblematic one? Coupled with the first characteristic, intent, one might also ask: What was the photographer (or his organization) *trying* to "say"? What does the photograph *itself* say? Why? How do the visual image and its associated caption interact? What is the image-producer's agenda? How do/can we know? In many ways the ultimate meanings of such images depend largely on the unique experiences, knowledges, cultures, ideologies, environments, and so on of the individual image-producer(s) and the members of his or her (or their) variously positioned audience(s).

Thus, the variety of *understandings*—the third element—of the image-producer and those who experience the image is significant, even vital. Does the image-producer understand the image to be accurate? Is this understanding apparent in the image itself? How? What of the audience members? What, deep down, do both groups *think* it *means?* The character of these understandings affects fundamentally whether perspectives or viewpoints are reinforced and reproduced, how they are (in)acted upon, and whether images are accepted as true or false (e.g., in the example, whether or not one buys that school violence indeed is increasing). Such understandings, then, cannot easily be dismissed, nor can their interpretive importance be ignored. They must, however, be approached via the various contextual settings within which images themselves are formed and construed. It is such a questioning, underlying perspective that informs this book and its (dis)orienting settings.

Themes

Throughout this book we assert a number of critical themes, each of which we believe is necessary to understanding contemporary public schooling vis-à-vis the dynamic and multiple meanings of image and education. We contend first that image matters. More precisely, we argue that in order to make sense of twenty-first-century schooling one must be able to make sense of the production, maintenance, implementation, and consequences of image(s). As we suggest, the relationships between images and education have grown—and continue to grow—more complex and fundamentally challenging. As a result, the mechanisms by which to contemplate image and education must therefore become more sophisticated as well. It is in this light that we probe the possible utility of newer fields such as visual studies, media studies, cultural studies/popular culture, and film studies, as well as the still (at least in educational scholarship) underappreciated and underexplored philosophies of authors such as Guy Debord, Jean Baudrillard, Daniel Boorstin, Roland Barthes, Mikhail Bakhtin, and Marshall McLuhan.

Second, contra both Debord (e.g., 1967/1995) and Michel Foucault (e.g., 1975/1979), we maintain that (post)modern, global society is neither solely a society of spectacle nor solely a society of surveillance, but in fact is a society of *both*—of surveillance *and* spectacle, of *surveillance-spectacle.* That is, ours is a society in which surveillance and spectacle coexist if not, in fact, converge. Moreover, it is within this coexistence or convergence that images (including those related to education) appear and establish their effects. And just as surveillance-spectacle provides the setting in which images are produced, further, the broader cultural, social, economic, political, scientific, and ideological environment(s) create(s) the climate in which surveillance and spectacle operate. Although a near infinite range of contextual factors, forces, and frameworks are discernible, as are their rather innumerable and unpredictable internal and external interactions, we choose to focus on three that we suggest are especially relevant: (1) *recent technological developments* (e.g., the Internet/World Wide Web/Web-Netcams); (2) *standardization* (i.e., the domination of classroom/school purpose, curriculum, instruction, and assessment by a politically, culturally, and economically powerful minority—as well as *the* current US school reform priority); and (3) *globalization* (i.e., the US-centered, asymmetric expansion of international, information-based, corporate, statist, commodity capitalism). For in effect these conditions constitute an image-power/surveillance-spectacle/technology-SBER-globalization conjunction—a coercive complex—that increasingly situates American schooling.

Further, and within this context, we claim that image is an effect of power, and vice versa, such that image-power or power-image creates, reflects, and reinforces—and is created, reflected, and reinforced *by*—certain disciplinary tendencies and repercussions, particularly in terms of democracy, oppression, authenticity, and the collective good.

Lastly, yet in many ways most importantly, we suggest that the potentially disciplinary ends of this image-power/surveillance-spectacle/technology-SBER-globalization regime can—indeed *should,* even *must*—be countered in schools and classrooms, and advance to that viewpoint critical media literacy, Foucauldian resistance, de Certeau's (1984) *"la perruque"* and the Situationist International's (SI's) notions of *dérive* and *detournement* as plausible modes of pedagogical and social resistance.

Organization

In part I, "Image and Education," we introduce our principal interests and concerns and position them within several developing and shifting areas of contemporary interdisciplinary scholarship. In this first chapter we have laid out and elucidated our purposes; the contexts and settings within which our arguments emerge and take form; various definitions of "image"; and our contingent, localized, constructed, and particularistic themes. In chapter two, "The Visual: Popular Culture, the Media, and Film," we explore the relatively new and evolving disciplines of visual culture, popular culture/cultural studies, film studies, and media studies as (a) the substructure within which the study of image has acquired its contemporary significance; (b) the grounding according to which we begin our own pursuit of educational image/images of education; and (c) a set of domains offering a range of useful and critical concepts and methodologies via which to interrogate both pedagogical images and images of the pedagogical.

In part II, "Contexts and Foundations," we delineate several current, framing conditions within which image and education—and educational images and images of education—are constituted and thus must be interpreted. In "Surveillance *and* Spectacle," chapter three, we build on the work of Foucault (e.g., 1975/1979) and Debord (e.g., 1967/1995) to argue that (a) contemporary US (Western, global, capitalist, information-based) society is *both* a "society of surveillance" *and* a "society of spectacle" (i.e., that surveillance and spectacle have merged or that they at least coexist—as opposed, that is, to the notion that ours is *either* a society of surveillance *or* a society of the spectacle), one of both voyeurism *and* exhibitionism; (b) that the convergence of surveillance and spectacle provides *a* (if not *the*) milieu within which (post)modern images emanate and must therefore be understood; (c) that this surveillance-spectacle convergence/mutuality creates a problematic and dangerous, new and dynamic "disciplinarity" for the establishment and implementation of public education (especially with respect to democracy, authenticity, the collective good, and anti-oppression); and (d) that such a disciplinarity implies (following Foucault, 1975/1979) specific reciprocal meanings for architecture (here we delineate our conceptions of "teletecture" [e.g., schools as "virtual buildings"] and "cosmotecture" [e.g., schools as casinos]). Further, we appropriate the work of Jean Baudrillard as a critical and substantial yet still underexplored extension of and/or alternative to the theorizing of Foucault and Debord regarding image and the implications of "the gaze." We, lastly, introduce our conceptualizations of "image-power" and "controlling images."

In chapter four, "Education as Public Issue: Technology, Globalization, and SBER," we consider advances in technology (e.g., the Internet, Webcams), the expansion of global capitalism, and standardization. We confront these as further contexts within which to understand the production, proliferation, and meaning of educational images and as possible (if not *likely*) sources of a hierarchical (power-induced) and exploitative mechanics of coercion and intimidation.

In chapter five, "Critical Frameworks," we employ an array of theoretical/philosophical viewpoints from which images of education/educational images might effectively be scrutinized, including Roland Barthes's (1977) "rhetoric of the image," Mikhail Bakhtin's (e.g., 1981) "chronotope," Daniel Boorstin's (1961/1992) "pseudo-event," Jean Baudrillard's (1995) "simulacra and simulation," and Marshall McLuhan's (1964/1994) thesis that "the medium is the message."

In "Pedagogical Image and Everyday Life," chapter six, we examine critically the relationship(s) between images of education and the "realities" of everyday life. We draw here on the work of Jackson (1968/1990), Vaneigem (1967/1972), Perlman (1969), de Certeau (1984), Brown (1973), and Lefebvre (1947/1992, 1968/1971).

Lastly, in part III, "Teaching in the Face of the New Disciplinarity," we address the potential significance of our work for public schooling. In chapter seven, "Image and Teaching Resistance," we offer the strategies of critical media literacy, Foucauldian resistance, *la perruque,* and the SI's conceptions of *dérive* (i.e., "transient passage through varied ambiances") and *detournement* (i.e., "negation, prelude, and supersession") as *potential* modes of resistance—and modes of pedagogy—against the disciplinary tendencies of pedagogical image as constructed within the environment of surveillance, spectacle, and surveillance-spectacle (or, perhaps more directly, the merging of exhibitionism and voyeurism)—that is, as a counterhegemonic means of "teaching in the face of the new disciplinarity." In "Applications: Popular Film and NCLB/SBER (standards-based educational reform)," chapter eight, we apply our work to several noted and popular educational examples, including the films *Dead Poets' Society* and *Dangerous Minds* and SBER/the No Child Left Behind Act of 2001 (NCLB).

Lastly, in chapter nine, "Summary and Conclusions: 'What Now?' and 'So What?'," we reiterate our main points and positions and interpret them in terms of their significance and meanings via contemporary, democratic, and authentic modes of public schooling (including curriculum, instruction, assessment, policy, scholarship, and so on), as well as against the culture, economics, politics, and ideologies of early twenty-first-century school-society relationships. It is here that we consider the implications of our work for schools and classrooms, and for the situated realities—the lived experiences—of teachers, students, scholars, citizens, and other concerned and committed stakeholders.

Our Position: A Final Note

As educators and scholars we maintain our own commitments to issues such as social justice and radical democracy. Although our backgrounds are in social studies education, teacher education, and critical pedagogical theory, our orientation includes a broad dedication to the lives of teachers and children and to creating or re-creating schools that are the best that they can be. Most recently our work has dealt with the problematics of standards-based educational reform, particularly standardized testing and curriculum standards, and with the disciplinary aspects of schooling, including those implicated via pedagogical image. We bring our own understandings of teaching and learning, curriculum theories and practices, educational foundations, research, teacher education, and critical philosophy to the present work, one influenced by a range of both modernism/structuralist and postmodernist/poststructuralist understandings.

We intend this book to be useful to both scholars and practitioners, and to provide a dynamic, subjective, and open-ended set of means by which to critique, interpret, and resist the potentially problematic effects of image, on both the pedagogical and social levels. We aim, that is, to provide both a theoretical explication of the meaning and consequences of images, and a primer on methods for dealing with teaching in the contemporary age of image, surveillance, spectacle, globalization, technological change, and standardization. We hope that teachers as well as university-based scholars (if not others) find it useful.

✳CHAPTER TWO

The Visual: Popular Culture, the Media, and Film

SIMPLY PUT, IMAGE MATTERS. And as society becomes evermore visual, or gaze-oriented, the importance of image subsequently increases and intensifies (even traditional print culture—the novel, for example—increasingly takes on image as its subject matter; see, e.g., Egan, 2002; King, 1995/2002). Whether one interprets this as a *positive* development (e.g., if one makes the argument that regardless of the threat to privacy, the proliferation of security cameras has increased public safety and thus justifies any potential inconvenience or intrusion) or as a *negative* development (e.g., if one makes the argument that security cameras pose an undue threat to privacy and thus do not justify any improvements in public safety), understanding image has become fundamentally more necessary and complex.

Thus, at the very least, our means of understanding image must also become more sophisticated. In part this is due to the ubiquitous and interconnected, hierarchical, dynamic, and power-laden existences of *viewer* and *viewed*—the fact that cameras and monitors are literally everywhere, in airplanes, airports, minivans, ATMs, classrooms, corridors, homes, highways, malls, and arenas (*ad infinitum*), and that few spaces exist where individuals are not watching or being watched, if not, in fact, doing both. But, further it is because the means of production, distribution, and consumption of images have themselves become so elaborate and esoteric that only a relatively small number of people actually understands their implicated technological mechanisms and their underlying processes, meanings, possibilities, and social/economic/political/cultural consequences. How, then, might we make sense of image?

Even more difficult is understanding the relationships between image itself and education; that is, the procedures by and settings within which the two maintain a shifting yet always important interconnection. Do pedagogical images influence and/or reflect the workings of schools and classrooms?

How and to what extent? In what ways do films, television programs, political cartoons, and so forth impact educational research, practice, and policy? Are popular images normative? Are they reproductive? To what ends?

In this chapter we consider the utility of visual culture, cultural studies/ popular culture, media studies, and film studies—relatively new areas of inquiry for educators—as critical interpretive alternatives. We provide first an overview—or set of definitions—of each of these particular fields. We conclude by identifying and engaging key conceptual points and questions derived from these views that *might* contribute to some theoretical and/or applied understanding of the myriad effects, significances, and meanings of exemplary (and arguably powerful) pedagogical (thus societal) visual images.

Visual Culture

> Modern life takes place onscreen. Life in industrialized countries is increasingly lived under constant video surveillance from cameras in buses and shopping malls, on highways and bridges, and next to ATM cash machines. More and more people look back, using devices ranging from traditional cameras to camcorders and Webcams. At the same time, work and leisure are increasingly centered on visual media, from computers to Digital Video Disks. Human experience is now more visual and visualized than ever before from the satellite picture to medical images of the interior of the human body. In the era of the visual screen, your viewpoint is crucial. For most people in the United States, life is mediated through television and, to a lesser extent, film. The average American 18 year old sees only eight movies a year but watches four hours of television a day. These forms of visualization are now being challenged by interactive visual media like the Internet and virtual reality applications.... In this swirl of imagery, seeing is much more than believing. It is not just a part of everyday life, it *is* [emphasis added] everyday life. (Mirzoeff, 1999, p. 1)

> You look into the eyes of these people, and you know they are looking at themselves in the mirror. There is nothing to them but their own image. There's just nothing.... We are drowning in images. We don't know fantasy from reality. Especially the generation coming up. Something happened. Anything that is so accessible becomes disposable. (Joni Mitchell, in Wild, 2002/2003, p. 28)

It seems almost too obvious to point out that the visual pedagogical image might be understood as an example of, and within the context of, the study of visual culture. Yet over the past few years visual culture has attained the status of a legitimate area of academic pursuit, one increasingly identified with such fields as cultural studies, media studies, and film studies (among others) and, therefore, can no longer be ignored by educational researchers whose concerns frequently focus on the lived experiences of American youth. That postmodern society can be approached by way of the visual rests, in part, on such phenomena as (1) the fact that "[s]omeone is nearly always watching and recording" and (2) that "the visualization of everyday life does not mean that we necessarily know what it is that we are observing" (Mirzoeff, 1999, p. 2). Our primary aims in this section, therefore, are to (1) define visual culture and (2) explore its potential relevance via contemporary schooling and the interpretation of pedagogical images.

"The gap between the wealth of visual experience in postmodern culture and the ability to analyze that observation marks both the opportunity and the need for visual culture as a field of study. While the different visual media have usually been studied independently, there is now a need to interpret the postmodern globalization of the visual as everyday life" (Mirzoeff, 1999, p. 3). Certainly this is this case with present-day schooling. In this chapter, following Mirzoeff (1999; see also Mirzoeff, 1998), we take the study of visual culture to include not only a specifically positioned definition, but also the concepts of "visualizing," "visual power," "visual pleasure," "visuality," "culture," and "everyday life."

So, then, what is *visual culture?* According to Mirzoeff (1999),

> Visual culture is concerned with visual events in which information, meaning, or pleasure is sought by the consumer in an interface with visual technology. By visual technology [is meant] any form of apparatus designed either to be looked at or to enhance natural vision, from oil painting to television and the Internet. (p. 3)

> [It is] a tactic with which to study the genealogy, definition and functions of postmodern everyday life from the point of view of the consumer, rather than the producer. The disjunctured and fragmented culture that we call postmodernism is best imagined and understood visually, just as the nineteenth century was classically represented in the newspaper and the novel. (pp. 3-4)

It involves, further,

> ...concentrating on the determining role of visual culture in the wider culture to which it belongs.... [and] highlight[ing] those moments where the visual is contested, debated and transformed as a constantly challenging place of social interaction and definition in terms of class, gender, sexual and racialized identities. [As such, i]t is a resolutely interdisciplinary subject.... [It is, finally,] a tactic, not an academic discipline. It is a fluid interpretive structure, centered on understanding the response to visual media of both individuals and groups. Its definition [therefore] comes from the questions it asks and issues it seeks to raise. (p. 4)

Visual culture, thus, deals in part first with the ideas of surveillance and spectacle—the idea that we are always watching and being watched as a means of disciplinarity (see chapter three). But, further, visual culture recognizes that although seeing—the gaze—is of critical importance, in many respects who is watching and who is being watched, and what is seen and who is seeing it, are difficult to comprehend. It contends, moreover, that the visual aspects (the "imaginaries") of society, including schooling, matter and therefore make a significant and possibly fundamental difference. It insists that technologies that encourage the visual—film, TV, cartoons, the news media, etc.—must be understood if we are to make any sense at all of contemporary, postmodern society, including schools. Lastly, it focuses on *divergence,* and the competing and contested ways in which asymmetrically positioned subjects interpret and utilize the image. It takes seriously, therefore, the possibility that pedagogical images—test scores, film representations, TV shows, headlines, cartoons—mean different things to different people, and that these differences in meaning are implicated in relations of power *and* have practical consequences for the practice of everyday (and authentically experienced) classroom (and social) life.

The study of visual culture also seeks some engagement with the concept of *visuality.* This implies, most directly, approaching

> modern visual media...collectively, rather than [as] fragmented into disciplinary units such as film, television, art and video. [For i]n place of the traditional goal of encyclopedic knowledge, visual culture has to accept its provisional and changing status, given the constantly shifting array of contemporary visual media and their uses. (Mirzoeff, 1999, p. 13)

Visuality, then, focuses on the visual writ large—as opposed, that is, to the disjointed televised, filmed, or videotaped event per se—in its pursuit, for instance, of the so-called (and dynamically complex) visual event. As Mirzoeff (1999) suggests:

> The constituent parts of visual culture are, then, not defined by medium so much as by the interaction between viewer and viewed, which may be termed the *visual event* [emphasis added]. By visual event [is meant] an interaction of the visual sign, the technology that enables and sustains that sign, and the viewer. (p. 13)

The visual event supposes an interdisciplinary back and forth between viewer and viewed—seer and seen—that works within the interpretation of some (image-based) phenomenon. It implies that interpreting visual images is important, and that it influences on at least some level the actualization of a specific action (or set of actions). In terms of schooling, this means taking on such virtual representations as those offered via film, TV, and the news media and (1) approaching them as interdisciplinary events; (2) treating them as important vis-à-vis the implementation of teaching and learning; and (3) recognizing that images are both produced and consumed within hierarchical settings of power and social/cultural/political/economic privilege.

Another feature of visual studies rests on its commitment to the status of *visualizing*. For:

> [o]ne of the most striking features of the new visual culture is the growing tendency to visualize things that are not in themselves [inherently] visual. Allied to this intellectual move is the growing technological capacity to make visible things that our eyes could not see unaided.... This remarkable ability to absorb and interpret visual information is the basis of industrial society and is becoming even more important in the information age....

> In other words, visual culture does not depend on pictures themselves but the modern tendency to picture or visualize experience. This visualizing makes the modern period radically different from the ancient and medieval worlds. While such visualizing has been common throughout the modern period, it has now become *all but compulsory* [emphasis added]. (Mirzoeff, 1999, pp. 5-6)

Thus, in terms of schooling, what is important is that when we try to make sense of visual culture, to interpret it, to understand it, we tend toward visualization, toward *visualizing* schooling. Hence the importance of contemporary film, television shows, newspaper accounts of education policy, and political (op-ed) cartoons.

Scholars of visual culture, moreover, recognize key contradictions surrounding the contingencies of *visual power* and *visual pleasure,* particularly in terms of the image. This is so first because

> [m]ost theorists of the postmodern agree that one of its distinctive features is the dominance of the image. [And, w]ith the rise of virtual reality and the Internet in the West, combined with the global popularity of television, videotape and film, this trend seems set to continue. (Mirzoeff, 1999, p. 9)

Thus, the postmodern world *is* visual, a world *of* the image. Yet:

> The peculiar dimension to such theory is...that it automatically assumes that a culture dominated by the visual must be second-rate. This almost reflex action seems to betray a wider doubt about popular culture itself. Such criticism has a long history, for there has always been a hostility to visual culture in Western thought. (p. 9)

This hostility has roots in Plato's "idealism" and can be traced as well to early Christian "iconoclasts." It is, moreover, related to lingering, elitist distinctions favoring "high" culture over the "popular" and those who engage in its visceral and/or sensual pleasures.

The study of visual culture also insinuates a particularist notion of *culture* itself. Yet as Mirzoeff (1999) argues:

> For many critics, the problem with visual culture lies not in its emphasis on the importance of visuality [alone] but in its use of a cultural framework to explain the history of the visual. (p. 22)

How, then, visual culture moves within the broader cultural sphere remains problematic. In part, as is likewise the case according to some scholars of cultural studies and popular culture, this is because

> The rush to condemn culture as a frame of reference for visual studies relies on it being possible to distinguish between the products of culture and those of art. However, any examination of the term quickly shows that this is a false opposition. Art is culture both in the sense of high culture and in the anthropological sense of human artifact. There is no outside to culture. Rather than dispose of the term, [then,] we need to ask what it means to explain certain kinds of historical change in a cultural framework[.] How does visual culture relate to other uses of the term culture? Using culture as a term of reference is both problematic and inescapable. Culture brings with it difficult legacies of race and racism that cannot simply be evaded by arguing that in the (post)modern period we no longer act as our intellectual predecessors did, while continuing to use their terminology. Nor can an assertion of the importance of art—whether as painting, avant-garde film or video—escape the cultural framework. (p. 23)

In the end,

> In forming approaches to visual culture, a key task is to find means of writing and narration that allow for the transcultural permeability of cultures and the instability of identity. For despite the recent focus on identity as a means of resolving cultural and political dilemmas, it is increasingly clear that identity is as much a problem as it is a solution for those between cultures—which, in the global diaspora of the present moment, means almost all of us. (p. 26)

For schooling, for addressing the pedagogical image, this implies a sense of culture as something that is dynamic and fluid—not fixed—yet something that both contains and yet contributes to the visual. It implies culture *as* art *and* culture *as* way (or ways) of life, and as such depends on the visual on at least two fronts—the visual *qua* artifact *and* the visual *qua* (artistic) means of expression. Thus the visual representation of education—editorial cartoons, headlines—might be understood (culturally) as human social construct (i.e., part and parcel of everyday life) *and* (culturally) as visual narrative (i.e., creative means of subjectivity).

Lastly, visual studies concedes the mutuality of the visual and *everyday life* (see also chapter six). As Mirzoeff (1999) sees it, "The transcultural experience of the visual in everyday life is, then, the territory of visual cultural" (p. 26). Citing de Certeau (1984), he asserts that

> Visual culture in this sense is an event resulting from the intersection of the everyday and the modern that takes place across the "wandering lines" marked by consumers traversing the grids of modernism. (Mirzoeff, 1999, p. 26)

Simply (see also Steinberg & Kincheloe, 1997), the visual *is* everyday life and everyday life *is* visual. Merely by virtue of our existence as consumers within a capitalist, profit-driven system, a system that exploits technological change for its own "efficient" benefits, we face, as we continuously negotiate our quotidian and image-mediated existences, the constant bombardment of ourselves (our bodies, our senses, our minds, our souls) by myriad visible/optical representations (e.g., advertisements, "action figures," e-mail, PSAs, video-clips, "breaking" news, and so on). Fundamentally, visual culture and everyday life meet and are mutually (re)productive, (re)inforcing, and (re)empowering.

With respect to education and schooling, we must first accept that in the (post)modern era schools and classrooms—teaching, learning, assessment, policy, and so on—are *visual,* and that the relevant actors (teachers, students, administrators, parents, etc.) are meant to be *seen.* We must face, further, simply, that watching and being watched does not automatically mean that we understand *what* is being watched—what and who we are watching and being watched by. We must accept that schooling, as an element of society, as a component of everyday life, *is* visual, both *internally* (in that pedagogical practices today frequently make use of TV, videotape, the Web, etc.)—and *externally* (in terms of the growth of "distance education," for example, but also vis-à-vis the fact that the public often confronts schooling in terms of both news and entertainment media accounts of its procedures and dominant/dominating policies and practices). Lastly, we must see that visual culture exists interactively with everyday life, and that it involves *both* the visual *and* the cultural, such that schooling only exists within the conjunctions of the visual, the cultural, and the everyday. As such schooling/visual culture is multiply-disciplined, difficult, shifting, multifaceted, and so on. It produces and is produced by both surveillance and spectacle and the various (if not also insidious) disciplinary consequences this essential existence implies.

Popular Culture/Cultural Studies

"The revenge of popular culture on those who take it too seriously."

The remark had an impact.... But then he thought, How can I not be serious? What's not to be serious about? What could I take more seriously than this? And what's the point of waking up in the morning if you don't try to match the enormousness of the known forces in the world with something powerful in your own life? (DeLillo, 1997, p. 323)

"Cultural studies" is perhaps one of the most difficult contemporary academic terms to define.[1] Yet its growing importance, in education as well as across the academy, is evident. In education, one need only refer to the ever-increasing number of books and articles informed by its assumptions and methodologies, including recent works by Steinberg and Kincheloe (1997), Giroux (1994a, 1994b; Giroux & [with] Shannon, 1997), and Hytten (1999a, 1999b). Introductory textbooks such as those produced by John Storey (1994, 1996, 1998), and treatments in non-specialized journals such as the now defunct *Lingua Franca* (Schudson, 1997) indicate that its reach and influence have extended throughout recent scholarship.

But what is cultural studies? According to Casella (1999), cultural studies can be defined "according to six theoretical orientations" (p. 526).

These include: (1) its interdisciplinary nature, (2) its challenges to hierarchies in culture, (3) its criticisms of ethnographic fixations on sites, (4) its manner of linking cultural, historical and economic analyses, (5) its emphasis on concepts [i.e., how people use and conceive of certain notions, such as "judgment," "pleasure," "sexuality," and "fascination" (p. 530)], and (6) its distaste for behavioral models of the world. (p. 526)

And yet, problems of definition are, paradoxically, one of the hallmarks of many definitions of and efforts to define cultural studies. As Casella himself notes: "There is one certainty upon which most theorists and researchers in cultural studies can agree: that there is no means of defining exactly what is cultural studies" (p. 526).

In his rather critical examination Schudson (1997) asserts that:

Cultural studies refuses to be defined or to define itself. Still, some of its features can be discerned. It is something like the extension of literary studies to subjects outside a conventional canon—including science fiction, pornography, rock music, MTV, television generally, popular culture at large. It tends to embrace an anthropological understanding of culture as a whole way of life rather than as a set of privileged aesthetic objects. But if this new discipline sees culture as the universe of social practices, it also redefines social practices as an ensemble of texts, all susceptible to interpretation or deconstruction. Cultural studies seems to promise a socio-logically enriched analysis—that is, one that locates cultural objects in relation to the social context in which people produce and use them. (p. 50)

Further reflecting such difficulty, although more sympathetically, Steinberg and Kincheloe (1997) state that:

Attempts to define cultural studies are delicate operations in that the field has consciously operated in a manner that avoids traditional academic disciplinary definitions. Nevertheless, cultural studies has something to do with the effort to produce an interdisciplinary (or counterdisciplinary) way of studying, interpreting, and often evaluating cultural practices in historical, social, and theoretical contexts. Refusing to equate "culture" with high culture, cultural studies attempts to examine the diversity of a society's artistic, institutional, and communicative expressions and practices. Because it examines cultural expressions often ignored by the traditional social sciences, cultural studies is often equated with the study of popular culture. (pp. 5-6)

And according to Giroux (1994a):

It is generally argued that cultural studies is largely defined through its analysis of the interrelationships between culture and power. This is particularly evident in two areas. First, cultural studies has strongly influenced a shift in the terrain of culture, as Stuart Hall [1992] has noted, "toward the popular." Second, it has broadened the traditional idea of reading to encompass a vast array of cultural forms outside of the technology and print culture of the book. Not only has this resulted in a critical approach to the production, reception, and diverse uses of popular texts, but it has also expanded the meaning of more conventional works. (p. 129)

Taken together, these examples indicate several general, though contested, characteristics of contemporary cultural studies. First, they imply a decentering of culture itself, one that seeks to disrupt the hegemony of the traditional meaning and privileged status of "high" culture, a decentering that works to establish and maintain the (at least) equal significance of "popular" culture. Second, these definitions suggest the importance of the contextual and subjective nature of culture, and of the interdisciplinary imperatives of its study. Cultural studies thus opposes any essentialized, fixed, decontextualized, or ahistorical conceptualization of culture and of its many components. Third, these definitions portray culture as open to interpretation—as fluid, shifting, and dynamic—and acknowledge and even encourage the possibilities of critical deconstruction. Lastly, they orient culture within a complex of, and as an effect of, power and power relationships.

Perhaps, though, the most problematic, difficult aspect of cultural studies involves its approach to, engagement with, and definition of "popular culture." According to Storey (1998), for example, there are at least six definitions. As he states, "An obvious starting point in any attempt to define popular culture is to say that popular culture is simply culture that is widely favoured or well liked by many people" (p. 7). Accordingly, popular culture here can be delineated simply via the processes of quantification; it represents, in effect, purely the results of a "popularity contest."

"A second way of defining popular culture," Storey (1998) continues, "is to suggest that it is the culture that is left over after we have decided what is high culture" (p. 8). Here,

> Popular culture...is a residual category, there to accommodate cultural texts and practices which fail to meet the required standards to qualify as high culture. In other words, it is a definition of popular culture as *substandard* [emphasis added] culture. (p. 8)

This is a view of popular culture as less than, as not as good as so-called high culture. It is that which does not fit into the somewhat "arrogant" or "snobbish" perspectives on and of culture established and maintained by variously identified members of some cultural elite. Such distinctions might oppose, for example, *opera* as a model of high culture and *rap/hip-hop* as a model of popular (or "low") culture (see, e.g., Fenstermacher & Soltis, 1998). This orientation clearly implies among "the powerful" (who *may* subsequently seek to impose their views on others) the existence and ultimate goodness of a dominating and normalizing set of cultural hierarchies.[2]

Storey (1998) identifies a third approach in which popular culture is defined as "mass culture" (p. 10). Accordingly:

> The first point that those who refer to popular culture as mass culture want to establish is that popular culture is a hopelessly *commercial* [emphasis added] culture. It is mass-produced for mass consumption. Its audience is a mass of non-discriminating consumers. The culture itself is formulaic, manipulative.... It is a culture which is consumed with brain-numbed and brain-numbing passivity. (p. 11)

From this perspective, mass culture is imposed on "the masses" by corporate economic powerhouses. It is an "artificial" creation, one used to produce and maintain markets. While it exists ostensibly to provide entertainment, it is in fact more insidious, working subtly and seductively to manipulate consumer demand, sell products, promote power-laden ideologies, and boost profit margins (see, e.g., Giroux, 1994a, 1994b; Giroux & [with] Shannon, 1997).

As Storey (1998) continues,

> A fourth definition contends that popular culture is the culture which originates from "the people." It takes issue with any approach which suggests that popular culture is

something imposed on "the people" from above. Popular culture is thus the authentic culture of "the people." It is popular culture as folk culture. It is a culture of the people for the people. As a definition of popular culture, it is "often equated with a highly romanticised concept of working class culture construed as the major source of symbolic protest within contemporary capitalism." (pp. 12-13; citing Bennett, 1980, p. 18)

Here, popular culture is taken as an "indigenous," "quaint" yet powerful production of the working classes. While certainly not high culture (within the mindset of the powerful), it is (in their view) perhaps "worthy" of study as an important force within the constitution of society. It is in a sense "revolutionary" thus indicative of the perceptions and perceived conditions both created by *and* imposed upon the variously constructed subjectivities of the oppressed.

A fifth approach to popular culture distinguished by Storey (1998) "is one that draws on the political analysis of the Italian Marxist Antonio Gramsci, particularly on his development of the concept of hegemony" (p. 13). Citing Gramsci, Storey defines "hegemony" as "the way in which dominant groups in society through a process of 'intellectual and moral leadership' win the consent of the subordinate groups in society" (p. 13). Thus:

> Those using this approach, sometimes referred to as neo-Gramscian hegemony theory, see popular culture as a site of struggle between the forces of "resistance" of subordinate groups in society, and the forces of "incorporation" of dominant groups in society. Popular culture in this usage is not the imposed culture of the mass culture theorists, nor is it an emerging-from-below spontaneously oppositional culture of "the people." Rather, it is a terrain of exchange between the two; a terrain, as already stated, marked by resistance and incorporation. (pp. 13–14)

Here, popular culture represents the playing field of a contest, a "contested border," a shifting space created according to an oppositional dialectic, one actualized, then, vis-à-vis the interactions between resistance and incorporation. This understanding accepts the dynamic nature of popular culture (and of all culture), as well as the continuity between popular culture and high culture. Here, that which is today identified as popular culture tomorrow becomes high culture; what is today's high culture is tomorrow's popular culture (and so on).[3] Popular culture is then, in a sense, the outcome of contact as dominant groups seek to "incorporate" it into high culture, and subordinate groups seek a mode of cultural "resistance" (or "anti-hegemony").

Lastly, "A sixth definition of popular culture is one informed by recent thinking around the debate on postmodernism" (Storey, 1998, p. 16). Thus, for Storey:

> The main point to insist on here is the claim that postmodern culture is a culture
> which no longer recognizes the distinction between high and popular culture....
> [F]or some this is a reason to celebrate an end to an élitism constructed on arbitrary
> distinctions of culture; for others it is a reason to despair at the final victory of com-
> merce over culture. (p. 16)

This is a view in which cultural categories collapse, with the boundaries between them blurring endlessly and simultaneously one into another.
"Authentic" and "commercial" merge, as do "high" and "low" and "art" and
"entertainment." One might think here of recent critiques of the blending of
"serious" and "tabloid" journalism, "information" and "entertainment" (i.e.,
"infotainment"[4]), and of various collaborations between "popular" and "classical" musicians.

According to Storey (1996), "what all these definitions have in common
is the insistence that whatever else popular culture might be, it is definitely a
culture that only emerged following industrialization and urbanization.... It
is a definition of culture and popular culture which depends on there being in
place a capitalist market economy" (p. 17). What he means is that these notions of popular culture necessitate the existence of socio-economic classes
and class differences. We would extend his analysis to include more broadly
the necessity of dominance and subordination, and of an unequal distribution
of *power*. There must, that is, be people "charged with" legitimating certain
social practices as acceptable manifestations of *high* culture in order for these
definitions of *popular* culture to make sense. Further, various institutional
mechanisms must be in place in order to maintain and extend this cultural
dominance, this cultural imperialism (see, e.g., Young, 1992). Today these
conditions generally reside within the circumstances of injustice, inequality,
and oppression situated as they are according to complex, multiple, and fluid
relationships grounded in localized constructions of gender, race, class, ideology, age, sexuality, culture, religion, and language (among others).

For our purposes, we take popular culture to refer to those social practices and cultural artifacts produced by and/or for a "popular" audience, an
audience including (but not confined to) young people of "traditional" school
age (preK-graduate school). (We note that we are to some extent limiting
ourselves to the popular culture of youth in the United States, increasingly
global in reach, or what some have called "American youth culture.") Popular culture here is *intentionally* popular culture. While at times "popularly"
created, it nonetheless manifests itself principally through various "big media" productions (e.g., TV shows, music, films, toys, books, computer
games, advertising, etc.) and provides, in part, the context within which multiple and subjective (and *popular*) identities are formed and ultimately chal-

lenged. It is, thus, both *impositional* and *oppositional*—economically, politically, ideologically. It represents the expression of voice and the creation, manipulation, and fulfillment of desire, and plays upon unstable and situated notions of difference. Both its construction and its maintenance—its very naming—take place within a contested and fluid, unequal complex of power.[5]

> At its most basic level cultural studies historically was, and still is, a critical, interventionist, and ethical project that builds upon a fundamental commitment to disempowered populations. It is aligned [generally] with Left political movements that aim at exposing how power operates in society to privilege some and disempower others. As a critical project, practitioners interrogate the power dynamics behind the valuation of only certain forms of cultural capital and show how social institutions, the media, and schools often help to reproduce, rather than to challenge, inequitable social relations. (Hytten, 1999b, p. 530)

Hytten's (1999a, 1999b) recent explorations of cultural studies and education suggest that although cultural studies potentially has much to offer contemporary schooling, especially in terms of reorienting both theorists and practitioners toward a deeper consideration of everyday cultural and classroom life (as opposed, say, merely to mechanics or method), many educators, due in part to certain institutional obstacles, remain unfamiliar with its growing, increasingly relevant, literature. Although cultural studies and education as an area of inquiry is complex, at its most basic:

> There seem to be two different traditions within cultural studies of education. On the one hand, there is a more general and playful study of cultural artifacts (such as movies), in order to get a better understanding of them. On the other hand, in the more critically oriented tradition, the goal is to use this understanding to alter situations in empowering ways. (Hytten, 1999b, p. 528)

In terms of education, the best known scholars of culture studies (e.g., Giroux) have made their greatest theoretical inroads and have been most significantly influential vis-à-vis "critical pedagogy" and "within ethnic and diversity studies" (p. 530).

Among the various cultural studies of education, Hytten distinguishes and develops four recent and evolving themes that together suggest key implications for contemporary pedagogical work. These themes are

1.   the popular as pedagogical
2.   critical literacy
3.   the [engaged] role of educators and intellectuals [and]
4.   rethinking diversity as pedagog[ies] of difference. (pp. 534-539)

Moreover, these themes culminate in and "are united in that they are all underscored by a vision of the possibility of developing a truly democratic social life in which the voices and contributions of all citizens are taken into account, and in which all forms of oppression and exploitation are diminished" (p. 539).

As such, for Hytten, they suggest five principal pedagogical implications:

> First, educators must acknowledge the value-ladenness of their positions and of knowledge itself. This means curriculum choices need to be seriously investigated for the explicit and implicit messages that they send, and that dissenting voices to the status quo need to be included. Second, educators need to relate curricula more directly to students' lives, aspirations, and cultures. Using popular culture as a way to bridge home and school learning is an important start. Third, issues of diversity need to be more paramount in schools. Specifically, students need to know how power and privilege get constructed in society—often in problematic ways. Fourth, educators should teach students how to express themselves and gain more control over their daily lives so that they are not [merely] passive consumers of disabling social messages. And fifth, educators must experiment with new models for teaching and learning that better connect what occurs in the classroom to efforts at social transformation. (pp. 540-541)

Thus, cultural studies/popular culture offers one way of interrogating pedagogical images in terms of production-reproduction and in terms of engaging the shifting and difficult relationships between contemporary schools and society. Overall, cultural studies/popular culture enables a range of critical responses to the advent of visual technology and with respect to the actualization of educational purpose, curriculum, instruction, assessment, and policy.

Media Studies

> I have been reading and writing about media for more than twenty-five years now, from varying angles, in different moods, modes, and styles, in scholarly studies and popular magazines, coolly and not so coolly, rethinking here and there but persuaded in general that *media matter greatly, that it takes effort to work out just how they matter, and that, if properly understood, they cast light on how our world works, though not necessarily as the engineers, proprietors, or users may have intended.* [emphasis added] (Gitlin, 2002, p. 1)

> ...how did it happen that the world I had known...had been processed by the news industry into pictures and slogans that seemed quite different from, even contrary to, what I knew with my own senses.... [T]he media are, in relation to social reality, fun-house mirrors, selective in their appetites, skewed in their imagery. The news is

not in any simple way a "mirror" on the world; it is a conduit for ideas and symbols, an industrial product that promotes packages of ideas and ideologies, and serves, consequently, as social ballast, though at times also a harbinger of social change. The news is a cognitive warp. The world is this way; the media make it appear that way. (Gitlin, 2002, p. 2)

When we watch TV or surf the Web, we are creating our own meanings and emotions. We need to understand our own work as creative and become critical users of other people's media.... [For t]he media mediate.... [In] all human communication, [information and/or content] has to be put into a material form—words, gestures, songs, pictures, writing. The point of mediating things is to communicate across space and time with as many people as possible. So the first thing to consider is that the media can reach **vast numbers of people.** Second, the messages nowadays are mediated by **highly advanced technology.** Third, while there is the choice of making our own music or drawing our own cartoons, most of us opt to be **consumers** of the professional productions of relatively few corporations. These mega-companies are pretty much closed and centralized, but the reception is **public** and **dispersed.** Fourth, there is virtually no communication between the *source* and the *receiver*. [bold and italics in original] (Sardar & Van Loon, 2000, pp. 5-6)

Simply, media studies involves the interdisciplinary study of the media—film, TV, the World Wide Web, cartoons, and so on—from a complex and critical set of orientations grounded in such academic areas as linguistics, sociology, cultural studies, the sciences, film studies, communications, history, philosophy, economics, and political science, etc. It "looks at the whole of the media industry from a number of different perspectives..." (Sardar & Van Loon, 2000, p. 20), and asks:

What is produced?
How is it produced?
What do these products mean?
Who controls the means of production?
What impact do media products have on society?
How are various groups of people represented by and in the media?
Who buys and consumes media products? [and]
How do the consumers interpret media products? (Sardar & Van Loon, 2000, p. 20)

As with any academic area, there are, of course, a variety of ways in which scholars approach and study the media, including those concerned with and grounded in institutional studies, professional ideologies, the politics of integrity, negotiated autonomy, structuralism, poststructuralism, political economy, and cultural studies (Kellner, 1994b; Sardar & Van Loon, 2000). Undoubtedly, though, any reasonable and in-depth treatment of these orientations goes well beyond the scope of this work. Luhmann (1996/2000), however, offers one relatively straightforward and succinct view that holds perhaps special critical relevance for understanding pedagogical images (i.e., within the context of media studies more broadly). Arguing from a starting point that "Whatever we know about our society, or indeed about the world in which we live, we know through the mass media...[,]" he goes on to delineate (and demonstrate) the roles played by the mass media in both "the construction of reality" and "the reality of construction," particularly in terms of what he calls the three principal "programme strands" of "news and in-depth reporting," "advertising," and "entertainment." He suggests that

> we should think of the knowledge of the world that the system of the mass media produces and reproduces. The question now goes: which description of reality do the mass media generate if one has to assume that they are active in all three programme strands? And if one were able to reach an opinion about that, the next question would immediately present itself: which society emerges when it routinely and continuously informs itself about itself in this way? (p. 76)

Thus, we might—*must?*—consider and make sense of the pedagogical image vis-à-vis its capacity as news/in-depth reporting (e.g., headlines), advertising (e.g., advocacy of a particular framework or philosophy—phonics, testing, etc.—or [surprisingly?] corporation—e.g., Chris Whittle's Edison schools), and entertainment (e.g., films, TV, cartoons). In other words, Luhmann implies that interpreting image via the mass media—especially given the recent emphasis on education in both the print and electronic press—necessitates engaging its mediated proclivity to "really construct reality," albeit in complex and dynamic, if not rather chaotic, ways and according to a variety of difficult and controversial mechanisms. Moreover, we must take seriously the idea that media matter, that they present skewed images of reality, that the public nature of media technology makes a difference, and that there are myriad ways of confronting and interpreting their significance and underlying impact. In effect, the media—the mediation of education and schooling—influence, *create,* the reality of education and schooling, and determine to a certain extent the range of personal pedagogical subjectivities and understandings that are possible, legitimate, nameable, desirable, privileged, and ultimately even speakable. As Maeroff (1998) states: "...the media...play an undeniable role in fixing impressions about education in the public consciousness.... [And m]any critics...remain persuaded that the media—above all other forces—affect beliefs about schooling" (p. 2; see also Wadsworth, 1998). And yet, there is at least some evidence that, perhaps no less importantly, the media—especially in terms of propagating various "negative" images—reflect rather than create public understandings (e.g., Wadsworth, 1998). In fact, there is even some question as to the reality or verisimilitude of some dominant media views, especially those of American schoolchildren as non-achievers (e.g., Berliner & Biddle, 1995).

With respect to schooling and education, this means that the media play a mediating role, that the press and popular outlets serve to connect our understandings of classroom practice with classroom practice itself, and that they form an intermediate bridge between schools and society and between the micro worlds of teaching and learning (and curriculum and instruction, etc.) and the macro worlds of context—culture, economics, politics, ideology, and so on. In effect, these facts make clear the inescapable obligation to pursue the media their significations most critically.

Film Studies

Mattering [i.e., why film and film studies *matter*] has tended to be affirmed in one of two ways: the formal-aesthetic and the social-ideological. The first argues for, or assumes, the importance of film in terms of its intrinsic worth...and the latter focuses on film's position as symptom or influence in social processes. (Dyer, 2000, p. 2)

If movies were our primary source of information on the state of American education, teacher shortages in urban schools would skyrocket. Quite simply, any teacher lacking the physical strength to throw gang bangers against walls or through windows would not apply. Movies tell us that suburban public schools have fewer gangs and less violence than their urban counterparts, but they are virtually run by bored, anti-intellectual adolescents majoring in sex, drugs, and delinquency. Of course, the alternative to public schools, according to Hollywood, is not so great either. The elite prep schools with their ivy-covered walls and high-status curriculum are oppressive institutions full of snobby and obnoxious brats. Their main purpose appears to be beating the life out of children who thought education was about questioning and exploring ideas and not simply about maintaining tradition and upper-class solidarity. (Wells & Serman, 1998, p. 181)

The only hope, in the celluloid world of education, is the heroic teacher—that superhuman agent of change, able to help promising students overcome all adversity, including poverty, gangs, peer pressure, and unreasonable parents. But they do not stop there. Our Hollywood teacher heroes frequently take on the entire corrupt educational "system," which generally encompasses a mass of self-interested school administrators, school board members or trustees, teachers, unions, and lawyers, as well as the rules and regulations they create. (Wells & Serman, 1998, p. 181)

As a very expansive and evolving field, film studies includes a multitude of disciplinary and technical approaches to studying, interpreting, and critiquing (obviously) film—the popular Hollywood-type cinema, certainly, but also documentaries, newsreels, and sporting events (among other useful and influential examples). According to Dyer (2000), film studies, as well as recent film criticism, has at its heart the notion that films matter—that is, that they are important, either "intrinsically" (i.e., that "film matters for its artistic merits...film as art" [p. 2]) or "extrinsically" (i.e., that film is laden with, and within, specific worldviews via economics, culture, power, and so on). In education, the latter has been more influential, particularly as, generally, scholars have taken a "cultural studies" approach to film/pedagogical image (e.g., Giroux, 1994a). For Dyer, this perspective is one that

> stresses the importance of power, the different statuses of different kinds of social group and cultural product, [and] the significance of control over the means of cultural production. Equally, cultural studies does not assume that cultural products are unified expressions of sections of society, but may often treat them as products of contestation within such sections or else of struggles of such sections against other social groups. (p. 6)

Yet as he cautions:

> The aesthetic and the cultural cannot stand in opposition. The aesthetic dimension of a film never exists apart from how it is conceptualized, how it is socially practised, how it is received; it never exists floating free of historical and cultural particularity. Equally, the cultural study of film must always understand that it is studying film, which has its own specificity, its own pleasures, its own way of doing things that cannot be reduced to ideological formulations or what people (producers, audiences) think and feel about it. (p. 7)

In terms of education and schooling, this means that the importance of any individual film regarding pedagogy and/or pedagogical image rests *both* on its merits (e.g., its critical acclaim, its popularity, its quality, and/or its lack of critical acclaim or popularity or quality) *and* its modes of politics, representation, and culture (among other characteristics and elements; e.g., the work produced in response to the film *Dead Poets' Society* [see, e.g., Carton, 1989; McBride, 2002]). This, perhaps, is especially important to the degree that "education as depicted in the entertainment media does not always bristle with verisimilitude" (Maeroff, 1998, p. 2).

Understanding the historical treatment of educational topics by Hollywood, and its implications for both theorizing and implementing various aspects of schooling (e.g., teaching, learning, curriculum, policy, etc.), requires a range of sophisticated orientations and methodologies. Film scholars advocate a number of diverse and potentially relevant frameworks, including those grounded in social theory and philosophy (e.g., postmodernism, Marxism, feminism, critical theory; see, e.g., Freeland & Wartenberg, 1995), technology, narrative, semiology, genre, representation, and textual and discourse analysis (for these various approaches see Freeland & Wartenberg, 1995; Hill & Gibson, 2000; Nelmes, 1999; Perez, 1998). Each of these offers insights into not only the quality of filmic depictions per se, but also their constructive meanings relative to the actualizations, interpretations, and outcomes of schooling and educational practice (e.g., Doherty, 2002; Wells & Serman, 1998).

Conclusions

Visual culture, cultural studies/popular culture, the media, and film are increasingly recognized by educational and other social scholars as important and as critical hermeneutic perspectives to be taken seriously. Typically, many authors claim that these approaches have provided useful and relevant insights into school/classroom/youth culture, research methodologies, school-society relationships, formal educational policy, and teaching practices (e.g., Bennett, 1980; Broudy, 1989; Carton, 1989; Dalton, 1999; Edelman, 1990; Emmison & Smith, 2000; Farber, Provenzo, & Holm, 2000; Fischman, 2001; Giroux, 1994a, 1994b; Giroux & [with] Shannon, 1997; Giroux & Simon, 1989; Harper, 1998; Hytten, 1999a, 1999b; McLaren, et al., 1995; Maeroff, 1998; Prosser, 1998; Rogoff, 1998; Sholle & Denski, 1994; Steinberg & Kincheloe, 1997; Vinson, 2001a, 2001b).

More specifically, what these views offer are (a) critical perspectives for making sense of pedagogical images, including in terms of their socio-peda-gogical/ideological meanings, influences, and consequences; (b) questions with which to engage or interrogate pedagogical images relative to their "mediation" of schools and society, policy and practice, and theory and classroom life; and (c) implied awarenesses of the workings, mechanisms, and technologies of image production, proliferation, maintenance, and change vis-à-vis power, pedagogy, dominance, and radical resistance.

The study of visual culture asks that we accept the status of seeing and being seen—watching and being watched. It recognizes the increasingly quotidian character of the visual, and the increasingly visual character of the quotidian. Moreover, it suggests that "merely" seeing is not the same as seeing and *understanding*. In confronting specific pedagogical images (such as we attempt to do in chapter eight), it indicates such questions as:

1. How do pedagogical images mediate the relationships between schooling and everyday life? Between classroom culture and culture more broadly?
2. How, and to what ends, are pedagogical images contested visual terrain? How might educators (critically) interpret this?

3. How do various stakeholders "visualize" schools and classrooms—teaching, learning, curriculum, instruction, and policy? Why? With what consequences?
4. How does classroom life—teaching and learning, curriculum and instruction, etc.—operate as "visual event?" What does–or *might*–this mean?
5. How do visual pedagogical images connect the thinking of viewer and viewed? How do they link the statuses of producer/creator, visual sign, visual technology, and audience?
6. Why do we take pleasure in visual pedagogical images? Who exerts power over such images—and, conversely, over whom do they exert power? What are the relevant repercussions? and
7. To what extent are visual pedagogical images fixed as opposed to fluid? Who decides what they mean? How and why, if at all, do the answers to such questions make a difference?

Cultural studies and the study of popular culture demand first that we acknowledge the *status* of popular culture—that is, the status of those cultural artifacts crucial to our children and their lives. Such work defends the at least equal status of "youth culture" with "formal school culture," especially that school culture officially sanctioned by powerful and elite educational managers. From Hytten (1999b), cultural studies seeks both to provide perspectives on the productions of popular culture as well as to mine such productions as and for empowering mechanisms of resistance. Cultural studies/the study of popular culture (again following Hytten) necessitates, then, interrogating pedagogical images via questions such as:

1. Who is included and who is not? How are various understandings of image and schooling implicated in hierarchies of power (and economics and ideology, etc.)? Whose knowledge is privileged and whose is marginalized? Who benefits from particular pedagogical representations? Why?
2. To what extent are pedagogical images related to the everyday lives of students (and teachers)? In what ways are they, or are they not, "authentic" (versus being "mere" images)? With what consequences?
3. In what ways, if at all, do dominant pedagogical images (films, TV shows, news depictions, etc.) either promote or inhibit meaningful discourses of diversity and inclusivity?
4. How might the construction of pedagogical images—and their utility and functionality via curriculum and instruction—influence the critical expression of student voice and identity? and
5. Are particular and specifically positioned pedagogical images transformative or reproductive? How? And to whose benefit?

As a field, media studies suggests first that we grasp the importance of the mediating role of the media—that is, those technologies that make possible, enact, and influence the production, distribution, and consumption of visual images—and that we discern the complexities of the media in their capacity to "construct reality." Moreover, media studies insists that we comprehend the media as reality-altering phenomena—and not, in Gitlin's (2002) words, as "'mirrors' on the world" (p. 2). With particular respect to individually construed pedagogical images, and to the media that present them (in "skewed" and "warped" ways), and that therefore mediate the social relationships that surround them, we follow Sardar and Van Loon (2000) in asking such critical questions as:

1. What image/s is/are produced and how? What does/do it/they mean?
2. Who controls the production of pedagogical images?
3. What relations exist between media-produced pedagogical images and the larger society?
4. How are particular individuals and groups of people represented? By whom? For what purposes? and
5. Who "consumes" such pedagogical images, and what sense do these "consumers" make of them?

Lastly, the interdisciplinary study of film beckons a critical take on both the aesthetic quality of any given work and the socio-ideological context it represents and seeks to present. In terms of education and schooling, this might first connote an analysis grounded in *accuracy*—Does a certain movie adequately portray some recognizable notion of "real" classroom life? Does it ring true? Is it (either subjectively or objectively) consistent with some manifest experience to which we (or even all of us) can relate? If so, how does it go about accomplishing this? If not, then why? And what, instead, does it, in fact, portray?

Perhaps more importantly, film studies asks that we approach critically the socio-ideological implications of any specific filmic effort, that we interrogate its politics and its social, economic, and cultural underpinnings and (implicit or explicit) pronouncements. Who is represented? What of indications of race, class, gender, power, and so forth? What of teacher-student relationships? Curriculum? "Effective" methodologies? Social transformation, social justice, the status quo? As with the other orientations discussed here, contemporary film studies perhaps assists most by way of the questions it (ideally) might elicit among education's various stakeholders.

In the end, these perspectives may shed light on the extent to which pedagogical images reflect and/or influence the theory and practice of schooling—and, importantly, the degree to which pedagogical images mediate the relationships between schooling and the larger society (e.g., Ayers, 1993). They may, in part, help us make sense of the role played by images in terms of how we understand education—how we pursue and implement policy; define effective teaching; legitimize and assess formal learning; establish or resist particular purposes; create, reinforce, or seek to reform curriculum; and make decisions about the "proper" place of schooling within the contexts of culture, social structure, economics, politics, and ideology.

In the next chapter we consider critically the philosophical ideas of surveillance and spectacle as conjoined settings within which pedagogical and other images are constructed, maintained, proliferated, interpreted, and/or resisted. For it is within the surveillance-spectacle environment that images come to be and to evolve, and that some become dominant (or come to dominate) and some become marginalized. It is, arguably, within this context that image *might* work as a complex and visual mode of conformative disciplinarity.

Notes

1. For Giroux (1994a), this definitional complexity stems in part from the current struggle over the history—and thus meaning—of cultural studies. As he states: "It is becoming increasingly difficult to assess what cultural studies is either as a political project or as a postdisciplinary practice" (p. 127). In part, as we know, this is because the concept of culture itself is still so controversial, even among professional anthropologists (a point that applies to our earlier discussion of visual culture/visual studies as well). Readers should refer to the recent debate in *American Anthropologist* for a relevant, and extremely important, discussion (see Borofsky, 2001).

2. Such a dominant and elitist hierarchy stereotypically might include "high brow" culture (e.g., opera, "classical" literature), "middle brow" culture (e.g., musical theater, the "Book-of-the-Month Club"), and "low brow" culture (e.g., rock music, romance novels).

3. Storey (1998) illustrates this approach by offering the "seaside holiday" as an example of a cultural practice that began within the domain of dominant groups but eventually evolved into an instance of popular culture, and "film noir" as an example of what began as popular culture but developed into a respected form of "high" art (see, especially, pp. 13-14).

4. Interestingly, and anecdotally, as an example, "infotainment" appears in our word processor's spell-checker even though we have never added it.

5. This definition does not mean that we necessarily oppose the postmodern position—we do not. In fact, we are sympathetic to many characteristics of what is called postmodernism. We simply accept the continuing (yet dangerous) *influences* of traditional and dominant distinctions, such as class.

❋PART II

Contexts and Foundations

❦CHAPTER THREE

Surveillance and *Spectacle*

UNDERSTANDING PEDAGOGICAL IMAGE involves more than merely analyzing the explicit contents of some given representation (or "picture"). It entails as well attempting to make sense of the peculiar contexts within which images are created and (thus) within which they proliferate, evolve, and execute their considerable and powerful consequences. It is a complex process, or set of processes, requiring a broad orientation toward both the general and the specific, the text and the context, the public and the private, an awareness of the importance of facing critically both the forces of the visible and the forces of the invisible, the overt and the covert. It suggests a radical confrontation with the contingencies of seeing *and* with the problematic pragmatics of simultaneously being seen by multiple and multiply positioned others.

In this chapter we explore one such image-grounding context, namely the contemporary status of "surveillance," "spectacle," and their potential convergence or (at least) coexistence (i.e., surveillance-spectacle or spectacle-surveillance). We approach these jointly as one critical setting within which the position of image emerges and within which its mechanisms, utilizations, and effects ultimately must be engaged and interpreted. We consider as well the possible significances of this image-surveillance-spectacle system for twenty-first-century schooling (as a brief example of surveillance in schools, see Reid, 2001; on spectacle, see Coleman, 1987; Eilenberg, 1975; Matthews, 1975; Miller-Kahn & Smith, 2001; Ohanian, 2002; Senese & Page, 1995).

By no means, though, do we hold that surveillance-spectacle exhausts the range of relevant environments (nor does it explain the contextualizations of spectacle and surveillance themselves), for as we suggest in the next chapter the very place of education today as a major public (and private?) issue necessitates taking a wider and critical contextual perspective toward its meanings and manifestations. As we argue in chapter four, such a perspective must take seriously the notion of pedagogical image vis-à-vis its connections to various social, cultural, technological, economic, ideological, and political (among other) conditions that are, paradoxically, at once both diverse/divergent and conformative/convergent.

In this chapter we contend that pedagogical image operates within a setting of surveillance *and* spectacle, one that enforces and reinforces, produces and reproduces, a certain *disciplinarity* that challenges the democratic, collective, authentic, and anti-oppressive potentialities of education—one that, in effect, privileges certain (i.e., dominant/dominating) interests (those of the wealthy and powerful few) over others (those of the majority). We begin by exploring the work of Michel Foucault, Guy Debord, and Jean Baudrillard. We contemplate here not only their capacity to help us understand the gaze-based, visual, disciplinary character of (post)modernity in terms of spectacle and surveillance, of exhibitionism *and* voyeurism, but also the implications of this "new" disciplinarity relative to contemporary education.

Foucault: Surveillance, Discipline, and the Panopticon

In *Discipline and Punish: The Birth of the Prison,* originally published in 1975, Michel Foucault (1975/1979) presented perhaps his first *major* and best-known investigation of power in modern "disciplinary" society. Subsequently, his conception of Bentham's Panopticon, and of power and its circular relation to knowledge, was applied by an array of scholars in an assortment of fields to an enormous range of social institutions and issues, including schooling/education and its connection to society, and in a multitude of formats and within and according to a complex setting of interests, desires, topics, theses, and pedagogical/philosophical formulations.

Foucault did not, though—perhaps more fairly *could* not—know or predict the monumental transformations that would come to define (post)modern society and to which his understandings ultimately—and frequently—would be employed. For between *Discipline and Punish*'s initial release and Foucault's untimely death in 1984, and perhaps even more strikingly between then and the early twenty-first century, Western society underwent a period of fantastic, if not fundamental, change. The explosion of personal media technology (e.g., the growth of the Internet/World Wide Web; the advent of mega-channel, 24/7 cable/broadcast/satellite television; wireless "connectivity"; access to personal video cameras; affordable two-way audio-visual communication devices—e.g., Net/Webcams, PalmPilots, etc.); the globalization of US-based, corporatist-statist, infotech capitalism; and the death of politics (i.e., the liberal-conservative, consensus-driven political race to the "middle of the road" and its inherent "will to standardize"), have altered in unprecedented ways, and at previously unimaginable rates, the so-cial, cultural, economic, political, and philosophical landscapes of everyday life beyond any reasonably anticipated expectations (see chapter four).

Our starting point is Foucault's (1975/1979) interpretation of surveil-lance and the Panoptic characteristics of "modern" disciplinary power, as established most notably in *Discipline and Punish*. As he argued:

> Antiquity had been a civilization of spectacle. "To render accessible to a multitude of men [*sic*] the inspection of a small number of objects": this was the problem to which the architecture of [ancient] temples, theatres and circuses responded. With spectacle, there was a predominance of public life, the intensity of festivals, sensual proximity. In these rituals in which blood flowed, society found new vigour and formed for a moment a single great body. The modern age poses the opposite prob-lem: "To procure for a small number, or even for a single individual, the instantane-ous view of a great multitude." In a society in which the principal elements are no longer the community and public life, but, on the one hand, private individuals and, on the other, the state, relations can be regulated only in a form that is the exact re-verse of the spectacle: "It was to the modern age, to the ever-growing influence of the state, that was reserved the task of increasing and perfecting its guarantees, by using and directing, towards that great aim the building and distribution of buildings intended to observe a great multitude of men [*sic*] at the same time." (p. 216)

Modernity did so, accordingly, by way of "Panoptic," disciplinary power, that is for Foucault (2000)

> one of the characteristic traits of our society. It's a type of power that is applied to individuals in the form of continuous individual supervision, in the form of control, punishment, and compensation, and in the form of correction, that is, the molding and transformation of individuals in terms of certain norms. This threefold aspect of panopticism—supervision, control, correction—seems to be a fundamental and char-acteristic dimension of the power relations that exist in our society. (p. 70)

For Foucault, surveillance—or "supervision"—was one aspect (the oth-ers being "examination" and "normalization," or "correction") upon which Panopticism, the dominant and generally diffused disciplinary organization of modern societies, rested (and in many ways still rests; e.g., Dowd, 2002a, 2002b).[1] Founded upon Jeremy Bentham's (in)famous model prison, the Panopticon, Panopticism represented, according to Foucault, a description "in the most exact manner [of] the forms of power in which we live...[and] a marvelous and celebrated little model of this society of generalized orthopedics..." (Foucault, 2000, p. 58).[2] Although the Panoptic structure is well known, simply its most critical attribute is a "central tower [in which] there is an observer...[whose] gaze can traverse the whole cell...so everything the individual does is exposed to the gaze of an observer who watches through shuttered windows or spy holes in such a way as to be able to see everything without anyone being able to see him [*sic*]" (p. 58); and, most importantly, without the observed even being certain whether anyone is there watching at all. For in its purest and most perfect form Panoptic discipline operates invisibly, unverifiably, and automatically, and as such is unrivaled in its efficiency, insidiousness, and effectiveness (Foucault, 1975/1979). What distinguished it most directly was (1) "[the] constant supervision [or surveillance] of individuals by someone who exercised a power over them" (Foucault, 2000, p. 59)—because of what they *might* do if not "properly" supervised, examined, and controlled—and (2) its broad applications to a range of regulatory institutions, including not only prisons but asylums, factories, hospitals, and schools as well (see, especially, Foucault, 1975/1979, pp. 133-228; see also Burchell, Gordon, & Miller, 1991; Dumm, 1996; Gore, 1998; Popkewitz & Brennan, 1998).

As a modern creation what was new about Panoptic, surveillance-based discipline—in addition to its invisibility, automaticity, unverifiability, and so on—and, indeed, what was most dangerous and potent, was its ability to produce at the same time both "silent" (or "docile") and "obedient" (or "useful") bodies. This meant for Foucault the capacity of Panopticism to at once increase *and* decrease the forces of the body by managing as closely as possible the individual's time, space, and movement: to *increase* them (the *positive* nature of power) vis-à-vis "economic utility," and to *decrease* them (the *negative* nature of power) vis-à-vis "political docility" (see esp. Foucault, 1975/1979, pp. 135-138).

For Foucault (2000), then, this power, this "constant supervision of individuals by someone who exercised a power over them—schoolteacher, foreman, physician, psychiatrist, prison warden" (p. 59)—created the possibility of "constituting a [new type] of knowledge concerning those [who were being] supervised" (p. 59). That is:

A knowledge that now was no longer about determining whether or not something had occurred...[but] rather...about whether an individual was behaving as he [*sic*] should, in accordance with the rule or not, and whether he was progressing or not. This new knowledge was no longer organized around the questions: "Was this done? Who did it?" It was no longer organized in terms of presence and absence, of existence and nonexistence; it was organized around the norm, in terms of what was normal or not, correct or not, in terms of what one must do or not do...a new knowledge [therefore] of a completely different type, a knowledge characterized by supervision and examination, organized around the norm, through the supervisory control of individuals throughout their existence. (p. 59)

This, as Foucault (1980) notably asserted, linked power and knowledge (or "truth") in a circular "regime of truth," a disciplinary setting in which "Truth is a thing of this world...[and] is produced only by virtue of multiple forms of constraint.... [It is, therefore, that which] induces regular effects of power" (p. 131; see also Gore, 1993). Moreover, in fact,

> Each society has its [own distinctive] régime of truth, its "general politics" of truth: that is, the types of discourse which it accepts and makes function as true; the mechanisms and instances which enable one to distinguish true and false statements, the means by which each is sanctioned; the techniques and procedures accorded value in the acquisition of truth; the status of those who are charged with saying what counts as true. (p. 131)

Here "'Truth' is linked in a circular manner with systems of power which produce and sustain it, and to effects of power which it induces and which extend it. Thus, a 'régime' of truth" (p. 133)—a circle, a state of affairs rooted in the Panoptic and maintained according to the singular implementation of surveillance, examination, and normalization.

While rightly exploring the modern workings and underpinnings of disciplinary surveillance, Foucault's interpretation perhaps somewhat downplayed the contemporary disciplinary status of spectacle (even as he defines it). It does clearly intimate, however, numerous, potentially relevant insights into recent, increasingly intrusive Panoptic developments established and practiced by the government (e.g., the FBI's Carnivore, the NSA's Echelon, President Bush's new Cabinet-level Department of Homeland Security, the USA Patriot Act) and by society more widely (e.g., the use of private surveillance cameras, Webcams, etc.). More precisely, in terms of schooling his work helps make transparent the links between the control of knowledge (e.g., curriculum standards tied to high-stakes standardized tests) and the implementation of gaze-based power, or observation—*watching*—for instance, in the "control" exhibited by test publishers and upper-level educational, political, corporate, and media management over the "normal" set of procedures by which assessment mechanisms—and schooling processes more generally—should proceed, be represented, and, finally, be interpreted.

Debord: *The Society of the Spectacle*

1 THE WHOLE LIFE of those societies in which modern conditions of production

prevail presents itself as an immense accumulation of *spectacles*. All that once was directly lived has become mere representation.

2 IMAGES DETACHED FROM every aspect of life merge into a common stream, and the former unity of life is lost forever. Apprehended in a *partial* way, reality unfolds in a new generality as a pseudo-world apart, solely as an object of contemplation. The tendency toward the specialization of images-of-the-world finds its highest expression in the world of the autonomous image, where deceit deceives itself. The spectacle in its generality is a concrete inversion of life, and, as such, the autonomous movement of non-life.

4 THE SPECTACLE IS NOT a collection of images; rather, it is a social relationship between people that is mediated by images. (Debord, 1967/1995, p. 12)

Foucault (1975/1979) contrasted the modern society of disciplinary surveillance (i.e., Panopticism) with the ancient society of disciplinary spectacle (e.g., circuses, temples), and maintained that the mechanism of surveillance, "[t]o procure for a small number, or even for a single individual, the instantaneous view of a great multitude," usurped the mechanism of spectacle, "To render accessible to a multitude of men [*sic*] the inspection of a small number of objects" (p. 216). In effect, according to Foucault, in the absurdly disciplinary state of modernity, surveillance won.

Guy Debord and his Situationist International (SI) colleagues provide a contrasting notion of modern society, "the society of the spectacle," one that can be meaningfully—*critically*—read against Foucault's somewhat more famous surveillance-grounded approach. Foucault's Panopticism can be interpreted (we think plausibly) as a critique of Debord's work (although to our knowledge Foucault does not mention Debord by name).[3] Our contention is that Debord's insights *indirectly* (in that *Society of the Spectacle* appeared before *Discipline and Punish*) challenge Foucault's understanding by suggesting a greater place within modernity for *spectacle*—for that which Foucault relegated and confined to antiquity—and that they do so precisely because of Debord's hermeneutic complexity, his more nuanced and sophisticated conceptualization of both spectacle and late capitalist society (see, e.g., Bracken, 1997; Debord, 1967/1995, 1988/1990; Jappe, 1993/1999; Jay, 1994; Knabb, 1981; Marcus, 1989; Plant, 1992; Sussman, 1989). Simply, in the "battle" between surveillance and spectacle, Foucault elevated surveillance. Debord's view levels this dichotomy by reconstructing spectacle and bringing it up to an equal status (as opposed to Baudrillard's [1995] work that does so by taking Panopticism [and spectacle for that matter] down).

For Debord, spectacle defines a society in which everywhere reality (and "real" human experience) is replaced by *images*—images that obtain and pursue a "life of their own" distinct (not merged with) reality. It, spectacle, presents a form of capitalist-induced alienation in which "being" means "appearing" and where the image, as commodity, as distorted and disconnected, mediates all social relationships. For Debord (1967/1995) the components and characteristics of this context include:

1. the dominance of image over lived experience
2. the privileged status of the commodity
3. the promotion of abstract (exchange) value and labor
4. alienation
5. passive observation (by spectators) and contemplation (over living or experiencing)
6. a specific economics and ideology
7. isolation/separation/fragmentation/lack of community, and
8. the denial of history. (see esp. chapter 1)

Spectacle, further, maintains its own regime of control and discipline, one opposed fundamentally to surveillance and to the Panopticon, one rooted in the fact that it exists purely for its own reproduction and thus subordinates all of human life to its needs. It controls by isolating and fragmenting, denying history, distorting reality, alienating, and monopolizing communication (one way, to its advantage). It ultimately works to deny that which can promote change (e.g., community, dialogue) in that those who want it maintained control images—the dominant form of social life—such that they might further mystify underlying and hierarchical relations of economic/capitalistic power. They, therefore, govern *social* relationships, and do so via the spectacular mechanisms of isolation, fragmentation, distortion, and the appearance of unity/unification/the whole at the site of the disconnected, and disconnecting, commodity-image itself.

Although Foucault and Debord defined spectacle in contrasting ways, their views nonetheless intersected at several critical points—and are not, therefore, innately incompatible; they may, in fact, be complementary. Both saw spectacle as a unique mode of social control favoring some groups and individuals over others. Both, moreover, attached it to historical, political, and (especially for Debord's fundamentally Marxist critique) economic circumstances. But whereas Foucault consigned spectacle wholly to civilizations of the past, Debord saw spectacle as an essential property of all (capitalistic) modern societies. Foucault distinguished spectacle as *actively* seeing, Debord as *passively* seeing (or "contemplating"—spectating). Foucault conceived it as ancient *life*, as *unifying*, as *gaze*; Debord conceived it as *death*, as *isolating*, as *mediating image(s)*. For Foucault it was truth, for Debord deception, or even the deception of deception.

Baudrillard: The End of the Panopticon/
Abolition of the Spectacle

What this overview of Foucault and Debord suggests, perhaps, is a too narrow reading on the part of both. For Foucault *perhaps* misread the importance of spectacle by working too hard to distinguish it from "modern" surveillance, and Debord *perhaps* misread the importance of "merely" observing by downplaying the significance of the "active" disciplinary gaze. A stronger conception of spectacle, then, might well include elements drawn from Foucault *and* Debord so that spectacle is capable of privileging image as it *simultaneously* disciplines via the inspection of the few by the many. Representation might contextualize spectacular observation, *and* spectacular observation might contextualize representation. Far from abolishing Panopticism this possibility arguably empowers it as it enlarges the range of its visual origins and recognizes the disciplinary connotations of the spectacular commodity-image. It is a view to which we return, most importantly in terms of (1) understanding image and (2) its implications for contemporary schooling.

Against these views we introduce here Jean Baudrillard's (1995) unique critique, "The End of the Panopticon," a contrasting theory that in some ways refines the understandings offered by both Foucault and Debord. Baudrillard constructs his radically divergent interpretation by first utilizing TV and the 1971 PBS documentary on the Loud family. As he begins:

> The eye of TV is no longer the source of an absolute gaze, and the ideal of control is no longer that of transparency. "[For y]ou no longer watch TV, it is TV that watches you (live)," or again: "You are no longer listening to Don't Panic, it is Don't Panic that is listening to you"—a switch from the panoptic mechanism of surveillance (*Discipline and Punish* [*Surveiller et punir*]) to a system of deterrence, in which the distinction between the passive and the active is abolished. (p. 29)

This system is, he continues

> An about-face through which it becomes impossible to locate one instance of the model, of power, of the gaze, of the medium itself, because you are always already on the other side. No more subject, no more focal point, no more center or periphery: pure flexion or circular inflexion. No more violence or surveillance: only "information," secret virulence, chain reaction, slow implosion, and simulacra of spaces in which the effect of the real again comes into play. (pp. 29-30)

Contrasted with panoptic surveillance, today's society is, for Baudrillard, one not of discipline but of *deterrence,* one in which the gaze-founded relationship of observer to observed is blurred, dynamic, and absolutely and purely circular—if not, indeed, extinguished.

As Baudrillard (1987) sums up his critique of Foucauldian discipline:

> ...Foucault will only have given us the key to [anything] when it no longer means anything. The same goes for *Discipline and Punish,* with its theory of discipline, of the "panoptic" and of "transparence." A magisterial but obsolete theory. Such a theory of control by means of a gaze that objectifies, even when it is pulverized into micro-devices, is passé. With the simulation device we are no doubt as far from the strategy of transparence as the latter is from the immediate, symbolic operation of punishment which Foucault himself describes. Once again a spiral is missing here, the spiral in front of which Foucault, oddly enough, comes to a halt right at the threshold of a current revolution of the system which he has never wanted to cross. (p. 16)

And:

> With Foucault, we always brush against political determination in its last instance. One form dominates and is diffracted into the models characteristic of the prison, the military, the asylum, and disciplinary action. This form is no longer rooted in ordinary relations of production (these, on the contrary are modeled after it); this form seems to find its procedural system within itself—and this represents enormous progress over the illusion of *establishing* power in a substance of production or of desire. Foucault unmasks all the final or causal illusions concerning power, but he does not tell us anything *concerning the simulacrum of power itself.* Power is an irreversible principal of organization because it fabricates the real (always more and more of the real), effecting a quadrature, nomenclature, and dictature without appeal; nowhere does it cancel itself out, become entangled in itself, or mingle with death. In this sense, even if it has no finality and no last judgment, power returns to its own identity as a *final principle:* it is the last term, the irreducible web, the last tale that can be told; it is what structures the indeterminate equation of the word. (p. 40)

Interestingly, he takes on spectacle and the Situationists as well as Panopticism and Foucault:

> We are witnessing the end of perspectival and panoptic space (which remains a moral hypothesis bound up with all the classical analyses on the "objective" essence of power), and thus to the very abolition of the spectacular. Television, for example in the case of the Louds, is no longer a spectacular medium. We are no longer in the society of the spectacle, of which the situationists spoke, nor in the specific kinds of alienation and repression that it implied. (p. 30)

As opposed, then, to a society in which all social relationships—the *real*— are mediated by images, as per Debord, Baudrillard instead sees one in which the differences between the image and the real collapse, the two converge and become indistinguishable, a setting of "hyperreality" where in fact frequently the existence of the image is more real than the real itself, and such that at some point images live in the absence of any "authentic" original (or *reality*)—as *simulacra*.

According to Steven Best (1994), Baudrillard here moves beyond both Debord and Foucault in that he "claims that not only are political economy and the era of production dead, but also [that] more recent theorizations of the disciplinary society and the spectacle itself are obsolete" (p. 53). As Best argues:

> Baudrillard's point is that the distinctions and assumptions Foucault's and Debord's analyses depended upon—the subject/object distinction, a subject of alienation or repression, and objective reality—have been obliterated. Baudrillard claims that we are in a radically new situation of maximal implosion.... (p. 53)

Baudrillard suggests, in other words, that the Panopticon and the spectacle are dead because the very foundations upon which they were built have now been toppled. The significance of the gaze and representation disappears in that any real or meaningful distance between their constituent parts— "see" and "seen" (or "seeing" and "being seen") and "original" and "representation" (i.e., image)—have been destroyed.

In (post)modern society there is not only no longer any difference between the real and the copy, but there is as well no difference between the warden and the inmate or the observer and the observed. And yet, if all such differentiations have, as Baudrillard insinuates, "imploded," what then of the conditions of disciplinarity—of the connections between control and the gaze, power and knowledge, lived experience, commodification, and contemplation? Where, in this instance, does Baudrillard leave us with respect to the Panopticon and to the spectacle?

Baudrillard is correct to suggest that absolute, firm, eternal, or pinpointable distinctions between various antithetic limits have blurred and become evermore complex and mobile, yet that is not synonymous with establishing the end of the Panopticon (or for that matter the spectacle). For it is perhaps not that such differences have collapsed or dissolved, but rather that their mechanisms and effects have actually expanded and become even more volatile, mutual, able, and diffuse. It's not, in other words, certain that the Panopticon has *ended* as much as it is plausible that it simply has *evolved* beyond any clearly distinguishable boundaries. A society does not, therefore, need prisons in order to have prisoners and wardens (anymore than it requires schools to have teachers and students)—a range of locations or geographies (whether material or cyber/virtual/hyper) will do. For, in fact, the scope and breadth of the disciplinary gaze have grown such that distance and space no longer present any obstacle to the workings and effects of power—the notion of "régime of truth" now implies an upward and outward spiral in which surveillance and the power/knowledge circularity become magnified and explicitly dangerous—at once more concentrated and more dispersed, specific yet simultaneously multiple.

What has changed more definitively are the *conditions* of Panopticism—its contexts, its positions relative to technology, globalization, standardization, and so forth. Newer visual technologies, for example, have made the Panopticon both more powerful and farther-reaching (yet still remarkably efficient). Globalization has stretched the effects of surveillance (and normalization and the examination). Standardization—the contemporary will to standardize, political/economic/cultural consensus and homogeneity around various exclusive interests—has strengthened the consequences of Panopticism, made discipline more invisible, and intensified the status of power/knowledge so that it becomes increasingly and more generally "normal"/"normalizing" (as the ostensibly wide-ranging alliance—conservatives *and* liberals—supporting standards-based educational reform perhaps indicates).

If the lines between such binaries as observer and observed and real and image and warden and prisoner do indeed disintegrate, it is not likely because the fundamental *foundations* of surveillance-driven Panopticism have gone away, but rather because those of *spectacle* (as Foucault used the term) have caught up. It is not because the "disciplinary center" has vanished, but to the contrary, that disciplinary centers have proliferated—that they are contingent, situated, and circumstantial—so that we might in the same instance wield power over others while others wield power over us, watch and be watched, and so that any singular commodity might exist as both an original *and* as a copy (depending on the peculiarities of any given time and place). What might it mean, then, if anything, to ask with respect to schooling: Are standardized test scores real or *mere* representations? Do teachers brandish power (i.e., *do they discipline*), or is power brandished against them (i.e., *are they disciplined*)? What of the connections of both teachers and testing to the processes of (disciplinary) knowledge? And, to what extent do images—test scores, representations, simulations—mediate social and pedagogical relations to the detriment of authentic, lived experience?

Surveillance *and* Spectacle: Voyeurism *and* Exhibitionism

The society in which contemporary schooling operates—and in which image emerges and attains its position of power—is one characterized in part by both surveillance *and* spectacle (e.g., Polan, 1986). It is, therefore, one of seeing *and* being seen, often at one and the same time. This trait, moreover, seems somewhat typical of—if not in fact fundamental to—not only twenty-first-century schooling, but other social institutions as well. In effect, ours is a society of both voyeurism and exhibitionism—not only in terms of the *possibility* of simultaneously seeing and being seen (theoretically all the time), but also of the *desire* to see and be seen. Although the question of *why* exceeds the scope of this chapter, clearly the convergence of technological development and cultural change plays significant roles). The advent of Webcams and "reality" TV, for example—and the presence of a 24/7 electronic visual media period—are key.

In any event, we feel the need to peer into the lives of others (often at a "safe" distance) and to allow others to peer into our lives—even, at times, while bemoaning our loss of privacy and the "tabloidization" of even "serious" news outlets (i.e., "infotainment"), as they (and the government) place individual citizens under increased scrutiny and an ever-expanding disciplinary gaze. We argue over the "need" for this—the public's "right to know" (e.g., the various Clinton scandals) and/or the need for public safety or national security (e.g., Echelon, Carnivore, and the Department of Homeland Security; see, e.g., Becker, 2002a, 2002b; Bumiller & Sanger, 2002; Tumulty, 2002; Tyler, 2002). Nevertheless, the visual-disciplinary ethos remains in place.

Regarding schools, this means a strengthened role for such "reforms" as SBER, a powerfully hierarchical regime of both surveillance and spectacle (see also chapter four). Here, curriculum standards and high-stakes testing work to monitor—watch—teacher, student, and school (as well as district and state) "performance" or "achievement." This represents the conformative—gaze-based disciplinary—qualities of surveillance, as relatively small groups of officials watch both how and that standards are implemented and how and that they are assessed. Spectacle—in both its Foucauldian and Debordian forms—surfaces in the name of accountability as such indicators of "success" as test scores and pass rates evermore frequently appear in the media. This means that larger groups—theoretically the entire news-interested public—watch smaller ones (teachers, students, classrooms, schools, etc.) as a means of control (as encouragement toward a particular level or type of legitimate knowledge acquisition and/or behavior). This may certainly involve both the few watched by the many (following Foucault) *and* the mediation of social relationships by the image (following Debord). Regarding the first, public display, consider the example related by Susan Ohanian (2002) of "administrators in a Washington school who decided to line graduates up at high school commencement according to their Grade Point Average" (p. 51). In effect, this amounts to the pedagogical equivalent of *Survivor* or *Jerry Springer*—a performance open to all in which the conceivable pressures to succeed, to conform to certain "achievement expectations," to entertain, weigh heavy, and operate as a publicized performance, a stage play, or a sideshow.

Regarding the second—social relationships mediated by images—think of the extent to which individuals with little or no recent firsthand experience with classrooms or schools make decisions about, and construct meanings about, the effectiveness or goodness of public education based merely on the publication of test scores (and perhaps popular film and television). People "know," that is, whether and which schools are good or effective irrespective of any authentic knowledge of actualized teaching practices, curricula, student needs, and so on according principally to representations—images— reported in the press. Hence, the relationship between school and society— teachers and students and the larger public—is in fact mediated, at least in part, by images, by test scores which may or may not indicate anything at all about the day-to-day workings of contemporary classroom and school-based life (or even student achievement for that matter).

In society more broadly this indicates a status described in *The New York Times Magazine* by Frank Rich (2000; see also Rich, 2003) as the "age of the mediathon," the era of O. J. Simpson, Monica Lewinsky, John Wayne Bobbitt, Chandra Levy/Gary Condit, Martha Stewart, and so on, all coverage— surveillance-spectacle/exhibitionism-voyeurism—all the time, one about which columnist Maureen Dowd (2002a) writes, "For years people have been complaining about the media's invasions of privacy. But the flip side is equally disturbing—the incredible hunger that so many Americans have to have their privacy invaded by the media" (p. 13). It is a condition in which we demand privacy for ourselves, but expect or even insist upon surveillance and spectacle, voyeurism and exhibitionism, for others (e.g., "Arab-looking" men, *The Osbournes,* characters on *Survivor* or *Dog Eat Dog;* even upscale restaurants reportedly use hidden cameras to determine when diners are ready for their next course; McNamee, 2002), even as we chase after our own fifteen minutes of fame. Yet in the postmodern age such lines and distinctions continuously, contingently, and unpredictably blur such that perhaps more than ever before *we become the others* and *the others become us*—the exhibitionists-voyeurs, the surveillors-surveilled, the spectators-spectatees are all of us; they are everyone.[4]

At its most direct level the relationship between spectacle and surveillance—or exhibitionism and voyeurism—operates in a fairly straightforward and clearly discernible way, and according to a relatively rudimentary mechanism pertinent to both schools and the wider realm of society. It is circular, and may in part be characterized according to certain assertions established within the evolving interdisciplinary fields of "systems thinking" and "dynamic modeling."[5]

Arguably, spectacle and surveillance function as potential solutions to problems caused by their specific and mutual consequences, such that the appropriate response to spectacle is the strengthening of surveillance, and the appropriate response to surveillance is the strengthening of spectacle. Often, however, the "benefits" of such reactions include with them a number of unwanted and unintended consequences. Consider two examples.

First, the spectacular but tragic events of September 11, 2001, the deadly commandeering of four commercial airliners subsequently used as weapons in the destruction of New York City's World Trade Center towers and Washington's Pentagon (and in an aborted effort to strike other major targets that was impeded by passenger intervention over Pennsylvania). The formal and official response was stepped up surveillance, most notably at US airports, for the purpose of preventing future such deadly spectacles. The intended, hoped for, and anticipated consequence is safety—homeland security, as it were—and public confidence in the government's ability to lead and in its efforts to provide domestic security. A "necessary evil," one justified by the risk posed by "the Evildoers," is a certain loss of privacy and freedom—as, for example, persons and personal belongings are increasingly and more thoroughly examined at airports. A potential unintended consequence is the likelihood that in addition to—or even instead of—greater safety and security, those who wish to engage in such destructiveness will simply get better at it—will become more effective and efficient in their use of the horrific and the spectacular in reply to augmented attempts at surveillance; they will learn to "beat the system." Thus, we will continue to lose privacy and freedom, and contrary to official pronouncements, we may simultaneously gain no greater degree of security, but may in fact face even more frightening and potent threats. In essence, we may confront the worst of both worlds—loss of privacy/freedom without any real corresponding growth in national protection or emotional/psychological comfort.

As a second, though clearly less critical and devastating, example, take the case of SBER. The perceived need to hold teachers and schools "accountable" leads to the almost inevitable expansion of surveillance—the demand/desire to peer inside classrooms as a means of observing/controlling what goes on there and in an effort to "make sure" teachers and students are meeting "important" goals. This, in turn, influences educational leaders to increasingly make public (via the media) the works (i.e., the results of testing) of their schools (spectacle) in a demonstration of "effectiveness" or "success"—such that, subsequently, societal interactions with education require diminishing amounts of any personal contact. For if the illustrious and illustrative test scores tell it all, why then bother with any genuinely human encounters with schools themselves? In the end, what may in fact take place is the growth of an externally disciplinary system, as teachers, students, classrooms, schools, and so forth work under the disciplinary gaze, without any clearly discernible improvement in teaching (as, perhaps, teachers already "perform well") and/or student learning (which is always incredibly difficult to measure anyway via currently predominant systems of testing). Again, the worst of both worlds.

In terms of disciplinarity, regarding both schooling and society, what exists is a regulatory and monitorial system of surveillance and spectacle that induces certain conformative and power-laden modes of both thinking and activity. It is, following Baudrillard, a system not only of discipline, however, but also of deterrence. For as surveillance encourages a certain notion of "how to act," spectacle encourages a certain notion of "how not to act." It represents, in the mindset of even conservative commentators such as Francis Fukuyama (2002), the exponential joining of the dangers posed by both Orwell's *1984* and Huxley's *Brave New World.* As Fukuyama writes:

The two books were far more prescient than anyone realized at the time, because they were centered on two different technologies that would in fact emerge and shape the world over the next two generations. The novel *1984* was about what we now call information technology: central to the success of the vast, totalitarian empire that had been set up over Oceania was a device called the telescreen, a wall-sized flat-panel display that could simultaneously send and receive images from each individual household to a hovering Big Brother. The telescreen was what permitted the vast centralization of social life under the Ministry of Truth and the Ministry of Love, for it allowed the government to banish privacy by monitoring every word and deed over a massive network of wires.

Brave New World, by contrast, was about the other big technological revolution about to take place, that of biotechnology. Bokanovskification, the hatching of people not in wombs but, as we now say, in vitro; the drug soma, which gave people instant happiness; the Feelies, in which sensation was simulated by implanted electrodes; and the modification of behavior through constant subliminal repetition and, when that didn't work, through the administration of various artificial hormones were what gave this book its particularly creepy ambiance. (pp. 3-4)

Ours is a government intent on a terrorist-free utopianism, one that demands toward this end a terrifying dystopianism, one in which everyone behaves, thinks, knows, and feels the same. Regardless of the eventual effects of Fukuyama's Huxleyan biotechnology, or even Orwell's perhaps more immediately recognizable Big Brother, without some rational and human/humane intervention, schools, sadly, will continue to be merely and unquestionably complicit in this dangerous and brave new world.

Consequences

In part, the potential pedagogical consequences of surveillance-spectacle originate in its peculiar disciplinary character—architecturally, visually, and so forth—and include those particular threats to the contemporary (and to some extent historical as well) aims and conditions of schooling that recognize a connection or connections between school and society and between formal education and everyday life. In our view these threats risk (re)imposing and/or (re)inforcing a pedagogy that is at once anti-democratic, oppressive, anti-the collective good, and inauthentic, threats that must be re-understood as quite possibly even more ominous within the growing contexts of technological change, education as a national public and private issue, globalization, and standards-based reform (all of which we address in chapter four). It is, ultimately, the risks posed by these threats that we seek to challenge in chapter seven.

Overall, each of these risks stems from the expansion of Panoptic disciplinarity, the convergence of spectacle and surveillance, and the concentration of visual, gaze-based power into the hands of a relatively small number of individuals and groups (e.g., the new federal Department of Homeland Security, multinational media conglomerates and their CEOs, etc.). In terms of democracy/anti-democracy, we rely principally on Dewey's (1916/1966) *Democracy and Education,* especially in light of its longstanding and widespread importance to US education and schooling. With respect to oppression/anti-oppression, we draw on both Paulo Freire's (1970) *Pedagogy of the Oppressed*—a landmark work in the evolution of critical or radical pedagogy—and Iris Marion Young's (1992) "five faces of oppression," a work that offers a sophisticated and newer alternative to Freire, though not necessarily an incompatible one. With respect to threats to the collective good and authenticity we utilize our own previous writings (e.g., Vinson, 1999, 2001a;

Vinson, Gibson, & Ross, 2001), those of Dewey, and the principles advocated by the progressive Whole Schooling Consortium (WSC; see Peterson, Beloin, & Gibson, 1998).

Democracy and Anti-Democracy

A first potential consequence of surveillance-spectacle-based disciplinarity is its threat to democracy, including its explicit dangers to democratic education and democratic schooling.[6] Although there are, obviously enough, numerous frameworks for approaching democracy and education, we choose the political-educational philosophy of John Dewey as our starting point because of (1) its consistency (generally, if not entirely) with our own viewpoints and (2) its tremendous impact on twentieth- and twenty-first-century educational theory (though to a lesser extent actual curricular and instructional practice). We argue, in short, that the image-privileging context of surveillance-spectacle presents no less than an *un-* or *anti*-democratic mode of society *and* an *un-* or *anti*-democratic mode of schooling, one antithetical to the means of preparing children for an engaged democratic social and political life, a life that might on some level assist them in combating the negative characteristics of modern disciplinarity (so that, in effect, the system risks becoming self-perpetuating).

In his monumental work *Democracy and Education: An Introduction to the Philosophy of Education,* Dewey (1916/1966), in some of the best-known words in the entire history of Western educational thought, presented his construction of democracy as a unique and desirable way of social life. In pursuing "the democratic ideal," he wrote that

> ...two elements in our criterion both point to democracy. The first signifies not only more numerous and more varied points of shared common interest, but greater reliance upon the recognition of mutual interests as a factor in social control. The second means not only freer interaction between social groups (once isolated so far as intention could keep up a separation) but change in social habit—its continuous readjustment through meeting the new situations produced by varied intercourse. And these two traits are precisely what characterize the democratically constituted society. (pp. 86-87)

And, most critically in terms of schooling (here Dewey is worth quoting at length):

> Upon the educational side, we note first that the realization of a form of social life in which interests are mutually interpenetrating, and where progress, or readjustment,

is an important consideration, makes a democratic community more interested than other communities have cause to be in deliberate and systematic education. The devotion of democracy to education is a familiar fact. The superficial explanation is that a government resting upon popular suffrage cannot be successful unless those who elect and who obey their governors are educated. Since a democratic society repudiates the principle of external authority, it must find a substitute in voluntary disposition and interest; these can be created only by education. But there is a deeper explanation. *A democracy is more than a form of government; it is primarily a mode of associated living, of conjoint communicated experience* [italics added]. The extension in space of the number of individuals who participate in an interest so that each has to refer his [or her] own action to that of others, and to consider the action of others to give point and direction to his [or her] own, is equivalent to the breaking down of those barriers of class, race, and national territory which kept [individuals] from perceiving the full import of their activity. These more numerous and more varied points of contact denote a greater diversity of stimuli to which an individual has to respond; they consequently *put a premium on variation in his [or her] action* [italics added]. They secure a liberation of powers which remain suppressed as long as incitations to action are partial, as they must be in a group which in its exclusiveness shuts out many interests. (p. 87)

Surveillance-spectacle, the disciplinary regime of the image, challenges democratic schooling and society initially to the extent that it itself is an undemocratic structure—it is ruled by an unrepresentative set of powerful and power-laden societal interests. It reduces shared and common interests to those characteristic of those in charge—or, perhaps even more dangerously, does so by demanding that broader interests take a back seat to more exclusive ones vis-à-vis the coercive mechanisms of gaze-based conformity. Surveillance-spectacle reduces the amount of social interaction and diminishes the quantity and quality of social intercourse as it eliminates the necessity (if not opportunity) for face-to-face contact (as contact is mediated by the image) and as the threat of someone watching and/or you watching someone else serves as a dualistic and systematic means of both discipline and deterrence (such that fewer options and less freedom exist). It limits the number of people truly involved in making decisions about their lives, and lessens the chance of variation in thought and action. Not only, then, is image-spectacle-surveillance disciplinary and conformative, it is disciplinary and conformative in support of the most powerful and well-heeled few. What "readjustment" occurs, then, involves merely a hyper-entrenchment of their undemocratic and controlling interests, and an associated commitment to those changes (technological, cultural, economic, etc.) that allow the mechanisms and routines of surveillance and spectacle to become more effective and more efficient.

Oppression and Anti-Oppression

A second risk involves oppression, simply a setting in which, whether intentionally or not, the interests of society's most powerful (the *minority*) are privileged at the expense of those of the least powerful (the *majority*).[7] In our analysis we draw on the work of two leading political and educational thinkers: Paulo Freire (1970), namely his *Pedagogy of the Oppressed,* and Iris Marion Young (1992), namely her "The Five Faces of Oppression."

In *Pedagogy of the Oppressed* Freire (1970) linked oppression to his celebrated conceptualization of "banking education," in which schooling

> turns [students] into "containers," or "receptacles" to be "filled" by the teacher....
> The more completely [the teacher] fills the receptacles, the better a teacher she [or
> he] is. The more meekly the receptacles permit themselves to be filled, the better
> students they are.... Education [thus] becomes an act of depositing, in which the students are the depositories and the teacher is the depositor.... The scope of action allowed to the students extends only as far as receiving, filing, and storing the deposits. (p. 53)

Banking education is identified with the fundamental conditions of oppression to the extent that:

> One of the basic elements of the relationship between oppressor and oppressed is
> *prescription.* Every prescription represents the imposition of one individual's choice
> upon another, transforming the consciousness of the person prescribed to into one
> that conforms with the prescriber's consciousness. Thus, the behavior of the oppressed is a prescribed behavior, following as it does the guidelines of the oppressor.
> (pp. 28-29)

For Freire, traditional schooling *is* oppressive as it consciously and purposefully prescribes, coerces, and banks.

A more recent yet also significant framework was established by Iris Marion Young (1992) in her work, "The Five Faces of Oppression," in which she tracks oppression beyond its

> traditional [grounding] in the exercise of tyranny by a ruling group [so as to include
> also its] new left...designat[ion of] the disadvantage and injustice some people suffer not because a tyrannical power intends to keep them down, but because of the
> everyday practices of a[n apparently] well-intentioned liberal society.... [It] refers to
> systemic and structural phenomena that are not *necessarily* [italics added] the result
> of the intentions of a tyrant [but are in fact] part of the basic fabric of a society, not a
> function [simply] of a few people's choices or policies.... Oppression refers to
> structural phenomena that immobilize a group...[where t]o be in a...group is to

share with others a way of life that defines a person's identity and by which other people identify him or her. (pp. 175-177)

For Young oppression is more subtle yet actually no less dangerous than in the definition set forth by Freire. What is oppressive from her perspective is the everyday workings of "the system," the structure, say, of public education itself. For once in place, well-intentioned though it may be, the system works automatically, if not absolutely, to control the lives of fundamentally oppressed teachers, students, and classroom/school communities (significant social groups), a condition synonymous with the conditions of injustice and disadvantage.

Young identifies five faces or types of oppression, recognizing that each presents its own unique mode or class of oppression whether in the presence or absence of any of the various others. Namely, these faces are

exploitation: [A state of] domination [that occurs] through a steady process of the transfer of the labor of some people to benefit others...[via a] relation of power and inequality [that] is produced and reproduced through a systematic process in which the energies of the have-nots are continuously expended to maintain and augment the power, status, and wealth of the haves (pp. 181-186);

marginalization: [The creation of] people...the system of labor markets cannot or will not employ...[a] most dangerous form of oppression [in which a] whole category of people is expelled from useful participation in social life, then potentially subject to severe material deprivation and even extermination; it deprives dependent persons of rights and freedoms that others have...[and] blocks such opportunity to exercise capacities in socially defined and recognized ways (pp. 186-188);

powerlessness: The absence of genuine democracy...[where] most people do not participate in making decisions that regularly affect the conditions of their lives and actions.... [I]t describes the lives of people who have little or no work autonomy[,] little creativity or judgment in their work, have no technical expertise or authority, express themselves awkwardly, especially in public or bureaucratic settings, and do not command respect; [it refers to those] lack[ing an] orientation toward the progressive development of [their] capacities...[and who lack] autonomy...authority, expertise, or influence (pp. 188-190);

cultural imperialism: [T]he experience of existing in a society whose dominant meanings render the particular perspectives and point of view of one's own group invisible at the same time as they stereotype one's group and mark it out as "other"; [it consists] in the universalization of one group's experience and culture and its establishment as the norm; [it] involves the paradox of experiencing oneself as invisible at the same time one is marked out and noticed as different (pp. 191-193); and

violence: [A condition in which the] members of some groups live with the *fear* [italics added] of random, unprovoked attacks on their persons or property, which have no motives but to damage, humiliate, or destroy them.... [It] may also take the form of name-calling or petty harassment intended to degrade or humiliate, and always signals an underlying threat of physical attack.... [I]t is directed at any member of the group simply because he or she is a member of that group...[and it] is usually legitimate in the sense that most people regard it as unsurprising, and so it goes unpunished.... [It is based upon] irrationality...[and] functions to help keep oppressed groups subordinate. (pp. 193-194)

For Young these faces denote singular and precise categories of oppression, each with its own contingent meanings, mechanisms, and modalities. With respect to contemporary schooling, we contend here that (1) *each* face exists and operates, independently *and* dependently, within classrooms, schools, and society at large; (2) taken together, the five faces approximate the experiences—the oppressive conditions—of many groups and individuals; and (3) teaching and learning present both oppressive and anti-oppressive possibilities, that is, the potential to challenge and disrupt as well as the potential to maintain and strengthen.

Fundamentally, image-spectacle-surveillance exposes its proclivity toward oppression mainly through two of its defining and characteristic features—(1) its establishment and maintenance by a politically, economically, socially, technologically, and culturally powerful few, and (2) its prevalent and routine place as part of everyday twenty-first-century life (see chapter six).

As representatives of powerful interests, those who control the settings of the imaginary—disciplinary and conformative, including those that make surveillance, spectacle, and surveillance-spectacle both possible and operative (see also the contexts discussed in chapter four)—work to impose their interests on others, and to coerce others into supporting them. They encourage them how to think; they prescribe. They make use of the work of teachers and students to further their own agendas (exploitation, as when educational managers claim the success of "their" programs when test scores rise, but blame teachers and students when they fall). They favor their own normalized and unchallenged and privileged positions—overwhelmingly white, male, wealthy, Christian, heterosexual, English-speaking, and so forth—as they continue to pretend the workings of meritocracy (with no input from those most affected by such assertions; cultural imperialism). They ignore— or "leave behind"—those who refuse to or cannot conform (marginalization), and threaten violence (either *physical,* as in the threat of arrest and imprisonment of Arabs, Arab-Americans, and Muslims [though this form here is also *cultural*]; or *social,* as in the punishments inflicted on teachers and students who dare to be themselves).

In essence, these *are* the effects of deterrence-based/disciplinary visuality—and the oppressiveness of the gaze—and what largely identifies the many missed opportunities inherent in public schooling.

The Collective Good

A third risk encompasses the threat posed by surveillance-spectacle to what might be called the "collective good," an ideal conceptualization distinguishable from both the individual (or private or personal good) and the common good, particularly in terms of key differences regarding their distinctive treatments and interpretations of interests. In short, each represents a unique, archetypal position along a single and theoretical continuum.[8]

In our view, the *individual good* is that state in which what is "good" is that which is *perceived* by a given person as what is in *his or her (individual, private, personal) best interests* regardless of any consideration of anyone else's best interests (e.g., the unbridled accumulation of private wealth or political power either for its own sake or for purely personal—selfish?—reasons). The *common good* refers to that which is *perceived* by a majority of individuals to be in *the best interests of a majority of individuals, or* what is perceived by a *powerful minority* to be in their best interests and then *imposed on others* as "therefore" in their best interests as well (a la "false consciousness" and/or "hegemony"; consider, for example, former GM president Charles Wilson's famous statement that "what's good for General Motors *is* good for the country").

The *collective good—as an ideal construct*—is that which is *authentically perceived by everyone to be in the best interests of everyone.* It takes seriously the realities of diversity and of the differentially constructed meanings of everyday lived experience. It represents an *intentionally maximized* coalition of communal interests, and demands in turn a *maximized* setting of democracy, a *maximized* context of equality in the distribution of power, *maximized* equality of opportunity, a *maximized* commitment to difference, and *maximized* conditions of social and economic justice. Again, an ideal type.

Most directly, image-spectacle-surveillance threatens the collective good in that those who manage its workings benefit individually from its consequences. When they don't, they portray their interests as the common good and seek in the process a degree of broader support. Although still an ideal, what keeps the collective good in opposition to the gaze is at the heart of the new disciplinarity—a lack of care and dedication toward such critical concepts as democracy, community, power-sharing, opportunity, difference, and justice. For the powers that be, they are solely distractions, for what is good for AOL Time-Warner and the FBI *is* good for the rest of America (and the world), evidently regardless of the havoc wreaked.

Authenticity and Inauthenticity

A final threat is that posed to the ideals of authenticity and to the goals of authentic education.[9] At its most basic level the risk is one in which the demands and effects of image or representation displace or supercede the imperatives of everyday classroom and social life (and their variously subjective, constructed, and confronted realities). For as Debord (1967/1995) himself implied, image and authenticity are incompatible; for in the society of the spectacle (and, as we see it, of surveillance, too), nothing is "really" lived. And authenticity signifies nothing if not the living of real experiences and the experiences of really living.

As Mathison (2001) argues (writing here specifically about assessment), that which is authentic in schooling is that which not only has "meaning" or value in "school contexts," but also more general meaning or value, especially in lived experience contexts, particularly as they persist and are created within the broader quotidian settings of modern global society writ large. Authenticity implies a focus on the daily lives, needs, and interests of classroom and school participants (especially teachers and students); a concern with lived and felt experiences; and a certain connectivity that challenges the alienating tendencies inherent in some aspects of contemporary formal education. The image-surveillance-spectacle complex makes any meaningful authenticity nearly impossible.

Perhaps the most famous treatment of authentic education was provided by John Dewey, specifically in the anti-traditional approach he espoused in works such as *The Child and the Curriculum* (Dewey, 1902/1956) and *Experience and Education* (1938/1963). It was in *Experience and Education,* in fact, that he contrasted traditional education with his own, more authentic and "genuine" approach. For Dewey (1938/1963), in traditional education:

> The main purpose or objective is to prepare the young for future responsibilities and for success in life, by means of [the] acquisition of the organized bodies of information and prepared forms of skill.... Since the subject-matter as well as standards of proper conduct are handed down from the past, the attitude of pupils must, upon the whole, be one of docility, receptivity, and obedience. Books, especially textbooks, are the chief representatives of the lore and wisdom of the past, while teachers are

the organs through which pupils are brought into effective connection with the material. Teachers are the agents through which knowledge and skills are communicated and rules of conduct enforced. (p. 18)

But for Dewey, in contrast, "all *genuine* [or *authentic*; italics added] education comes [and must come] through experience" (p. 25), that is as an "interaction" *between* "objective and internal conditions," or what he called a *"situation"* (p. 42). Dewey asserted that a "progressive" education must consider both the objective and the internal and resist the temptation to overemphasize either one. He maintained that since all students come to school with individual and unique *experiences,* they must then encounter unique and individual *educations* as well; the "material for learning...must be derived from materials which at the outset fall within the scope of ordinary life-experience" (p. 73). Only then can come "the progressive development of what is already experienced into a fuller and richer and also more organized form, a form that gradually approximates that in which subject-matter is presented to the skilled, mature person" (pp. 73-74). It is "incumbent," Dewey argued, on educators to "be aware of the potentialities for leading students into new fields which belong to experiences already had, and [to] use this knowledge as [their] criterion for [the] selection and arrangement of the conditions that influence their [students'] present experiences" (p. 76).

In *The Child and the Curriculum* Dewey (1902/1956) insisted first that educators must "get rid of the prejudicial notion that there is some gap in kind...between the child's experience [and that which defines] the [formal] course of study" (p. 11). They must, he continued:

Abandon the notion of subject-matter as something fixed and ready-made in itself, outside the child's experience; cease thinking of the child's experience as also something hard and fast; see it as something fluent, embryonic, vital; and we realize that *the child and the curriculum are simply limits which define a single process* [italics added]. Just as two points define a straight line, so the present standpoint of the child and the facts and truths of studies define instruction. It is continuous reconstruction, moving from the child's present experience out into that represented by the organized bodies of truth that we call studies. (p. 11)

Clearly, Dewey's interpretation of genuine, or authentic, education took seriously the import of the child, his or her experiences as well as his or her personal understandings. Yet the key problem with dominant modes of schooling—the traditional approach—was "the failure to keep in mind the double aspect of subject-matter which causes the curriculum and the child to be set over against each other..." (p. 23), such that "[t]he [instructional] material is not translated into life-terms, but is directly offered as a substitute for, or an external annex to, the child's present life" (p. 24). Because of this, "[t]hree typical evils result: In the first place, the lack of any organic connection with what the child has already seen and felt and loved makes the material purely formal and symbolic" (p. 24). The material becomes, in effect, "not a reality, but just the sign of a reality which *might* be experienced if certain conditions were fulfilled..." (p. 25).

"The second evil in this external presentation is lack of motivation. There are not only no facts or truths which have been previously felt as such with which to appropriate and assimilate the new, but there is no craving, no need, no demand" (p. 25). Teachers and children still work, of course, and technically still "teach" and "learn," because even the most "unpleasant, because meaningless, activities may get agreeable if long enough persisted in" (p. 28). For, as Dewey continued, *"It is possible for the mind to develop interest in a routine or mechanical [or inauthentic or un-genuine] procedure if conditions are continually supplied which demand that mode of operation and preclude any other sort"* [italics added] (p. 28).

Dewey's "third evil is that even the most scientific matter, arranged in most logical fashion, loses this quality, when presented in external, ready-made fashion, by the time it gets to the child" (p. 6). That is

[i]t has to undergo some modification in order to shut out some phases too hard to grasp, and to reduce some of the attendant difficulties. What happens? Those things which are most significant to the scientific man [*sic*], and most valuable in the logic of actual inquiry and classification, drop out. The really thought-provoking character is obscured, and the organizing function disappears.... [Content] is presented as stuff only for "memory." This is the contradiction: the child gets the advantage neither of the adult logical formulation, nor of his [or her] own native competencies of apprehension and response. (p. 26)

In effect, schooling becomes *hypersimplified*—inauthentic and disconnected and alienating. Teaching and learning become denatured to the point that they exist solely for those involved to appear a certain way—knowledgeable, able to behave "properly"—and as a means purely for collecting, storing, and retrieving mere facts and rote ideas (rather like Freire's banking education). Education develops toward the unproblematic and unproblematized, the unassailed and unassailable; it becomes imaginary, a simulation designed to portray and symbolize an absolute and conformative Truth.

Dewey's solution derives from what he termed "psychologization," a process or set of processes grounded in "the need of reinstating into experience the subject-matter of the studies, or branches of learning" (p. 22). Schooling here "must be restored to the experience from which it has been abstracted. It must [that is] be psychologized: turned over, translated into the immediate and individual experience within which it has its origin and significance" (p. 22). As against the "evils" of the disconnected, alienating, and inauthentic propensities of dominant and traditional education, Dewey argued that:

> The legitimate way out is to transform the material; to psychologize it—that is, once more, to take it and to develop it within the range and scope of the child's life. But it is easier and simpler to leave it as it is, and then by trick of method to arouse interest, to make it interesting; to cover it with sugar-coating; to conceal its barrenness by intermediate and unrelated material; and finally, as it were, to get the child to swallow and digest the unpalatable morsel while he [or she] is enjoying tasting something quite different. (p. 30)

Such is, ultimately, the unpalatable morsel, for example, of high-stakes standardized testing.

A second, more recent notion of authenticity resides in the efforts of the Whole Schooling Consortium (WSC), an organization that promotes a more holistic and community-based pedagogy than that typically found in traditional modes of schooling (Peterson, Beloin, & Gibson, 1998). From its perspective, whole schooling consists of five principles, namely, the effort to:

1. Empower citizens in a democracy
2. Include all
3. Teach and adapt for diversity
4. Build community & support learning [and]
5. Partner with families & the community. (Peterson, Beloin, & Gibson, 1998, p. 2)[10]

More specifically, these five principles mean that:

1. the goal of education is [and should be] to help students learn to function as effective citizens in a democracy;
2. all children [should] learn together across culture, ethnicity, ability, gender, [and] age;
3. teachers [should] design instruction for diverse learners that engage[s] them in active learning in meaningful, *real-world activities* [italics added]; [and] develop accommodations and adaptations for learners with diverse needs, interests, and abilities;
4. the school [should be one that] uses specialized school and community resources...to build support for students, parents, and teachers; [to] build community and mutual support within the classroom and school; [and to] provide proactive supports for students with behavioral challenges; [and]
5. educators [should] build *genuine* [italics added] collaboration within the school and with families and the community; engage the school in strengthening the community; and provide guidance to engage students, parents, teachers, and

others in decision-making and [the] direction of learning [and] school activities. (pp. 2-5)

Bluntly, surveillance-spectacle, the context within which image arises, and that setting within which contemporary schooling and society must be at least in part interpreted, makes authentic education unfeasible, if not in the end impossible. It does so in several distinctive and menacing ways.

First, given its requisite gaze-based disciplinarity, it completely ignores the realities of children's everyday lived experiences (although they, too, are increasingly constructed within an environment of image, surveillance, and spectacle). For, simply, they don't matter. Under the hierarchical power of observation, where image rules and where being means appearing, what does matter is knowing the "right" thing, behaving the "proper" way, regardless of any explicit individual and diverse life circumstances.

Second, surveillance-spectacle sets content and the learner against one another, opposing therefore the child and the curriculum and experience and education and schools and society, such that unique persons are irrelevant; whoever is there, the subject matter of knowing and behaving is consistent and constant—and ensured as such. Names, backgrounds, and identities, and the existential conditions of hearts, minds, and souls, take second place to the dominant/dominating wishes of various political, economic, social, and cultural elites.

Third, and in terms of Dewey's "evils," schooling becomes merely symbolic, a deceitful substitute rather than a part of actualized and experienced life (think here standardized test scores and the pressure among educators to raise them). *Real* motivation is nonexistent, but so-called motivation instead is coerced through forceful external demands (and induced by forceful external rewards). If teachers and learners *seem* to be enjoying themselves, it is merely a false conditioning—an *image*—built up via a one-sided discourse, repetition, and "sugar-coating." What might be scientific, logical, or thought-provoking is lost, as doing what others say to do—thinking and acting like (or even "better than") everyone else—*conform or else, because we are watching and you are being watched*—carries the most weight. Image-spectacle-surveillance, in effect, creates the ideal and absolute situation of *antipsychologization.*

Fourth, this climate contradicts the promising principles of whole schooling and repudiates its ambitions relative to authenticity and genuineness. Within such an arrangement, democratic empowerment cannot occur in that the context itself is perpetually anti-democratic; everyone cannot be included because those who either choose to not or cannot conform to the externally implicated visual disciplinarity are "left behind"; diversity is renounced in the name of homogeneity—we're watching, at multiple micro and macro levels, so *behave correctly,* or *don't behave incorrectly*; community disintegrates as relationships that might be real become mediated by images, or else "community" is forced in the name of competition (i.e., "beating" other local, national, and/or international communities); and, lastly, partnerships become solely alliances of convenience and disconnected modes of successfully strengthening, reproducing, and reinforcing the established governing order.

In Sum

The contemporary convergence or coexistence of surveillance and spectacle forms in part the context within which image attains its power. Yet this state of affairs poses specific and critical threats to the enactment of meaningful schooling and to the evolution of global society. These threats include those related to democracy, authenticity, anti-oppression, and the collective good, current and historical goals of public education, and those commitments that might effectively challenge the problematics of disciplinarity. Moreover, surveillance-spectacle brings specific architectural consequences (as noted by Foucault), that both reinforce and are reinforced by the system itself, including the implementation of schooling. In the next section we consider the architectural import of image-surveillance-spectacle and its new disciplinary regime, and argue that (1) image-surveillance-spectacle implies (or creates or compels) a particular architectural structure (or set of structures); (2) this architectural structure strengthens and is strengthened by gaze-based disciplinarity; and (3) it produces and reproduces the dangers to schooling described in the preceding discussion.

Architecture: "Teletecture" and "Cosmotecture"

Just as Foucault identified the architectural dimensions of visual power-knowledge—the Panoptic prison with respect to surveillance, circuses and temples with respect to spectacle—we suggest that the implications of surveillance-spectacle, the image-based new disciplinarity, might carry as well architectural implications relevant to schooling and contemporary society, implications that will (circularly) strengthen/be strengthened by the hegemony of representation and the threats to democracy, authenticity, the collective good, and anti-oppression posed by image and surveillance-spectacle.

These implications may be both far-reaching and significant with respect to contemporary education. The new disciplinary architecture, which soon may come even to characterize schooling, might, in fact, move *beyond* the Panoptic prison model proper and instead veer toward, say, the casino, the international airport, the empty (or "any") space (given wirelessness), the sports coliseum or arena, and/or the mega-shopping mall (noting, for instance, that some schools already manifest the equivalent of a food court, even accommodating McDonald's). For what these new archetypes share is a context of *both* spectacle *and* surveillance, where in terms of discipline, in each case structures are in place so that the many can observe the few, the few the many, and so that image essentially rules.

Speculatively, then, two inclusive architectural *types* might emerge as the post-Panopticon, the new (and "improved") general disciplinary form grounded in the technology of the gaze. The first, what might be called "teletecture," would describe the virtual space/building/time of connectedness/connectivity (hyperspace, virtual space, cyberspace). It would involve the means by which seer and seen could interact through and across the absence of any enclosing space—or between separate enclosing spaces. With the evolution of the Internet, including its wireless, modem, and broadband modes of access, and Net/Webcams, the possibility increasingly exists of a visual disciplinarity among individuals without any direct and/or proximal contact. Thus, the workings of image, surveillance, and spectacle can extend throughout all imaginable confines of time and space, such that the few can watch and control the many anywhere and anytime (or *every*where and *every* time), *and* the many can watch and control the few anywhere and anytime (or *every*where and *every* time). In effect, what this means is the construction of a Panoptic shape without walls—or with walls with no apparent or discernible, and thus, perhaps, with no fundamentally *knowable,* bounds.

The second, what might be called "cosmotecture," would describe the effort to build all under one roof an entire "universe"—replete with monitors and cameras, the international airport or casino (or [post]modern school?), for example—large-scale but insistently bounded (a la the megamall). Here surveillance and spectacle would work together in a setting of the *super*-Panoptic—the extension of the prison model beyond its typical size to that of a structure with ever-expanding walls, and with nearly every amenity located all within a single bordered location.

Today's (and tomorrow's) Panopticon may in fact best be thought of not as a traditional prison at all, but either (paradoxically) as an *infinite* sociocultural-behavioral-economic-pedagogical space, *or* as a *null* socio-cultural-behavioral-economic-pedagogical space. With respect to disciplinarity, surveillance and spectacle here would work together so that discipline is not only a function of *being seen*—the many being observed by the few—but also of *seeing*—the few being observed by the many—with both occurring (potentially) simultaneously in that today one can plausibly observe and be observed at once, particularly given advancements in interactive visual and digital technologies.

As we have argued, surveillance works disciplinarily in that we discipline ourselves because we might be (or are) the *objects* of the gaze, while spectacle works disciplinarily in that we discipline ourselves because we might be (or are) the *subjects* of the gaze. It's a matter of disciplining *others* to behave or think like *us* (the dominant/dominating) and/or of disciplining *us not* to behave or think like (the dominated) *others*. In the post-Panoptic setting, the mishmash of exhibitionism and voyeurism, then, for schools the threats posed by the image-surveillance-spectacle framework—those threats to democracy and the collective good and of inauthenticity and oppression—might only grow more dangerous and frightening, especially given the incredible efficiency and effectiveness brought on by the new mechanisms of visual control.

Conclusions

Our main argument has been that in order to understand the meaning of pedagogical image—or of any particular pedagogical image—one must understand as well the contexts within which it is produced, actualized, and maintained (or not), *and* within which it and its producers effect its experienced consequences. In this chapter, we have explored surveillance, spectacle, and surveillance-spectacle as one such set of contexts, particularly as it relates to schools/schooling and society.

Moreover, we have maintained that this setting—image-surveillance-spectacle—in fact creates and is created by a unique and new disciplinarity, one that can be at least somewhat understood according to the singular philosophical views of Michel Foucault, Guy Debord, and Jean Baudrillard. It is a critical climate in which seeing and being seen dominate—what we have labeled exhibitionism and voyeurism—an environment which harbors clear and distinctive dangers relative to education and its variously construed historical and present-day goals.

Several further critical and necessary contexts surface, though, within which it is useful to locate the underlying arguments of this chapter in terms of contemporary schooling and society, and image and Panopticism, in addition to those of the co-mingling of surveillance and spectacle (see, e.g., Debord, 1967/1995; Foucault, 1975/1979), most directly the recent expansion of economic globalization (i.e., global-corporate-statist infotech capitalism), technological proliferation (e.g., two-way Web/Netcams), and standardization (especially, for schooling, mandated high-stakes standardized testing and curriculum standards), namely, in terms of their problematic and significant possible consequences (e.g., the privileging of "image" over variously constructed "authenticities" and the inducement of exclusivist practices [oppression, anti-democracy, de-privileging the collective good] via knowledge and behavior).

In the end we argue that it is imperative to approach schools and society and the preeminence of image as they are actualized within the *convergence/ coexistence of surveillance and spectacle.* That is, we conclude (with respect primarily to education) not that ours is a society of surveillance *or* spectacle, but that it is instead a society of surveillance *and* spectacle, that both have joined or at least now function concurrently.

This is not to say, however, that elements of each do not exist independently; they certainly do. For example, in schooling, surveillance emerges in the ever growing technologies by which a small group of people (test administrators, managers, superintendents, etc.) inspect the processes, procedures, contents, and outcomes of larger groups (teachers, students, parents) engaged in standardized testing. Spectacle appears according to the extent that key media outlets publish—publicize—scores, so that a larger group (potentially all of society) may observe the cultural and pedagogical "actions" of a smaller one (schools, principals, teachers, students, etc.). In terms of the broader society surveillance operates within such technologically enabled phenomena as nannycams, Carnivore, and Echelon, as well as within increased governmental efforts to monitor once private areas of individual and personal conduct (e.g., the Department of Homeland Security). Spectacle surfaces in the remarkable array of reality and tabloid television shows (even post-Springer, including *Survivor, Fear Factor, The Osbournes* [a 2002 Emmy Award winner for "Best Reality Series"], *American Candidate* [in which US presidential candidates will be selected], *My Life is a Sitcom*—believe it or not, a show for families who think their lives are funny enough for network TV—and so on, including even more stupid examples such as *Joe Millionaire* and *The Bachelorette*) presently on the air (e.g., Vinson & Ross, 2001a).

More significant, though, is the evident degree to which both coexist, if not in fact unite. For ours is a society of both nannycams *and Survivor,* of surveillance *and* spectacle, a state of affairs that creates, in effect, a *new* disciplinarity, one founded on the theoretical yet absurd possibility of *everybody watching everybody all the time* (unlikely, perhaps, but *possible*). It is further a situation that (re)produces and is (re)produced by a number of interconnected factors, including the desire and opportunity to see and be seen, technological development and proliferation (especially interactive [including wireless] multimedia connectivity), and the "triumph" of US culture (via both global capitalism and the direct exportation of powerful "American" artifacts). Arguably, US society today is one in which image trumps any reasonable interpretation of authenticity(ies), a perpetual mediathon, a regime in which voyeurism and exhibitionism meet and meld one into the other, exposing and reinforcing a power-based compilation of visual mechanisms of control (e.g., Rich, 2000; Vinson, 1999, 2001a; Vinson & Ross, 2001a). It is within such a broader and deeper milieu, *where we ask others to allow an invasion of their privacy and where others ask us to invade their privacy,* that contemporary schooling must be approached (e.g., Dowd, 2002a). Such is a (if not *the*) condition of contemporary schools and society.[11]

What Debord and Baudrillard indicate with respect to Foucault's perspective thus is not the end of the Panopticon at all, as much as it is the expansion, evolution, or restructuring/re-orientation of its fundamental and disciplinary features.

What Debord and Baudrillard's critiques hint at is that Foucault erred in downplaying—or even mis- or underdefining—spectacle as (1) a feature distinctly characteristic of ancient civilizations, and (2) solely the antithesis of surveillance. Although Foucault's passing precluded his witnessing and interpreting the technological revolution of the late twentieth and early twenty-first centuries, such change has in fact raised the status, significance, and possibility of spectacle as well as the critical position of the image. Spectacle is not, then, just the *opposite* of surveillance, but is in addition a dominant feature of the (post)modern, late capitalist world, a world in which images mediate the social. Plainly, Foucault (perhaps unavoidably) overlooked the standing of spectacle in favor of that of surveillance.

Second, surveillance itself has evolved, such that the Panoptic structure is not necessarily still *the* dominant/dominating disciplinary framework of our society. Today, perhaps, instead of the prison, and considering visual/technological developments, disciplinarity—still gaze-based—rests more on the prevalence of two-way cameras than direct observation, or on connectivity instead of proximity. It may metaphorically be symbolized via the casino, international airport, mall, stadium, and/or cyber/hyper/virtual space (basically, then, *anywhere*) and not solely the Panoptic prison.

Third, the very scope or domain of disciplinarity has expanded, as we think Debord and Baudrillard imply. Although Foucault recognized surveillance as a key power-component of modernity, he located it vis-à-vis related and delineated *institutions* (e.g., the prison, of course, but also the hospital, asylum, school, and so on). Debord and Baudrillard imply a deinstitutionalization of power/disciplinarity, of Panopticism itself, as the means by which the gaze can operate *mutually*—back and forth—and by which it can (and has and does) infiltrate the most intimate of human environments.

Does the Panopticon then still work as a tropic and conceptual disciplinary mechanism? Yes, but in ways beyond those initially identified by Foucault. It operates in conjunction with spectacle (the many observing the few *and* relationships mediated by image), between the cracks of formal/formalized institutions, and in ways independent of (and "bigger than") Bentham's architecture. Ours is not simply a society of spectacle or of Panoptic surveillance or of the "end" of Panopticism, but is instead one of surveillance *and* spectacle *and* surveillance-spectacle *and* their complicated and dynamic expansion, evolution, and restructuration.

What occurs, in effect, is a structure of *image-power*—or *power-image*—parallel to Foucault's (1980) celebrated notion of power-knowledge. Here, *image* "is a thing of this world...[and] is produced by virtue of multiple forms of constraint.... [And, therefore, it] induces regular effects of power" (p. 131). *Image* "is linked in a circular manner with systems of power which produce and sustain it, and to effects of power which it induces and which extend it. Thus, a 'régime' of [*image*]" (p. 133). Within the setting of surveillance-spectacle, image produces power which produces image which produces power, *ad infinitum.* Power becomes a function of *controlling images*—that is, control *by* images (i.e., images *that* control), and the control *of* images (i.e., images *that are* controlled).

Of course all of this needs to be more fully explored and interpreted within the current milieu of (1) public education's place as a growing national public/private issue (see chapter four), and (2) post-9/11 US and global society (where even the image of the United States itself has been called into question; e.g., Dao, 2002). With respect to education's growing status, what perhaps matters most today is the recent passage and enactment of the No Child Left Behind Act of 2001 (NCLB), one mandate of which specifies increased SBER/high-stakes testing. If we are correct, this provision may well contribute to the elevated standing of image and to the developing consequences of surveillance-spectacle/disciplinarity and its respective pedagogical risks.

The meaning of image and of surveillance-spectacle post-9/11 emerges in at least two principal ways. First, in the circular and mutual relationship that will exist between spectacle and surveillance as one serves as the preferred and spiraling response to the other. Second, in what is and will be the strengthening of domestic spying as the new Department of Homeland Security becomes a veritable clearinghouse for secret information—a Department of Homeland *Surveillance* managed by an appointed *Secretary of Surveillance* (Tom Ridge)—a surveillance *czar* (especially given the Bush Administration's support for the Terror Information and Prevention System [TIPS], the Foreign Intelligence Surveillance Act [FISA] Court, and the USA Patriot Act of 2001 [PL 107-56]; see Mitchell, 2002). The call, of course, will be for someone to "watch the watchers"—for spectacle and surveillance to enforce/reinforce one another.

For education, this complexity signals a number of critical implications, for curriculum, instruction, assessment, teacher education, scholarship, policymaking, and so on. It means taking image seriously, considering both its Panoptic and spectacular dimensions, and engaging in a project of facing the meanings, causes, and possible consequences for teaching and learning within such an organization. Its means, moreover, confronting the dangerous and changing potentialities of education within the social complex of a fused surveillance-spectacle, a complex that demands that all educators (and other concerned individuals and groups) work to critique, interrogate, and problematize what they do, and that we all undertake to hold up our work against the ideals of democracy (for instance, the "criteria" advanced by Dewey), authenticity, anti-oppression (e.g., following Freire and Young), and the collective good.

For as the efficacy with which disciplinarity functions continues to evolve and intensify—as Panopticism continues to work even within and surrounding schools—the crucial threat is against the least powerful and the least wealthy, and most relevantly here against the majority of schoolchildren and their teachers, as they endure the remarkable evolution of image-power, standardization, and the gaze.

Notes

We rely here heavily on our own previous work, especially Vinson (2001b, 2002) and Vinson and Ross (2001a, 2001d, 2003).

1. Clearly things have to some extent changed since 9/11. Yet our fundamental arguments, we think, still hold up. First, since the attacks on the World Trade Center and the Pentagon the federal government has, for both good and bad, stepped up its efforts at surveil-

lance (e.g., Dreyfuss, 2002), seeking in the process evermore efficient and effective mechanisms of inspection, observation, and control (e.g., at major airports and sporting events). Second, arguably, the media presentations of the events of 9/11 themselves indicate the (post)modern workings of spectacle, although, albeit, via a contemporary and evolving (global) state of affairs in which the overt stakes are horrifically greater.

2. Although well beyond the scope of this work, it should be noted that Foucault does to some extent go into the origins of this Panoptic system, an "invention" of the late eighteenth and early nineteenth centuries. As he suggests, and as we further interpret, the "move" from "spectacle" to "surveillance" (i.e., Panopticism) as a mode of discipline evolved along with (though not necessarily as a cause or effect of, or even simultaneously with or parallel to) other phenomena, including ideas established via the Enlightenment, philosophical developments such as liberalism and conservatism, the increased influence of both church and state, capitalism, urbanization, and various "popular" revolts—particularly as "social control" moved from a lower-middle class, morals-based defense *against* state power to an aristocratic and elitist move *toward (re)inforcing* state power (e.g., Foucault, 1975/1979, esp. pp. 60-70).

3. It is, however, likely that Foucault and Debord knew of one another's work, particularly given Debord's notoriety as a "leader" in the events of 1968 and the fame of his *The Society of the Spectacle,* and Foucault's status as one of France's most famous public and international intellectuals.

4. That image, surveillance, and spectacle are important current and historical issues is easy to demonstrate via even a simple review of the academic and scholarly literature. The possible examples are too many to make even a modestly exhaustive listing practical here, however. Although typically a range of topics is covered, most recent analyses tend to focus on the threats posed by increased surveillance (versus its benefits), the meaning or even (somewhat ironically) the *authenticity* of images, and the past and present effects of the spectacular and those media that make it possible. See, among others: Apple (2001); Bate (2002); Benedict (2001); Calvert (2000); Corn (2002); Deconstruct This (2000); Dowd (2002a, 2002b); Dreyfuss (2002); Elkins (2001); Fendrich (2002); Fukuyama (2002); Gitlin (2002); Goodheart (2000); Hockney (2001); James (2001, 2002); O'Reilly, 2002); Piper (2002); Rich (2000); Roman, 1996; Rosen (2000); Schwartz (2001); Shulevitz (2001); Simpson (2001); and Smith (2001).

5. We wish to thank Jennifer Toll for her helpful and insightful clarifications of these orientations.

6. We rely heavily here on Vinson, Gibson, and Ross (2001).

7. We draw extensively here on Vinson, Gibson, and Ross (2001) and Vinson (2001c).

8. See Vinson, (2001a).

9. See Vinson, Gibson, and Ross (2001) and Vinson (1999). In this section, "authentic" and "genuine" are used synonymously.

10. Page number references to Peterson, Beloit, and Gibson (1998) refer to the on-line version, available at: http://www.coe.wayne.edu/CommunityBuilding/WSPaper.html.

11. Readers interested in some of the phenomena we discuss might wish to see Arthur Lubow's (2003) recent piece in *The New York Times Magazine* on the architects Elizabeth Diller and Ricardo Scofidio. Regarding their work, they discuss the architectural possibilities related to "the simultaneous acts of seeing and being seen" (p. 40) and of "an immaterial building, a spectacle without substance" (p. 41).

✸CHAPTER FOUR

Education as Public Issue: Technology, Globalization, and SBER

And his [Feuerbach's] premonitory complaint has been transformed in the twentieth century into a widely agreed-on diagnosis: that a society becomes "modern" when one of its chief activities is producing and consuming images *[emphasis added], when images that have extraordinary powers to determine our demands upon reality and are themselves coveted substitutes for firsthand experience become indispensable to the health of the economy, the stability of the polity, and the pursuit of private happiness.* (Sontag, 1977, p. 153)

IN THE PREVIOUS CHAPTER we explored the complexities and consequences of the contemporary convergence, or coexistence, of surveillance and spectacle—*surveillance-spectacle*—as *a* significant context or set of contexts from within which the (post)modern image emerges and attains its position of relative power (*image-power, controlling images*), especially in terms of twenty-first-century US public schooling. In this chapter we seek simply to broaden our approach, our contextualization, to include several additional societal developments and recent trends, namely (1) the growing status of education as a national public (and private?) issue, (2) the continuing "successes" of technological evolution and innovation, (3) the demands of economic (capitalistic, Western/US-controlled, information-based) globalization, and (4) standards-based educational reform (SBER) and the current "will to standardize" (or the "standardization imperative"). We maintain that these settings situate not only image itself, but also surveillance, spectacle, and surveillance-spectacle. In effect, this depiction presumes and presents a multiple layering in which the workings of education as a national public issue, technological change, globalization, and SBER surround the mechanisms of surveillance-spectacle, *and* in which *both simultaneously* set up the critical environmental positionality of image. We argue that these mutual and interdependent circumstances make possible and encourage the burgeoning dominance and intensity of (the) pedagogical (and other) image(s)—even to the extent of (a) mutual relationship(s) existing between public education as national issue on the one hand, and technological change/globalization/SBER on the other. That is, schooling becomes even more significant nationally as technology, globalization, and standardization schemes proliferate, strengthen, and mature.

Schooling: A *National* Public (and Private) Issue

Historically, schooling has been the responsibility of states and local districts. Interpreted constitutionally as a Tenth Amendment issue, as one of the "powers not delegated to the United States by the Constitution, nor prohibited by it," it has been construed therefore as "reserved to the states respectively, or to the people." State executives and legislatures and local educational agencies (LEAs) have, thus, traditionally retained for themselves control over curriculum, policy, teacher certification, assessment, instructional methods, funding, building construction, and so on. But with the *relative* domestic activism of mid-twentieth-century administrations (and to some extent congresses—conservative *and* liberal), especially in the aftermath of the Supreme Court's 1954 *Brown vs. Board of Education* decision; social movements demanding civil rights (including high quality education) for African Americans, women, the disabled, gays and lesbians, immigrants, non-English speakers (or those who speak English as other than their first language), and the economically disadvantaged; and the federal government's 1983 publication of *A Nation at Risk* (National Commission on Excellence in Education, 1983; see also Department of Education, 1990, 1991), increasingly the president and Congress—Republican *and* Democratic— have sought influence over and federal input into, if not *control over*, public education—perhaps especially so since the 1979 establishment of the Department of Education out of the old Department of Health, Education, and Welfare. Public schooling has indeed now become so important nationally and has attained such an enormous and controversial place in national electoral politics and political debate and discussion that no serious candidate for national office can run without taking *some* engaged position (whatever it might be) on at least the "major" topics (e.g., school vouchers, school choice, school prayer, the Pledge of Allegiance, standardized testing/SBER, bilingual education, charter schools, etc.).

This augmented "official" national attention works in conjunction with public opinion, which, perhaps, always has considered education an important, nationwide concern. Most likely, public opinion influences increased formal national/governmental attention, *and* greater national attention influences public opinion. For as recent polls indicate, the voting public perceives education as one of the (if not, in fact, *the*) most important modern domestic issues (even in light of the events of 9/11 and present-day revelations about stock market/investor/management corruption). In fact, only "the economy" (post-Enron) and "terrorism" (post-9/11) come even close to matching the rationalized magnitude of public education and schooling in the minds of many Americans (see, e.g., Deily, 2002; Johnson & [with] Duffett, 1999; PollingReport.Com, 2002; Rose & Gallup, 2002; Saad, 2002).

All of this was driven home during the 2000 US presidential election campaign and in the platforms of all the major candidates (Bush, Gore, Buchanan, and Nader). As contemporary polls made clear, politicians ignored public schooling only at their own electoral risk (e.g., Gallup, 2000; Jones, 2001; Robelen, 2001a, 2001b). Once considered principally a Democratic issue—in part because of the post-*Brown* reforms spearheaded by Democratic President Lyndon B. Johnson during the 1960s and the subsequent (post-Democratic Carter, of course) efforts by Republican President Ronald R. Reagan during the 1980s to eliminate the Democratically created Department of Education and to privatize public schools as an antidote to "tax and spend big government liberalism"—today both Republicans and Democrats (and many Third Parties) consider a federal role in education to be crucial to their aims; they attempt, therefore, to place their particular (and ideological) positions as "the one best way" to save or improve American schools (and by extension American culture, society, and the economy; see here, e.g., the writings of former Secretary of Education and Drug Czar Republican William Bennett [e.g., 1988, 1994]; see also Hirsch, 1987, 1996).

Today, perhaps, this is most evident via the No Child Left Behind Act of 2001 (NCLB; see No Child Left Behind, 2001; [The] *No Child Left Behind Act of 2001*, 2001). Supported both by current Republican President George W. Bush (whose father, ironically, was President Reagan's vice president during the latter's efforts to dismantle the Department of Education) and a majority of members of Congress (a bipartisan effort led in large part, surprisingly or not, by Democratic Senator Edward Kennedy of Massachusetts working with the Bush White House), the NCLB Act represents arguably the most wide-ranging and potentially influential federal education legislation passed in more than a generation.

Its most notorious component, an increased and unprecedented commitment to standardized testing, (re)inforces the dominant/dominating position of pedagogical image, downplaying any relevance for the arguably more authentic, and, in fact, most ominously demonstrates the complex and troubling workings of surveillance-spectacle. Although we address SBER more thoroughly later, its features not only undergird present national policy but also set the stage for the underlying disciplinary contexts of contemporary public schooling.

Interestingly, at the same time schooling surges in national, *public* attention, it grows as well as a major *private* issue—especially in view of such recent initiatives as charter schools, school vouchers, school choice, and corporate sponsorships (granted, not all of which are *purely* privatization endeavors, but are [or may be or reflect] the influence of the private sector on the government).

What matters most here, though, is how this heightened public-private standing of education and schools effects a new contingent set of conditions relative to surveillance-spectacle and image. This public-private administrationing of schooling means an increased place for the visual as a means of control (and, subsequently, an increased desire for the official control of the visual). As schooling becomes an evermore magnified and compelling national question, and, simultaneously, an evermore profit-driven private venture, the disciplinary-visual imperative becomes all the more significant. What occurs, in essence, is a reciprocal demand that schools and schooling become (a) increasingly *watched* and thus (b) increasingly *watchable*. This occurs at both the micro and macro levels. At the micro level this suggests an enhanced attempt to "see" what goes on in individual schools (say through media-reported within-district test scores). At the macro level it means observing schools via interstate competitions, international testing results, "accountability" schemes (e.g., Mathison & Ross, 2002), and the conceivable connections between international economic advantage and teaching and learning. All of this we maintain rests on the immediacy of technological change (and what it enables/encourages), globalization, and standardization-SBER, *and* social/cultural/political/economic standardization more broadly construed.

Technology: Seeing and Being Seen 24/7

One hundred and fifty years ago, Karl Marx gave a one-sentence summary of his theory of history: "The hand mill gives you society with the feudal lord; the steam mill, society with the industrial capitalist." Today he could have added: "The jet plane, the telephone, and the Internet give you a global society with the transnational corporation and the World Economic Forum.

Technology changes everything—that was Marx's claim, and if it was a dangerous half-truth, it was still an illuminating one. As technology has overcome distance, economic globalization has followed. (Singer, 2002, p. B9)

The evolution of technology, of course, changes the conditions, mechanisms, and needs of the gaze—in that the needs of the gaze and technological change mutually affect one another. Their interaction, in terms both of possibility and desire, thus alters the processes, potentialities, chronologies, and geographies of seeing and being seen, and in effect establishes a new order with respect to image and a new set of constructed and contested meanings for surveillance and spectacle (for schools as well as societies). What exists today is the baffling if not absurd *ability*—even, perhaps, the *urge*—to see and be seen continuously, 24/7, as a complex and mutual circumstance of disciplinarity. In a world of watching and being watched, nonstop, image increasingly rules.[1]

We are not, certainly, anti-technology Luddites; technology makes many good and positive things possible—quicker, easier, safer, more reliable, and so on (e.g., in medicine, information, research, travel, etc.). Our contention, simply, is that the convergence or coexistence of surveillance and spectacle (and the technological shifts that in part make it possible), have remade and strengthened the enactment and impact of disciplinarity. In effect the move has been from the *ancient* application or threat of a sovereign's *physical force* (following Foucault's notion of antiquity as an age of *spectacle*), to *modernity's* gaze-based *surveillance* (following Foucault's take on Bentham's Panopticon), to *postmodernity's surveillance-spectacle contextualized regime of controlling and dominant/dominating visual image(s).*

Without question human civilizations have always sought and been characterized by some degree of technological change; as such, today is not unique. But what has been transformed is the very scope, pace, and amount of such technological change, and, surely, what it might *represent* and how it might be *represented*.

We propose first that *all* technological change—ancient, classical, medieval, modern, or postmodern (or whatever)—may be distinguished as more or less *vertical* and more or less *horizontal* (positioned, say, on a grid of Cartesian axes). *Vertical* technological change—whether evolutionary, revolutionary, both, or something else entirely—represents the degree to which new technology replaces, or substitutes for, older technology (e.g., the way in which the automobile usurped the status of the horse-drawn carriage). *Horizontal* technological change—again, whether evolutionary, revolutionary, both, or something else—involves the extent to which new technologies complement, or work with, older ones rather than replace them altogether (e.g., the way CD burners work with earlier PCs).

Technological change today occurs within an overall environment of relative rapidity and expansion. Although both vertical and horizontal mutations take place, vertical substitution proceeds comparatively slowly while horizontal complementarity proceeds comparatively swiftly. Fewer technologies are *quickly* and *completely* supplanted; through the possibilities provided by "peripherals," "interfaces," "networking," "compatibility," and the like, newer technologies such as the PC remain more or less constant over longer periods of time. While substitution/replacement does happen, generally newer technologies are only *gradually* displaced (the CD over the cassette tape, DVD over VHS) and are instead more often designed to work together (e.g., television sets with connections for both DVD and VHS recorders/players).

Until the onset of modern industrialization, the pace of technological change was fairly negligible (at least from a twenty-first-century perspective), almost imperceptible, and may be understood perhaps as a case of what evolutionary biologists Stephen J. Gould and Niles Eldredge (1977) famously called "punctuated equilibria"—periods of apparent stability separated by periods of detectable and dramatic (even catastrophic) variation. (Think book publishing before and after Gutenberg.)

Industrialization brought increased technological transformation—faster substitution or replacement (the automobile vs. the horse-drawn carriage) and (relatively) slow complementation (as new developments superceded rather than worked with existing technologies).

But today's (postmodern) orientation toward the horizontal and away from the vertical presents a number of important and challenging implications. First, it suggests a relatively long lifespan for the dominant contemporary disciplinary regime. It seems, that is, that surveillance-spectacle is here to stay. Surveillance-spectacle and its privileging of image will be replaced only exceedingly slowly, if at all, and may in fact represent the very death of disciplinary evolution. But second, and arguably more important, this dominant contemporary disciplinary regime of surveillance-spectacle-image will be strengthened. We are, and will get, "better" at it—faster, more effective, more efficient. The disciplinary structure of society will continue to depend upon and necessitate seeing and being seen, surveillance-spectacle, and changing technological possibilities will only make this situation more proficient, profitable, potent, and indeed fundamentally more prevalent (as cheaper and more widely available digital video cameras continue to replace already inexpensive and widely available VHS, for example).

Globalization

For most of the eons of human existence, people living only short distances apart
might as well, for all the difference they made to each other's lives, have been living
in separate worlds.... Over the past few centuries the isolation has dwindled, slowly
at first, then with increasing rapidity. Now people living on opposite sides of the
world are linked in ways previously unimaginable. (Singer, 2002, October 11, p.
B9)

Perhaps *the* buzzword of the late twentieth/early twenty-first-century epoch is *globalization,* a concept that depicts the increasing interconnectedness
and interdependence of the world's disparate peoples and nation-states.
Driven by the economic opportunities associated with newer modes of trans-
portation and telecommunications, and by the possibilities of "new" market-
enabled profitization, globalization supports and is supported by surveillance-spectacle-image, and in part sets up the present disciplinary status of
both the visual and the visualizable.

As news coverage indicates, globalization is, of course, controversial (an
understatement to be sure), as the disputes and contentions between its various advocates and detractors first made widely known during the 1999 protests known as "the battle in Seattle" demonstrated.[2] Globalization's supporters maintain that the expansion of free market, corporate capitalism provides
(and will continue to provide) economic opportunities for workers and consumers in developing areas as well as a/the springboard for attaining higher
socio-economic standards of living. Its critics, however, reason that it merely
leads to a status of the undemocratic and exploitative concentration of wealth
and power in the hands of an elite, providing, among other dangers, the
framework for US-led Western and imperialistic political/military/cultural/
economic hegemony, the consequences of which include environmental deg-
radation, low wages, and corporate selfishness (among others). The issue for
US public education is whether, and to what degree, schools should/do/must
work in support of this powerful, ever-intensifying economic scheme (for an
introduction and overview, see, e.g., Spring, 1999). For our purposes, what
matters most is how (if at all) and by what mechanisms globalization sur-
rounds and helps to explicate the widening reach and heightened import of
pedagogical images/images of the pedagogical.

One must first understand here the absolute imperative of US corporate-
competitive victory (although the reasons are complex, they may involve
such factors as nationalism, xenophobia, "American exceptionalism," fear,
the "old-boy network," and avarice, among others). For at least since the release of *A Nation at Risk* (National Commission on Excellence in Education,

1983), economically and politically powerful Americans have claimed a direct correspondence between national and international *educational* "success" or "failure" and national and international *economic* "success" or "failure." There has been, and continues to be, a naive and patronizing view in support of some "trickle down" sort of connection between capitalism and public schools. The argument, in its most overly simplified form, goes something like this: In order for US corporations to win at the "game" of international economic competition (i.e., to maximize profits at all costs), US schools must win at the game of international pedagogical competition (i.e., produce higher standardized test scores than schools in other countries)—*properly* thriving schools lead to a *properly* thriving economy (and vice versa). (Needless to say, we hope, the wealthy and powerful tend to benefit most from this structure and so tend as well to be its most active and vocal cheerleaders.)

In that, generally, corporate leaders possess more power than educators (although at the "highest levels" such distinctions frequently dissolve), what globalization means for schooling is principally greater economic (political/ corporate) scrutiny of and control over public education. Hence, over time, schools become more businesslike—market driven, management oriented, "homogenous" (e.g., Barlow & Robertson, 1997), and so on. This increased scrutiny and control (read need for disciplinarity) implies a greater level of surveillance and spectacle—coupled with the need to "win" as others "lose," it implies an enhanced demand for seeing/being seen, watching/being watched, and visualizing/visualization. The status of "our success" rests on the numbers and their presentation—economic data and test scores, for example, become evermore authoritative and conformative/conforming. The pedagogical image—images of schooling, schooling as image—circulates via other controlling images. The consequences can be appalling. The economy is good or not (because GDP says so) even as and whether millions of Americans are un- or underemployed, discriminated against in the workplace, live in substandard housing, and cannot afford higher education (because evidently that's okay as long as McDonald's, Nike, and Philip Morris can expand into previously untapped markets and pay their workers in other countries less than a pittance). Schools are good or not (because test scores tell us) regardless of what actually goes on inside them. In whose interests, indeed, does this fundamental and ultimately one-sided regime operate?

SBER

...two questions arise: 1) why do those who have power in our modern capitalist society want you to learn what you do and in the way(s) you do it? And, 2) starting
from your own needs and interests, what would you like to learn and how would
you like to learn it? (Ollman, 2001, pp. 6-7)

We already have too many people on the board, in the media and in the Legislature
telling everyone what's wrong with education but who have no knowledge of what
is actually needed in the classroom. (Murphy, 2002, p. B6)

It is very unfair to label schools because it does not truly measure the effort teachers
make to help students learn. *People see these labels and immediately assume they
are a reflection of the teaching that goes on at the school* [italics added]. (Pedersen,
2002, p. B6)

The criticisms of SBER—especially high-stakes and other standardized
testing schemes—are well known, and have been most notably and elo-
quently delineated by organizations, teachers, and scholars such as the Alliance for Childhood (2001); Berliner and Biddle (1995); Dianda, McKeon,
and Kapinus (n.d.); Kincheloe, Steinberg, and Weil (2001); Kohn (1999,
2000); Levin (1998); McNeil (2000); Mathison (2001); Ohanian (1999,
2002); Ollman (2001); Popham (2001); and Wolf (1998). In addition, a great
deal of this critique has focused on President Bush's controversial educational work as former governor of Texas and his espoused views as a presidential candidate in election year 2000 (as well as his actualization, as president, of NCLB and the efforts of former Houston superintendent and current
Secretary of Education Rod Paige; see, e.g., in addition to those critical
works cited earlier, Bush, 2001; Haney, 2000; Klein, et al., 2000; Olsen,
2001; Stutz, 2001; Tumulty, 2002). Our own previous work has emphasized
especially the extent to which such pedagogy is anti-democratic, oppressive,
anti-the collective good, disciplinary, and inauthentic (see, Ross, 2000; Vinson, 1999, 2001a, 2001c; Vinson, Gibson, & Ross, 2001; Vinson & Ross,
2001a, 2001b, 2001c, 2001d, 2001e, 2003). What makes SBER important
here, however, is its place in the broader contemporary setting of standardization—the will to standardize, the standardization imperative—and its
privileging of the pedagogical image and of images of the pedagogical.

Fundamentally, SBER is but one part of a larger, and evolving, social/
political/cultural/economic, pro-standardization coalition or alliance, one in
which both liberals and conservatives, Democrats and Republicans, seek
some patriotic, safe, and noncontroversial middle-of-the-road. In fact, leaders
from across the ideological spectrum set out jointly to claim and control this

ostensible center such that, in the end, little real difference exists, or can exist, between the two major US political parties. This condition, of course, provided a principal reason for (a) the 2000 presidential candidacies of Nader and Buchanan and (b) the troubling or at least odd development of the "compassionate conservative," the "new Democrat," and the "Blair-Clinton Project" of "conservative-liberalism" (or something like that). The need to *appear* "mainstream"—an image-driven aspiration—forces "natural" allies (Nader via the Democrats, Buchanan via the Republicans) to abandon ship. The desire among mainstream Democrats is to *appear* liberal but not *too* liberal, and among mainstream Republicans to *appear* conservative but not *too* conservative. In essence, this defines the end or death of politics and the "triumph" of the US one-party state. Yet, incredibly, in this setting, stripped of all meaningful conflict, SBER makes a certain amount of selfish and self-interested sense.[3]

This pro-standardization coalition explains, further, why scholars from across the political-pedagogical spectrum seem to unite around SBER, regardless of their differences on other (often related) issues. Hence pedagogical conservatives and pedagogical liberals agree on the basic indispensableness of developing a broad system of content and assessment standards (even if they disagree over some of the specific and applicable components).

Over the past several years the range of SBER supporters has extended to include a variety of ostensibly strange bedfellows, such as conservative Diane Ravitch (e.g., 1995, 2000; Ravitch & Finn, 1987) and liberal Gary Nash (Nash, Crabtree, & Dunn, 1997). That SBER, then, has evolved into the predominant mode of contemporary school reform and has acquired a mind-boggling array of committed and active advocates comes in part as no great surprise (especially in light of steady governmental endorsement; see, e.g., [The] Business Roundtable, 2001; Finn & Petrilli, 2000; Tucker & Codding, 1998; see also, perhaps, standards documents produced by professional education organizations such as the National Council for the Social Studies and the National Council of Teachers of Mathematics, among others, that might be usefully read against this backdrop).

Though frequently at odds over issues of purpose, curriculum, instruction, and/or assessment—and in view of the fact that their work can sometimes be (and *has* sometimes been) controversial—what most SBER adherents today agree on is (1) that students do not "know" enough (however *know* is defined) and that, by extension, teachers do not "teach" enough (however *teach* is defined), and (2) that a systemic and structural approach to subject matter/content scope and sequence—selection and organization—is necessary, accompanied, of course, by a "rigorous" and comparison-oriented program of assessment or testing so that teachers, students, schools, states, and so on can somehow be held "accountable."

SBER and its supporters, obviously, have not been immune from criticism. At the risk of oversimplification, this criticism has fallen (and still falls) rather neatly into four broadly constructed and overlapping categories: *the philosophical, the pedagogical, the personal,* and *the political.*

Philosophical interpretations rest primarily on SBER's perceived incompatibility with the "appropriate" goals of public education or with SBER's underlying inconsistencies or conceptual defects. Much of this work draws upon the larger traditions of critical and progressive educational theory (including that of authors such as John Dewey and Paulo Freire). Recent writings by Alfie Kohn (1999, 2000) and Francis Schrag (1995) provide relevant and representative examples. (Note that although Schrag's [1995] best known work, *Back to Basics,* does not focus on standardization per se, it does effectively challenge philosophically the assumptions upon which it and its recommendations often are built.)

Pedagogical critiques argue that SBER espouses or represents ineffective or poor pedagogy—that is, is gets teaching, learning, assessment, curriculum, motivation, and so forth "wrong." The best and most noted recent examples are Kohn's (1999, 2000) *The Schools Our Children Deserve: Moving Beyond Traditional Classrooms and "Tougher Standards"* and *The Case Against Standardized Testing: Raising the Scores, Ruining the Schools.*

Personal (or "anecdotal") views rely on stories (or "anecdotes") about the negative emotional, physical, and psychological consequences students and teachers face as a result of schooling regimes that enforce various aspects of SBER (especially high-stakes standardized testing), such as anxiety, illness, low self-esteem, academic failure, threats of job loss, dangers via creativity and diversity, and so forth. Susan Ohanian's (2002) *What Happened to Recess and Why Are Our Children Struggling in Kindergarten?* provides one such model of this approach.

Political criticism highlights concerns such as those related to social and economic (in)justice, racism, sexism, and classism (etc.). Our own prior work on SBER, especially in terms of social studies education, high-stakes testing, and curriculum standards (e.g., Ross, 2000; Vinson, 1999, 2001a; Vinson, Gibson, & Ross, 2001), as well as that of Bertell Ollman (2001), offer contemporary and indicative examples.

Of most interest here, however, is the extent to which SBER (whether viewed within the larger setting of standardization or not) contextualizes the mechanisms and statuses of surveillance-spectacle and image. In fact, it does so in at least two significant ways. First, it makes possible, if not insists upon, the predominance of image at the expense of authenticity—principally by way of the growing trend toward publishing/publicizing standardized test scores. Here, how something (or someone; e.g., schools, teachers, students, etc.) *looks* matters more that how it *is* (even granting that how it "is" may be multiple, diverse, subjective, contingent, situated, and so forth). As a result of the watchability imperative, how education is *seen*—its *image*—takes precedence over the actualized experiences of school/classroom life. Thus, based on test scores, the public at large makes decisions about the effectiveness of teachers, schools, and students not on what actually occurs in everyday formal education, but instead on how such teachers, schools, and students appear in the media and the press. We "know" which schools are "good" or "successful" (or, for that matter, "bad" or "unsuccessful") because of test scores (frequently correlated with wealth, not "ability" or "intelligence," which, absurdly, also are frequently so correlated), not because we generally have any firsthand experiences of what "really" goes on inside them (for instance, in terms of teaching techniques, teacher-student relationships, and/or curriculum).

The second issue rests on the importance of seeing/watching and being seen/being watched—surveillance-spectacle—and the problematic repercussions of such processes and applications. SBER increases the *exposure* of schooling. Though this is not *inherently* bad—and may indeed be rather good in some situations—it does so only on a superficial level. This means visual/representational shortcuts—the ability to *watch* schools without really *seeing* them, and for teachers and students the knowledge that schools (and they themselves) are *being watched* without really *being seen.* The safest way for those involved is to conform to the demands of dominant interests and to suffer under those normative aspects of power-laden standardization that threaten democracy, authenticity, the collective good, and an anti-oppressive society.

Conclusions

The emerging agenda for research and theorization is to recognize that both globalization and the new technologies can be profoundly transformative and can constitute whole new domains of the social, ones marked by profound and complex imbrications of the new and the old. These domains need in turn to be constructed as objects for research and theorization. This entails at least a partial move toward seeing globalization and technology not only as causing changes in existing domains but also as constituting new types of social domains. (Sassen, 2002, p. B4)

Indeed, today, our society is one that privileges, perpetuates, controls and is controlled by, commodifies, and buys and sells the image. It is our own preferred postmodern means of pedagogy and disciplinarity—if not, in fact, of everyday life itself. Technological change, globalization, standardization, and the new-fashioned import of education as a national and nationalized issue instigate and are subsequently instigated by this considerable phenomenon.

Increasingly what is "known" about schools and societies depends upon manipulations of (and manipulating the) visual image. *Mere* representation has displaced and continues to displace authentic experience and existence. This holds true, certainly, for both schools and the greater society at large. Why this occurs and what it means reflect and are reflected by the contemporary position of surveillance-spectacle. Even more important, perhaps, today, is the extent to which image, surveillance, spectacle, and image-surveillance-spectacle are further contextualized vis-à-vis the recent developments described in this chapter.

As we have argued, the contemporary status and power of (the) image(s) rests within a complex set of interactions between surveillance and spectacle. Our theme in this chapter, though, has been simply to further and more elaborately situate surveillance and spectacle themselves (in addition to image) by and according to their status relative to education as a public/private issue, standardization, globalization, and technological change. In this difficult and dynamic web of commensurate concepts, each reinforces and strengthens, and is reinforced and strengthened by, the various others.

In chapter two we pursued avenues for understanding the state of the pedagogical (and other) image via newer (inter)disciplinary philosophies, views, and perspectives. In chapter three we explored the meanings and mechanisms of surveillance, spectacle, and surveillance-spectacle as foundations for making sense of the workings and characteristics of image. In the next chapter, chapter five, we offer and take on a series of critical philosophical frameworks that might, hopefully, elucidate the functioning and significance of image even more fully and even more forcefully.

Notes

1. See Gould and Eldredge (1977) on "punctuated equilibrium." See also Maier, Smith, and Keyssar (2002) and Gleick (2002) on the implications of technological innovation.
2. On globalization and its various arguments for and against, see Waters (2001), Mander and Goldsmith (1997), and Stiglitz (2002).

3.   What "lessons" both parties learn from the 2000 presidential and 2002 congressional and state elections remain to be seen. For the Democrats, losers in both, two options seem plausible. First, they could interpret their defeats as evidence favoring an even stronger move toward the center-right—that is, they could see the elections as proof that they've not yet gone far enough. But second, some Party leaders could construe their electoral shortcomings as an indication that what they've been doing is wrong and as a call to re-establish their traditional center-left (or "liberal") values and stands. For why, they might argue, would people who want to vote center-right vote for Democrats *acting* like Republicans when they can just as simply vote for *real* Republicans? Moreover, this might stem the continuing drain of liberal-left voters from the party (e.g., those who have followed Nader and the Green Party).

✖CHAPTER FIVE

Critical Frameworks

PEDAGOGICAL AND OTHER image an be explored according to an array of theoretical frameworks. Surveillance and spectacle (i.e., the work of Foucault and Debord described in chapter three), and their multiple and peculiar socio-pedagogical settings (as explored in the previous chapter), present but one such set of critical interpretive possibilities. The recent, "post-disciplinary" scholarship that we reviewed in chapter two—work drawn from the relatively "new" fields of visual culture (Mirzoeff, 1998, 1999), media studies (e.g., Gitlin, 2002; Herman & Chomsky, 1988; Luhmann, 1996/2000; Sardar & Van Loon, 2000), cultural studies (e.g., Storey, 1994, 1996, 1998), and film studies (e.g., Hill & Gibson, 2000; Nelmes, 1999)—offers some of the alternative, broader, and potentially most useful orientations. In fact, educators have already taken up, to some extent, many of the challenges posed by both surveillance-spectacle and these newer modes of inquiry and have made significant contributions, not only to educational theory but also to understanding the shifting impacts and technologies of representation (i.e., image) more generally. Works by scholars such as Apple (1996), Dalton (1999), Fischman (2001), Giroux (1994a, 1994b; Giroux & [with] Shannon, 1997), Hytten (1999a, 1999b), McLaren (McLaren, et al., 1995), Maeroff (1998), Popkewitz and Brennan (1998), Senese and Page (1995), and Steinberg and Kincheloe (e.g., 1997) are indicative of the directions these efforts have taken.

Since this range of critical options in itself poses a potential difficulty, in both quantity and quality, in this chapter we have chosen to focus upon only five "classical" theorists who have written specifically and extensively on the concept of image and its numerous and complicated meanings. Their attempts, we think, can help educational theorists and researchers (if not also practitioners, policymakers, and other interested stakeholders) to make sense of the production, use, diffusion, interpretation, and effects of pedagogical images, especially given the increasingly visual—and, perhaps, *representational*—status of our society.

We include here namely the ideas of Mikhail Bakhtin, Roland Barthes, Daniel Boorstin, Jean Baudrillard, and Marshall McLuhan. We argue that although their perspectives remain complex, they nonetheless hold out the possibility of facilitating a more productive engagement with the mechanics and significances of the pedagogical (and social) image. We maintain, further, that although their views do not offer any absolute or universal Truth per se, the questions they can incite and the interpretations they can elicit make working through their difficulties critically and fundamentally worth the effort. As such, we conclude this chapter by identifying key questions and views suggested by these perspectives, those that might well (we think) assist in addressing image itself as well as its myriad and often fluid socio-pedagogical consequences. In chapter eight we apply our understandings of their work, along with our understandings of surveillance-spectacle and the post-disciplinary fields of visual culture, cultural studies/popular culture, media studies, and film studies, to several distinguished and diversely presented examples of contemporary pedagogical images.

Bakhtin: The Chronotope

For Mikhail Bakhtin (1981, 1984), understanding image involves exploring the processes by which a given imaginary work (or category or genre of work) succeeds in "assimilating" or "appropriating" various and "isolated aspects of time and space" (Bakhtin, 1984, p. 84), especially vis-à-vis their fundamental and "intrinsic[ ] interconnectedness" (Morson & Emerson, 1990, p. 367). More directly, it requires an analysis grounded in his conceptualization of the "chronotope."

> We will give the name *chronotope* (literally, "time space") to the intrinsic connectedness of temporal and spatial relationships that are artistically expressed in literature [or other artistic works]. This term (space-time) is employed in mathematics, and was introduced as part of Einstein's Theory of Relativity. The special meaning it has in relativity theory is not important for our purposes, we are borrowing it for literary criticism almost as a metaphor (almost, but not entirely). What counts for us is the fact that it expresses the inseparability of space and time (time as the fourth dimension of space). (Bakhtin, 1981, p. 84)

> In the literary artistic chronotope, spatial and temporal indicators are fused into one carefully thought-out, concrete whole. Time, as it were, thickens, takes on flesh, becomes artistically visible; likewise, space becomes charged and responsive to the

movements of time, plot and history. *This intersection of axes and fusion of indicators characterizes the artistic chronotope* [italics added]. (p. 84)

The chronotope as a formally constitutive category determines to a significant degree the image of man in literature as well. The image of man [sic] is always intrinsically chronotopic [italics added]. (p. 85)

As Morson and Emerson (1990) rightly suggest, chronotope is an exceedingly difficult concept to define. But as they approach it, it indicates first "a way of understanding experience; [or] a specific form-shaping ideology for understanding the nature of events and actions" (p. 367) as they are (and must be) produced within particular and immediate contexts. These contexts "are shaped fundamentally by the kind of time and space that operate within them" (p. 367). It is here, according to Morson and Emerson, that Bakhtin makes his "crucial point…that time and space vary in *qualities*; different social activities and representations of those activities presume different kinds of time and space. Time and space are therefore not just neutral 'mathematical' abstractions" (p. 367).

Drawing on Bakhtin's own reference to Einstein, Morson and Emerson (1990) argue that a comparison of chronotopic space-time with the theory of relativity illuminates and helps clarify Bakhtin's approach in at least five important ways:

1. In the chronotope, as in Einsteinian physics, time and space are not separate but are rather "intrinsically interconnected"; each chronotope specifies a *"fused"* sense of time and space;
2. The very formulation of Einstein's theory, as Bakhtin understands it, demonstrates that there are a *variety* of senses of time and space available;
3. Different aspects or orders of the universe cannot be supposed to operate with the same chronotope…[because, for example] different social activities are also defined by various kinds of fused time and space…;
4. It follows from the variety and multiplicity of chronotopes that they may change over time in response to current needs; they are in fact, and in potential, historical; [and]
5. Chronotopes are not so much visibly *present* in activity as they are the *ground* for activity. (pp. 367-368)

For Morson and Emerson (1990), a specific and "well-developed" chronotope offers answers to a number of questions implied by the more general concept of chronotope. These include those related to the association between action and context, the "replaceability" of some particular space, the ordering or directing of time (e.g., is time reversible?), the mutual dependence of time-space and context, and the characterization (fluid, fixed, etc.) of human identity, character, and image (among many others).

With respect to image, as Clark and Holquist (1984) note, Bakhtin's chronotope presents "a way not to take leave of reality…[but] precisely the opposite, a concept for engaging reality" (p. 278). For

> [o]ver the centuries people have organized the world of their immediate experience into a number of different world pictures. The fundamental categories for creating these images are time and space…. Bakhtin…insists on the inseparability of these categories…[and] that at different times, differing combinations of space and time have been used to model exterior reality. (p. 278)

For the purposes of this chapter, Bakhtin's chronotope provides one mechanism by which to interrogate, critique, and investigate contemporary pedagogical images. More precisely, it offers *a* means by which to explore image and reality via the inseparability and utility of time and space, and how "our particular totally integrated sense of space and time shapes our sense of reality…[as] we…engage[ ] in the activity of *re*-presenting the signals we get from our exterior environment, shaping those signals into a pattern…" (Clark & Holquist, 1984, p. 279). What "sense of space and time" is indicated via an image? How might an audience's understanding of space and time interact with that of an image/image producer as both work to re-present some sense of some reality (and/or some experience and/or some activity)? In terms of schooling—of image and education—Bakhtin's work demands that we take seriously the implications of that merged sense of time and space (re)presented by a specific pedagogical image: How does a given image, that is, chronotopically shape and contextualize ideologically some experience—some *story*—or some characteristic aspect of school and/or classroom reality? To what politico-pedagogical ends? Why, and *how,* does it matter?

Barthes: The Rhetoric of the Image

> According to an ancient etymology, the word *image* should be linked to the root *imitari.* Thus we find ourselves immediately at the heart of the most important problem facing the semiology of images: can analogical representation (the "copy") produce true systems of signs and not merely simple agglutinations of symbols?

> [G]eneral opinion…has a vague conception of the image as an area of resistance to meaning—this in the name of a certain mythical idea of Life: the image is re-presentation, which is to say ultimately resurrection, and, as we know, the intelligible is reputed antipathetic to lived experience. Thus…the image is felt to be weak in respect to meaning. (Barthes, 1977, p. 32)

As Barthes (1977) understands it, images do, nonetheless, (explicitly or implicitly) express messages—intentionally or unintentionally—and do, therefore, signify something—that is, present some meaning, even if rudimentary in comparison to other symbol/signification systems such as formal (symbolic) language. He takes on image according to three principal questions:

1. How does meaning get into the image?
2. Where does it end? and
3. [If] it ends, what is there *beyond?* (p. 32)

By "submitting the image to a spectral analysis of the messages it may contain" (pp. 32-33), he suggests, answers to these questions, as well as to those crucial to the structure of meaning itself, might emerge.

According to Barthes, all images offer, in their most fundamental distinction, a *linguistic* (or "textual") and a *symbolic* (or "iconic") *message.* The linguistic message (which is both denotational and connotational) can be discerned, for instance, "as [or in the form of a] title, caption, accompanying press article, film dialogue, comic strip balloon [etc.]" (p. 38). It serves two characteristic purposes: (1) "anchorage" and (2) "relay." *Anchorage* works to help the viewer "choose *the correct level of perception,* [and] permits [him or her] to focus not simply [his or her] gaze but also [his or her] understanding" (p. 39). It functions to "guide" both "identification" (i.e., What *is* it?) and "interpretation" (i.e., What does it *mean*?), ultimately seeking to inhibit "the [possible] connoted meanings from proliferating" (p. 39) and/or drifting off. The *relay* function of the linguistic message serves to complement the symbolic message, extending, advancing, and/or completing it (e.g., as a film's dialogue does via its pictures—it helps "tell the story").

The symbolic message encompasses two components—a denoted message or image and a connoted message or image. The denoted message is, for Barthes, "utopian" in that it exists only in an ideal sense. It is both "evictive" (i.e., "what is left in the image when the signs of connotation are mentally deleted") and "sufficient" (i.e., "it has at least one meaning"—i.e., one recognizes it as *some*thing). It is received precisely regardless of culture and is, therefore, "perceptual," "literal," and "non-coded." And, "cleared utopianically of its connotations, [it] become[s] radically objective, or, in the last analysis, innocent" (p. 42). The connoted message, conversely, is exceedingly "cultural," "non-literal," and "coded." It offers the possibility of multiplicity and variation in readings, each depending "on the different kinds of knowledge—practical, national, cultural, aesthetic—invested in the image"

(p. 46) *and* residing in any given individual image sender or receiver or medium. Thus:

> The image is penetrated through and through by the system of meaning, in exactly the same way as man [*sic*] is articulated to the very depths of his being in distinct languages. The language of the image is not merely the totality of utterances emitted..., it is also the totality of utterances received.... (p. 47)

Connotation includes "typical" signifiers and "common" signifieds. This set of signifiers (or "connotators") constitutes a "rhetoric of the image," which, in turn, signifies an *ideology*—one "which cannot but be single for a given society and history [rather like Foucault's *episteme*], no matter what signifiers of connotation it may use" (p. 49).

What Barthes makes possible is a specific and critical analysis of the image—in this case, the pedagogical image—grounded in its linguistic and iconic messages, both literal and symbolic, both denoted and connoted. He allows an interpretive undertaking relative to the structure of the image, and to its intended and unintended meanings, its connotator-signifier-rhetoric, and its connoted-signified-ideology. In terms of education this means facing a series of questions relating not only to image itself, but also to the creation and function of image-based meaning. For instance: How do words and pictures work together? How do pedagogical images seek to limit or define the number and range of possible interpretations? To what effects? How is what is *directly depicted* different or similar to what is *implied?* And, how and to what degree do such images implicate a particular rhetoric and a specifically constituted, contextually bounded ideology?

Boorstin: The Pseudo-Event

> We are haunted, not by reality, but by those images we have put in place of reality. (Boorstin, 1961/1992, p. 6)

> The making of the illusions which flood our experience has become the business of America, some of its most respectable business. I am thinking not only of advertising and public relations and political rhetoric, but of all the activities which purport to inform and comfort and improve and educate and elevate us.... (Boorstin, 1961/1992, p. 4)

Daniel Boorstin's prophetic words first appeared in his 1961 work *The Image: A Guide to Pseudo-Events in America*. Arguing that contemporary US society had become one of "image" instead of "reality," or "pseudo-events" instead of "real" events, Boorstin (1961/1992) effectively delineated and positioned the evolving role and status of the media and information in the contemporary United States. He defined the "pseudo-event...[as first] a happening that:

1. Is not spontaneous, but comes about because someone has planned, planted, or incited it. Typically, it is not a train wreck or an earthquake, but an interview.
2. Is planted primarily (not always exclusively) for the immediate purpose of being reported or reproduced. Therefore, its occurrence is arranged for the convenience of the reporting or reproducing media. Its success is measured by how widely it is reported. Time relations in it are commonly fictitious or factitious; the announcement is given out in advance "for future release" and written as if the event had occurred in the past. The question, "Is it real?" is less important than, "Is it newsworthy?"
3. Is relat[ed] to the underlying reality of the situation...ambiguously. Its interest arises largely from this very ambiguity. Concerning a pseudo-event the question, "What does it mean?" has a new dimension.... [T]he interest in an interview is always, in a sense, in whether it really happened and in what might have been the motives. Did the statement really mean what it said? Without some of this ambiguity a pseudo-event cannot be very interesting. [and]
4. Is [u]sually...intended to be a self-fulfilling prophecy. (pp. 11-12)

In *The Image* Boorstin justifies his understanding by establishing the affiliation between the predominance of the pseudo-event and the development among Americans of certain "extravagant expectations." As he states: "We demand anything and everything. We expect the contradictory and the impossible. We expect compact cars which are spacious; luxurious cars which are economical.... We expect to be...made literate by illiterate appeals for literacy" (p. 4). In fact, he continues, "[w]e are ruled by extravagant expectations":

1. *Of what the world holds.* Of how much news there is, how many heroes there are, how often masterpieces are made, how exotic the nearby can be, how familiar the exotic can become. Of the closeness of places and the farness of places. [and]
2. *Of our power to shape the world.* Of our ability to create events when there are none, to make heroes when they don't exist, to be somewhere else when we haven't left home. Of our ability to make art forms suit our convenience, to transform a novel into a movie and vice versa, to turn a symphony into mood-conditioning. To fabricate national purposes when we lack them, to pursue these purposes after we have fabricated them. To invent our standards and then to respect them as if they had been revealed or discovered. (pp. 4-5)

He then situates the pseudo-event within what he terms the "Graphic Revolution," when, beginning in the nineteenth century with the perfection

of the telegraph, the human "ability to make, preserve, transmit, and disseminate precise images—images of print, of men and landscapes and
events, and the voices of men and mobs—now grew at a fantastic pace" (p.
13). This revolution included such inventions as photography, the telephone,
the phonograph, radio, motion pictures, television, and, more recently, the
personal computer and the Internet.

Although historical in origin, for Boorstin, the speed and force with
which the pseudo-event has evolved, and continues to evolve and to dominate, have created a state of affairs in which pseudo-events now in fact
"overshadow [more] spontaneous events..." (p. 39). This is because:

1. Pseudo-events are more dramatic [in that they] can be planned to be more sus-
   penseful....

2. Pseudo-events, being planned for dissemination, are easier to disseminate and
   to make vivid. Participants are selected for their newsworthy and dramatic interest.

3. Pseudo-events can be repeated at will, and thus their impression can be re-en-
   forced.

4. Pseudo-events cost money to create; hence somebody has an interest in dis-
   seminating, magnifying, advertising, and extolling them as events worth
   watching or worth believing. They are therefore advertised in advance, and re-
   run in order to get [someone's] money's worth.

5. Pseudo-events, being planned for intelligibility, are more intelligible and hence
   more reassuring....

6. Pseudo-events are more sociable, more conversable, and more convenient to
   witness. Their occurrence is planned for our convenience....

7. Knowledge of pseudo-events—of what has been reported, or what has been
   staged, and how—becomes the test of being "informed".... [and]

8. Finally, pseudo-events spawn other pseudo-events in geometric progression.
   They dominate our consciousness simply because there are more of them, and
   ever more. (pp. 39-40)

Although Boorstin addressed most directly the cultures of politics and
celebrity, his case holds unmistakable relevance for the study of pedagogical
images. Do such images, in fact, meet the characteristics of pseudo-events
(i.e., consider film portrayals and media-reported test scores)? Are they un-
spontaneous, planted, ambiguous, and self-fulfilling? Do they at all relate to
irrational and "extravagant" expectations—for example, the view that ("of
course") the United States will "lead" the rest of the world in everything (or
that, following Lake Wobegon, all US children can and will be above average)? And lastly, to what extent—if at all—do they inhibit the spontaneous
event, effectively privileging image over authenticity and/or the illusion over
the experiential?

Baudrillard: Simulacra and Simulation

Simulation is no longer that of a territory, a referential being, or a substance. It is the generation by models of a real without origin or reality: a hyperreal. The territory no longer precedes the map, nor does it survive it. It is nevertheless the map that precedes the territory—*precession of simulacra*—that engenders the territory. (Baudrillard, 1995, p. 1)

In *Simulacra and Simulation,* Jean Baudrillard (1995) presents a fourth critical theory of the image, albeit one *ostensibly* less practical or directly applicable (perhaps) than the others to the contingencies of contemporary schooling. At heart, his work is a complex and dynamic, if not downright frightening, interpretation of postmodernity, one constructed via a nuanced reading of not only image itself, but of simulacra, simulation, hyperreality, and truth as well (see also Kellner, 1994a).

Baudrillard's critique rests first on the recognition that today the image-reality relationship has changed fundamentally *away* from one of *representation* and *toward* one of complete and ideal *disconnect*—of the annihilation of any referential link whatsoever between the original and the copy. As such, the present implies a break from the "classical" and "modern" pasts. Whereas for earlier "simulators" the intent was to make their models coincide with the real, now "present-day simulators attempt to make the real, all of the real, coincide with their models..." (p. 2). And yet, for Baudrillard, in fact, even this explanation falls short of adequately characterizing the postmodern society. For in terms of the postmodern,

it is no longer a question of either maps or territories [and which comes first and/or which is real]. Because, [in effect] [s]omething has disappeared: the sovereign difference, between one and the other, that constituted the charm of abstraction.... This imaginary of representation.... No more mirror of being and appearances, of the real and its concept. No more imaginary coextensivity.... The real...no longer needs to be rational, because it no longer measures itself against either an ideal or negative instance. It is no longer anything but operational. In fact, it is no longer really the real, because no imaginary envelops it anymore. It is a hyperreal, produced from a radiating synthesis of combinatory models in a hyperspace without atmosphere. (p. 2)

Ultimately both a *technological* (computer-based) and *biological* (genetic) effect, this new image-reality (non)relationship implies Baudrillard's earlier "orders of simulacra," especially in the transitional space between modernity and postmodernity—or the modern and the postmodern. As Tseëlon (1994) succinctly summarizes these "orders" in her historical analysis of Western fashion:

The first order, that of *imitation* characterizing the classical period, presupposes dualism where appearances disguise reality. In the second order, *production,* appearances create an illusion of reality. In the third order, *simulation,* appearances invent reality. No longer concerned with the real, images are reproduced from a model. And it is this lack of a reference point which threatens the distinction between true and false. (p. 120)

Further:

In terms of signification relations the three orders can be summarized as follows: the order of imitation involves *direct* [italics added] signifier-signified links. The order of production involves *indirect* [italics added] signifier-signified links. The order of *simulation* involves signifier-signifier links, i.e., *links between signifiers that are divorced from relations to signifieds* [italics added]. These links subvert signification in favor of a play of signs. (p. 120)

For Baudrillard (1995), it is this third order of simulacra that characterizes postmodernity, or

...the era of simulation [which] is inaugurated by a liquidation of all referentials.... It is no longer [therefore] a question of imitation, nor duplication, nor even parody. It is a question of substituting the signs of the real for the real.... A hyperreal henceforth sheltered from the imaginary, and from any distinction between the real and the imaginary.... (pp. 2-3)

That is, a circumstance in which the copy (or image) is indistinguishable from the original (the real or authentic).

Still, as Baudrillard himself asks, what does—or could—all this *mean?* He begins with what he terms "the divine irreference of images" (p. 3), and grounds it initially in the distinction between "dissimulation" and "simulation."

To dissimulate is to pretend not to have what one has. To simulate is to feign to have what one doesn't have. One implies a presence, the other an absence. But it is more complicated than that because simulating is not pretending.... Therefore, pretending, or dissimulating, leaves the principle of reality intact: the difference is always clear, it is simply masked, whereas simulation threatens the difference between the "true" and the "false," the "real" and the "imaginary." (p. 3)

Simulation, then, contains "the knowledge that truth, reference, [and] objective cause have ceased to exist" (p. 3).

He next differentiates *simulation* from "representation."

Representation stems from the principle of the equivalence of the sign and of the real (even if this equivalence is utopian, it is a fundamental axiom). Simulation, on the contrary, stems from the utopia of the principle of equivalence, *from the radical negation of the sign as value,* from the sign as the reversion and death sentence of every reference. Whereas representation attempts to absorb simulation by interpreting it as a false representation, simulation envelops the whole edifice of representation itself as a simulacrum. (p. 6)

For Baudrillard, then, dissimulation suggests merely "faking it," so that there is still a "true" difference between appearance (or image) and reality, simply a difference that is masked. He uses here the example of faking an illness. Representation, though, implies *some* match—an *equivalence*—between some image and some reality. In the postmodern situation of simulation, however, signs exist as "mere" signs, without "real" reference, essentially dissociated from any "signified"—any linked or linking (*real*) concept. Just signs. For Baudrillard, then, in this condition, "the whole system becomes weightless, it is no longer anything but a giant simulacrum—not unreal, but a simulacrum, that is to say never exchanged for the real, but exchanged for itself, in an uninterrupted circuit without reference or circumference" (pp. 5-6).

These conceptions of dissimulation, representation, and simulation lead Baudrillard to posit logically "the successive phases of the image" (p. 6).

[First,] it is the reflection of a profound reality;
[Second,] it masks and denatures a profound reality;
[Third,] it masks the absence of a profound reality; [and]
[Fourth,] it has no relation to any reality whatsoever: it is its own pure simulacrum. (p. 6)

Moreover:

In the first case, the image is a good appearance—representation is of the sacramental order. In the second, it is an evil appearance—it is of the order of maleficence. In the third, it plays at being an appearance—it is of the order of sorcery. In the fourth, it is no longer of the order of appearances, but of simulation. (p. 6)

For the pedagogical image, for schooling and education, Baudrillard's work beckons theorists and researchers to (re)consider the relationships between signifier and signified, image and reality. Taking, for example, the types of images we address in chapter eight—Hollywood films such as *Dead Poets' Society* and *Dangerous Minds* and policies such as the No Child Left Behind Act of 2001 (NCLB)—it asks that scholars interrogate the link between model and real, or being and appearance. It challenges us to pursue whether any meaningful referential connection exists between the image and reality—for example, the test score and classroom life—and whether the real produces itself, or the real produces the image, or the image produces the real, or, in fact, *the image produces the image.* It demands that we consider the "truth" of the image—the film, the headline, whatever—and whether or not it works purely as detached sign or as some representation, some equivalent, of some authentically experienced—and recognizable— pedagogical life.

McLuhan: The Medium is the Message

In a culture like ours, long accustomed to splitting and dividing all things as a means of control, it is sometimes a bit of a shock to be reminded that, in operational and practical fact, *the medium is the message* [italics added]. This is merely to say that the personal and social consequences of any medium—that is, of any extension of ourselves—result from the new scale that is introduced into our affairs by each extension of ourselves, or by any new technology. (McLuhan, 1964/1994, p. 7)

Marshall McLuhan's (1964/1994) *Understanding Media: The Extensions of Man* is notable for a near countless number of reasons, including, arguably, its groundbreaking role in the creation of contemporary media studies as a legitimate academic discourse. Although McLuhan is best known today for phrases such as "the medium is the message," "generation gap," and "global village," his work remains a complex and insightful mechanism for the investigation of images—pedagogical and otherwise—most importantly, perhaps, those made possible by technological change and innovation.

For this chapter, we limit our focus primarily to McLuhan's statement that "the medium is the message," yet consider as well the probability that, commutatively, "the message is the medium." Recall here that in deriving his thesis, McLuhan first *redefined* "medium" away from its common usage as transmitter of information (e.g., the press, newspapers, TV, films, etc.), and suggested instead that a "medium [is] an[y] extension of ourselves" (p. 7), "our human senses" (p. 21). Further, he redefined "message," opposing the more traditional notion of "information" or "contents" with his view that "the 'message' of any medium or technology is the change of scale or pace or pattern that it introduces into human affairs" or "the psychic and social consequences of the designs or patterns [of some medium] as they amplify or accelerate existing processes" (p. 8). But since, as he saw the world, in effect, "it is the medium that shapes and controls the scale and form of human association and action" (p. 9), the medium then *is* the message. But because the content of any medium is always another medium (e.g., as the content of a film is a novel or story or opera or nonfiction narrative, and so on), in fact, then, the message is the medium as well.

What McLuhan argues is that the "message" of a "medium" exists irrespective of the specific informational nature of its "contents." Media/messages create their social and psychological contents no matter the specificity of specifically denoted data. The message of the medium of television, for example, depended originally not on the particular contents of its images, or even on how it was used, but was in actuality contained in the medium itself. As a medium, an extension of ourselves, an extension of our eyes and ears, television's message, "the change of scale or pace or pattern that it introduce[d] into human affairs" or "the psychic and social consequences of [its] designs or patterns...as they amplif[ied] or accelerate[d] existing processes" (p. 8), was structural to television itself—*was* television itself—in how it "shape[d] and control[led] the scale and form of human association and action" (p. 9). In the end, "objective" contents and uses were less important to meaning than were the medium itself and its psychological, social, technological, and cultural outcomes.

The idea that the medium is the message (and that the message is the medium) enables a unique approach to investigating pedagogical images. It asks that scholars re-aim their focus, and that the point of inquiry shift from the contents (the dialogue or picture of a film or the test scores themselves—and what these might mean) to the various media (films, comics, TV news, newspaper headlines, soundbites) as extensions of the human senses (ears, eyes, and so forth) and to their consequences writ socially and psychologically and culturally (i.e., via their impact on human association and their ability to "eliminate time and space factors in human association" [McLuhan, 1964/1994, p. 9]). To what extent, then, do the media of films, cartoons, newspaper headlines, and so forth work as sensory extensions? How? To what extent do their effects, as opposed to those of their contents, operate socially, psychologically, and culturally relative to human relationships? More bluntly, what is medium and what is message, and are such questions and their possible answers in any way significant? How and why?

Conclusions

Although necessarily brief (and inevitably oversimplified), our treatment of each of these frameworks offers scholars a unique perspective from within which to pursue the creation, proliferation, and consequences of pedagogical images. Although, of course, these frameworks do not all apply equally well to all images (thus, for instance, Boorstin's pseudo-event is *perhaps* more useful with respect to newspaper headlines than to cartoons, and so on), in each case the relevant concepts and ideas do suggest at least a certain hermeneutic utility that can help clarify the significance and potential impact of such popular and dynamic depictions.

Bakhtin's *chronotope* demands that we interrogate pedagogical images relative to their expressed fusions of qualitative time and space, and, further, how (if at all) they (1) represent unique and localized socio-historical settings, (2) function ideologically, and (3) interact with subjective and meaningful modes of educational and social experience.

Barthes's *rhetoric* presents an approach grounded in an understanding of image as meaning*ful,* that is one that accepts the status of image as more than incidental, as more than merely analogical. His work challenges us to treat images as complex constructions in need of a distinctive and sophisticated mechanism of critical interpretive analysis, one aimed toward exposing (1) the interplay between connotation and denotation *and* between "text" and "icon"; (2) the means by which signifiers and signifieds constitute a situated and dominant "rhetoric"; and (3) the ideological workings of a given image via its peculiar, power-laden, and epistemic characteristics, circumstances, and influences.

Boorstin's *pseudo-event* questions the assumed connections between image and reality, or, rather, the (un)likelihood that what we take for reality is really reality at all. He denounces the substitution of image for reality, yet nevertheless identifies this phenomenon as a key feature of contemporary US society. He hypothesizes, moreover, its existence as a logical outgrowth of Americans' illogical commitment to extravagant—*unreal*—expectations that can never really be satisfactorily and authentically fulfilled (i.e., they are *unrealizable*). Against the pedagogical image, Boorstin's work implies such questions as: (1) Is it spontaneous or is it planned and/or planted (think here of media reported standardized test scores)? (2) Is it produced solely to be reproduced—that is, how, why, and to what level is the image simply newsworthy (vs. somehow "real"), and in what ways did (or does) this issue ultimately matter? (3) How (un)ambiguously is it related to some intended and "underlying reality?" and (4) To what extent is it meant as—and/or might it become—a "self-fulfilling prophecy"?

Baudrillard's notion of *simulacra* asks that we confront pedagogical images in terms of their association with a *real*—whether, in fact, there is any referential connection at all between image and some original thing. His work indicates a postmodern (pedagogical) society built on images with no relation at all to any reality, or in which the two are indistinguishable, and in which images or signs "signify" no more than other images or signs, a situation of simulation in which separations or boundaries between true and false, real and imaginary, and copy and original implode. Perhaps more importantly, though, Baudrillard's work begs the question of whether reality produces images or images produce reality—or whether, in fact, images only produce other images.

McLuhan's notion that the *medium is the message* downplays the traditional critical focus on information or contents (the stereotypical "message," the specific image itself) and instead insists that we consider the possibility that the real message of any medium is in fact that of the medium itself—namely, in its effects relative to its impact on the scale or pace of "human affairs" and on the psychological and social "consequences" it brings to bear on everyday human interactions. In short, McLuhan suggests that the importance of any pedagogical image rests in its propagating medium, that the meaning of an op-ed cartoon on schooling springs from the cartoon itself as an extension of ourselves, of our eyes and ears and brains.

In chapter eight, "Applications: Popular Film and NCLB/SBER," we revisit these perspectives as we apply them (as well as those we presented in chapters two through seven) to particular instances of pedagogical image(s). Our purpose in the end is to show how (1) pedagogical images might be interpreted and understood and (2) the potentially disciplinary features of such images might critically and effectively be resisted.

We turn now to the connections between (pedagogical) image and everyday (pedagogical) life.

❧CHAPTER SIX

Pedagogical Image and Everyday Life

AN IMPLICIT THEME throughout this work has been the predominant role(s) played by image(s) within the various settings of *everyday life*. For it is within these settings of the everyday that we are continuously confronted by physical images, and that we also necessarily make use of them in the complex processes by which we seek to make sense of ourselves and our society and by which we act on ourselves and our society. Not only, therefore, do we create, maintain, propagate, and transform image(s), but we are in turn created, maintained, propagated, and transformed *by* image(s)—all within the environs and performances of the everyday.

This holds true throughout all aspects, institutions, and manipulations of everyday life, including schooling, increasingly so as we face the evolving imperatives of "the visual society" and the immediacies of seeing and being seen ("publicly" as well as "privately"; e.g., Rothstein, 2000). As we have argued, this condition operates according to the dynamic convergence/coexistence of surveillance and spectacle—as voyeurism and exhibitionism—and as further positioned by such contemporary societal characteristics as the will to standardize, technological change, and globalization.

The consequences of this framework, as we've indicated, encompass such perils as anti-democracy, oppression, the devaluation of the collective good, inauthenticity, and disciplinarity—specifically via what we have termed "controlling images" and "image-power"—all of which in conjunction affect and are affected by the structures and mechanisms of (post)modern everyday life (see Vinson & Ross, 2003).

We maintain an intimate link between everyday life and image wherein image plays a role in the workings of everyday life, and everyday life plays a role in the workings of image. Given image's ubiquity (see, e.g., Steinberg & Kincheloe, 1997), the two in effect become nearly indistinguishable as each ceaselessly and intentionally pervades the other's domain. In some ways, each is a subset of the other. Moreover, the two share significant and troubling characteristics and mechanisms, such that the effects of everyday life can be just as oppressive, anti-democratic, anti-the collective good, disciplinary, and inauthentic as can the effects of image. In some ways, the two work together and are mutually reproductive and reinforcing.

In this chapter we contend principally that in order to understand the impact and significance of social and pedagogical image one must as well be able to understand the impact and significance of everyday life—especially if one aims to combat the negative possibilities identified previously. It is toward this interpretive end that we employ the critical theoretical and empirical work of Philip W. Jackson (1968/1990), Raoul Vaneigem (1967/1972; 1967/2002), Fredy Perlman (1969), Michel de Certeau (1984), Bruce Brown (1973), and Henri Lefebvre (1968/1971).

Throughout we presume a fundamental and mutual set of relationships between schooling and everyday life whereby each influences and is a part of the other. Accordingly, we hold that *there is an everyday life of schooling* and *a schooling of everyday life.* We accept that everyday life is an inextricable component of schooling and that schooling is an inextricable component of everyday life. We suggest that image, and all that it entails, mediates the dynamics of school-everyday life interplay: that the *social* image works and is worked against within the confines of schooling, and that the *pedagogical* image works and is worked against within the larger confines of society. Our underlying question is, simply, how to understand and transform the conditions, mechanisms, and practices of everyday life such that the potential consequences of dominant/dominating pedagogical images (controlling images, image-power) might be counteracted, transcended, or superceded. We conclude by considering the implications of this work for contemporary educational (in the broadest sense) practice.

Jackson: *Life in Classrooms*

In his classic work, *Life in Classrooms,* Philip W. Jackson (1968/1990) first introduced many educators to the importance of the quotidian details of everyday classroom life. His book remains, even after thirty-five years, an indispensable starting point. In *Life in Classrooms* Jackson argued chiefly that scholars of education must take the "trivial" events of schooling at least as seriously as they take the "more important" ones. For as he reminded us:

> School is a place where tests are failed and passed, where amusing things happen, where new insights are stumbled upon, and skills acquired. But it also a place in

which people sit, and listen, and wait, and raise their hands, and pass out paper, and stand in line, and sharpen pencils. School is where we encounter both friends and foes, where imagination is unleashed and misunderstanding brought to ground. But it is also a place in which yawns are stifled and initials scratched on desktops, where milk money is collected and recess lines are formed. Both aspects of school life, the celebrated and the unnoticed, are familiar to us, but the latter, if only because of its characteristic neglect, seems to deserve more attention than it has received to date from those who are interested in education. (p. 4)

Significantly, Jackson titled his first chapter "The Daily Grind." It is here that he lays out his conception (qualitatively, empirically based) of the "unnoticed" minutiae of the modern school/classroom experience for both teachers and students. He initially characterized classroom life around three facts: (1) that children are in school for a very long time (compared, for instance, with the amount of time they spend in religious institutions, at home, sleeping, etc.); (2) that school settings are highly uniform (day-to-day, across grade levels and schools, and so on), repetitive, and ritualized; and (3) that students are in school—and usually must be in school—whether they want to be or not (rather like the cases of prisons and psychiatric hospitals). For Jackson, essentially, the everyday life of schools and classrooms is so important in part because it involuntarily comprises such a large and normative portion of the everyday lives of children.

Several further qualities distinguish the everyday lives of classrooms, including their crowdedness, their positioning as spaces of evaluation and praise (i.e., in terms of success and failure), and their functionality as situations of hierarchical power. According to Jackson, these properties constrain or restrict the conduct of both teachers and students in ways that are at once complex, problematic, and influential (via future life experiences).

Crowdedness leads teachers to perform several distinctive and powerful (or disciplinary) roles, including that of "gatekeeper" (i.e., manager of classroom talk), "supply sergeant," granter of privileges, and "official timekeeper." For students, it instigates: (1) "the experiencing of delay"; (2) "the denial of desire"; (3) "interruptions"; and (4) "social distraction" (that is, "the recurring demand that the student ignore those who are around him [or her]"; p. 16).

The evaluative character of classrooms teaches students to please others (both teachers and peers), to conform to normative expectations, and to perform tasks primarily for external/extrinsic reasons. Yet for the "proper control" of educational tasks, and for producing obedient adults, it is "needed." Students must learn the dynamics of praise and punishment, of getting along. What makes this difficult, however, are the multiple and organic sources (teachers, peers), referents (the unique operations of schools as institutions), values (consistency, reciprocity), and conditions (public, private, secret, open) according to which evaluation in classrooms occurs.

But for Jackson, it is "[t]he fact of unequal power...[that] provides the most salient feature of the social structure of the classroom and its consequences relative to the broader conditions of freedom, privilege, and responsibility as manifest in classroom affairs" (p. 29). It furnishes the climate within which children learn to take orders from adult strangers and where they discover that power can be both "prescriptive" (i.e., what one *must* do) and "restrictive" (i.e., what one *must not* do). Also within such differences they come to accept the substitution of a stronger person's goals for their own. They perceive distinctions between work and leisure (that is, they conceptualize *job*), and they strive to gain favor with the teacher who is, effectively, "the student's first 'Boss'" (p. 31).

As Jackson states: "From kindergarten onward, the student begins to learn what life is really like in The Company" (p. 37). They learn, in effect, the elements and mechanisms of power, and who holds it and why. They discern their "appropriate" ranks and responsibilities as cogs in the larger capitalist machine. They increasingly master the skills of taking orders, of behaving "properly," and of conforming to pre-established norms. And they learn, of course, to expect to receive (or "merit") "fair" and "deserved" rewards for their compliance and submissiveness. They ascertain that everyday life is, indeed, a "daily grind," and that authenticity might only be achieved by somehow escaping it.

Regarding pedagogical image—controlling images, image-power—what is important is that teachers and children jointly form a captive audience conditioned to the stipulations of disciplinarity and conformity. Thus, classroom and school communities are easily manipulated—they are used to following orders, to seeking praise, to obeying rules, and to being compensated as successful for doing so. Further, they are easily represented or imaged/imagined, programmed as they are to act as one and to exert little *overt* individual difference—to become their own stereotypes, their own caricatures (or their school's test scores). Perhaps, in the end, what is most striking in *Life in Classrooms* is the degree to which so many of Jackson's observations still hold up.

Although we return to Jackson's work later, we consider now several critical philosophical and social theories directed toward everyday life, each of which we think offers potentially useful insights into understanding and challenging the dominance of pedagogical image and its associations with the everyday.

Vaneigem: Revolution

Because of its increasing triviality, daily life has gradually become our central pre-occupation.... No illusion, sacred or deconsecrated..., collective or individual, can hide the poverty of our daily actions any longer.... The enrichment of life calls inexorably for the analysis of the new forms taken by property, and the perfection of the old weapons of refusal.... (Vaneigem, 1967/2002, p. 21)

...making workers' demands the sole basis of a [critical Marxist] project...What is certain is that it is sheer madness...when the economy of consumption is absorbing the economy of production and the exploitation of labor power is submerged by the exploitation of everyday creativity. The same energy is torn from the worker in his [*sic*] hours of work and in his [*sic*] hours of leisure, and it drives the turbines of power which the custodians of the old theory lubricate sanctimoniously with their purely formal opposition.

People who talk about revolution and class struggle without referring explicitly to everyday life, without understanding what is subversive about love and what is positive in the refusal of constraints—such people have a corpse in their mouth. (Vaneigem, 1967/2002, pp. 25-26)

The new wave of insurrection tends to rally young people who have remained outside specialised politics, whether right or left, or who have passed briefly through these spheres because of excusable errors of judgment, or ignorance. All currents merge in the tide-race of nihilism. The only important thing is what lies beyond this confusion. *The revolution of daily life will be the work of those who, with varying degrees of facility, are able to recognise the seeds of total self-realisation preserved, contradicted and dissimulated within ideologies of every kind—and who cease consequently to be either mystified or mystifiers* [italics added]. (Vaneigem, 1967/2002, p. 168)

In *The Revolution of Everyday Life,* Raoul Vaneigem (1967/2002), a former Situationist International (SI) colleague of Guy Debord's, argues that it is the dominant perspective of power—"power's perspective"—that undergirds all alienation in terms of "modern" everyday life. Although in many ways a fundamentally Marxist critique, Vaneigem's view contends that no longer can the oppression of workers (as a class) be understood in isolation from the oppression that occurs throughout the totality of human existence, especially to the extent that capitalist economics, continuous consumption capitalism, has extended its reach even into the ostensibly private, or "subjective," aspects of contemporary experience.

For Vaneigem, the alienating, oppressive, and exploitative *power of power* rests in its capacity to make the authentic—*really living*—impossible by prohibiting the ability of individuals to relate to one another, to connect, to escape boredom, and to construct the situations of themselves *qua* selves.

In fact, power perpetuates, and perpetuates itself by way of, an interlocking threefold problematic (i.e., *power's perspective*): (1) "The impossibility of participation: power as sum of constraints" (which Vaneigem identifies with five "mechanisms of attrition and destruction: humiliation...isolation...suffering...[the decline and fall of] work...[and] decompression"—where "Decompression is the permanent control of... antagonists by the ruling class"—think of today's US Democratic and Republican parties; pp. 27 & 57); (2) "The impossibility of communication: power as universal mediation" (i.e., "the false necessity wherein people learn to lose themselves rationally...by the dictatorship of consumption...by the predominance of exchange over gift...[and] by the reign of the quantitative..."; p. 65); and (3) "The impossibility of realisation: power as sum of seductions" (p. 105). On this third, arguably the most important and complex, Vaneigem is worth quoting at-length:

> Where constraint breaks people, and mediation makes fools of them, the seduction of power is what makes them love their oppression. Because of it people give up their real riches: for a cause that mutilates them...for an imaginary unity that fragments them...for an appearance that reifies them...for roles that wrest them from authentic life...for a time whose passage defines and confines them.... (p. 105)

In sum, power (i.e., "the rulers") alienates, oppresses, and exploits by demolishing any opportunity for participation, communication, and self-realization. It denies individuals the chance to build communities, to connect to one another, and to become who and what they might become. It isolates and fragments, passes off false relationships as human (i.e., as "real"), and defines subjective persons objectively—all in large measure as everyday life becomes less about joyous and creative and loving and playful interhuman experiences and more about the capitalistic imperative always to consume (if not also eventually to *be* consumed).

Perhaps obviously, then, Vaneigem's "revolution" calls for a "reversal of perspective," one opposed to the hierarchical workings of power, one he designates as "The unitary triad: self-realization, communication, [and] participation," one incompatible with what he calls "survival sickness" and "spurious forms of opposition." As he states:

> The repressive unity of Power is three-fold: constraint, seduction and mediation are its three functions. This unity is merely the reflection of an equally tripartite, unitary project, its form inverted and perverted by the techniques of dissociation. In its chaotic, underground developments, the new society tends to find practical expression as a transparency in human relationships which promotes the participation of everyone in the self-realisation of everyone else. Creativity, love and play are to life what

the needs for nourishment and shelter are to survival.... The project of self-realisation is grounded in the passion to create...; the project of communication is grounded in the passion of love...; the project of participation is grounded in the passion for play.... Wherever these three projects are separated, Power's repressive unity is reinforced. Radical subjectivity is the pressure—discernible in practically everyone at the present time—of an individual will to build a passion-filled life.... The erotic is the spontaneous coherence which gives practical unity to attempts to enrich lived experience.... (p. 236)

And:

The project of self-realisation is born of the passion for creation, in the moment when subjectivity wells up and aspires to reign universally. The project of communication is born of the passion for love, whenever people discover that they share the same desire for amorous conquest. The project of participation is born of the passion for playing, whenever group activity facilitates the self-realisation of each individual. (p. 237)

But for Vaneigem, these three passions must be connected in a meaningful totality. For:

Isolated, the three passions are perverted. Dissociated, the three projects are falsified. The will to self-realisation is turned into the will to power; sacrificed to status and role-playing, it reigns in a world of restrictions and illusions. The will to communication becomes objective dishonesty; based on relationships between objects, it provides the semiologists with signs to dress up in human guise. The will to participation serves to organise the loneliness of everyone in the crowd; it creates the tyranny of the illusion of community. (p. 238)

Thus in order to combat the alienation, oppression, and exploitation inherent in everyday life, created and promoted by power, Vaneigem explores the possibilities of self-realization (creation), communication (love), and participation (playing). It is only through these *passions* that the everyday can transcend the banalities—the threats—of power-based consumer capitalism and fragmented disconnection.

With respect to image and education, *The Revolution of Everyday Life* demands that we consider schooling and its various representations according to their complicity in reinforcing the effects and techniques of power and their limitations on the actualizations of creativity, love, and playfulness. Do test scores and popular films, for example, restrict or promote the deadness of isolation, or do they instead promote its opposite (i.e., self-realization, communication, and participation). Are such imaginary depictions designed to liberate, to maximize subjectivity, or to extend the consequences of consumption further into the realm of schooling? And, finally, to what degree does (or can) formal education contradict the effects of images via the every-day, *and* to what degree does (or can) the everyday contradict the effects of images via schooling?

Perlman: Reproduction

In *The Reproduction of Daily Life,* Fredy Perlman (1969) argues that "Through their daily activities, 'modern men [and women]'...reproduce" their social situations, "the inhabitants, the social relations and the ideas of the[ir] society; they reproduce [that is] the social form of daily life" (p. 2). In short, within a capitalist system, they reproduce capitalism and the conditions of their own oppression. For Perlman, this is in part because the individual members of a capitalist society unknowingly "carry out two processes: [1] they reproduce the form of their activities, and [2] they eliminate the material conditions to which this form of activity initially responded" (p. 3). That they don't see this, and that they continue to participate, relates in Perlman's view to what represents perhaps the two most dominant features of modern every-day life: "alienation" and "fetish worship."

On reproduction:

Like the tribe and the slave system, the capitalist system is neither the natural nor the final form of human society; like the earlier social forms, capitalism is a specific re-sponse to material and historical conditions.

Unlike earlier forms of social activity, everyday life in capitalist society [systemati-cally] transforms the material conditions to which capitalism originally responded... [T]he subject of analysis is not only how practical activity in capitalist society re-produces capitalistic society, but also how this activity itself eliminates the material conditions to which capitalism is a response.

In the performance of their daily activities, the members of capitalist society simul-taneously carry out two processes: they reproduce the form of their activities, and they eliminate the material conditions to which this form of activity initially re-sponded. But they do not know they carry out these processes; their own activities are not transparent to them. They are under the illusion that their activities are re-sponses to natural conditions beyond their control and do not see that they are them-selves authors of those conditions. The task of capitalist ideology is to maintain the veil which keeps people from seeing that their own activities reproduce the form of their daily life; the task of critical theory is to unveil the activities of daily life, to render them transparent, to make the reproduction of the social form of capitalist ac-tivity visible within people's daily activities.

Under capitalism, daily life consists of related activities which reproduce and expand the capitalist form of social activity.

The aim of the process is the reproduction of the relation between the worker and the capitalist. (Perlman, 1969, pp. 1-10)

On alienation: .

Academic sociologists, who take the sale of labor for granted, understand this [notion of] alienation of labor as a feeling: the worker's activity "appears" alien to the worker, it "seems" to be controlled by another. However, any worker can explain to the academic sociologist that the alienation is neither a feeling nor an idea in the worker's head, but a real fact about the worker's daily life. The sold activity is in fact alien to the worker; his [or her] labor is in fact controlled by its buyer.

By selling their labor, by alienating their activity, people daily reproduce the personifications of the dominant forms of activity under capitalism, they reproduce the wage-laborer and the capitalist. They do not merely reproduce the individuals physically, but socially as well; they reproduce individuals who are sellers of labor-power, and individuals who are owners of means of production; they reproduce the individuals as well as the specific activities, the sale as well as the ownership.

Every time people perform an activity they have not themselves defined and do not control, every time they pay for goods they produced with money they received in exchange for their alienated activity, every time they passively admire the products of their own activity as alien objects procured by their money, they give new life to Capital and annihilate their own lives.

The worker alienates his [or her] life in order to preserve his [or her] life. If he [or she] did not sell his [or her] living activity he [or she] could not get a wage and could not survive. However, it is not the wage that makes alienation the condition for survival.... It is people's disposition to continue selling their labor, and not the things for which they sell it, that makes the alienation of living activity necessary for the preservation of life. (Perlman, 1969, pp. 1-10)

And on fetishism and fetish worship:

Thus economics (and capitalist ideology in general) treats land, money, and the products of labor, as things which have the power to produce, to create value, to work for their owners, to transform the world. This is what Marx called the fetishism which characterizes people's everyday conceptions, and which is raised to the level of dogma by Economics. For the economist, living people are things...and things live.... The fetish worshipper attributes the product of his [or her] own activity to his [or her] fetish. As a result, he [or she] ceases to exert his [or her] own [power] (the power to transform nature, the power to determine the form and content of daily life); he [or she] exerts only those "powers" which he [or she] attributes to his [or her] fetish (the "power" to buy commodities). In other words, the fetish worshipper emasculates himself [or herself?] and attributes virility to his [or her] fetish.

But the fetish is a dead thing, not a living being; it has no virility. The fetish is no more than a thing for which, and through which, capitalist relations are maintained. The mysterious power of Capital, its "power" to produce, its virility, does not reside in itself, but in the fact that people alienate their creative activity, that they sell their labor to capitalists, that they materialize or reify their alienated labor in commodities. [I]n other words, people are bought with the products of their own activity, yet they se[e] their own activity as the activity of Capital, and their own products as the products of Capital. By attributing creative power to Capital and not to their own activity, they renounce their living activity, their everyday life, to Capital, which means that people give themselves daily, to the personification of Capital, the [so-called] capitalist.

The daily transformation of living activity into Capital is mediated by things, it is not carried out by the things. The fetish worshipper does not know this....

The fetishism of commodities and money, the mystification of one's daily activities, the religion of everyday life which attributes living activity to inanimate things, is not a mental caprice born in men's [and women's] imaginations; it has its origin in the character of social relations under capitalism. Men [and women] do in fact relate to each other through things; the fetish is in fact the occasion for which they act collectively, and through which they reproduce their activity. But it is not the fetish that performs the activity. It is not Capital that transforms raw materials, nor Capital that produces goods. (Perlman, 1969, pp. 1-10)

Alienation implies that today the work of laborers is no longer authentically their own, but instead exists under the control of someone else—its buyer. Fetish worship suggests (1) that labor (the efforts of individuals) is a *thing,* and (2) that "things live." Under a fetishistic system, such as that which operates within contemporary capitalism, people attribute their own power to things, inanimate things, and thus de-actualize their own roles— their own real power—in the (re)constitution of society.

To make use of Perlman's work within the context of image, education, and everyday life, it helps first to locate schooling—classroom life, if not necessarily schooling as a social institution—within the setting of contemporary global capitalism. We must consider (1) that a product—a thing—is produced, distributed, consumed, bought, and sold (ostensibly "education" or "achievement"), and (2) that the major actors in the processes of schooling represent distinctive social classes—say the capitalist (or ruling, or powerful, or oppressor) class (e.g., school boards, politicians, bureaucratic management, corporations, and so on) and the working (or laboring, or teaching-learning, or oppressed) class (e.g., teachers, students, and parents). (Of course we recognize here the risks of reductionism, oversimplification, and overgeneralization.)

Perlman's work implies, to the extent that schooling is a part of everyday life and that, in turn, everyday life is a part of schooling, that contemporary education is reproductive—it doesn't work to transform or even "improve" society. It works to maintain it, to rationalize and mystify it, and to present it (and schooling itself, therefore) as right, natural, and neutral, but not as a means to promote, for example, social justice or radical democracy. Moreover, contemporary schooling and society work to reduce if not eliminate the conditions that brought on current pedagogical practices—yet, current pedagogical practices continue to grow. The recent move toward SBER, for example, stems from the alarm initially raised two decades ago by *A Nation at Risk* (National Commission on Excellence in Education, 1983), which argued that schooling must change because the United States was "losing out" in terms of international economic competition—especially with respect to Japan and Germany—and that US schoolchildren were not performing as well as their European and Asian peers. Although both now have been effectively debunked (e.g., Berliner & Biddle, 1995; current Japanese and German economic woes as against the global hegemony of US mega-corporations), SBER continues forward.

These circumstances extend and reinforce, and are extended and reinforced by, alienation and the worship of fetishes. As we argue, this primarily occurs around pedagogical image(s), image(s) that in many ways link(s) everyday classroom life and everyday social life—such that teachers and students (and to some degree many parents) no longer "control" the images of their work, but the images of their work are now (and increasingly) controlled by their buyers according to the rules of a system that those buyers create and that privilege their dominant/dominating situations (noting, as we have already suggested, that image has displaced authenticity). These images are treated as things and credited with power—with change (again, think test scores)—as if simply having tests and curriculum standards make schools better instead of it being because of the work of individual classroom participants. As we have heard frequently though anecdotally from teachers and students, when test scores increase, those who sanctioned the tests take credit (superintendents, managers, legislators, etc.). When they decrease, teachers and students take the blame (i.e., are held "accountable")—thus reinforcing current divisions.

Although we treat these contingencies in more detail later, as we consider everyday life and schooling vis-à-vis popular film and SBER, we suggest that the relationship between the reproduction of daily life and alienation entails teachers and students doing the system's work—that is, performing tasks designed, developed, more or less implemented, and evaluated by the buyers of its results (the powerful—school officials and political and corporate leaders, for example). The link between the reproduction of daily life and fetishism involves the worship represented in certain images of particular ideologies, scores-as-things, and specific disciplinary characteristics depicting the good/effective (or bad/ineffective) teacher, student, principal, parent, and/or school (e.g., as depicted in popular films).

We next explore the work of anthropologist and cultural theorist Michel de Certeau and his critical perspectives on the "practice" of everyday life.

de Certeau: Practice

> The imaginary landscape of an inquiry is not without value, even if it is without rigor. It restores what was earlier called "popular culture," but it does so in order to transform what was represented as a matrix-force of history into a mobile infinity of tactics. It thus keeps before our eyes the structure of a social imagination in which the problem constantly takes different forms and begins anew.... The landscape that represents these phenomena in an imaginary mode thus has an overall corrective and therapeutic value in resisting their reduction by a lateral examination.... This return to another scene thus reminds us of the relation between the experience of these practices and what remains of them in an analysis. It is evidence, evidence which can only be fantastic and not scientific, of the disproportion between everyday tactics and a strategic elucidation. Of all the things everyone does, how much gets written down? Between the two, the image, the phantom of the expert but mute body, preserves the difference. (de Certeau, 1984, pp. 41-42)

> This essay is part of a continuing investigation of the ways in which uses—commonly assumed to be passive and guided by established rules—operate. The point is not so much to discuss this elusive yet fundamental subject as to make such a discussion possible; that is, by means of inquiries and hypotheses, to indicate pathways for further research. This goal will be achieved if everyday practices, "ways of operating" or doing things, no longer appear as merely the obscure background of social activity, and if a body of theoretical questions, methods, categories, and perspectives, by penetrating this obscurity, make[s] it possible to articulate them. (p. xi)

Michel de Certeau (1984), in *The Practice of Everyday Life,* offers most usefully a depiction of and differentiation between "strategies" and "tactics," a dual means by which to make sense of the workings of experience, including the character of image and how best to combat its potentially negative effects. For de Certeau, a *strategy* essentially is the calculus of force-relationships which becomes possible when a subject of will and power (a proprietor, an enterprise, a city, a scientific institution) can be isolated from an "environment." A strategy assumes a place that can be circumscribed as *proper* (*propre*) and thus serve as the basis for generating relations with an exterior distinct from it (competitors, adversaries, "clientèles," "targets," or "objects" of research). Political, economic, and scientific rationality has been constructed on this strategic model. (p. xix)

A *tactic* is

a calculus which cannot count on a "proper" (a spatial or institutional location), nor thus on a borderline distinguishing the other as a visible totality. The place of a tactic belongs to the other.... A tactic insinuates itself into the other's place, fragmentarily, without taking it over in its entirety, without being able to keep it at a distance. It has at its disposal no base where it can capitalize on its advantages, prepare its expansions, and secure independence with respect to circumstances. The "proper" is a victory of space over time. On the contrary, because it does not have a place, a tactic depends on time—it is always on the watch for opportunities that must be seized "on the wing." Whatever it wins, it does not keep. It must constantly manipulate events in order to turn them into "opportunities." The weak must continually turn to their own ends forces alien to them. This is achieved in the propitious moments when they are able to combine heterogeneous elements (thus, in the supermarket, the [shopper] confronts heterogeneous and mobile data—what she [or he] has in the refrigerator, the tastes, appetites, and moods of her guests, the best buys and their possible combinations with what she [or he] already has on hand at home, etc.); the intellectual synthesis of these given elements takes the form, however, not of a discourse, but of the decision itself, the act and manner in which the opportunity is seized. (p. xix)

And:

Many everyday practices (talking, reading, moving about, shopping, cooking, etc.) are tactical in character. And so are, more generally, many "ways of operating": victories of the "weak" over the "strong" (whether the strength be that of powerful people or the violence of things or of an imposed order, etc.), clever tricks, knowing how to get away with things, "hunter's cunning," maneuvers, polymorphic simulations, joyful discoveries, poetic as well as warlike.

In our societies, as local stabilities break down, it is as if, no longer fixed by a circumscribed community, tactics wander out of orbit, making consumers into immigrants in a system too vast to be their own, too tightly woven for them to escape from it....They also show the extent to which intelligence is inseparable from the everyday struggles and pleasures that it articulates. Strategies, in contrast, conceal beneath objective calculations their connection with the power that sustains them from within the stronghold of its own "proper" place or institutions. (p. xx)

Moreover:

> A distinction between *strategies* and *tactics* appears to provide a more adequate ini-
> tial schema. I call a *strategy* the calculation (or manipulation) of power relationships
> that becomes possible as soon as a subject with will and power (a business, an army,
> a city, a scientific institution) can be isolated. It postulates a *place* that can be de-
> limited as its own and serves as the base from which relations with an *exteriority*
> composed of targets or threats (customers or competitors, enemies, the country sur-
> rounding the city, objectives and objects of research, etc.) can be managed. As in
> management, every "strategic" rationalization seeks first of all to distinguish its
> "own" place, that is, the place of its own power and will, from an "environment"....
> [I]t is an effort to delimit one's own place in a world bewitched by the invisible
> powers of the Other. It is also the typical attitude of modern science, politics, and
> military strategy. (p. 36)

The distinction, most importantly:

> By contrast with a strategy (whose successive shapes introduce a certain play into
> this formal schema and whose link with a particular historical configuration of ra-
> tionality should also be clarified), a *tactic* is a calculated action determined by the
> absence of a proper locus. No delimitation of an exteriority, then, provides it with
> the condition necessary for autonomy. The space of a tactic is the space of the other.
> Thus it must play on and with a terrain imposed on it and organized by the law of a
> foreign power. It does not have the means to *keep to itself*, at a distance, in a posi-
> tion of withdrawal, foresight, and self-collection: it is a maneuver "within the en-
> emy's field of vision," as von Bülow put it...and within enemy territory. It does not,
> therefore, have the options of planning general strategy and viewing the adversary
> as a whole within a distinct, visible, and objectifiable space. It operates in isolated
> actions, blow by blow. It takes advantage of "opportunities" and depends on them,
> being without any base where it could stockpile its winnings, build up its own posi-
> tion, and plan raids. What it wins it cannot keep. This nowhere gives a tactic mobil-
> ity, to be sure, but a mobility that must accept the chance offerings of the moment,
> and seize on the wing the possibilities that offer themselves at any given moment. It
> must vigilantly make use of the cracks that particular conjunctions open in the sur-
> veillance of the proprietary powers. It poaches in them. It creates surprises in them.
> It can be where it is least expected. It is a guileful ruse.... In short, a tactic is an art
> of the weak. (pp. 36-37)

And finally:

> In sum, strategies are actions which, thanks to the establishment of a place of power
> (the property of a proper), elaborate theoretical places (systems and totalizing dis-
> courses) capable of articulating an ensemble of physical places in which forces are
> distributed. They combine these...types of places and seek to master each by means
> of the others. They thus privilege spatial relationships. At the very least they attempt
> to reduce temporal relations to spatial ones through the analytical attribution of a
> proper place to each particular element and through the combinatory organization of

the movements specific to units or groups of units. The model was military before it became "scientific." Tactics are procedures that gain validity in relation to the pertinence they lend to time—to the circumstances which the precise instant of an intervention transforms into a favorable situation, to the rapidity of the movements that change the organization of space, to the relations among successive moments in an action, to the possible intersections of durations and heterogeneous rhythms, etc. In this respect, the difference corresponds to two historical options regarding action and security (options than moreover have more to do with constraints than with possibilities): strategies pin their hopes on the resistance that the *establishment of a place* offers to the erosion of time; tactics on a clever *utilization of time,* of the opportunities it presents and also of the play that it introduces into the foundations of power. Even if the methods practiced by the everyday art of war never present themselves in such a clear form, it nevertheless remains the case that the two ways of acting can be distinguished according to whether they bet on place or time. (pp. 38-39)

de Certeau extends a formula for understanding and enactment instituted in the scope of and disparity between strategies and tactics. It provides both a sense-making mechanism and a mechanism for action; it asserts a framework for theorizing everyday movements and practices as more than mundane, banal, and trivial, or as less "real" or "important" than some "larger" or "more meaningful" or "more revolutionary" ones.

de Certeau's strategy-tactic distinction indeed proves useful on several levels, including those of critical empiricism (what to look for), critical interpretation (how to make sense of), and critical resistance (how to respond). It assists in disentangling the conduct and motives of the powerful and the powerless, and in unearthing the dynamics within which the behaviors of the two encounter and confront one another.

For de Certeau, strategies are planned, coordinated, and come into play when target-subjects can be isolated via places of identifiable power and power relations. They imply recognizing and locating others as "them" or as "the enemy." In some sense, they entail establishing a front, a border circumscribed by battle fronts or positions. Although in our reading we infer from de Certeau the prominence of strategies as the political maneuverings of the powerful (as he repeatedly refers to armies, scientists, businesses, governments, etc.), in our view their basis in physical space, discourse, and institutions (and so on) does not preclude strategic actions on the part of the relatively powerless. In each case, strategies seek to (1) value place as a defense against the movement (or "erosion") of time and (2) camouflage their own internal connections to and maintenance of hierarchies of power—upheld or "justified" by the spatial separation kept up between contending forces.

Strategic thinking and behavior can be found in the actions of both the relatively powerful and the relatively powerless. It occurs when both set up and seek to protect their domains—as when a school district's central office and those who rule it attempt to keep others out and when they establish and preserve their authority over curriculum, policy, and assessment, or when principals and teachers champion autonomy over "their" own schools and classrooms. With respect to image, and to its potentially problematic consequences, strategic work takes place when administrators, managers, politicians, and corporate leaders (among others) stake their claim as the proper authorities over what counts, or should count, as achievement, knowledge, good or effective schooling, and good or effective teaching. For these comparatively powerful players, strategies represent a blueprint for solidifying their position and for barricading their specifically identified place. Strategic work on the part of the comparatively powerless—teachers, students, parents—transpires, for example, in organized protests, marches, letter-writing campaigns, and unionization.

Tactics, on the other hand, are the practices of everyday life—"talking, reading, moving about, shopping, cooking"—and for de Certeau are specifically available to the less powerful ("the art of the weak"). They involve taking advantage of time and making the most of opportunities when they arise. They involve cleverness and guile, using one's opponents' means against them while operating within these same opponents' spaces. Sabotaging standardized test results, for instance, or using "school time" to do personal or even resistance-based work, such as debating the merits of SBER. Tactics involve what can be done within the "ordinary" confines of everyday life, a life that, in terms of schooling, generally develops and takes place within a setting governed by someone outside the classroom, someone other than teachers and students. In effect, strategies exist according to the ability to locate and get at an enemy, to distinguish the locus of power geographically. They involve a "we are here" and "they are there" attitude, a willingness to claim and to cede and to fight for space. Tactics, conversely, work within everyday settings, those controlled by the powerful, but those nonetheless within which the relatively powerless make sense of and engage their experiences. Regarding schooling, image, and everyday life, each is vitally important.

Brown: Marx and Freud

In *Marx, Freud, and the Critique of Everyday Life: Toward a Permanent Cultural Revolution,* Bruce Brown (1973) contends that critical theory and practice must consider not only the external and "objective" conditions of social, economic, and political oppression, those that demand a revolution grounded in class consciousness and class struggle, but that they recognize as well the psychological and subjective "natures" of oppression, those that demand a revolution grounded in personal expression, creativity, and self-actualization. What he calls for is a new critical theory and a reconstructed practice, one that combines the insights of (neo)Marxism and psychoanalysis, Marx and Freud, and one that takes seriously both the political and the personal, the psychological along with the economic, the structural, and the social. By drawing on the work of such critical scholars as Reich, Fromm, Marcuse, Horkheimer, Lefebvre, Habermas, and the Situationists, he attempts to discern how capitalist forms and mechanisms become internalized by individuals, such that their oppression is not only political and economic, but also psychological. His "permanent cultural revolution" would seek to make sense of and overthrow both manifestations of oppression.

For Brown, critical understanding and revolutionary praxis must incorporate at the same time both the individual and the group. It must begin "with the recognition that in a society whose bureaucratic apparatus has so profoundly invaded even the deepest roots of the individual experience, the projects of self-transformation inaugurated within face-to-face groups can progress only to the extent that they succeed in simultaneously subverting the institutional contexts in which they have arisen" (p. 184). "This means," further, "analyzing, discrediting, and disassembling these institutions in such a way as to undermine their apparent universality and rationality and, by thus stripping away the mask of reification and mystification, to reveal their real origins as the objectification of human purpose and activity.... [E]ven before hierarchical power can be encountered and contested on the political or economic level," then, "it must be attacked in the realm of the social imagination..." (pp. 184-185). In other words, a "socio-analytical" critique of society must begin with a psychological critique of oppression.

And yet,

At the same time, the cultural revolutionary process which has been launched by [such] actions cannot remain solely within the sphere of the imaginary.... The new utopian culture which is the object of the revolutionary reconstruction of everyday life is not something which can first be imagined in its entirety and then created; it must be created and imagined at the same time. This requires not only the occupation of "mental space," but of a "space" which is material as well as symbolic.... The new images of utopia cannot bear fruit unless they materialize themselves by actually entering into the social division of labor. Otherwise [they risk] leaving the summits of bureaucratic power and their roots in the economic base undisturbed.... A cultural revolutionary project which aims at the actual transformation and not just the suspension of everyday existence must be capable of countering such attempts to

impose the reorganization of everyday life from above with a concrete project of its
own aimed at reconstructing social life from below. (p. 188)

Brown's point is that by itself the personal—the individual, the imaginary—
is not enough, but that in order to be revolutionary, to combat the subjective
or psychological oppression surrounding everyday life, it must contend concurrently with the problematics of social oppression. His argument is not to
dump either Marxist critique or psychoanalysis, but rather to join them in a
radical effort to eradicate both aspects of contemporary oppression.

As Brown states:

The specifically utopian functions of cultural contestation must be supplemented by
a strategy of anti-institutional struggle, and "the long march through the institutions"
recognized as the only road to the realization of the new utopian culture. In general
terms, this means a fusion of the cultural and political revolutions into a new conception of politics, within a struggle "to extend the community realm of choice and
decision over the entirety of social life in the interests of needs that do not require
domination...." What emerges is a new model of the revolutionary process, simultaneously involving destruction and creation, negation and affirmation, and uniting
individual self-realization with social consciousness. (pp. 188-189)

His program for cultural revolution is, therefore, multiple:

1. It begins with the individual's personal experience of oppression and of the
    fragmentation of experience which makes authentic experience impossible for
    him or her;

2. It leads from the discovery of this alienation to the individual's refusal of it
    through a process which is best described as the politicization of oneself and
    which aims at a retotalization of the individual's experience;

3. It develops further through the individual's collision with the inertia of an op-
    pressive social reality in his or her search for authenticity;

4. With this recognition of the social sources of the individual's malaise, it leads
    to the inauguration of a radical contestation of existing institutions on the level
    of everyday life carried out by small groups and collectives, and extended
    through their spontaneous multiplication as micro-social centers of resistance;
    [and]

5. It finally attains a truly social dimension, uniting the struggle for the creation of
    a new self with the struggle for the creation of a new society, through the emer-
    gence of new needs and capacities for self-organization within broad sectors of
    the population and the attempt on the part of these groups to engender the crea-
    tion of new forms of self-management (or, as the French call it, *autogestion*)
    throughout every sphere of social activity. (p. 189)

Thus:

> [f]rom all sides, the eruption of localized centers of contestation and the further politicization of these contesting currents lead to the demand for a new collective self-regulation of life, for a generalization of self-management throughout society. In this sense, self-management becomes both the principal means and method for the reconstruction of everyday life and, simultaneously, the principal goal of this reconstruction. (pp. 189-190)

In the end, Brown calls for a cultural revolution that is "cumulative...a project which incorporates into itself all the unrealized or incompletely realized liberatory aims of the earlier struggles, thus giving a new power of expression to all those revolutionary needs and energies that had previously always remained more or less implicit and submerged" (p. 196). It would take on:

> The individual, through the release of hitherto suppressed creative needs and passions; the social, through the liberation of language, the revival of a collective spirit of festivity and free play and the reassertion of all those modes of community and communion which have hitherto been suppressed by the reductive logic of hierarchical power; [and] the planetary, through the expansion of reciprocal exchange between civilizations and modes of experience which have hitherto been subordinated, ignored, or evaded, and which will become the new modalities for the emergence of the men and women of the future. (p. 197)

What Brown offers is twofold. First, he provides a means for understanding critically the oppressive potential of everyday life—and, by extension, schooling, given (1) the reciprocal and interconnected relationship between everyday life and schooling (i.e., the schooling of everyday life and the everyday life of schooling) and (2) the image-mediated overlap between everyday life and schooling (i.e., in that image plays a major role with respect to both). Second, he spells out a program of radical resistance, one appropriate not only to the characteristics of everyday life as he sees them, but also to the problematic aspects of schooling and pedagogical image. Brown elucidates the dual framework of oppression, with one side being psychological/individual/subjective/personal and the other social/economic/objective/political. He advances a revolutionary program based on progressing from the personal and individual experiencing of oppression to developing a mode of social resistance in which the goal is uniting the struggle for a new self with the struggle for a new society, an anti-oppressive existence in which class struggle prevails against objective material conditions *and* the individual obtains a measure of creativity, expression, and autonomy.

In terms of schooling and pedagogical image Brown suggests an alternative way of theory and practice. His interpretive caution reflects the balanced importance of the social and the psychological and the imperative not to conceive of image and education (within the setting of everyday classroom and social life) solely, or overly, on the basis of only one of these contexts alone. Moreover, Brown indicates a critical praxis according to which both modes of oppression might be fought, one equally applicable to any or all of the threats posed by prevailing pedagogical image(s). In the end his orientation provides here a unique perspective from which to conceive of the complex natures of oppression and resistance and the difficulties in pinpointing a single point at which to attack the negative tendencies of image-power and controlling images.

Lefebvre: Alienation

[Charlie] Chaplin gave us a *genuine reverse image* of modern times: its image seen through a living man, through his sufferings, his tribulations, his victories. We are now entering the vast domain of the *illusory reverse image*. What we find is a false world: firstly because it is not a world, and because it presents itself as true, and because it mimics real life closely in order to replace the real by its opposite; by replacing real unhappiness by fictions of happiness—and so on. This is the "world" of most films, most of the press, the theatre, the music hall: of a large sector of leisure activities.

How strange the split between the real world and its reverse image is. For in the end it is not strange at all, but a false strangeness, a cheap-and-nasty, all-pervasive mystery. (Lefebvre, 1947/1992, p. 35)

Marxism describes and analyses *the everyday life of society* and indicates the means by which it can be transformed. It describes and analyses *the everyday lives of workers* themselves: separated from their tools, connected to the material conditions of their labour solely by the "contract" which binds them to an employer, sold like commodities on the labour market in the (legal and ideological) guise of the "free" labour contract, etc.

The real, everyday life of the worker is that of a commodity endowed, unhappily for him [or her], with life, activity, muscles—and with a consciousness which the concerted pressure of his [or her] Masters seeks to reduce to a minimum or to divert into inoffensive channels....

Thus Marxism, as a whole, really is a critical knowledge of everyday life.

It is not satisfied with merely uncovering and criticizing this real, practical life in the minutiae of social life. By a process of rational integration it is able to pass from the individual to the social—from the level of the individual to the level of society and of the nation. And vice versa. (Lefebvre, 1947/1992, p. 148)

In *Critique of Everyday Life,* an essentially Marxist work, Henri Lefebvre (1947/1992) identifies alienation as the key characteristic underlying the oppressiveness of everyday life. Further, he presents the modern regime of image as an industry of falseness and as evidence of the disconnectedness between men and women and the world of their everyday lived experiences. Although Lefebvre's work remains remarkably complex and multidimensional, what matters most here, for our purposes, is his reading of Marxism as inherently a critique of everyday life, one joining such concepts as mystification, fetishism, and alienation with a critique of the meaning-laden technologies and effects of image.

For Lefebvre, this Marxist critique of everyday life includes six more specific and elemental critiques, each with its own "central theme," namely, the

(a) *Critique of individuality* (Central theme: the "private" consciousness);
(b) *Critique of mystifications* (Central theme: the "mystified" consciousness);
(c) *Critique of money* (Central theme: fetishism and economic alienation);
(d) *Critique of needs* (Central theme: psychological and moral alienation);
(e) *Critique of work* (Central theme: the alienation of the worker and of [individuals]); [and]
(f) *Critique of freedom* (Central theme: [human] power over nature and over [human] nature). (pp. 148-170)

For Lefebvre, Marx's (and Lefebvre's own) critique of individuality meant a critique of selfish self-consciousness, of individualism, of a subjectivity in which human beings see their individuality as distinct and separate from that of others. This form of individuality, this "private consciousness," assumes individuality as private property, as possession, as natural, and as competitive (and is what consistently is represented in the traditions of the Liberal West and its constitutions). For Lefebvre this tendency, initiated by the objective conditions of the structure of labor—fragmentation and specialization, for example—reduces "the human" to "the merely biological." It makes everything else which is human, aside from one's own "humanity," alien, unknown, and even adversarial.

The critique of mystifications, of mystified consciousness, has at its roots the power of the capitalist and the bourgeoisie as imposed on and toward the proletariat, the worker, and as ideological conceptualization of and control over everyday life. Here, several contradictions come into play. The bourgeoisie function as a class even as its members claim and assert and privilege their status as individuals, their individuality (although they dress, talk, and often think alike). At the same time they work to encourage the proletariat to identify as individuals and to not act as a class. Both, in effect, are classes of individuals, yet the bourgeoisie acts as a class while claiming the priority of the individual, and the proletariat is a class but is encouraged to act as individuals. In Lefebvre's view this mystification, like others, involves a hiding or manipulation or denying of the truth, of working class consciousness and the capitalist threat to transformation.

Implied in the critique of money (with its major themes of fetishism and economic alienation) are the notions (1) that money becomes an end in and of itself—and a marker of class—and (2) that money, and what money can "do," becomes a substitute for the creative, expressive, and authentic activities—work, the *human being*—of human beings.

Lefebvre's interpretation of the critique of needs (emphasizing psychological and moral alienation) suggests that:

> Money becomes inflated out of all proportion, as does the fundamental need (in capitalist regimes) which bears witness to its presence in men's [and women's] hearts. And every other need is adjusted and revised according to the need for money. As a set of desires, the human being is not developed and cultivated for himself [or herself], but so that the demands of this theological monster may be satisfied. The need *for* money is an expression of the needs *of* money [italics added].

> On the one hand, therefore, every effort is made to create fictitious, artificial, imaginary needs. Instead of expressing and satisfying real desires, and of transforming "crude need into human need," the capitalist producer inverts the course of things. He starts with the object which is the simplest or the most lucrative to produce, and endeavors—mainly through advertising—to create a need for it. (pp. 161-162)

And:

> ...Marx has demonstrated the "idealist" character of this operation, which begins with the external, abstract concept of the object in order to stimulate a desire for it. This idealism culminates in fantasy, whims, the bizarre.... [T]he producer becomes the pimp for the individual and his [her] own self: he [she] 'places himself [herself] at the disposal of his [her] neighbour's most depraved fancies, panders to his [her] needs, excites unhealthy appetites in him [her], and pounces on every weakness, so that he [she] can then demand the money for his [her] labour of love.

> But at the same time, for all those unable to pay, needs die, degenerate, become more simple. As a result the worker stops feeling the simplest needs, which are also the most difficult needs for workers to satisfy: the need for space, for fresh air and freedom, for solitude or contemplation.... (pp. 161-162)

Therefore, the individual

> sinks even lower than an animal. Needs and feelings no longer exist in a human form; they no longer even exist in a dehumanized form, therefore 'not even in animal form'. Not only does man [or woman] cease to have human needs, but he [or she] loses his [or her] animal needs: to move about, to have contacts with beings of the same species....

> It is a state of affairs that the bourgeois economist finds eminently satisfactory; it means that all is well in the capitalist economy. Money reigns; everyone serves it in their particular way, according to the position they hold in "human nature": the bourgeois worship it in a refined, even artistic, way, while the workers' homage is humble and austere. (pp. 161-162)

Under capitalism, then, what passes as needs are principally the needs of money that displace or cover-up more authentic human ones. Genuine human desires—psychological, biological, sociological—are manipulated into the demand for the artificial. Producers convince men and women of the necessity of some product—sometimes even before the product exists—and then insist on money as a reward for "generously" satisfying, or making possible the satisfaction of, such "needs." Even "simple"—or natural?—needs require money, and, therefore, frequently move ever farther out of reach for the less wealthy. In fact, the wealthy can and do monopolize the meeting of needs. Everyday life thus becomes the quest to fulfill the money-mediated necessities of the economy. Human beings in effect de-evolve, or evolve rather into commodities and into the non-human, externally defined and externally useful, tools of money and of economic power.

Regarding the critique of work/the alienation of the worker and, more generally, of [persons]:

> The relation of every humble, everyday gesture to the social complex, like the relation of each individual to the whole, cannot be compared to that of the part to the sum total or of the element to a "synthesis," using the term in its usual vague sense. Mathematical integration would be a better way of explaining the transfer from one scale of greatness to another, implying as it does a qualitative leap without the sense that the "differential" element (the gesture, the individual) and the totality are radically heterogeneous.

> Within the parameters of private property, this relation of the "differential" element to the whole is both disguised and distorted. In fact, the worker works for the social whole; his [or her] activity is a part of "social labour" and contributes to the historical heritage of the society (nation) to which he [or she] belongs. But he [or she] does not know it. He [or she] thinks he [or she] is working "for the boss." And he [or she] is indeed working "for the boss": he [or she] provides him [or her] with a profit. In

this way the portion of the social value of his [or her] labour which does not come back to him [or her] in the form of wages is retained by the boss (surplus-value). The only *direct* relations the worker has are with the boss. He [or she] is ignorant of the overall or total phenomena involved. He [or she] does not know that the totality of surplus-value goes to the bosses as a group or capitalist "class." He [or she] does not know (at least, not spontaneously) that the sum total of wages go to the proletarian "class"; he [or she] is even more ignorant of the fact that the way the sum total is distributed—surplus-value, wages, products, rates of profit, purchasing power, etc.—obeys certain laws. (p. 164)

Simply, one's labor and its creations belong to others. Though often represented as individual, as healthy, as good for its own sake, and as a component of a personal relationship—between, say, worker and supervisor—or even as craft, skill, talent, vocation (etc.), it is in reality anything but. As work develops into labor-power to be bought and sold, undifferentiated, alienation takes hold. It functions to subjugate, to dehumanize, and to enable the worker's further oppression. It benefits the capitalist. Work becomes necessary not for authentic human living, but in terms instead of the welfare of the economic system that depends upon it. And it is in the interests of the economically powerful to downplay, or even deny, this fact of life (though in some cases they themselves are ignorant of it). For Lefebvre, in sum:

The human being—ceasing to be human—is turned into a tool to be used by other tools (the means of production), a thing to be used by another thing (money), and an object to be used by a class, a mass of individuals who are themselves "deprived" of reality and truth (the capitalists). And his [or her] labour, which ought to humanize him [or her], becomes something done under duress instead of being a vital and human need, since it is itself nothing more than a means (of "earning a living") rather than a contribution to [human] essence, freely imparted.

...Therefore, for every individual, worker or expert, the division of labour is imposed from without, like an objective process, with the result that each [person's] activity is turned back against him [or her] as a hostile force which subjugates him [or her] instead of being subjugated by him [or her].

In this way a dehumanized, brutally objective power holds sway over all social life; according to differing aspects, we have named it: money, fragmented division of labour, market, capital, mystification and deprivation, etc. (p. 166)

Work within the context of everyday life, then, succeeds in denying human beings their possibility of being fully human; it, instead, alienates, objectifies, and subdues.

Lastly, in his critique of freedom and its central theme of "[the individual's] power over nature and over his [or her] own nature," Lefebvre contrasts freedom's "bourgeois" definition (that of classical, Western, liberal capitalism) with that provided by Marx. Citing the French Constitution of 1793 and the *Declaration of the Rights of Man* of 1791, he characterized the bourgeois definition: "Liberty is the power which belongs to man [*sic*] to do anything that does not harm the rights of others; Liberty consists in being able to do anything which does not harm others" (Lefebvre, 1947/1992, p. 170). It is, in this view, "the right of the 'private' individual, and in its practical application consists essentially of the right to 'private' property" (p. 171).

Such freedom reflects a "what's mine is mine, what's yours is yours" and a "to each his own" mentality. It establishes our possessed or owned right to be free from others and others' right to be free from us, to exert maximum individualism within the boundaries its sets between multiple individuals. It privileges, in effect, a market orientation, a supply and demand analysis of freedom in which a competitive equilibrium between positing one's own liberty while minimizing that of others presents the ideal.

In contrast, according to Lefebvre, "The Marxist definition of freedom is concrete and dialectical.... The realm of freedom is established progressively by *'the development of human powers as an end in itself'*" (p. 171). Moreover:

> The definition of freedom thus begins with the *power* [individuals] increasingly [have] over nature (and over [their] own nature, over...self and the products of their activity). It is not a ready-made freedom; it cannot be defined metaphysically by an "all or nothing": absolute freedom or absolute necessity. It is won progressively by social man [and woman]. For *power*, or, more exactly, *the sum total of powers* which constitute freedom belong to human beings grouped together in a society, and not to the isolated individual. (pp. 171-172)

Accordingly:

> In the first place, then, freedom must be won; it is arrived at through a process of becoming: there are therefore *degrees of freedom*.

> In the second place, the freedom of the individual is founded upon that of his [or her] social group (his [or her] nation, his [or her] class). There can be no freedom for the individual in a subservient nation or class. Only in a free society will the individual be free to realize his [or her] full potential.

> In the third place, there are *freedoms* (political and human, both on the social and the individual level) rather than "freedom" in general. All freedoms imply the exercise of *effective* power. Freedom of expression, effective participation in the running of the social whole, these are political freedoms. The (complementary) rights to work and to leisure—the possibility of attaining the highest consciousness and development of the self through culture—contribute to *concrete* individual freedom.

All power is liberating.... "Spiritually" and materially, the free individual is a totality
of powers, i.e. of concrete possibilities. (p. 172)

Here freedom is both individual and societal such that "real" individual freedom requires "real" societal freedom. Freedom is gradually won. An individual is free only if his or her group (nation, society, class, etc.) is free.
Freedom is multiple—political, social, cultural, *and* individual. And ultimately freedom involves the totality of powers, the individual's possibil-
ity(ies) to become and to develop maximally. It is positive in that it depends
on an authentic relationship, or authentic relationships, with others; not negative—in the sense of bourgeois freedom—in which liberty depends on separation, distinction, competition, and isolation.

For Lefebvre, everyday life then risks privileging individualism over individuality, mystified consciousness, the fetishism of money and economic
alienation, false needs, the alienation of workers, and a narrow and limiting
view of freedom. With respect to image and education, what Lefebvre provides is a means by which to understand and to act against image's potentially negative effects. How do, for example, pedagogical images reflect or
reinforce the conditions of everyday life? Do they push individualism at the
expense of individuality, and so on? Do they hyper-support money or depict
alienation in a somehow positive or productive light? Does the chasing of
test scores mirror or parallel the fetishism of money? Do they disconnect
students from one another and/or from their teachers? Teachers and students
from their potential, their power to grow? From their academic work? Are
his and Marx's concerns at all related to our own concerns of anti-democracy, oppression, inauthenticity, disciplinarity, and anti-collectivity? Can
they make more transparent the mechanisms of image-power and controlling
images? And how, if at all, can Lefebvre's insights help counteract the imperatives of disciplinarity, anti-democracy, inauthenticity, oppression, and
anti-collectivity?

Conclusions

At the heart of this chapter lay a number of relationships crucial to understanding image and education. We assume, in sum, a set of connections
between schooling and everyday life mediated by image(s). More directly,
we suppose the importance of image to both schooling and everyday life and
that this importance serves in part to link them. Perhaps more ominously,
however, we maintain that the possible negatives of pedagogical image and
those of everyday life to some extent merge, such that the two become ever-

more nearly indistinguishable. Everyday life, therefore, risks the same threats of anti-democracy, inauthenticity, oppression, and anti-collectivity as those posed by dominant/dominant image(s), and dominant/dominating image(s) risk(s) the same threats of alienation, reproduction, and so forth as those posed by everyday life.

The theories of everyday life presented here provide at least two significant contributions: a mode of critical understanding and a mode of critical action. The work of Jackson, Vaneigem, Perlman, de Certeau, Brown, and Lefebvre suggest mechanisms by which to engage not only everyday life per se, but also the workings of pedagogical image and of contemporary schooling itself. They ask educators to consider the importance of the "trivialities" of schooling, the alienating aspects of schooling, and how much of schooling can be interpreted as "fetishism" or "fetish worship" (perhaps standardized test scores?). They imply a mode of resistance grounded in both strategies and tactics, the psychological and the political, and in play, creativity, and connectivity, each of which seems pertinent to the demands of image-power and controlling images. They present unique ways of knowing relevant to the complexities of pedagogical image and how its effects in fact might function anti-democratically, oppressively, inauthentically, and anti-collectively (i.e., maybe "alienation" or "fetish worship" or "reproduction" undergirds these effects of image?).

These perspectives, for example, might help educators and scholars make some new sense of the quotidian world of classrooms explored earlier by Philip Jackson. How, and to what benefit, might the actions of students be understood via the conceptions explored here? How might these views help us address the workings and outcomes of image(s), including the effect(s) of image(s) on creating and reproducing a certain set of little known classroom characteristics? To what extent are how students line-up, obey rules, and so on alienating, reproductive, influenced by image(s), and/or a result of or reproductive of the fetishizing of test scores/achievement/performance? Of resistance? Does life in classrooms indicate any level of strategic and/or tactical behavior? How are test scores, and the "idealized" representations presented in films and television, like money? To what consequences?

Image most likely will continue to constitute a major feature of everyday life, especially as, in the aftermath of 9/11, surveillance and spectacle, technological change, standardization, and globalization will continue to grow and to exert their own singular and troublesome influences (e.g., Brzezinski, 2003, for one set of insights into what post-9/11 everyday life might become). Thus, studying everyday life and its back-and-forth relationships with schooling, as well as the mediating effects of image, should remain important—critically so, particularly as our everyday lives and as schooling further evolve into the playing field of voyeurism and exhibitionism.

For the practice of schooling, the theories of everyday life examined in this chapter mean that educators and scholars of education must be increasingly sensitive to the everyday lives of children and other relevant stakeholders. For as Jackson implies, classroom life prepares students, for good and bad, for the conformity, the disciplinarity, of capitalist life, most prominently by way of classroom life's forced and institutional hierarchies. Of course, the economy desires and perpetuates this image, and rewards schools for going along, so that the image of schools as the system's reproductive training ground serves to connect everyday life and classroom life.

Overall, we must consider the potential relationships between theories of everyday life and the actualities of classrooms and schools. From Vaneigem, we must address the possible ways in which "the system" precludes meaningful participation, authentic communication, and self-realization. From Perlman, we must consider the extent to which the problematics of schooling reproduce the problematics of everyday life, and vice versa, particularly via the mechanisms of alienation and fetish worship. From de Certeau, we must interpret the interplay in schools between the relatively powerful and the relatively powerless in terms of the strategic and tactical behavior of both. From Brown, we must work through the likelihood that the everyday life of classrooms, bound as it is to image, oppresses and/or represses not only socially/objectively/politically/economically, but individually/subjectively/psychologically/personally as well. And, lastly, from Lefebvre, we must critique how, if at all, the practices of contemporary schooling might be implicated in the workings of individualism, mystification, money, false needs, and misplaced understandings of freedom. In the end, curriculum, instruction, assessment, policy, teaching, learning, and so on must include a significant and critical theorization relative to the practices and implications of everyday life.

In the next chapter we consider specific modes of classroom-based resistance to the various problematics of image and education that we have identified. We investigate, namely, the techniques of critical media literacy, Foucauldian resistance, *la perruque, dérive,* and *detournement.*

And in chapter eight we look at specific examples of pedagogical image and seek to demonstrate how the approaches, ideas, and positions we've explored thus far—for instance, various views of the visual (e.g., visual culture, popular culture/cultural studies, media studies, and film studies), critical frameworks (including those developed by Bakhtin, Barthes, Boorstin, Baudrillard, and McLuhan), surveillance-spectacle, technology/globalization/

standardization, and the theories presented in this chapter relative to everyday life, can help interested stakeholders both critically engage and critically respond to their functionings. Specifically, we take on two popular films, *Dead Poets' Society* and *Dangerous Minds,* and the No Child Left Behind Act and the broader movement toward standards-based educational reform.

PART III

Teaching in the Face of The New Disciplinarity

❊CHAPTER SEVEN

Image and Teaching Resistance

SO WHAT TO DO? That is, how might classroom teachers and students (and other educational stakeholders) work to combat the potentially harmful effects of pedagogical image? Of controlling images? Of image-power? How might concerned schoolfolk resist their possible consequences—anti-democracy, oppression, inauthenticity, disciplinarity, and anti-collectivity? How might they meaningfully contest the consequences of these threats relative to their daily lives, situated as they are according to the prevailing and dominant/dominating contexts of surveillance, spectacle, standardization, globalization, and technological change?

Historically, the field of critical pedagogy has provided a number of relevant techniques and strategies, and, in fact, can claim today a long and admirable tradition of pursuing within both schools and society a commitment to social justice, diversity, democracy, and opportunity. It has fought the social, pedagogical, cultural, religious, economic, and political forces of privilege, social reproduction, and conformity, and has consistently espoused countermeasures to the racist, sexist, and classist aspects of contemporary schooling while simultaneously supporting schooling's more liberatory and emancipatory elements. Drawing on such varied perspectives as social reconstructionism, progressivism, pragmatism, feminism, multiculturalism, critical race theory, (neo)Marxism, postmodernism and poststructuralism, and cultural studies (among many others), this view advocates for a radically democratic schooling, one in which such pedagogical practices as authentic instruction, authentic assessment, transformative pedagogy, culturally relevant teaching and learning, multicultural education, whole language, multilingual education, and democratic education itself (among others) can both claim space and make a serious and broad-based difference.

We should not forget, moreover, that educators and activists—students, teachers, parents, etc.—have a long history as well of incorporating and engaging in more widely known and at least equally effective modes of mass critical resistance, those such as boycotts, strikes, demonstrations, letter/op-ed writing campaigns, teach/sit-ins, marches, and other forms of protest.

Of course we welcome, applaud, and encourage such efforts. We sympathize with and even participate in the work of both critical/radical pedagogues and of educator-activists (often one and the same), all like-minded transformationists. In fact, we hope to contribute to and expand upon these heritages of critical theory and critical practice. Yet in this chapter we do attempt to identify and distinguish explicit procedures and mechanisms more directly aimed at the technologies of image and its concomitant problematics. More specifically, we examine a number of practical classroom methods constructed out of our earlier and ongoing theoretical investigations, namely those of: (1) critical media literacy; (2) *la perruque*; (3) Foucauldian resistance; (4) *dérive*; and (5) *detournement*.

Strategies for Media Literacy

> We are immersed from cradle to grave in a media and consumer society and thus it is important to learn how to understand, interpret, and criticize its meanings and messages. The media are a profound and often misperceived source of cultural pedagogy: they contribute to educating us how to behave and what to think, feel, believe, fear, and desire—and what not to. Consequently, the gaining of critical media literacy is an important resource for individuals and citizens in learning how to cope with a media environment and how to resist media manipulation and to empower oneself in relation to our media and culture. (Kellner, 1995, p. xiii)

> The issue of critical media literacy is thus part of a process of critical pedagogy that teaches individuals how their culture, society, and polity are structured and work. Critical media pedagogy involves teaching how to activate students and citizens so that they can learn to more actively create their own meanings, lives, and society. The media themselves are forms of pedagogy[,] so critical media pedagogy needs to counter media pedagogy by teaching individuals how to read and criticize the media and how to produce alternative media and culture. (Kellner, 1995, p. xv)

As Kellner (1995) indicates, critical media literacy assumes its importance in relation to the ever-increasing dominance of image relative to everyday life. Critical media *literacy* involves assisting students to understand—to *read*—(1) what roles the media play in terms of creating individual and group subjectivities and (2) how to counteract the manipulative and depowering tendencies of the media as they work to control, dictate, monopolize, determine, and perpetuate hierarchies of social, cultural, economic, political, ideological, and pedagogical power.

In the book *Rethinking Media Literacy* (McLaren, et al., 1995), Shirley Steinberg (1995) in effect creates an applied pedagogy of critical media literacy by inquiring into and extending the methodological insights of several distinguished media and educational scholars (Rhonda Hammer, Susan Reilly, David Sholle, & Peter McLaren). Essentially, this approach includes: (1) theoretical development within the practical domain (Hammer); (2) theorizing experience (McLaren); (3) critiquing existing texts and creating new media programs (Reilly); and (4) modeling media systems (Sholle). In our view, each of these components makes sense not only in terms of its potential versus the negativities of pedagogical image, but also in terms of its educational utility as a practical, implementable, and sophisticated classroom technique. (Although we address each of these one-by-one here, we return to them more generally in our summary and conclusions.)

Rhonda Hammer (in Steinberg, 1995) suggests first the need for "theoretical development within the practical domain" (p. 226). She means by this the integration of theory and practice in a dialectical relationship in which neither one is privileged or deprivileged and in which "the students' frame of reference" (p. 227) supplies the situative context and starting point for theory construction and utilization. She argues against *merely* or *simply* transmitting some theory to students (and/or, by extension, teachers or future teachers) and then insisting on their (enforced?) willingness to apply it to some given or selected "reality." Rather, she supports the imperative of student experience (both "positive" and "negative") with the media and with media representations (e.g., of American youth, women, immigrants, etc.), *and* the collaborative efforts of teachers and students (perhaps interacting with existing theoretical views) to form their own critical comprehensions and interpretations.

Peter McLaren (in Steinberg, 1995) considers the pedagogical need to "theorize experience" by first exploring his own professorial work, a project in which students (generally teachers, administrators, or future teachers and administrators) have regularly "resisted theory and looked to experience as their final court of appeal" as if "somehow experience magically speaks for itself" (p. 253).

> As if experiences are self-observances, are auto-didactic, something that gives us an accurate notion of the world. Joan Scott, myself, and others have argued that knowledge is not gained through the unmediated apprehension of a world of transparent objects. As if somehow experiences precede interpretation or rhetoric. Interpretation, in fact, occurs at the very moment of perception. The problem is that teachers really see theory as the enemy of experience. So I try a little epistemological disrobing by way of critical theory. When I'm successful, and there is certainly no guarantee that I will be, eventually students confront the challenge of viewing expe-

rience as both a construction—an ideological effect—and as constitutive of reality....
[W]e have to understand experiences as never transparent or self-present but always
occurring within a textual economy.... So experience can be understood as having
always already occurred yet paradoxically having still to be produced.... Having experiences are important—it's different than reading about experiences—but I think
that having certain experiences does not guarantee a particular politics. What's important are the languages we use to understand our experiences—to help us transform them. Language is not fixed and can represent the same social relation in different ways. It can construct different meanings. By this I mean simply that language can both constrain and enable understandings.... (pp. 253-254)

McLaren's position, basically, is that experience is neither natural nor neutral, and that it must, therefore, somehow be "theorized." That is, images,
pedagogical and otherwise, do not interpret themselves. Instead, they must be
actively understood. He asserts that teachers, students, and future teachers be
introduced to, that they must confront, theory, but not as a substitute for experience. They must see that unexperienced theory is no better than untheo-
rized experience. Media representations do not speak a transparent "truth,"
but one that can only be comprehended situationally, one that cannot be understood without being challenged, one that "says" many things, both more
and less than what its power-laden appearance(s) ostensibly espouse(s) on its
ideological and non-mediated surface. Image—experience—risks meaning-
lessness, then, in the absence of critical theoretical work.

Yet as Susan Reilly (Steinberg, 1995) implies, exploring the connections
among theory, real-life experience, and pedagogical practice only accom-
plishes so much without students also engaging in the acts of critique, creation, and creation-critique. As she states:

Critical analyses of existing media texts are a good place to start, but eventually students need to create their own media programs. In these programs, students can advance border narratives which break the bonds of hegemonic discourse and provide
oppositional readings of history and social practice. (p. 236)

What Reilly makes clear is that in order to combat, to resist, the power of
media images, students not only need to interpret them critically, but also to
create *counterimages*—that is, those that enable students (and teachers) to
present their own imaginings, their own stories, their own demands and desires, and their own subjective identities as against those provided for them
by the dominant/dominating powers that be. Ideally, for Reilly, these would
be counterhegemonic, and would, in fact, narrate what rarely (if ever) gets
narrated. Formats might include multimedia presentations, videotapes, photographs, DVDs, musical compositions, and/or other examples of artwork.
They would tell alternative tales, include what is often excluded, and require

that students consider the settings within which "mainstream" or "conventional" (i.e., "conservative") images are constructed, propagated, and left unexamined.

The suggestion by David Sholle (Steinberg, 1995) in favor of "modeling media systems" represents what might be the most radical and most intriguing instructional application of critical media literacy/critical media pedagogy. Here he dares teachers and students to (re)create, in effect, the entire structure of contemporary media and cultural practices. His concern, first, is that students come to construe the media and media work as more than solely the formal mechanics of production (e.g., lighting, broadcasting, taping, scripting, etc.); for in his view it includes as well the dynamic and complex set of cultural politics that functions within the interplay among the production, distribution, and consumption of significant texts. And second, he considers the fundamental relationship between media and media studies and democracy and democratic citizenship.

To this end, Sholle begins by positing three framing guidelines: (1) "teachers should avoid forcing interpretations of the text"; (2) "the media text needs to be put in context—the reading needs to be situated in both a theoretical and historical setting"; and (3) "discussion of a particular text must evolve from a confrontation with the act of consumption" (p. 241). He asserts that the interrogation of media images should start from exemplars (written, visual, etc.) that are of special interest to students, and that, ideally, it "should lead to self-reflection and [to a] give and take between [the] affirmation of popular culture's contribution to everyday life and its potential problems" (p. 241).

Following James Curran (e.g., 1991a, 1991b) and John Keane (e.g., 1991), Sholle proposes the modeling of "democratic media systems" (p. 247). Here:

> Students would participate in the formation of associations that function as public media organizations of various kinds...includ[ing] a private enterprise sector, a general purpose public service system, a civic sector (consisting of party and subcultural tiers), and an autonomous professional sector. Students would participate in setting up the system and thus, would experience and work through the problems inherent in forming genuinely radical democratic institutions.

> The result would be a [publicly] regulated sphere of media activity with the students acting in various positions of authority—from media producers, to organizational heads, to public representatives. This would be a direct experiment in citizenship....
> (pp. 247-248)

Further: "This media public sphere would provide an arena, where student concerns, experiences, histories, discourses and desires could be aired and contested" (p. 248).

What Sholle offers teachers and students is a critical practice grounded in situated interpretation, democracy, and authentic cultural pedagogy. His is a program that could apply across grade levels and subject matter areas, especially given that his modeling could work via any image-creating system (e.g., TV, film, music, broadcast journalism, etc.) and toward a range of specific goals and objectives. For Sholle, what matters most is that the various media be confronted holistically, that students and teachers role play the positions of multiple stakeholders—including what they bring to and take from variously located and intentioned representations—and that all voices are genuinely heard. His tact encourages both imagining a radically inclusive and democratic public media sphere and a critique of what exists instead in the "real world" in terms of complex, evolving, and sometimes anti-democratic shortcomings.

Overall, critical media literacy entails a multiple and dynamic classroom practice encompassing at least three distinct, though related, elements: (1) theory construction; (2) critique and creation; and (3) system modeling. At best, each of these would contribute to a radical pedagogical project consistent with resisting the hegemonic tendencies of controlling images and image-power.

Regarding theory construction, teachers and students first need to operate knowing that theory, practice, and experience are intimately connected. They would work, then, to fashion their own theories of image and representation, seeking ultimately to theorize their own experiences and actions as well as those of others. They would conjointly choose content—imaginary productions of interest to them—and pursue meaning, rationale, utility, and consequences. Certainly they could make use of formal or "high" theory, but pragmatically, not in an uncritical or blindly accepting way. Teachers and students would investigate the nexus among their own lives, the lives of image-makers and image-viewers, and the production, distribution, and consumption of mainstream representations—Who produces them? Who gets represented and how? Within what contexts? Why are they produced and others not produced? What do they mean? Who decides and how? And how and why do some come to dominate? Most probably students would perceive a relationship or set of relationships linking who they are, what they do and have experienced, and how they interpret the work of the media. Moreover, they might discern significant differences between some image consumers and some image-producers and distributors. They may, in fact, grow to question critically the total media ensemble and to inquire into its workings relative to contemporary society, politics, ideology, culture, economics, power, and schooling.

La Perruque

The operational models of popular culture cannot be confined to the past, the countryside, or primitive peoples. They exist in the heart of the strongholds of the contemporary economy. Take, for example, what in France is called *la perruque,* "the wig." *La perruque* is the worker's own work disguised as work for his [or her] employer. It differs from pilfering in that nothing of material value is stolen. It differs from absenteeism in that the worker is officially on the job. *La perruque* may be as simple a matter as a secretary's writing a love letter on "company time" or as complex as a cabinetmaker's "borrowing" a lathe to make a piece of furniture for his living room. Under different names in different countries this phenomenon is becoming more and more general, even if managers penalize it or "turn a blind eye" on it in order not to know about it. Accused of stealing or turning material to his [or her] own ends and using the machines for his [or her] own profit, the worker who indulges in *la perruque* actually diverts time (not goods, since he uses only scraps) from the factory for work that is free, creative, and precisely not directed toward profit. In the very place where the machine he [or she] must serve reigns supreme, he [or she] cunningly takes pleasure in finding a way to create gratuitous products whose sole purpose is to signify his [or her] own capabilities through his [or her] *work* and to confirm his [or her] solidarity with other workers or his [or her] family through *spending* his [or her] time in this way. With the complicity of other workers (who thus defeat the competition the factory tries to instill among them), he [or she] succeeds in "putting one over" on the established order on its home ground. Far from being a regression toward a mode of production organized around artisans or individuals, *la perruque* reintroduces "popular" techniques of other times and other places into the industrial space (that is, into the Present order). (de Certeau, 1984, pp. 25-26)

[Mr. Hand]: Am I hallucinating here? Just what in the hell do you think you're doing?
[Jeff Spicoli]: Learnin' about Cuba and havin' some food.
[Mr. Hand]: Mister Spicoli you're on dangerous ground here. You're causing a major disturbance on my time.
[Jeff Spicoli]: You know, I've been thinking about this Mister Hand. If I'm here and you're here, doesn't that make it *our* time? (student Jeff Spicoli [played by Sean Penn] to teacher Mr. Hand [played by Ray Walston] in *Fast Times at Ridgemont High,* after Spicoli orders a pizza delivered to his social studies classroom; Heckerling & Crowe, 1982)

La perruque represents what might be the most subversive mode of resistance relative to the disciplinarity of pedagogical image. But in order to grasp its utility, its import, several convictions must first be considered. Schooling must, for instance, be seen as "our time" and not simply a managed or enculturating time, unquestioned labor-work, controlled by and supportive of the authorities (though frequently this is the case). Moreover, we must remember why a critical pedagogy of the image is necessary in the first place; the rationale for enacting *la perruque* must be consistent with promoting democracy, collectivity, and authenticity and opposed to oppression. Third, *la perruque* must be about capabilities and solidarity, that is, it must empower teachers and students to chase their interests, desires, skills, and abilities while simultaneously encouraging them to connect and form communities with one another—within and across classrooms and within and across schools.

What matters most then is that here students and teachers effect a program aimed at counteracting the visual-based problematics of image. Thus, for example, representations that posit particular views of, say, the good teacher or good student or good school, and/or that privilege certain constructions or relationships of race, ethnicity, class, gender, sexuality, language, and religion, etc., must be vigorously and critically challenged. Teachers and students should pursue, therefore, their own everyday lives in schools, as schools make sense only within the everyday lives of teachers and students.

To illustrate, *la perruque*-inspired instruction might admit school "assignments" that attack school assignments. If schools have a homework policy, for instance, teachers and students might create projects in which they examine critically homework's positive and negative aspects. They might develop "tests" in which essays ask students to critique standardized testing. They might use "their" time to critique and create their own content standards. Of course teachers and students might simply use their time to do things other than mandated schoolwork, perhaps even operating directly against formal dictates. (We are not necessarily advocating any particular techniques, but merely offering samples of what might be done. We encourage teachers and students to develop their own situated pedagogies. We note, too, that this section might lead one to think of the actions of student Eddie Pilikian [played by Ralph Macchio] in the movie *Teachers* [Hiller & McKinney, 1984] as he succeeds in videotaping the many absurdities that occur at his school in the name of education.) What is at stake, at minimum, is who controls school time and to what ends, who gets to decide what education is, what forms of teaching and learning matter, and what, finally, it actually means to matter. We are not suggesting that teachers and students "waste" time or that they engage in unimportant activities.

What these actions do, though, is clarify how the potentially controlling effects of image might be countered through *la perruque* and within the demands of democracy, authenticity, the collective good, and anti-oppression. Teachers, students, and schools would be playing with their stereotypical images, whether as good or bad or mediocre or hardworking or lazy or whatever. Schools, teachers, and students typically seen as good, hardworking, and mainstream now would be seen as radical and bad, perhaps even as failing. Those viewed as failing would be able to claim that they are hardworking (they are doing homework and taking tests after all) and as successful as those against whom they are usually held up to as competitors. Ideally, all would come to challenge the mechanisms of image and education, especially its potentially negative consequences, and to question the evidence upon which such images are produced and disseminated and the motives of those who perpetuate them.

Further, teachers and students would begin seeing their broad and intimate relationships with one another, across classrooms, schools, and districts, and that under dominant circumstances some are unfairly held up while some are unfairly held down (i.e., because of economics, power, race, ethnicity, neighborhood, language, religion, and so forth). Such work would be radically democratic as it would reside primarily in the hands of students and teachers themselves. It would be anti-oppressive to the extent that it frustrates Freire's conception of banking education and that it negates the five faces outlined by Young (see chapter three). It would be authentic as it would reflect the lived experiences of teachers and students and as it took their individual and collective wants, needs, desires, interests, backgrounds, and subjectivities as uniquely legitimate.

Foucault

Foucault's work on "resistance" is perhaps more straightforward than might be expected, even though, arguably, he never laid out an explicit program for liberation or revolution. As Gordon (1980) rightly suggests, "it may be objected that Foucault never locates his theoretical enterprise 'on the side of' resistance by undertaking to formulate a strategy of resistance" (p. 256). But what this means in effect, though, is the plain possibility that "the cunning of [any given revolutionary] strategy is taken as being the exclusive property of [distinct] *forms* [italics added] of domination" (p. 256). It is, in other words, localized and specific, contingent. But for Foucault this does not mean that revolutionary resistance can't occur—it does occur, period—but only that any particular resistant act is neither inherently and universally good nor inherently and universally bad; it is inherently neither better nor worse than any other such act. And yet, "People do revolt; that is a fact" (Foucault, 2000, p. 452). Revolution and resistance are neither predictable nor inevitable nor objective. But they do happen.

His thinking rests on a number of premises, most importantly, the understanding "that power, with its mechanisms, is infinite," though not *necessarily* "evil" or "omnipotent" (Foucault, 2000, p. 452). He cautions against various resistant tendencies in which some individuals have the authority to distinguish appropriate or proper revolutionary behaviors at the expense of others, and recognizes that revolutionaries must take into account not only those actions that are most directly "political," but also those that are "merely" of "evasion or defense." He warns of the problematics of some revolutionary strategies by which one regime charged with normalizing is replaced by another charged with the same coercive capacities (Foucault, 1980). And yet, for Foucault (2000), power in all its guises demands some mode of resistance of the strongest sort: "The rules that exist to limit [power] can never be stringent enough; the universal principles for dispossessing it of all the occasions it seizes are never sufficiently rigorous. Against power one must always set inviolable laws and unrestricted rights" (p. 453). He implies, subtly, the potential, according to Gordon (1980), of an even more anarchic or hyperdemocratic and "profounder logic of revolt" in which the "whole species of rationality and the status of a whole regime of truth can be made to open itself to interrogation..." (p. 258), a striking and radical resistance aimed toward the entirety of disciplinary power.

With respect to pedagogical image, and within the convergence of surveillance and spectacle and the statuses of standardization, globalization, and technological change, this view allows for a number of tangible (and more typical) techniques, including those of boycott, refusal, organizing, political action, letter-writing campaigns, and so on. What Foucault frankly contests is the universal and immanent or natural rightness of one over the other, the preeminence of some action as against other actions, the certainty that what replaces today's system will *necessarily* be an improvement, and the rash confidence that the essential problematics of pedagogical power simply will fade away.

Resistance, then, must first be continuous and flexible. It must as well be democratic in the extreme. It must focus upon all aspects of whatever system is in place and must seek both understanding and change. Regardless of the specific techniques pursued, it must at least seek to expose the links between power and knowledge (as represented, for example, in popular and journalistic media representations of teachers, students, and schools) and the disciplinary characteristics of the dominant regime (e.g., SBER/NCLB). Authenticity comes into play as teachers and students discern the power-ladenness of their lives in general, not just in school, and that and how they are disciplined into living inauthentically. Collectivity emerges as the invisible workings of power become visible, and as teachers and students see that the disciplinary workings of society are pervasive and widely felt.

Dérive and *Detournement*

Guy Debord and other members of the Situationist International (SI; see, e.g., Bracken, 1997; Jappe, 1993/1999; Knabb, 1981; Marcus, 1989) indicate other, somewhat less widely known techniques relevant to superceding "the society of the spectacle" and its effects, techniques not yet extensively explored for their conceivable and critical pedagogical significance, yet of special interest given their promise vis-à-vis the controlling and enforcing propensities of pedagogical image.

The first, the *dérive*, literally "drifting," implies "[a] mode of experimental behavior linked to the conditions of urban society: [it is] a technique of transient passage through varied ambiances..." (Definitions, 1958/1981, p. 45). According to Debord (1958/1981):

> The dérive entails playful-constructive behavior and awareness of psychogeographical effects; which completely distinguishes it from the classical notions of the journey and the stroll.

> In a dérive one or more persons during a certain period drop their usual motives for movement and action, their relations, their work and leisure activities, and let themselves be drawn by the attractions of the terrain and the encounters they find there. The element of chance is less determinant than one might think: from the dérive point of view cities have a psychogeographical relief, with constant currents, fixed points and vortexes which strongly discourage entry into or exit from certain zones. (p. 50)[1]

For the SI (Definitions, 1958/1981) "psychogeography" referred to "[t]he study of the specific effects of the geographical environment, consciously organized or not, on the emotions and behavior of individuals" (p. 45).

On the second, *detournement,* literally "diversion," the SI (Definitions, 1958/1981) wrote:

Short for: detournement of preexisting aesthetic elements. The integration of present or past artistic production into a superior construction of a milieu. In this sense there can be no situationist painting or music [per se], but only a situationist *use* [italics added] of these means. In a more primitive sense, detournement within the old cultural spheres is a method of propaganda, a method which testifies to the wearing out and loss of importance of those spheres. (pp. 45-46)

It "involves," according to Jappe (1993/1999), "a quotation, or more generally a re-use, that 'adapts' the original element to a new context" (p. 59).

It is [moreover] also a way of transcending the bourgeois cult of originality and the private ownership of thought. In some cases the products of bourgeois civilization, even the most insignificant ones, such as advertisements, may be reemployed in such a way as to modify their meaning; in other cases, the effect may be to reinforce the real meaning of an original element...by changing its form. (p. 59)

For Debord (1958/1981) himself *detournement* suggested

the reuse of preexisting artistic elements in a new ensemble [via t]he two fundamental laws of detournement...the loss of importance of each detourned autonomous element—which may go so far as to lose its original sense completely—and at the same time the organization of another meaningful ensemble that confers on each element its new scope and effect. (p. 55)

Together, *dérive* and *detournement* sprang from Debord and his colleagues' "dreams of a reinvented world" (Marcus, 1989, p. 170; see also Debord & Wolman, 1956/1981; Detournement as Negation and Prelude, 1959/1981) where one might "supercede dead time," a world of experiment and play, of "discovering that a world of permanent novelty could exist, and finding the means to start it up" (p. 168). According to Marcus (1989):

These means were two: [jointly] the "dérive," a drift down city streets in search of signs of attraction or repulsion, and "detournement," the theft of aesthetic artifacts from their contexts and their diversion into contexts of one's own device. (p. 168)

Ideally:

...to practice detournement—to write new speech balloons for newspaper comic strips, or for that matter old masters, to insist simultaneously on a "devaluation" of art and its "reinvestment" in a new kind of social speech, a "communication containing its own criticism," a technique that could not mystify because its very form was a demystification—and to pursue the dérive—to give yourself up to the promises of the city, and then to find them wanting—to drift through the city, allowing its signs to divert, to "detourn," your steps, and then to divert those signs yourself, forcing them to give up routes that never existed before—there would be no end to it. It would be to begin to live a truly modern way of life, made out of pavement and pictures, words and weather: a way of life anyone could understand and anyone could use. (p. 170)

As techniques of resistance aimed toward the enforcing elements of controlling images, within the settings of surveillance-spectacle, globalization, technological change, and standardization, what might *dérive* and *detournement* mean? What might they look like? How might they be applied? And how might they work? Especially with respect to democracy, anti-disciplinarity, the collective good, anti-oppression, and authenticity?

Applied to schooling and image, the *dérive,* the more difficult of the two, demands first a re-understanding of the geographical shifts brought on by changes in gaze-based technologies, the will to standardize, and the related global expansion of US capitalism. It requires a consideration of the architectural evolution induced by surveillance-spectacle and its effects (as discussed previously). Today, with respect to education, *dérive* necessitates "drifting" not only through the teletecture and cosmotecture of contemporary schools (schools as virtual space, schools as casinos) and society, but also through the cyberspace "city" of the Internet. It begs a critical confrontation with an entirely new set of psychogeographies.

In that *dérive* is a social act, students and/or teachers and/or other stakeholders would move communally, cooperatively, drifting as it were through buildings and landscapes, through cyberspace or virtual space, through cosmotectures and teletectures, as their emotions and behaviors were piqued. These drifters would, for instance, be free to enter or exit testing sites (physical or virtual) as they were encouraged or discouraged to do so, and they would seek simply to experience, to disrupt, and to play. They would surf Websites, confronting relevant images, come and go, utilize monitors and Webcams for "travel," compelled toward or away from various zones, from, say, official image bases, from control, and from the enforcing effects of standardization schemes. Conceivably, albeit more extremely, they could drift in and out of—even *hack* into—testing locales and interrupt them, create with them, toy with them. They could, moreover, enter and exit classrooms, schools, central offices, government domains, and corporate media positions where image production and distribution are enacted and where image consumption is influenced, and where, in the end, controlling images are most oppressively manipulated. Teachers and students could explore the vast geographies of their total worlds, drifting along the interiors and exteriors of the physical, the spiritual, the technological, the academic, and the social/personal, all as a means of resistance.

With respect to *detournement,* the implications for resistance are perhaps clearer, especially within the contexts of image, surveillance, and spectacle. Again, to quote Jappe (1993/1999), *detournement* involves "a quotation, or more generally a re-use, that 'adapts' the original element to a new context" such that a given image (1) "may be reemployed in such a way as to modify [its] meaning"; or (2) such that "the effect may be to reinforce the *real* [italics added] meaning of an element...by changing its form" (p. 59). Consider, for example, this plausible (though made-up) newspaper headline:

President Bush Announces Education Package—
Called No Child Left Behind, Plan Emphasizes Increased Testing

In and of itself, this seems (or may seem to some) relatively innocuous, even positive, in that the administration will be devoting federal attention to schools and seeking to ensure that no child is left behind by testing them all on a regular basis to measure their progress. Suppose, however, that as a mode of resistance the headline is juxtaposed next to a chart providing data on test scores, wealth, ethnicity, language, and "dropout" rates, for instance in Texas, President Bush's home state. The power and significance of the image then changes as it becomes evident that in Texas, under a system that the president aims to impose on the country as a whole, some children indeed are left behind and those who are share similar characteristics relative to wealth, language, and ethnicity. The image has been "re-used" or "reemployed" and its importance and meanings have shifted.

As a second example, imagine this headline:

State Assessment Scores Show Many Schools Failing

Suppose an accompanying chart with the names of schools or districts in one column and mean standardized test scores in a second column, perhaps with pass-fail cutoff scores indicated.

Now consider recent (mind-boggling but true) news reports that within a particular state funding has been provided to equip upper school system management with personal wireless telecommunication devices (at a cost of thousands of dollars) while because of budget cuts at the school level parents have been asked to donate supplies, including toilet paper, as a means to save money that might otherwise have to be diverted from instruction. (According to some reports, some schools actually have engaged in a system of bartering donated supplies, again, including toilet paper, in order to obtain necessary educational materials.) Now, re-imagine the image. The headline:

State Assessment Scores Show Many Schools Failing

The chart? Column one, names of schools or districts; column two, number of rolls of donated toilet paper (with appropriately arbitrary pass-fail levels reported). As with the first case, both meaning and significance have been changed.

Alternatively, and more simply, students could playfully, though pointedly, recreate the headline, selectively reorganizing its elements and/or its meanings. Perhaps *State Assessment Scores Show Many Schools Failing* might become *Schools' Scores Show State Assessment Failing* or *School Assessment Scores Show State Failing* or even *State Assessment Scores Show Society Failing Many Schools*. (Optimally this praxis would be actualized on "genuine" newsprint, perhaps even computer-enhanced to maximize its impacts and effects—think the "realism" of Orson Welles's 1938 *The War of the Worlds*). Think of the power of such resistance if efforts like these were published in school newspapers, as graffiti, on flyers distributed in school neighborhoods, or in the mainstream press or broadcast media.

These kinds of techniques would work as well for more directly visual images such as those indicative of TV, movies, or cartoons. Teachers and students could re-enact scenes from relevant popular films, for example, *Dead Poets' Society* or *Dangerous Minds*. Meaningful *detournement* might include restaging key scenes in which the characters and dialogue are the same as in the original, but the setting is changed to reflect some divergent meaning. Imagine, for instance, switching the settings between *Dangerous Minds* and *Dead Poets' Society* while keeping their other features intact. Conversely, critical scenes might be redone so that the only thing that varies is the dialogue. Suppose the production of a scene from *Dead Poets' Society* using the dialogue from *Dangerous Minds*.

These illustrations of *detournement* and *dérive* as pedagogy intimate a resistance schooling aimed at countering the negative effects of controlling images/image-power. For at heart they allow and encourage teachers and students some autonomy over what they see and how they are seen. They enable classroom actors to assert themselves into the generally hierarchical processes of image production, distribution, and consumption. Instructionally and as agents of resistance, they first represent a radically democratic mode of teaching and learning as students and teachers choose and unchoose and create and recreate as they deem useful, meaningful, and pertinent. Second, they suggest maximal authenticity. *Dérive* and *detournement* both take seri-ously the lived experiences, the everyday lives, of teachers and students, their surroundings, interests, desires, concerns, cultures, and beliefs. They cham-pion the collective good in that they are social performances, ones depicting connection, human relationships, and solidarity among a wide-ranging popu-lation of schooling's constituents, a class living within externally imposed, power-laden, disciplinary, and reproductive constraints. Lastly, *dérive* and *detournement* work as anti-oppressive tools of empowerment to the degree that they contest the perils of banking education and the hazards of cultural imperialism, exploitation, marginalization, powerlessness, and violence by presenting students and teachers a certain freedom and a certain equality, a fundamental level of sovereignty, individuality, and group identity.

Conclusions

Taken together, critical media literacy, *la perruque, dérive, detourne-ment,* and Foucauldian resistance offer a number of practical implications for classroom instruction. They suggest an applied alternative to the implied and explicit dangers of the hegemony of the image. [2]

As we have argued, images work according to their inherent characteris-tics and mechanisms of and toward controlling images and image-power. They operate, both socially and pedagogically, as disciplinary regimes of truth. Contextualized within the contemporary convergence of surveillance and spectacle and set further according to the manipulations of standardiza-tion, globalization, and technological evolution, the dominant/dominating image poses as its primary threats (1) anti-democracy, (2) inauthenticity, (3) oppression, and (4) a functional perspective antithetical to the collective good.

Pedagogically, the modes of resistance explored in this chapter suggest a radical re-examination of purpose, content, method, and assessment in light of these dangers. With respect to purpose, critical media literacy, following Kellner (1995), demands that teachers and students "learn how to understand, interpret, and criticize [media] meanings and messages...[and] that they learn how to cope with a media environment and...to resist media manipulation..." (p. xiii). *La perruque* insists that individuals be able "to signify [their] *work* and to confirm [their] own capabilities through [their] solidarity with other workers or...family..." (p. 25). From Debord and the SI, *dérive* and *detourne-ment* suggest the need to "supercede the society of the spectacle," that is the image-mediation of social relationships. And from Foucault, the aim of education, within the context of our work, becomes the absolute resistance to any and all concentrations of socio-pedagogical (and political and cultural and economic and so on) power.

As we have indicated, contemporary schooling must work to counter controlling images/image-power, and to challenge its (their) potential tendencies toward oppression, inauthenticity, anti-democracy, and anti-collectivity. Overall, an appropriate image-resistant pedagogy should aim to:

1. critique the enforcing/manipulative power of media representations (often racist, sexist, classist, nationalistic, imperialistic, Christian, etc.);
2. empower teachers and students (i.e., citizens) to control their own labor, time, and identities/subjectivities;
3. supercede the spectacular;
4. combat surveillance-based disciplinarity; and
5. counter the problematics of anti-democracy, oppression, inauthenticity, and anti-collectivity.

Taken together, the purpose of education would be, therefore, the radical resistance to dominant/dominating images and their possibilities of or roles in initializing, perpetuating, and reproducing the hierarchical control of humanness/human connectivity, normalization, marginalization, asymmetricity, and injustice. The broad goal would be to make sense critically of the workings of image-based power and regimentation and to act according to such knowledge.

Regarding curriculum and content, these approaches imply an organization that is interdisciplinary, nontraditional, fluid, and focused on dominant and dominating mainstream media and media images. Specific subject matter might include popular films, TV shows, Websites, and print-based journalism (among countless others), as well as theoretical perspectives from within which to develop and refine critiques (e.g., feminist theory, [neo]Marxism, critical race theory, queer theory, etc.). Ideally, this content would cut across (if not eliminate the need for) standard academic areas, as such a curriculum is intrinsically no more or less appropriate for social studies or English, for instance, than for math or science. Particular emphasis might be placed on such novel topics as: (1) the study of time and space as "boundless borders"; (2) the "explorative" curriculum; (3) representation; and (4) critical standards-based pedagogy. These areas, however, are neither exhaustive nor mutually exclusive.

The notion of boundless borders at first might seem somewhat illogical, even paradoxical, yet taken literally it makes a certain reasoned and practical sense. For time and space indeed are both boundless and borders. Teachers and students might, therefore, engage time and space as "limitless limits," as the given parameters within which they live and function but also as parameters that are flexible, unstable, and infinite. In other words, teaching and learning might take on time and space both as necessary contexts (i.e., given that human beings are historical beings) and as contexts that have no beginning or end. It is from this perspective that they might enact the thinking of Debord and the SI, explore the creation and interpretation of images and counterimages, appropriate time and space for their own uses, and pursue the implications of radically democratic social and pedagogical change.

The second possibility, the "explorative" curriculum, takes seriously the abilities of teachers and students as thinking, creative, and active persons. It assumes and accepts the desirability of their finding, formulating, choosing, moving through, and revising the curriculum for themselves. It encourages classroom groups and individuals to move, to go toward what attracts them and away from what repulses them. It perceives the curriculum as multidimensional and multi-environmental, so that individuals might wander or drift through its variously conceived milieus. They might progress, therefore, in and out of such curricular elements as the traditional (e.g., books, standards, etc.), the non-traditional (e.g., examples of popular culture), and the circumstantial, that is the physical, the technological, the formal academic, the artistic, and the personal/social. Accordingly, teachers and students might here consider the relationships between their experiences of schooling and their experiences of everyday life. Such explorativity might further enable them to pursue the selective production, distribution, and consumption of selective representations and their selective and constructed meanings.

Perhaps too obviously, the curriculum also must include the critical examination of representation—what representations are, why they exist, how they are chosen, what they mean, and how and why and by whom they are produced, distributed, and consumed. This examination would be twofold—critical and creative—so that teachers and students not only critique representation(s) but in addition construct and interpret their own (counter)representations. Such study, of course, might well draw and build upon the perspectives we delineated in chapters two and five—cultural studies/popular culture, media studies, the study of visual culture, and film studies, and the theoretical views of Bakhtin, Barthes, Baudrillard, Boorstin, and McLuhan. In any event, such a curriculum would have to be fluid, dynamic, complex, situated, and subjectively and democratically created—in constant motion.

Critical standards-based pedagogy takes as its starting point the principle that in contemporary schooling a certain set of rules and a certain dominant game have been sanctioned as official and as governing. While this is no doubt true for other times and places as well, as each given period and loca-tion legitimates is own peculiar set of rules and games (rather like Foucault's *episteme*), today it may be even more pertinent and influential than ever be-fore. What dominates today is SBER, a system that from our vantage point frequently and unfairly differentiates, punishes, and privileges based on race, ethnicity, class, power, language, geography, religion, gender, and sexuality. It risks, therefore, becoming or being anti-democratic, oppressive, inauthen-tic, and individualistic or competitive, and thereby warranting a most forceful and directed resistance.

Two options apparently exist. First, we could play the established game but change the rules. Second, we could use the established rules but play a different game. Either way the dominant system, its resultant representations, and any inferences that could be drawn between the two would be altered. Classrooms could, for instance, technically follow the provisions of SBER/NCLB (the established game) yet do so pursuant to their own self-instituted rules. Deliberately answering high-stakes standardized test questions incor-rectly provides a case in point, one that students in some schools and school districts have enacted, one that subverts the one-sided and asymmetrically powered image machine that unjustly privileges some children and punishes others (i.e., how would administrators, corporate leaders, and politicians be able to use media-reported test scores to distinguish "good" schools/teach-ers/students/parents from "bad" schools/teachers/students/parents or to re-ward them differentially if differences in test scores, associated as they so often and prejudicially are with race, class, gender, language, culture, dis-ability, and so on, disappear?). Even more interestingly, though, students could be taught content standards and tested on them in classes other than those for which such standards and testing mechanisms were developed. Consider the possibilities of using mathematics curriculum standards to teach social studies, or social studies curriculum standards to teach math. Consider standardized math tests as a way of assessing social studies, or vice versa. Such processes surely would work to resist any negative effects of image-based pedagogy and would almost certainly render virtually meaningless and uninterpretable any representations built by way of traditional educational ideologies. But even more importantly, such exercises would if nothing else (1) help students build and feel solidarity—collectivity—with less privileged peers and communities; and (2) demonstrate to all interested stakeholders the sometimes artificial and arbitrary nature of subject area distinctions and sepa-rations among educational purpose, curriculum, instruction, policy, and as-sessment.

Although we have introduced here a number of instructional tactics and strategies, we have made no claim to exhaustiveness or prescription. We encourage creativity, multiplicity, variability, individuality, and situatedness. While those that we have identified may well be unrealistic or too radical for many people concerned with schooling today, they are not, we believe, undoable or without a great measure of pedagogical worth. In sum, we have considered: critical media pedagogy, *la perruque,* Foucauldian resistance, *dérive,* and *detournement.* What these have in common are a commitment to the lived experiences of teachers and students, maximized democracy, the leveling of power, connectedness, and individual and community-located autonomy. They see that image-resistant pedagogy can never be coercive or static; it can never be a one-shot enterprise.

Finally, assessment, currently one of the most controversial issues surrounding public schooling. Although no single method would universally and uniformly suffice, clearly some are more relevant than others to the particulars of image and education. Generally speaking, these means of assessment might well be influenced by a number of germane assumptions, namely:

1. Assessments should be democratically and inclusively chosen;
2. School success can mean different things in different situations and for different teachers, students, and communities;
3. Multiple assessments and types of assessment should be used—they may, in fact, fluctuate with time, place, and individual; they should reflect individual, academic, and cultural differences;
4. Assessments should not be used to rank competitively; and
5. Modes of assessment should be numerous, varied, contingent, localized, and authentic—that is, as "real-world" oriented as possible.

For our purposes they should, of course, reflect the image-related imperative to critique and create. They should proceed in a manner as consistent with democracy, authenticity, and the collective good as possible, and in as potent a measure of hostility to oppression as feasible. One possible application might be the utilization of Sholle's take on media systems modeling (see preceding discussion), "assessed," perhaps, via peer evaluation or some similarly reflective mechanism.

All of this, of course, would have to take into account the various contexts within which image operates: its functionings in terms of controlling images and image-power; the convergence of surveillance and spectacle; and the implications of globalization, standardization, and technological change. It would compel educators, students, and others interested in schooling to cherish the goals of democracy, authenticity, and the collective good, and to actively confront the many dangers of oppression. It would accept and interrogate the attachment between image and everyday life and the importance of one to the other. In the end, such a transformative pedagogy would necessitate embracing schools as spheres of critique, creativity, social justice, and genuinely lived experience, and as more than simply the formally commissioned means by which to reproduce/reinforce the existing conditions—the status quo—of society.

Notes

An earlier version of portions of this chapter appear in Vinson and Ross (2003).

1. Debord and his colleagues work throughout their discussions of dérive to distinguish it from the better-known concept of Baudelaire's (and Benjamin's and others') flâneur, often defined too literally as one who more or less strolls aimlessly through the streets of a city, but which in fact carries deeper and more complex connotations (e.g., Tester, 1994; White, 2001; see also the Cultural Services of the French Embassy Website at: http://www.frenchculture.org).
2. We recognize that what we describe in this section perhaps holds more relevance for secondary than for elementary education. There is no reason, however, that some variation of these efforts wouldn't work for any level of schooling. We should also add—though we shouldn't have to—that our support for the ideas included in this section in no way means that we somehow don't support teaching children to read and write and to understand mathematics, science, and history, and so on. We know of no one who advocates such an absurd position—not even professors of education, despite the opinions of some conservative commentators.

✿CHAPTER EIGHT

Applications: Popular Film and NCLB/SBER

DURING THE 1980s and 1990s, in the wake of *A Nation at Risk* (National Commission on Excellence in Education, 1983), efforts at school reform took a decidedly new turn, one characterized by three distinct and extraordinary features. The first, what might be called "federalization," began in earnest with the creation by President James E. Carter in 1979 of the US Department of Education. Although the national government had been somewhat involved in education long before this (perhaps most notably during President Lyndon B. Johnson's "Great Society" and through the former Department of Health, Education, and Welfare), especially in the wake of Sputkik and *Brown vs. Board of Education,* until the 1980s and 1990s it clearly remained subordinate to the traditional, arguably constitutional, authority of states and local districts. Although initially a fairly partisan issue (keeping in mind the early commitment of Republican President Ronald R. Reagan to dismantle the Department of Education), by the time of the election of President George W. Bush in 2000, a place for an activist federal education policy had been firmly established and had garnered an impressive level of bipartisan political support.

The second attribute of the "new" school reform involved standards-based educational reform (SBER), and rested on the creation and implementation of "high standards" regarding curriculum (often developed or at least proposed by relevant professional organizations such as the National Council for the Social Studies and the National Council of Teachers of Mathematics), instructional method, assessment, and teacher education. Though technically under the auspices of state governments and state boards of education, the national government increasingly took on greater responsibility for SBER's evolution, execution, enforcement, and effectiveness. Its hallmark was the enactment of mandated, high-stakes, standardized testing.

The third component, "accountability," provided a mechanism—standardized test scores—by which states could punish or reward schools for their performance against the mandated curriculum standards. "Failing" schools would lose money or face state takeover, and their students might fail to graduate, while "successful" schools would gain resources and be held up as models. The public would know whether or not their children's schools were good because test scores would be published in the news media. Increasingly, various privatization schemes—school choice, vouchers, and so on—and a conservative cultural agenda became coupled with accountability frameworks.

Taken together, these three elements of contemporary school reform, federalization, SBER, and accountability, culminated in the most recent federal school policy legislation, the No Child Left Behind Act of 2001 (NCLB).

To some extent, all of this must be read against the "conservative restoration" initiated by the 1980 election of President Reagan and peaking with the 1994 "Republican Revolution" in Congress spearheaded by former Speaker of the House Newt Gingrich. This movement was one in which conservative, supply-side economics merged with the fundamentalist "Christian-values" discourse of groups such as Jerry Falwell's "Moral Majority." Of course Democrats played along. Fearing the loss of what was traditionally "their" issue, education, and being in the minority, they acted so as not to be seen as obstructionist, anti-high standards and academic performance, and/or as simply "tax-and-spenders" opposed to accountability, patriotism, and "real" knowledge. More fundamentally, though, these interrelated reforms sprung from the widespread beliefs that (a) US students weren't learning enough—and, therefore, their teachers weren't teaching enough; (b) poorly performing schools threatened the ability of the US economy to compete in the newly globalizing marketplace; (c) teachers and especially teacher educators were biased toward "liberalism"; and (d) students and schools in the United States generally were underperforming when compared to those in other developed and industrialized countries (especially Germany and Japan).

Simultaneously, a second yet not necessarily unrelated trend (in that, arguably, both were about strengthening the status quo) was taking hold, the rediscovery by Hollywood of teaching and schooling as legitimate, and profitable, subject matter for popular films. Although teaching and schooling had been portrayed in the past (e.g., *Goodbye, Mr. Chips; To Sir, with Love; The Prime of Miss Jean Brodie*), during the 1980s and 1990s education-centered films became a successful and acclaimed growth industry.

In this chapter we have chosen to focus on but two of the films that were produced during this period, *Dead Poets' Society* and *Dangerous Minds*. They were selected because of (a) their ostensibly marked differences in setting, theme, plot, and character, (b) their implied radicalness, and (b) their comparative critical praise.

We consider, in fact, both phenomena, the proliferation of popular film representations of teaching and schooling, namely those offered by *Dead Poets' Society* and *Dangerous Minds,* and NCLB, in terms of several principal and significant themes. First, we pursue the specific images they portray relative to the good teacher, the good student, and the good school, that is, how each of these is depicted in *Dead Poets' Society, Dangerous Minds,* and NCLB. Second, we critique their treatments of race, ethnicity, gender, language, and class. Third, we interpret them via the critical frameworks and theoretical perspectives that we included in chapters two through seven. Fourth, we challenge them according to what we presented earlier as the potential consequences of pedagogical image, specifically anti-democracy, anti-collectivity, disciplinarity, oppression, and inauthenticity. And, fifth, we pursue their implications relative to resistance, in terms both of how resistance is represented within the texts themselves, and how each might be appropriated for a resistance-based pedagogy in the classroom.

We begin with *Dead Poets' Society,* which then serves as a model for our treatment of *Dangerous Minds* and NCLB.

Dead Poets' Society

Dead Poets' Society (Weir, 1989) presents the story of John Keating (played by Robin Williams) as he returns to his alma mater to teach English. Set in 1959, the film takes place at Welton Academy, an elite New England prep/boarding school for boys. The plot revolves around Keating's attempt to turn his students into "Romantics," at least temporarily, through poetry (especially that of Walt Whitman), and his effort to convince them to live life to its fullest—to seize the day, *carpe diem*—to live each day as if it were their last.

The implied importance of Keating's work stems from the fact that at Welton everyday life for students is scheduled, organized, rigorous, and systematic; in a word, boring. The students are, in effect, ripe for Keating's methods. Students do, for the most part, what they are told (though they do engage in certain minor transgressions). Tradition, excellence, discipline, and honor are Welton's "four pillars," and they are strenuously and severely enforced.

Students Neil Perry (played by Robert Sean Leonard), Todd Anderson (played by Ethan Hawke), Charlie Dalton (played by Gale Hansen), and Knox Overstreet (played by Josh Charles), are the most receptive to Keating's project, and each undergoes at least some level of personal transformation under his influence. Anderson, whose brother had earlier been a standout student at Welton, enters school dreadfully shy, and is brought out of his emotional shell when Keating demands that he create a poem from scratch in front of the class. Overstreet takes *carpe diem* literally as encouragement to pursue the attentions of the girlfriend (Ginny Danbury, played by Laura Flynn Boyle) of another student from another school. Dalton enacts Keating's philosophies in the extreme, and becomes the most daring and inventive of the students—even initiating a phone call from God encouraging Headmaster Nolan (played by Norman Lloyd) to accept girls into Welton's student body.

The key conflict, though, involves Neil Perry, whose disciplinarian father (Mr. Perry, played by Kurtwood Smith) insists that he give up all extra-curricular activities in order to devote as much time as possible to his academic studies. Against his father's wishes, however, Perry auditions for, receives, and accepts the part of Puck in Shakespeare's *A Midsummer Night's Dream*. Intent on playing the role, he seeks Keating's advice, which is to talk to his father and to tell him how he feels about the theater. Too scared, Neil instead forges a letter of permission from his father and proceeds to act in the play. His father attends, becomes angry, takes Neil home, and informs him of his decision to withdraw Neil from Welton and to enroll him in a military academy. Convinced that he was good, that he truly could act, Neil commits suicide, (melo)dramatically shooting himself in the nude with his father's revolver. The subsequent investigation leads to Keating's dismissal, and to his students displaying their solidarity with him by climbing on top of their desks and calling him "Captain, My Captain" (his self-proclaimed Whitman-esque nickname).

Image: The Good Teacher, Student, and School

Dead Poets' Society presents clearly a certain perspective on the good teacher, the good student, and the good school. It does so via a series of either/or contrasts. Keating, unquestionably, represents the good teacher, and is implicitly positioned in opposition to most of Welton's faculty, especially its headmaster, Mr. Nolan, himself a former English teacher. The good here means anti-traditionalism, creativity, bucking the system, trying new things, fighting conformity, and forming caring relationships with students. The bad, on the other hand, means discipline and rigor, implementing the established (and "proven") curriculum, homework, memorization, rule-following (enforced by a system of demerits, threats, and beatings), and conformity.

The good student, represented to some degree by Perry, Anderson, Dalton, and Overstreet, is a risk-taker, independent, someone who is open to new ideas, to self-expression, and to the pursuit of freedom and life (though arguably, as we discuss later, Keating's students merely exchange one form of conformity for another). Good students are willing to trust themselves and those who are different and to engage themselves in living for the moment. The bad student, perhaps symbolized by Richard Cameron (played by Dylan Krussman), who "rats" on the Dead Poets, cares only for himself and for his own well being. He is happy simply following the crowd and abiding by what others expect of him.

Welton Academy itself exemplifies the paradigmatic bad school, interestingly in that it simultaneously represents what many people today would see as the ideal good school. Students come and go, nothing changes, tradition and discipline rule. Students sit in rows and columns memorizing formulas and Latin (of course) conjugations; they "behave." That which is new is quickly shut down. Students are expected to care about little more than their grades, their pending Ivy League educations, and their future careers as doctors, lawyers, or businessmen. Enforcement matters, and may even include corporal punishment. In contrast, from the point of view of the film, the good school would be humanistic, existentialist, and Romantic; it would be built around the Keating approach. There would be movement, activity, free thinking, and creative self-expression—a Keating in every classroom.

Race/Ethnicity/Class/Gender/Language

Welton's and *Dead Poets' Society*'s treatment of race, ethnicity, class, language, and gender seems, on the surface, pretty simplistic. And, perhaps, it is. The year is 1959 and Welton is a school attended only by wealthy, white, young men. Period. If any racial or ethnic difference exists at Welton, among faculty as well as students—even with respect to students of the local public school—it is well masked. And, of course, the only language other than English presented at all is Latin. Yet, for all that, there are subtleties and complexities that demand attention.[1]

For instance, why 1959? One might argue that the filmmakers' intent was to produce a movie faithful to a particular time and place, historically accurate. Maybe. Maybe the screenwriter or director or producer or someone was recounting his own high school experiences. Possibly. But suppose, instead, that *Dead Poets' Society* is legitimately fiction, and that what mattered most to the production were the film's particular themes and questions and ideas. Then what? Now why 1959? Why not make the same movie set today, where quite possibly the themes it presents (e.g., the goodness of anti-standardization) would still be relevant?

Why 1959? First, were *Dead Poets' Society* set today in a school similar to Welton, viewers and critics most likely would immediately charge elitism and deplore the film for not existing in the real world (and would also, hopefully, decry the use of corporal punishment). By choosing 1959, the filmmakers do not have to worry about such charges; for 1959 is not, so to speak, the real world, but it is the past, memory (for some), and distant. The year 1959 "allows" the filmmakers to get away with things that they otherwise would have to have addressed. They can ignore the 1960s and that decade's social unrest that so influenced students of later eras. The underlying racism, sexism, and classism can be "dismissed" as "that's just the way things were then." In effect, *Dead Poets' Society*'s racism, sexism, and classism can hide behind its alleged and intended "realism."

The only person of color in the entire film is a cook (one from whom Overstreet actually steals bread). Women, what few appear, are depicted either as sex objects (Ginny Danbury) or as quiet, complacent, and subservient (Mrs. Perry, played by Carla Belver). Clear class distinctions are made between Welton and the public school that Danbury and her boyfriend attend. Students, presumably middle class, from the local public high school have parties, drink, make-out, fight, and play football. Welton students read poetry, study trigonometry, build radios, attend medical school, and compete in rowing.

A similar film could have addressed the experiences of an innovative teacher entering an elite boarding school today, or even an urban public school today. Such an effort might well have been very interesting. But, it could not have so easily overlooked diversity and privilege and the difficult questions such issues raise. *Dead Poets' Society,* in effect, takes the easy way out, and represents sexism, racism, and classism in such a way that it tries to avoid its responsibility for depicting and ultimately reproducing them.

Critique

Surveillance, spectacle, and image. One gets the feeling in watching *Dead Poets' Society* that if surveillance cameras had been more widespread in 1959, Welton Academy surely would have deployed them. Even without them, though, the faculty and administration do their best to see and to watch the students as much as possible (a situation that causes the students to sneak around and to hide). The students engage in the spectacular, both for their own benefit and for the viewers', for example in their re-forming the Dead Poets' Society and holding meetings in a cave, Dalton's phone call from God, and Overstreet's delivering flowers and reciting poetry to Danbury in her classroom. Here, in terms of both surveillance and spectacle, the intentions and outcomes are disciplinary and work to induce, or to try to induce, particular forms of behavior and governmentality.

Throughout the film and its various settings, image clearly matters and mediates many of the relationships we see. From the faculty and administration's commitment that Welton be seen as a first-rate and demanding institution ("better" than the public school), to Overstreet's pursuit of Danbury based almost solely on his physical attraction toward her; from Mr. Perry's relationship with Neil, mediated by Neil's academic (and pointedly not his extracurricular) success as opposed to any real physical or emotional or parental bond, to the students viewing themselves, and wanting to view one another, as special and radical free thinkers; from the headmaster's positioning of young people as objects to be disciplined, to Keating's positioning of them as in need of genuine experience; each of these demonstrates the dedication of the film to the importance and power of image.

Everyday life and technology, globalization, and standardization. With respect to the everyday life of students, Welton Academy makes two things clear: first, its purpose is to reproduce society as it exists (especially vis-à-vis class, race, language, and sex/gender), and second, that in order to live authentically, to seize the day/*carpe diem,* one needs to escape the confines of formal schooling (e.g., to party with the public school students, to hold poetry reading meetings in caves).

The film also demonstrates the differential between strategies and tactics, with strategies being the tools of the relatively powerful (e.g., Headmaster Nolan having students recite Welton's four pillars), and tactics being the tools of the relatively powerless (e.g., smoking, building forbidden radios, planning Dead Poets' Society meetings, etc.). It demonstrates that the everyday life of schooling is indeed alienating—disconnected from individual students and their interests and desires—and suggests, problematically, that the proper response, and the "real" meaning of schooling, should involve individual, psychological, and subjective transformation rather than social, political, economic, and objective revolution.

That the movie's setting is 1959 also, as is the case with race, sex/gender, language, and class, "allows" *Dead Poets' Society* to ignore the implications of globalization, contemporary technological change, and standardization, although Welton appears to encourage standardization above all else. Though only speculative, we can assume that the faculty and administration of Welton, for the most part, would have supported NCLB/SBER and vouchers/choice/privatization.

The visual—critical frameworks. The critical frameworks explored in chapter two, namely visual culture/studies, cultural studies/popular culture, media studies, and film studies, provide two key points of critical entry. First, they encourage certain forms of critical understanding; they discourage, in other words, knee-jerk and unreflective responses. Second, they imply various modes of action, or practice, relevant to contemporary schooling and to curriculum, instruction, and policy.

The study of visual culture proposes that *Dead Poets' Society* and any other popular film be interpreted as "contested terrain," that popular images reflect the competitive viewpoints of specifically interested individuals. Thus, although viewers might respond viscerally to the movie—"I really liked it" or "Mr. Keating was great"—a more meaningful perspective would require that audience members consider those responsible for creating, and financing, the film and to delve into the degree to which only certain positions were forcefully represented (e.g., those of the powerful) and to ask "Why?" and "Whose?" Further, interpreting *Dead Poets' Society* critically means considering how the viewer and the viewed are connected. What is the film trying to say to and/or about us? Why?

As praxis, visual studies speaks to the possibility of incorporating popular pedagogical images into the curriculum and as tools of classroom instruction. Certainly students could watch *Dead Poets' Society* in class and discuss it, rather like they might now discuss a more traditional literary text. More specifically to this film, however, such a discussion, from the perspective of visual culture, might revolve around questions such as: If one were to make a movie of our classroom, what would it look like? Would it be similar to *Dead Poets' Society?* Why? Who would you want to produce this movie? Who would you want to see it? Would, or could, it really represent what our classroom is like? Why do some people like particular films and others dislike them? Who might most like *Dead Poets' Society?*

Cultural studies and the study of popular culture suggest several themes for critical understanding and critical classroom action. Its concerns, principally, are those of inclusion, hierarchy, everyday life, dominance, voice, and transformation/reproduction. In approaching *Dead Poets' Society* both interpretively and more directly pedagogically, tough questions must be addressed. For instance: Why are all the students and teachers male? Why are they all white? Of all the film's characters, whose opinions seem to be most important? Why? Is this film "realistic"? How does the local public school and its students compare to Welton and its students? Can we (or you as students) relate to it? Is Mr. Keating a good teacher? Would he be successful here and now? Why? Does he want Welton Academy to change? Do you think it will change even though Mr. Keating gets fired? And, of course, should he have gotten fired at all?

Media studies insists first that we be clear that no representation can truly depict any instance of reality accurately. The media always mediate between the image and the viewer. Critically understanding *Dead Poets' Society* and incorporating it into the classroom requires asking questions such as who produced the movie and why? What relations exist between *Dead Poets' Society* and our society? Between *Dead Poets' Society* and US society in 1959? Who most likely watched *Dead Poets' Society* when it was first released, and what do you think different viewers thought of it? Why? We must, from this perspective, see that although the media contribute to our construction of reality, and may even be necessary to it, what they offer us, in fact, is ultimately skewed and warped.

Lastly, film studies encourages viewing *Dead Poets' Society* relative both to its aesthetic dimensions and to its socio-ideological contexts. We must ask, therefore, questions about the film's accuracy and quality and about its messages and their meanings. Such questions might include: Did the story make sense? Was it authentic or credible? Was the acting good? Would you like to have attended Welton? Would you have even been allowed to? What would you think of such a school if one like Welton existed here today?

In the end, we must as viewers and as educators ask why we feel the way we do about particular pedagogical representations. If we initially liked *Dead Poets' Society,* do we still? And, how might we (re)consider what it means?

Theories of image. The ideas of Bakhtin, Barthes, Boorstin, Baudrillard, and McLuhan, as presented in chapter five, offer unique and potentially useful insights into critically understanding the meanings and implications of pedagogical images—here, obviously, *Dead Poets' Society*. Although, admittedly, some of these are more relevant to popular film than others, each still provides at least some understanding that might assist interested stakeholders in interpreting and responding to specific representations.

Bakhtin's chronotope asks viewers to consider the peculiar relationships between space and time implicit in any given image, as well as how, and to what extent, space and time merge and exist as an explicit character. How do the time and place within which *Dead Poets' Society* is set influence our understanding of the film? For instance, are we more willing to excuse its treatment or lack of treatment of race, ethnicity, language, gender, and class because of its fusion of 1959 and New England? Are we led to more fully or less fully believe that things change or that they stay consistent? Moreover, how do our and our students' perceptions of this era and this location interact with how they are presented in the film? Again, the key question might be why the producers chose this setting and/or what it would have meant to set the film in a different time and space, such as the here and now. In *Dead Poets' Society* time and geography clearly overlap, even blend, into a specifically stereotypical chronotope. In and of itself, the year 1959 might signify any number of things—the conservative, suburban 1950s; the beginnings of the 1960s civil rights movements; the age of innocence; some idealized "better" time of "the good old days"; the Jim Crow South; and so on. New England might well represent urban Boston, the Red Sox, conservatism, elitism, or something else. But together, the elite New England boarding school of 1959 means, signifies, something, even if that something is different for each of us.

Barthes's rhetoric of the image suggests seeing *Dead Poets' Society* in terms of its linguistic or textual and its symbolic or iconic messages. On the linguistic/textual level, Barthes simply asks that viewers attend to things like what is shown versus what is not shown (an example of what is not shown might be Headmaster Nolan's private discussions with faculty after Perry's suicide) and how the audio text and the visual text work together. (As an interesting pedagogical exercise, students might either watch the film with the sound turned down or listen to the sound without the pictures, and then try to recreate or retell the movie's story; consider here, for instance, the famed differences between television and radio audiences to the Nixon-Kennedy debates.) On the symbolic/iconic level, Barthes intimates that viewers should compare and contrast what is directly stated—that is, the intended and explicit plot—with the film's indirect or even hidden ideology. What is said, for example, versus what is meant or implied? Are there any unintended meanings? Is what is stated, for example that students should "seize the day," the same as what the film (either intentionally or unintentionally) insinuates?

The notion of pseudo-event, Boorstin's philosophy of the image, is, granted, perhaps more appropriate to contemporary public affairs or journalism that it is to popular film. Yet, his grounding of the significance of image in "extravagant expectations" indicates a possible connection. To reiterate, he argues that the contemporary power of image stems from the fact that "[w]e are ruled by extravagant expectations" related to "what the world holds" and "our power to shape the world" (Boorstin, 1961/1992, pp. 4-5). For Boorstin, this means that the world, at least in our perceptions, can provide everything and that we can change the world to meet our complete desires—all of us. Thus, we might ask the extent to which the popularity and success of *Dead Poets' Society* represents our belief (a belief that is almost certainly nonsense) in the possibility and desirability of returning to an idealized and mythical earlier age when things were better (at least for some), if not, in fact, perfect or at least perfectible (again, at least for some).

The notion of simulacrum implies that *Dead Poets' Society*, while aiming to reasonably reflect a particular time, place, and set of events and circumstances, instead reflects a mere legend of some time, place, and set of events and circumstances. *Dead Poets' Society*, then, might reflect a reflection, and/or image an image. And yet, following Baudrillard, our tendency is to see it as authentic and appealing and plausible. More dangerously, our tendency is to idolize it such that we believe its re-creation is possible—even though it itself never existed. Here, Welton and 1959 New England, as represented in the film, is no more than The Land of Oz, Neverland, or Brigadoon.

And finally, for McLuhan, what is important about *Dead Poets' Society*, or any film, is not what it says directly, its particular contents, its plot and themes, but instead the medium and technology of film itself and what it enables. Film here acts as an extension of our senses, and obliterates time and space. *Dead Poets' Society*, in a certain manner, enables us to be somewhere else, in a different space and time, and to peer into it so that we might somehow "know" it. It allows us to associate with a previous generation, and in turn influences how we interact with one another today. It changes the level of human inter-involvement so that we all might have a common, though ideologically constructed, frame of experiential reference.

Consequences

Dead Poets' Society demonstrates clearly Welton-based examples of anti-democracy, disciplinarity, inauthenticity, oppression, and anti-collectivity. Decisions are top-down and authoritarian. Students are coerced, and threatened, into following the norm, into conforming and behaving "properly." They are encouraged not to be themselves, but to be everyone, the Welton archetype. Relationships are hierarchical, and banking education rules. The milieu is one of competition—for grades, Ivy League acceptances, and professional school placements. Even Keating, one might argue, does not support classroom democracy (he still, for example, expects to be the leader, the "Captain," and the principal decision-maker), anti-oppression (he forces Anderson to create), or the collective good (he sees freedom as an individual or psychological choice and experience, not as political, economic, and/or social). The question, of course, is whether Keating truly advocates a genuine transformation, or whether, instead, he advocates merely a parallel mode of disciplinary and reproductive conformity.

Resistance

Undoubtedly a certain mode of resistance is presented in *Dead Poets' Society*. Keating and his students react against the rigidity and conformity inherent in Welton's program (e.g., they rip out pages of textbooks, stand on their desks, smoke, break curfew, etc.). While multiple interpretations of this portrayed resistance are possible, several concerns do emerge. First, what resistance is demonstrated tends to be punished: Keating is fired, Perry commits suicide after being threatened by his father with military school, Dalton is expelled after being physically punished (spanked) by Nolan, and, quite possibly, the remaining Keating supporters among the students will face further official retribution (the movie does not say). There is at best, then, a murky representation of the relationship between resistance and punishment, a representation that is iffy regarding whether resistance actually does, or can do, any good.

Second, although the involved students reinstate the Dead Poets' Society, for the most part resistance involves only individual acts (such as Dalton's phone call from God), hedonism, and critical moments of personal defiance (albeit not without some level of personal growth). Nowhere in the film is privilege challenged or are statements made against racism, sexism (unless one counts Dalton's efforts to integrate Welton without questioning his motives), and/or classism. They, the elite students of Welton, should live freely and creatively and ecstatically, but what about others? Women, the less wealthy, people of color? *Dead Poets' Society* takes no intentional position with respect to collectivity or solidarity. As presumed future leaders, the film implies, if anything, little more than a vague duty among these students grounded in some underdeveloped sense of *noblesse oblige.*

Third, it is less than clear from the movie that resistance, as it presents it, makes any difference. The implication is that although deep inside the students might have experienced some subjective change, overall, post-Keating, things will go back to the way they were. The students will *feel* differently, but will more or less *act* the same. In the long run Welton will not change. Of even greater concern, however, is the extent to which Keating was at all successful. Did his students merely exchange one mode of conformity for another? One power-relationship for another (as in Keating's *forcing* Anderson to create a poem against his will)? Did these students become free thinkers or instead did they simply evolve from a state of "Welton-think" to one of "Keating-think?" And is this good or bad?

We can see, though, in the film, some examples of the kinds of resistance we identified in chapter seven. *La perruque,* for instance, is evidenced in students using "school time" for their own purposes (e.g., building radios, planning Dead Poets' Society meetings, and so on). But, even more importantly, as we also suggested in chapter seven, students and teachers themselves could in fact use *Dead Poets' Society* as a basis for their own enactments of classroom resistance. They could "rewrite" the film, changing settings, dialogue, meanings, and so forth (*detournement*) in some effort to promote, say, democracy or the collective good, even, as it were, to "improve" the film or its meanings. Moreover, and more practically, the movie itself could provide the content for a relatively stimulating and intense pedagogical discussion or project.

In fact, the film lends itself well to various resistance strategies via critical media literacy (as we describe in chapter seven). In that this requires a three-pronged approach of theory construction, critique and creation, and system modeling, a number of possibilities seem warranted. First, and most directly, students could be taught some level of formal media theory and be asked to interpret *Dead Poets' Society* within its framework (perhaps, for example, they could be introduced to an appropriate dose of the theories of image we explore in chapter five). But second, students could be asked to reflect on the film according to their own experiences, their lives, and make sense of it within their own subjective understandings. Here, the content of the film and students' real life knowledge play off one another pedagogically

and philosophically so that students, in effect, become their own media theorists. They could also, of course, react more personally with and against
Dead Poets' Society and critique it based purely on their experiences, without the assistance of formalized theory, based more on their unique and differentially situated understandings of how school works and of the real
world. Perhaps, as well, they could attempt to create their own such movie,
an alternative to *Dead Poets' Society,* about similar or even more pertinent
themes. They might, finally, create an entire system model, one in which
everyone involved in the production, distribution, and consumption of media
images (i.e., from financial backers to audience members) would be role-
played by the students. Again, the underlying goals of this work would be
learning to "read" what roles the media play in terms of creating and perpetuating identities and how to counteract the manipulative and depowering
tendencies of the media in contemporary society (as we indicated in chapter
seven, pp. 140-141).

In any event, it is admittedly somewhat difficult, in the end, not to like
this film, at least a little. Arguably, Keating and his students do what they
can to make the best of a bad situation, and who can argue with that? And,
no doubt, most of Welton's students indeed will go on to become doctors,
lawyers, and business leaders. Perhaps, in this context, Keating's efforts can
be seen as positive, and, hopefully, effectual.

Dangerous Minds

Dangerous Minds (Smith, 1995) presents the experiences of LouAnne
Johnson (played by Michelle Pfeiffer), an ex-Marine who abandoned her
commission in order to become an English teacher in a reputedly tough California high school. Although she is not fully certified, lacking student teaching, she is assigned students who have intimidated their previous teachers to
the point of resignation, and who are considered exceedingly difficult and
unruly, to say the least, by Johnson's colleagues. The story is of her efforts to
"reach" her students, especially via the "Dylan-Dylan" contest and through
various extrinsic rewards (e.g., candy, field trips to amusement parks, visits
home, etc.). Her techniques, simply, involve sweet and tender coercion, pressure, and bribery. Albeit, regardless of any criticisms, she clearly loves her
students and does what she believes is the best she can under the circumstances.

In sum, her story reflects principally her relationships with students Callie Roberts (played by Bruklin Harris), Raul Sanchez (played by Renoly

Santiago), and Emilio Ramirez (played by Wade Dominguez), each of whom struggles with some personal issue and its confrontation or interaction with schooling. Callie becomes pregnant and faces the decision of whether to continue attending her "regular" school; Raul makes a deal with Johnson, promising to graduate (in return for her excusing the debt he accrued by borrowing money from her, very kindly lent, in order to buy a dinner jacket); and Emilio, a class "leader," gets shot and killed, seeking to maintain face in representing himself as a "tough guy." The primary conflict involves whether Johnson will return for a second year (she will), especially given the opposition she encounters on the part of some parents and her ostensibly supportive and mentoring principal, Mr. George Grandey (played by Courtney E. Vance).

Image: The Good Teacher, Student, and School

From the perspective of *Dangerous Minds,* a film based on a true story, the good teacher is tough and hypermasculine, in this case an ex-Marine who uses karate to maintain her class's interest and disciplinary responsiveness. Receiving little real support from her administration, she gives up much of what she learned in "teacher school" (e.g., she laughs out-loud at the book *Assertive Discipline* and at the silliness of writing her students' names on the board, etc.) and dismisses the advice of her "superiors." In this situation, her role, as the good teacher, is twofold: First, to make her students (whom, privately, she refers to as "little bastards") "sit down and shut up"; and second, to make them perform well on the standardized curriculum (and presumably the tests that represent it). But, deep down, she truly does wish that they learn something about poetry, regardless of the official insignificance of this activity as portrayed via the attitude of Mr. Grandey.

The good student, represented especially by Callie, Raul, and Emilio, gives into, and trusts, the demands and requests of his or her teacher (especially if she provides candy and field trips to amusement parks), although not without the teacher somehow striving to deserve, and succeeding in deserving, such cooperation. Within the perspective of the film, *all* students are fundamentally good; they just need appropriate guidance. Even if students are, in fact, unruly or undisciplined, they merit, and can command, the teacher's love, attention, and best efforts. This point is driven home in Johnson's relationship with Callie, who, pregnant, returns to her home school even in the face of oppositional pressures; with Raul, who promises to graduate; and with Emilio, the film's most exceedingly macho character, who supports, and then leads the class to support, however gradually, Johnson's teaching (although, in the end, he is murdered).

Lastly, the good school is one in which students follow teachers' directions, right or wrong. It is one in which teachers and students are brave enough to challenge administrative mandates, but not so brave that they can challenge the official curriculum in its entirety or that students can completely get away with denying the "correctness" of the teacher's program. Good schooling, in the end, is that which is relevant (at least on the surface) and that which contradicts what many if not most principals espouse (in the view of the film).

Race/Ethnicity/Class/Gender/Language

An interesting dichotomy exists within the film between Johnson, a white woman, and her principal, a black man, especially given that most of Johnson's students are African American and Latino/a. On one level, the film, as is the case with many dominant/dominating pedagogical images, offers Johnson as savior, as redeemer, as "white knight," someone who can come in and "rescue" students from the conditions of their lives and educations. Although the principal is African American, and the parents who appear are predominantly African American and Latino/a, the karate-fighting, white, female, uncertified, ex-Marine, new teacher, for some reason, can relate better to the students than can anyone else.

On the surface, the system undoubtedly is biased against Johnson's students. Faculty and administration apparently make little or no effort to get to know the students or to learn anything about their lives (prior, of course, to Johnson's arrival). The implication, a pretty blunt one, is that the faculty and administration believe these children can't learn. Cultural diversity plays almost no role in matters of curriculum and instruction, except when brought up by students themselves; bilingual education is a non-issue, even though a large percentage of the students here come from a bilingual, Spanish and English speaking, background.

Complicating this situation is the fact that the principal is African American and male. For whereas normally it would be relatively easy to complain that the white system is keeping students down, here an African American represents that system. The ideology of the film simply is that the structure of schooling in this specific case so abuses and abandons students that is doesn't matter who runs the school; further, Mr. Grandey, though a "company man," cannot be seen entirely in opposition to his students' best interests—that is, arguably, he has their interests, at least as he perceives them, in mind. What is troubling, though, is that *Dangerous Minds* seems to suggest that education in this setting is a lost cause, and going nowhere, without the intervention of white-Marine-masculinized Johnson. No one cares, that is, before her entrance.

Although Johnson makes many, by her own admission, mistakes, they are somewhat forgiven—or intended to be forgiven—because of her inexperience. This is not, of course, entirely unfair, as nearly all professional educators make rookie mistakes that they would not later want to be held accountable for. On the other hand, she is portrayed as the only truly caring adult in many, though not all, of her students' lives, a certain absurdity, and as the one adult who really knows what is best for these particular kids, especially among their teachers. Yet even her most marked "success," the "Dylan-Dylan" contest, indicates, at best, a degree of social and cultural disconnect. For her one attempt to be most relevant, besides her classroom incorporation of the martial arts, unjustly reduced here merely to fighting, is to tie the ostensibly irrelevant and "formal" poetry of Dylan Thomas (especially his "Do Not Go Gentle into That Good Night") to the "relevant" and more "accessible" poetry of Bob Dylan (especially his "Mr. Tambourine Man"), an endeavor that demonstrates primarily what is meaningful in her own life, the significance of the poetic and lyrical arts for what is important to her, and not any meaningful concern with the experiences, other than death and drugs, of her students (who, as teenagers during the time in which this film is set, *probably* listened to other forms of music). The champion of the Dylan-Dylan contest, Raul, a young, urban Latino student, to all appearances Johnson's favorite is depicted, of course, as unfamiliar with the manners appropriate to dinner at a fine restaurant, his reward for winning. Still, Johnson perseveres, and does take a sincere interest in who her students are.

Critique

Surveillance, spectacle, and image. In *Dangerous Minds,* image permeates, at least at first, just about all publicly enacted social relationships, especially those between perceived (or at least assumed or possible) enemies, students and authority figures (nearly all adults), and strangers. In fact, for the students depicted in this film, image defines a large part of their overall experienced and everyday lives more generally. Usually, the students are quick to present themselves as tough, brave, independent, strong, skeptical, and streetwise—as opposed to their naive and relatively unsophisticated

teachers. Only in the most intimate settings, such as in the case of Raul's private, friendly, and innocent dinner with Johnson, are defensive guards let
down. On some level, the lives of these students parallel those of adolescents
everywhere, through boundaries of time and space, an age cohort for whom
how one appears to oneself and to others matters, and has likely always
mattered, greatly.

In part, this image mediation of social relationships defines spectacular
society as portrayed in *Dangerous Minds.* So too, however, does the fact that
within their complex, dangerous, and demanding environment, these young
people put themselves on display, for example, by fighting, so that they are,
in essence, disciplined—enforcing what to do or how to act, and what not to
do and how not to act—as the few observed by the many. Yet, simultaneously, these students also experience firsthand and pointedly the mechanisms
of disciplinary surveillance, both formally and informally. The school they
attend, for example, is policed by security guards; the regular police force
secures (monitors) the streets where they hangout. Here, then, these kids are
indeed the many observed by the few, disciplined by way of a vast and expansive Panoptic regime, layered. They even, throughout this whole cycle of
surveillance-spectacle-image, spy on one another.

These students' lives are lives of seeing and being seen, or, more accurately, of watching and being watched. They watch themselves, others, their
fronts, their backs, their friends, their enemies, the known, the unknown, the
powerful, and the powerless. Perhaps privileging image, for them, might be
afterall a rational and intentional and necessary skill for survival.

Everyday life and technology, globalization, and standardization. Little
direct mention is made in *Dangerous Minds* of globalization or technology.
Yet, we speculate two relationships. First, the coercive and disciplinary tendencies implied by the film would be even stronger and more apparent were
the film set today, as surveillance cameras and the possibilities of the Internet
are more discernible and more widely available (although, of course, wealth
would be a critical limiting factor). Second, we suggest that one point of the
movie is that Johnson's underlying aim, at least in part, is to enable her students to "rise above their status" and to provide them some opportunity for
"a way out," that is a way to escape their reproductive and nearly predestined
role as nothing more than minor cogs in the globalized capitalist framework.
Yet, no matter what, the film seems to imply that that will ultimately be the
fate (at best) of many of these young people. Regarding standardization,
what we see is a battle between the formal and official mandates of the system (represented by Mr. Grandey) and the alternative and contradictory de-

sires of Johnson, even if her program merely substitutes one form of discipline for another.

We witness the alienation of schooling via everyday life firsthand, as, at least at first (i.e., pre-Johnson), "official" education seems to have very little to do with these students' experiences or with who they are. What they do formally on a daily basis is wholly for someone else. Real communication between the powers that be and the relatively powerless are squelched (e.g., Emilio's attempt to talk with Mr. Grandey). Sanctioned elf-realization is nearly impossible—*My Darling, My Hamburger*, required reading, is too "important" for this. The goal of schooling here, whether intended or not, is to reproduce and perpetuated the system as it exists, the same goal that permeates these students' real lives and their more general existences. The students do try, as in their various attempts to make their school-based time and space their own (maybe or maybe not in reaction to or consistent with their success or failure in making the[ir] streets their own). Both as a class and as individuals, they are pushed down and out, and their lives are determined by others with opposing, and exploitative, interests. In the end, therefore, behaving properly, that is, following the dictates of those who are in charge, the "bosses," is fetishized, and becomes almost the be all and end all of schooling.

The visual—critical frameworks. All in all, *Dangerous Minds* elicits the same types of questions regarding the visual as does *Dead Poets' Society*. In sum, drawing on visual studies, cultural studies, media studies, and film studies, these are

1. Who is represented in the film and who is not? Why?
2. What connections are there between schooling as portrayed in *Dangerous Minds* and those of contemporary teachers and students? Why?
3. Is this film realistic?
4. Is Ms. Johnson a good teacher? Is Mr. Grandey a good principal? Are these students good students? Is this a good school?
5. What viewers would like this film? Dislike it? Why?
6. What roles do race, language, gender, and class play in this film?
7. Who produced this film? What were—or might have been—their intentions?
8. Is this a good film? Why? and
9. What does this film mean?

The point, from these perspectives, is to ask whether or not we can figure out the significance of *Dangerous Minds,* its quality, and whether or not we like it, and why? And, can we move beyond the purely emotional re-

action and toward a theoretically more sophisticated, and critical, interpretation?

   Theories of image. *Dangerous Minds* merges qualitative time and space
into a relatively commonplace chronotopic structure, namely the *contemporary urban*. Within this framework, certain stereotypes are implied that necessitate this unique blending. The contemporary urban is not timeless or intended to be universalizable, as opposed to the 1959 New England prep
school chronotope of *Dead Poets' Society*. It indicates a very particular set of
significant and organized characteristics: poverty, diversity, violence, vic-
timhood, and drugs. It represents a setting of seemingly no escape, yet one
from which individuals can either (a) be rescued by powerful and well-intentioned others, or (b) overcome nearly insurmountable odds, through hard
work, so that they might "rise above" their circumstances and their lives. In
both cases what is clear is that success demands nothing less than Herculean,
one-in-a-million heroics.

   Following Barthes, the textual message of *Dangerous Minds* is certain:
A classroom full of streetwise and overlooked students, abandoned by the
system and seeing no meaningful connections between schooling and their
existences, comes to life following the arrival of Ms. Johnson, a teacher
whose hard work, patience, love, and dedication help the students defeat the
neglect and low expectations of the powers that be so that they might learn,
might come to respect education, and might someday even become deserv-
edly successful—to become more "like us." All they need is the right person.
The iconic message is that these students are going nowhere unless an out-
sider, one who practices tough love and exudes high expectations, comes to
the scene as a savior. Otherwise, these students are condemned to who they
are, to their miserable surroundings, because clearly no one from their own
community cares enough, or is capable enough, to "fix" the way things are.

   In Baudrillard's schematics of simulacra, the question is, in some sense,
one of the relationship between image and reality. Is there a reality behind
the representation proffered by *Dangerous Minds?* What is it? To what extent does *Dangerous Minds* reflect it? Does the film reflect the reality, or
does the reality reflect the film? In our view, *Dangerous Minds* includes a
downright mind-boggling array of cliches and stereotypes, and, deep down,
likely does its very best to perpetuate them.

   Boorstin and McLuhan's works likely hold less relevance here than for,
say, NCLB and SBER. Possibly, Johnson's successes may be read as a
pseudo-even, although that might be stretching it. That the medium is the
message, as is the case with *Dead Poets' Society* as well, implies simply that

what matters most here is the extent to which film-as-mediator enables an ever greater number of outsiders to peer into situations other than their own, and to make judgments.

Consequences

Like *Dead Poets' Society, Dangerous Minds* is plainly less democratic and pro-collectivity and more disciplinary, inauthentic, and oppressive than it at first appears. The image championed by the film is one of Johnson and her students against the world; where the rest of the world is depicted as oppressive, competitive and individualistic, irrelevant, impositional, and conformative, Johnson is portrayed as dedicated to the holistic complexity of her work, and as creating for her students a dynamic environment grounded in community, justice, shared decision making, the real world, and liberation.

Johnson's classroom, however, runs on discipline and conformity, granted of a friendlier sort than that represented by the rest of the school/ school system. Johnson knows what she wants and how to get it—how to make her students do it, through bribes and rewards, but in such a way that her students seem to cooperate willingly and to maintain their respect for and support of her and her methods. The bottom line, though, in this image-dominated setting, is that teaching and learning are anything but democratic. In fact, Johnson's pedagogy is as disciplinary as any, though presumably more caring, as she seems willing to commit to almost anything to convince her students to do what she says, to follow and obey her lead.

In Johnson's favor, though, she does at least try to connect school to the lives of her students more than her colleagues do, or even seem capable of doing. That they like school, and that they perceive its potential links to who they are, in part accounts for Johnson's standing, and eventual popularity, among her students. And, significantly, she does attempt to learn about them, to bond with them, and to get to know their environment. But, again, her one greatest effort at authenticity, besides karate, the Dylan-Dylan contest, reflects more on Johnson's interests, background, and experiences than it does on those of her students.

Dangerous Minds, further, presents nearly all education, at least at this school, aside, of course, from that offered by Johnson, as oppressive, from the perspectives of both Freire and Young. Banking education predominates, and endorses, an official ideology of schooling, an ideology of the powerful, one where a prescribed curriculum and teacher-centered instruction intersect with a view of these students as uneducable and going nowhere, a virtual waste of time. (All of this, of course, is challenged by Johnson.) These students are kept down and denied opportunity not because some person stands constantly above them forcing them to stand in place, but rather because the system itself is structured and maintained to make it happen that way.

In her own mind, Johnson's struggle is collective, and her fight is not only on behalf of her own individual sense of right, but also for what she believes is best for her students. It's us versus them, the good teacher/good students versus the bad administration/bad system. And, clearly from the movie's point of view, Johnson's perspective and efforts are warranted. Yet within her classroom, Johnson has no problem with competition and individualism, with winners and losers—granted, though, a competition of a relatively benign type. The question, fundamentally unsettled throughout most of the film, is whether Johnson is actually looking out for herself (i.e., seeking to improve things for her or to simply implement her ideas instead of those of the establishment) or instead truly engaged in a revolutionary project of emancipation and authenticity via her students and their worlds.

Resistance

A particular version of resistance appears throughout *Dangerous Minds,* the gist of which involves Johnson confronting her principal on her students' behalf. She challenges Mr. Grandey on the official curriculum (suggesting, for instance, the stupidity of *My Darling, My Hamburger* as required reading), on the legitimacy of a non-sanctioned field trip to an amusement park, and on caring more about policy and procedure than children. In one memorable example, one of the film's central scenes, she blames Mr. Grandey and his coldness and inaccessibility for the shooting death of Emilio, who had been turned away by Mr. Grandey for not knocking on his door before entering; Emilio, in this case, attempted to see Mr. Grandey, at Johnson's behest, because he believed his, Emilio's, life to be in danger.

Initially, Johnson's students resist her as "white bread" and as merely an interchangeable part of the system. Only slowly do they come around to her, after a great deal of effort on her part, and only after Emilio begrudgingly takes the initiative and begins to cooperate. In each case, resistance involves a specific leader, someone in charge. What unites the students, and Johnson and her students, seems less a real sense of community, and instead more of a "hang together or hang separately" mindset.

In some ways, schooling exists in *Dangerous Minds* as an extension of the students' streetlife, as a context within which they continue or maintain their non-schooling activities and roles. As such, a peculiar notion of *la perruque* does occur, that is using school time to pursue non-school interests, yet not necessarily always in the direct and intentionally revolutionary manner favored by de Certeau. Similarly, with *dérive* and *detournement,* to the extent that they appear at all, any transformative rationale or pedagogical intent, while they may indeed be there, are never made transparent.

In terms of using *Dangerous Minds* as classroom-based resistance, the same principles apply as we described with respect to *Dead Poets' Society.* In this way, the film, or both films together, can be used to resist anti-democracy, anti-collectivity, disciplinarity, inauthenticity, and oppression via the methods of targeting the concentration of power, critical media literacy, *la perruque, dérive,* and *detournement.*

NCLB/SBER

The No Child Left Behind Act of 2001 represents the culmination of decades of evolving federal involvement in the creation and sanctioning of definitive principles and practices relative to US public schooling. According to the Bush Administration's Executive Summary, the law's chief components are

Increased accountability for States, school districts, and schools; greater choice for parents and students, particularly those attending low-performing schools; more flexibility for States and local educational agencies (LEAs) in the use of Federal education dollars; and a stronger emphasis on reading, especially for our youngest children. ([The] *No Child Left Behind Act of 2001,* 2001, p. 1; see also No Child Left Behind, 2001)

In essence, NCLB fulfills President Bush's, and Secretary of Education Rod Paige's, goal of implementing nationally the educational reforms, test-score based, that characterized the school improvement movement previously enacted in Texas (noting, of course, that prior to the 2000 presidential election Bush and Paige had been governor of Texas and Superintendent of Houston Public Schools, respectively).

Regarding increased accountability:

The NCLB Act will strengthen Title I accountability by requiring States to implement statewide accountability systems covering all public schools and students. These systems must be based on challenging State standards in reading and mathematics, annual testing for all students in grades 3-8, and annual statewide progress objectives ensuring that all groups of students reach proficiency within 12 years.

Assessment results and State progress objectives must be broken out by poverty, race, ethnicity, disability, and limited English proficiency to ensure that no group is left behind. School districts and schools that fail to make adequate yearly progress (AYP) toward statewide proficiency goals will, over time, be subject to improvement, corrective action, and restructuring measures aimed at getting them back on course to meet State standards. Schools that meet or exceed AYP objectives or close achievement gaps will be eligible for State Academic Achievement Awards. ([The] *No Child Left Behind Act of 2001*, 2001, p. 1)

This means, in essence, although the law might sound complicated, that the Administration "knows" what is right, and that it will force schools and school systems to conform to its whims, or else.

In addition, NCLB promises "more choices for parents and students," especially for schools "identified for improvement or corrective action under the 1994 ESEA [*Elementary and Secondary Education Act*] reauthorization" ([The]*No Child Left Behind Act of 2001,* 2001, pp. 1-2). Specifically, the law requires that:

1. students attending low performing schools be provided the opportunity to attend a "better public school," including a public charter school, at LEA expense;
2. students attending "persistently failing schools" be able to use Title I funds to obtain remedial or supplemental education in the public or private sector;
3. LEAs spend up to "20 percent of their Title I allocations to provide school choice and supplemental educational services to eligible students"; and
4. failing schools improve vis-à-vis achievement tests or risk (a) losing students and budgeting and/or (b) operating under state control in terms of "reconstitution under a restructuring plan." (pp. 1-2)

As this indicates, NCLB favors the possibility of using at least some public funding for private educations. Coupled with the Bush Administration's well known disregard for the separation of church and state, and its deep, though somewhat downplayed, support for vouchers and other privatization schemes, and given NCLB's threat of reconstitution, this all suggests a system in which (a) public schools must (even under often unfavorable conditions) out-compete one another or (b) risk being taken over and run directly by the state, a state of affairs that assuredly guarantees an even more coercive and restrictive and problematic framework for public education (even more absurd given that the state itself determines and enforces the criteria by which schools are and will be evaluated).

NCLB also asserts greater flexibility for states and LEAs by building on the "flexibility for accountability" approach established at the 1989 National

Economic Summit between US governors and President George H. W. Bush. The law's principal points here are that:

1. states can transfer up to 50 percent of the funds they receive from the federal Teacher Quality State Grants, Educational Technology, Innovative Programs, and Safe and Drug-Free Schools programs to any one of these programs or to Title I;
2. under the "State Flexibility Demonstration Program" up to 7 states can consolidate their federal education monies in return for entering 5-year "performance agreements" with the Secretary of Education; and
3. up to 80 LEAs can consolidate federal education funds received under the Teacher Quality State Grants, Educational Technology, Innovative Programs, and Safe and Drug-Free Schools programs in return for performance agreements with the Secretary of Education. (p. 2)

What this section implies, though, is less straightforward than NCLB seems to suggest. While in some ways it does offer limited fiscal flexibility, it does so only insofar as states, schools, and local districts willingly, and inflexibly, follow the testing and standardization mandates of the law. The implication, paradoxically, seems to be flexibility as long as you act inflexibly.

A fifth major provision of NCLB emphasizes reading, "putting reading first," and claims to back and expand upon "President Bush's unequivocal commitment to ensuring that every child can read by the end of third grade" (p. 3). This stress on reading includes two significant elements. The first, the "Reading First Initiative," grants, through the Reading First State Grant Program, money to states and LEAs for (1) diagnosis and assessment in order to identify students at-risk for reading failure and (2) K-3 professional teacher development. The second, the Early Reading First Program, provides funding to LEAs for early and preschool literacy education, especially for lower-income students. Its cornerstone, and that of NCLB's orientation toward reading more generally, is the reliance on "scientifically based reading research" as the basis for elementary school curriculum, instruction, assessment, educational policy, and teacher education.

Lastly, NCLB contains several other "miscellaneous" pieces, most notably (1) the combining of the Eisenhower Professional Development and Class Size Reduction Programs into a new Improving Teacher Quality State Grants Program that "focuses on using practices grounded in scientifically based research to prepare, train, and recruit high-quality teachers"; (2) the simplification of English language instruction for limited English proficiency students; and (3) the requirement that students be allowed to transfer out of "persistently dangerous schools" and into "safe schools," with LEAs also responsible for reporting school safety statistics and for using Federal Safe and

Drug-Free Schools and Community "funding to implement drug and violence prevention programs of demonstrated effectiveness" (pp. 3-4).

Image: The Good Teacher, Student, and School

NCLB endorses an overlapping and simplistic vision of the good teacher/student/school. What holds for one holds for the others, and they are inseparable. The good teacher produces students who obtain high test scores, who meet state content standards, especially in reading and math. He or she practices phonics—coded in NCLB as scientifically based research, even though research in whole language can be as "scientific" as anyone could want—implements narrowly defined best practices, and works to help his or her school out-compete other, similarly positioned, schools in the public school marketplace.

Good students, therefore, follow along and take in what official knowledge is taught. They achieve high test scores, meet state standards, and obtain among one another indistinguishable educations. Good students "overcome" differences in race, ethnicity, language, class, and gender; they are non-violent, drug free, and hardworking. And, they can all read identically well by the end of the third grade.

The good school simply is defined as one in which a majority of its students attain high achievement test scores. More subtly, it is as well one that is safe and drug free, and one that can beat other schools on a range of objective measures. Most certainly, the good school would never face restructuring or reconstitution. In fact, once a good school becomes a good school there is never a need to change; it can freeze and stand in place. No more innovation is necessary, so it is free to focus on maintenance, on treading water.

Race/Ethnicity/Class/Gender/Language

NCLB at least makes (in our admittedly most optimistic and idealistic view) some good faith effort to take race, ethnicity, class, and gender seriously. In fact, it goes further, and at least recognizes the fact of linguistic diversity. NCLB's point here is that schools, no matter how "good," will not be allowed to claim success unless their test scores go up across the board, for all identified groups of students, and not just on the aggregate and unqualified levels. In other words, NCLB seeks to guard against labeling schools high performing merely on the basis that their white, English-speaking, wealthy or middle class, and male students so outperform others that their achievement effectively skews the school's overall results.

On the other hand, one must wonder how seriously NCLB, and, therefore, President Bush and Secretary Paige, really takes diversity. NCLB recommends a one-size-fits-all approach to curriculum, instruction, and assessment, and advocates disaggregating test score data simply to ensure that conformity works even more effectively than it might otherwise—that is, to make sure that not only white, wealthy or middle class, native English speaking, and male students are effective and thriving conformers, but that everyone else is as well. Its philosophy, in essence—one consistent with its broader support of increased surveillance—is that the more we know about how someone is different from dominant groups, the better able we will be to erase their identities, to discipline them, and to make them more like us, that is to control them. And, perhaps most remarkably, NCLB makes absolutely no real mention of disability and/or the special needs of students currently receiving special education or inclusion-based services—that is, other than the belief that, through phonics, children will be less likely to be identified as special education solely because they can't read as a result of poor instruction.

Critique

Surveillance, spectacle, and image. NCLB, like SBER more generally, positions teachers, students, and schools as objects of both surveillance and spectacle. They are, here, the many observed by the few *and* the few observed by the many. Social relationships—among teachers, students, parents, administrators, and policymakers—are mediated under NCLB by images, test scores ostensibly representative of education. Teachers, students, and schools exist first within the gaze of administrators (surveillance) who work to promote a specific mode of disciplinary behavior (i.e., teaching to the test). In this case, how they appear to administrators and other powerful educational leaders becomes necessarily a classroom/school concern; for, of course, everyone wants to succeed and to be perceived as successful. Simultaneously, though, teachers, students, and schools exist within the gaze of the larger public (spectacle), principally by way of the media, and are thus on the stage. In some ways they are trapped within the spectacle-surveillance circle, and are led from both directions toward disciplinarity. With all this watching, how one appears becomes crucial. They are "known," regardless of what actually occurs within the everyday settings of classrooms, by how they look, whether they appear to be doing the "right" things (following a mandated curriculum) and whether they appear to be high performing (via media-reported test scores). Throughout, image matters more than authentic classroom experience.

Everyday life and technology, globalization, and standardization. NCLB makes little direct mention of the everyday lives of either students or teachers, other than, of course, the point that some teachers and students are more or less wealthy than others, that some have more or less English proficiency than others, and that drugs and violence are real experiences for some more than for others. All in all, its treatment of lived experience, such as it is, is superficial and generic. Likewise, NCLB says little about technology, except that LEAs and states now have more flexibility in terms of how they spend federal educational technology funding, including whether or not they spend it on educational technology. But, what NCLB clearly does is place schooling and education strongly within the contexts of globalization and standardization, as it takes as its fundamental rationales US economic competition and pedagogical conformity via enforced curriculum, instruction, and assessment standards.

Each of the approaches to everyday life presented in chapter six provides critical insight into NCLB and lived experience. From Vaneigem's (1967/2002) work, we can see, perhaps, NCLB's implication in "power's perspective." We can see, for example, its role in limiting participation in its taking teaching and learning out of the hands of teachers and learners and placing them in the hands of officially designated bureaucrats. We can see NCLB working against communication, where the communicative acts of teaching and learning become more and more totally mediated by the tools of power—test scores. We can, lastly, also see NCLB maneuvering against the possibility of self-realization, as the seductiveness of the system—the potential rewards and benefits of conformity (e.g., merit pay and promotion for teachers, test parties for students, higher property values for parents) draws them into it, reducing the likelihood that those involved will strive for their own subjective or genuine sense of personhood or self-actualization.

Perlman's (1969) emphasis on reproduction, alienation, and fetishism also offers a useful critical perspective on NCLB and everyday life. First, NCLB's reproductive nature rests on its insistence on thwarting change. By playing along, teachers and students in essence work to extend and perpetuate their own oppression, even though through NCLB (and SBER more broadly) they have little to gain in return for their efforts (other than certain of their schools being labeled as failing or, for some, a publicly financed private education). That the process, secondly, is alienating, stems from NCLB's determination to disengage schooling from the experienced lives of teachers and students, such that who teachers and students are as individuals and as members of classes becomes irrelevant. And third, of central importance to the entire NCLB/SBER movement, certain ideas and actions are fetishized, here, especially, accountability, phonics, and testing/test scores. Simply by virtue of their existence, NCLB/SBER supporters presume that schools are better; NCLB/SBER praises accountability and testing as *causing* schooling improvement; it *blames* teachers and students (and, sometimes, other stakeholders) for school failure. Accountability and testing take on a life of their own.

The works of de Certeau (1984), Brown (1973), and Lefebvre (1947/ 1992) perhaps present even more straightforward understandings. de Certeau's distinction between strategy and tactics, for instance, is pertinent here not because NCLB directly addresses it, but because it doesn't. And yet, NCLB clearly is a strategic action on the part of the powerful. Under its mandates, the powerful have identified their place, the "proper," as the location of the development and enforcement of curriculum, instruction, assessment, and related educational policies. They have, the powerful, isolated themselves from the geography of everyday schooling, distinguishing their own space of authority—in, say, central offices or in governmental departments. From this position, they can identify—and have identified—"targets" to be managed for their own hierarchical benefits, namely targets such as teachers, students, and schools (though, more cynically, some might add to this list the poor, racial/ethnic/linguistic minorities, and women). Brown's work provides further awareness of NCLB's relationships to everyday life by way of his focus on both the psychological/subjective and the social/economic/political modes of oppression. The significance of his view stems from its insistence that we see NCLB as impeding both self-actualization and self-growth and social and economic transformation and equality. NCLB inhibits both individuals (e.g., in denying teachers and students freedom) and social and economic classes (e.g., in leaving lower test-scoring schools and localities behind). And lastly, Lefebvre's stress on the strength and importance of alienation encourages a view of NCLB as placing the labor of some under the control and profit of others. Under NCLB, teachers and students have next to no autonomy with respect to their own work; their classroom lives are determined by others. Yet, the fruits of their labor go toward rewarding those external to the classroom, for instance in reelection campaigns and claims that power-laden policies, as opposed to teachers and students themselves, are working.

The visual—critical frameworks. Visual studies/visual culture, cultural studies/popular culture, media studies, and film studies imply the same questions for NCLB that they do for *Dead Poets' Society* and *Dangerous Minds*, though granting that, obviously, film studies offers fewer relevant insights. We must ask—teachers, students, and concerned citizens: (1) Whose views get represented? (2) To what extent is NCLB inclusive and not exclusive? (3) Is NCLB realistic? What does this mean? (4) Is NCLB more supportive of social change or social reproduction? (5) Under NCLB, who benefits most? (6) Who created and sanctioned NCLB, and why? (7) How does NCLB meld with our own views of public schooling, both positive and negative? and (8) What might the effects, outcomes, or consequences of NCLB be? As we hope we've made clear, our own view is that NCLB, and SBER more generally, unfairly privileges some over others, represents primarily the interests of the relatively powerful, presents an idealized view of public schooling, supports social and economic reproduction, benefits the economically and politically powerful, and risks the consequences of anti-democracy, anti-collectivity, inauthenticity, disciplinarity, and oppression. To say the least, regarding NCLB, we are not impressed.

Theories of image. In terms of Bakhtin's chronotope, first, it must be noted that Bush and Paige's NCLB does not at all mention time and space. Yet, it does have pertinent implications. What NCLB seeks is a universalization, or transcendence, of time and space, one that attempts to "invisible-ize" their causes and effects and interactions. From the NCLB perspective, what works works, and has always worked and will always work, regardless of specific locations, eras, and/or relativities.

Barthes's rhetoric of the image questions the relationship between what is said (directly) and what is meant (indirectly). Regarding NCLB, what is said is: "Since we want no child left behind, we need to have greater accountability. We are willing to grant states and local districts flexibility, but only in return for efforts that might produce higher test scores." But, what NCLB means is: "We are in charge. Do what we say or else. If you are willing to do what we say, we will give you *some* flexibility with respect to funding, but no more than that. If you are not willing to do what we say, we will take over your schools, relieve you of your students, and/or punish you financially." In effect, NCLB is a disciplinary archetype, a paradigm of power, coercion, and enforced conformity.

Perhaps Boorstin's notion of pseudo-event presents the most striking critique potential of any of these theories of image. If we consider his characteristics of a pseudo-event, then we see its possibilities as a framework for critically understanding NCLB. To paraphrase, a pseudo-event is planned or planted (that is, non-spontaneous) for the singular purpose of being reported or reproduced. It is only ambiguously at best related to the reality of the situation it seeks to characterize, interpret, or respond to. A pseudo-event, moreover, is intended to be a self-fulfilling prophecy (see chapter five, pp. 98-100). According to Boorstin, pseudo-events trump real events because, basically, pseudo-events are more dramatic and easier to disseminate and repeat than are real events. They succeed, further, because someone has a financial or power-based stake in their success. Lastly, they are more intelligible and convenient than reality, and are planned to be so. "Knowing" the pseudo-event means being well informed and up on the issue, a process that becomes even easier as pseudo-events engender even more pseudo-events.

Simply, NCLB is a pseudo-event. It was unquestionably planned for reporting, reproduction, and intelligibility, hence its sloganish name, No Child Left Behind—Who can forget that? Is it related to reality, most likely not, but who knows? The point, and Boorstin's message, is that it really matters very little. It will "succeed" because it was designed to be self-fulfilling: President Bush and Secretary Paige can now say that "we" are leaving fewer, if any, children behind because NCLB is in place. And, people will believe that; it will become "fact." Most people probably can't describe the features of their state or district's curriculum standards or assessment program. But they "know" they are good and necessary and beneficial. They "know" what schools are good or bad, whether or not they have even been in any of them. And, though they probably don't know the details, they "know" No Child Left Behind is the president's law, and that he cares about children, schooling, high-standards, effective teaching, and accountability. We can, then, almost guarantee that in the 2004 election campaign, the Bush Administration will "prove" its program is working; Bush will again be the "education president."

Baudrillard's simulacrum and McLuhan's "the medium is the message" are, in this specific case, more forthright than the other perspectives. Simulacra are copies of copies, representations without originals. And, deep down, that's what NCLB presents. Underlying NCLB is the idealized notion that today schools are bad, but they used to be good (i.e., "Back when I was a kid..."). It is, in short, a conservative enterprise. Bush and Paige's intentions are to return to a time that never existed, or, perhaps more accurately, never left. Their story? "In the good old days, teachers worked hard, used appropriate methods, and taught real content. They knew if their students learned anything because they tested them, frequently and rigorously. They practiced tough love, and punished kids when they misbehaved. But at some point, we lost our way. Today's classrooms are too touchy-feely, anti-American, and multicultural; nobody teaches kids how to read, write, or calculate, and nobody teaches them the basics of history, science, civics, and geography. *That's* why we need NCLB." The problem, though, is that, arguably, today's schools are better than ever (e.g., Berliner & Biddle, 1995). More children learn more stuff and graduate and go on to college and so on than at any other point in US history. Chances are, more contemporary schools are the way Bush and Paige remember from times past than they care to admit. There was never, however, a period of perfect schooling, nor will there ever be. And, most likely, what Bush and Paige want already exists to too great and expansive an extent. As such, NCLB will probably improve things very little.

That the medium is the message, with respect to NCLB, means simply that the multiplication of test scores, accountability schemes, and so on, wrestles with the demand, so to speak, to propagate them. McLuhan's insights suggest that what matters most about NCLB is the improved or increased ability of the American public to peer into schools. More people can look into schooling more frequently, more disciplinarily, and more effectively. Surveillance, spectacle, and image—that is the medium's (or the media's) message; they are also the message's medium (or media).

Overall, then, what NCLB enables is a focus on appearance over reality, one that privileges how teaching, learning, and schooling seem over how they are. As we have maintained, however, there are several, many, problematics entwined within this dangerous state of affairs, so that what NCLB claims is not necessarily or entirely what it means, or even what it *might* mean. The consequences of the entire regime, NCLB and SBER more broadly, as we have discussed, are crucial.

Consequences

From our standpoint, NCLB must be read within the larger context of SBER and within the present and dominant conservative-inspired but bipartisan will to standardize. As we have argued here (see chapter four) and elsewhere (e.g., Ross, 2000; Vinson, 1999, 2001a, 2001c; Vinson, Gibson, & Ross, 2001; Vinson & Ross, 2001a, 2001b, 2001c, 2001d, 2001e, 2003), these post-*A Nation at Risk* settings encourage such disciplinary consequences as anti-democracy, anti-collectivity, oppression, and inauthenticity. Moreover, NCLB's emphasis on standardized testing (especially high-stakes testing) not only endangers any connected and meaningful education, but also, perhaps ironically, threatens, in fact, to leave some children behind (Haney, 2000; Kohn, 2000; McNeil, 2000; Ohanian, 1999; Ollman, 2001; Popham, 2001).

NCLB is anti-democratic in that it imposes, with little opportunity for alternatives, a top-down system of schooling masquerading as a state and locally controlled program; those responsible for its operations pay too little attention to grassroots views. It is anti-the collective good in its emphasis on competition and its implied individualism. Its oppressive character appears in both its support for banking education and its underlying grounding in reproductive powerlessness (i.e., teachers and students are forbidden to speak for themselves) and cultural imperialism (i.e., the demand that all teachers, students, and schools obey the mandate for Americanization and uniformity). NCLB's inauthenticity springs from its refusal to take seriously the lived experiences, the everyday lives, of teachers and students. Overall, it only hints at freedom and choice, its self-proclaimed objectives, while actually and powerfully inducing an outcome of disciplinary and strict conformity.

Resistance

In all actuality, the very idea of resistance is moot with respect to the official textualization of NCLB. For despite Bush's rhetoric, in all its manifestations, the law is nothing if not reinforcing of the dominant and hegemonic status quo. For most certainly, NCLB was designed, ratified, and actualized with the straightforward intention to squelch any and all opposition that might surface and that might challenge its disciplinary preeminence. NCLB is, in fact, tantamount to the pure and perfect Panoptic regime of truth (see Foucault, 1980; Gore, 1993). Both ethically and politically, NCLB was designed to be implemented with no real oppositional counterforce, no contrary presence, allowed. With its enforcement mechanisms and fiscal self-empowerment, frankly it leaves educators, schools, and educational leaders no choice but to conform. Reproduction, in fact, seems the only reasonable and responsible interpretive framework. Still, the modes of classroom resistance addressed in chapter seven seem perfectly pertinent and more than appropriately applicable.

La perruque would mean, of course, using testing time, or time formally designated for teaching and learning the prescribed curriculum, for other things—perhaps researching or even protesting the state testing regime, or, less dramatically, pursuing more personally meaningful pedagogical (in the broadest sense) projects. The *dérive,* drifting, might invite students and teachers to wander—informally and whimsically—through other classrooms, or possibly outside the school, observing and feeling the effects of standardization, if not emphatically escaping them, following psychological and geographical sentiments as particular attractions emerged. *Detournement* would involve recreating or reconstituting curriculum standards and/or test questions or answers, in a "propagandistic" way, so to speak. It might also include "playing" with sanctioned teaching methods. For example, instructors and older students might *detourn* phonics by using it as a system to teach pig Latin. Lastly, with respect to Foucault, students and teachers might resist most directly by inquiring into the relationships between power and knowledge—Who is able to design and implement curriculum and testing standards? and What is the relationship between their interests and what counts as genuine and official knowledge?

In the end, and most fundamentally, the overall points of any resistance mechanism would be questioning, critique, and response. More specifically, the goal would be to approach NCLB democratically (i.e., involving as many people as possible in making decisions about curriculum, instruction, and assessment), collectively (i.e., with solidarity between higher scorers and lower scorers, especially if information regarding language, gender, class, race, and ethnic differences were discerned), anti-oppressively (i.e., fighting banking education, working against cultural imperialism, exploitation, violence, and so forth), and authentically (i.e., taking into account the real lives and lived experiences, similarities as well as differences, of teachers, students, and communities). For at the heart of NCLB rests a reform program grounded in the hegemony of the image, how teachers, students, and schools appear. And, as such, it must be challenged if not ultimately overturned or overthrown.

Conclusions

What these examples demonstrate, hopefully, is, first of all, the power of pedagogical images. For as we contend, they say a great deal, even more than we can possibly discuss in this format, relative to visual culture (writ broadly), surveillance and spectacle, understanding representation, everyday life, and classroom-based and other educational resistance. Second, again hopefully, they demonstrate how, to what extent, and the ways in which particular images might not "mean what they say," or how, to what extent, and the ways in which particular images might not "say what they mean," or, in fact, how such images end up saying more than they intend to or other than they intend to. Our point, most simply, is that understanding image and education is tougher than it might at first seem.

What we've attempted in terms of *Dead Poets' Society, Dangerous Minds,* and NCLB is appropriate, of course, for other representations, especially those now overwhelming the popular media. And, obviously, our efforts need not be confined solely to schooling and education, but may, in fact, hold wider and deeper meanings relative to other popular depictions (e.g., of the war against Iraq). Nevertheless, we hope, throughout the entire course of this book, to have at least encouraged questioning, critique, and doubt, and that we have, in the end, inspired further spirited investigation into some of the most important educational questions of our time.

Notes

1.   We acknowledge here the work of Carton (1989).

CHAPTER NINE

Summary and Conclusions: "So What?" and "What Now?"

> *A media culture has emerged in which sounds...and spectacles...help produce the fabric of our everyday life. Radio, television, film, and the other products of the cultural industries provide the materials out of which we forge our very identities, our sense of selfhood, our notion of what it means to be male or female, of sexuality, our sense of class, of ethnicity and race, of nationality, of "us" and "them." Media images help shape our view of the world and our deepest values: what we consider good or bad, positive or negative, moral or evil. Media stories provide the symbols and resources through which we constitute a common culture and through the appropriation of which we insert ourselves into this culture. Media spectacles demonstrate who has power and who is powerless, who is allowed to exercise force and violence, and who is not. They dramatize and legitimate the power of the forces that be and show the powerless that they must stay in their places or be destroyed.* (Kellner, 1995, p. xiii)

> *Unmistakably, reproduction as offered by picture magazines and newsreels differs from the image seen by the unarmed eye. Uniqueness and permanence are as closely linked in the latter as are transitoriness and reproducibility in the former. To pry an object from its shell, to destroy its aura, is the mark of a perception whose "sense of the universal equality of things" has increased to such a degree that it extracts it even from a unique object by means of reproduction. Thus is manifested in the field of perception what in the theoretical sphere is noticeable in the increasing importance of statistics. The adjustment of reality to the masses and of the masses to reality is a process of unlimited scope, as much for thinking as for perception.* (Benjamin, n.d.; see also Leslie, n.d.)

> *Far and away the creepiest new toy theme, though, is snooping. An outfit called Wild Planet is bringing out an entire line of spy gear for kids. The products include a motion sensor, a metal detector, a tracking device with perimeter alerts and a gizmo that looks like a portable CD player with earphones but is actually a listening device that can pick up conversations from the other end of the lunchroom. Wild Planet is marketing this one specifically for girls—on the assumption, presumably, that they talk about one another more than boys do—but surely it would appeal to*

most reasonably paranoid preteens, which is to say just about any seventh grader you can think of. (McGrath, 2003, p. 15)

IMAGE. PERHAPS NO TERM better represents the defining characteristic of the modern, or postmodern, age. Seeing and being seen, surveillance and spectacle, exhibitionism and voyeurism, our contemporary society, our social institutions, and our culture—everyone and everything—all today seem intent on watching, being watched, and disciplining through/being disciplined by the visual. Contemporary schooling, for better or worse, is no exception.

For some people, no doubt, this is good. For, the argument might go, we live in an age of terrorist threat and the continuous prospect of ongoing war. So, after all, what else can we do? We must watch, we must remain vigilant, even at the expense of some loss of privacy, lest we suffer a repeat of the tragic events of 9/11. For others, though, our commitment to surveillance within the society of the spectacle, the privileging of image, does indeed pose enormous threats to our ways of being, to the "American" way of life, and to our idealistic traditions of civil rights, liberty and equality, social justice, and civil liberties.

Yet either way, this situation, surveillance and spectacle and so on, pervades our society, and constitutes one critical way of characterizing the vast and fluid setting within which contemporary schooling operates.

Throughout this book we have sought answers to a number of difficult and complex questions. We have attempted to: (1) demonstrate the importance of pedagogical image(s)—especially via popular film and the No Child Left Behind Act (NCLB)/standards-based educational reform (SBER); (2) provide and explicate various ways of understanding—critically theorizing—image, including those suggested by the fields of visual studies/visual culture, popular culture/cultural studies, media studies, and film studies, and the orientations offered by Bakhtin, Barthes, Boorstin, Baudrillard, and McLuhan; (3) contextualize image according to the increasingly important settings of surveillance, spectacle, and surveillance-spectacle; (4) place image (and surveillance and spectacle) within the contemporary political geographies of technological change, standardization, and globalization; (5) explore the relationships between image (pedagogical and social), schooling, and everyday life; (6) interpret specific examples of pedagogical images, namely *Dead Poets' Society, Dangerous Minds,* and NCLB/SBER; and (7) consider plausible means of resistance (i.e., as classroom praxis; e.g., critical media literacy, *la perruque,* Foucauldian resistance, *dérive,* and *detournement*) to the possible negative consequences (e.g., anti-democracy, anti-collectivity, oppression, disciplinarity, and inauthenticity) of pedagogical image, especially vis-à-vis our conceptions of image-power and controlling images.

In this chapter, our specific questions, though, are "So What?" and "What Now?" That is, we pursue the potential significance, if any, of our work and what work still remains relative to image and education and to the meanings, settings, and mechanisms of its multiple, dynamic, shifting, and complicated functionings.

"So What?"

As the Kellner (1995) quote with which we began this chapter indicates, ours is a society of image. Today it is almost impossible in the course of our quotidian and everyday existence not to confront some capital/power-laden representation or another that claims to tell us either how we are or how we should or should not be. For image pervades the entirety of our social fabric, our social institutions, our (multi)cultural settings and actions, and our politics, economics, and ideologies. Certainly schools are no exception. What we think, what we know, what we think we know, and why and how, are all influenced by, if not, in fact, in part *determined* by, the omnipresent interplay among images, power, and relevant pedagogical/everyday experiences. Thus, to the extent that Kellner, and that we, are correct, understanding society— including schools and schooling—demands that we understand image.

We must, for instance, understand the contexts within which images are produced, distributed, consumed, manipulated, perpetuated, acted upon, and revised. We must do so so that we might acquire at least some insight into the processes by which certain images come to dominate and others fall by the wayside (or are actively squelched). We must explore the continuing— the evolving and strengthening—workings of surveillance and spectacle, and the contexts within which the image-surveillance-spectacle triad operates to the benefit of some groups and individuals and the detriment of others. Such contexts, as we have suggested, include technological change, what we have called the standardization imperative or the will to standardize, and globalization. To the extent that these surround the workings of schooling, and they do and apparently will continue to do so, *and* to the extent that they, therefore, influence and will continue to influence the practices of schooling as they do all social institutions, they are important, and must be viewed as legitimate. For today, given the present NCLB/SBER-based climate of nationalized school "improvement," the proliferation of TV/film representations of teaching and learning, the post-9/11 spread of fear and inspection-grounded regimes, the predominance of the standardized test score, and the hegemony of accountability as a movement, the disciplinary gaze, seeing and being seen, watching and being watched, matter and will persist in their risky and conformative power.

The links among schooling, image, and everyday life, and economics, politics, and culture, also in part help explain the possible significance of this study. For everyday life is increasingly surrounded by images; images and the theory and practice of everyday life infiltrate one another on a nearly nonstop basis. And as schooling and everyday life, like image and everyday life, also are intertwined, and given the recent preponderance of media images pertinent to schooling, how these forces interact and pervade the positions and existences of one another is crucial. It is imperative, then, that we take seriously meanings, critiques, interpretations of, and reactions to image, everyday life, and schooling as a dynamically constructed and ultimately powerful complex. For although their various connections are difficult, even confusing, comprehending their interworkings is essential to comprehending twenty-first-century US schooling. In the present age, one in which standardization, globalization, and technological change—all of which work to privilege, and in return are privileged by, the visual, which all together make possible and desirable the power of surveillance, spectacle, and image—we must maintain our commitment to grasp and to challenge the processes of image production, distribution, consumption, perpetuation, manipulation, and resistance.

As Kellner (1995) argues, and as we concur, the images propagated by the contemporary media make a lot of difference in how we live our lives—how we make sense of the world, how we identify and distinguish good and bad, how we name friends and enemies, and how we portray, define, and react to instances of power. They affect, if not limit and repress, our very identities and our senses of who we are. As with everyday life and the range of our social institutions, so it is with schools and schooling.

"What Now?"

Clearly, a great deal of work is still needed. On both the empirical (qualitative and quantitative) and theoretical/philosophical planes, our project remains, perhaps necessarily, incomplete.

We need, for instance, more information on the causes and effects of specific images—what leads to their creation and what contributes to their particular and situated impacts. Moreover, we need concrete data on the problematics of pedagogical image, both those we have specified as negative and troubling—those we named anti-democracy, anti-collectivity, oppression, inauthenticity, disciplinarity—and potentially others. Scholars, further, should pursue—again, theoretically as well as empirically—the various contexts within which relevant images operate, those of surveillance, spectacle, technological change, globalization, and standardization, of course, but also others, those that have yet to be identified and/or even fully investigated.

Perhaps most importantly, most fundamentally, educators must investigate the importance of pedagogical image relative to its impact on and connection to—its complicity in—schooling's purpose; the design, development, implementation, and interpretation of curriculum; the privileging of explicit instructional methodologies and theories; assessment; and the creation, development, and elaboration of public school policy.

In short, further research should seek data related to the following questions:

1. What is the relationship between images of education and the practice of education? Productive? Reproductive? Enforcing? Reinforcing?
2. How, if at all, do dominant/dominating images influence schooling? How are these images, in turn, influenced by schooling, if at all?
3. What role do image-based education reform movements (e.g., SBER) and popular media representations of schooling play relative to purpose, curriculum, instruction, assessment, and policy?
4. To what extent does image mediate the connections between schooling and everyday life? To what effects? What does this mean?
5. What images and image-systems matter most?
6. What are the consequences of pedagogical images? How sufficient is our own interpretation of anti-democracy, anti-collectivity, oppression, inauthenticity, and disciplinarity? To the extent that negative consequences do exist, how might they effectively be resisted? and
7. How might we as scholars, practitioners, teachers, students, policymakers, and concerned citizens better understand the potential importance of image and education? What should we do?

At the very least, the future study of image and education requires (1) theoretical rebuttal, expansion, or validation of what we have thusfar done, and (2) empirical data either demonstrating or building upon or refuting the soundness of our speculations and critical perspectives. Perhaps most of all, at least at this point, we need questions to be asked and re-asked, and answers to be rigorously pursued.

If nothing else, we hope we have encouraged others—educators, scholars, activists—to take pedagogical image seriously, in terms of understanding, critique, research, practice, and action. For if we have, then our greatest goal has been met, and we can know—or at least reasonably hope—that the educational needs of our children, whatever we and other concerned citizens might determine them to be, might be met in ways that contemporary school reform efforts often have overlooked, yet in ways that may be fundamental, imperative, and of the utmost educational, psychological, cultural, and societal significance. For the very future of US public schooling (if not all of US society) is at issue. How we see it, and how it sees us, may make all the difference.

❧REFERENCES

Alliance for Childhood. (2001). *High-stakes testing: A statement of concern and call to action.* College Park, MD: Author. (Available on-line: http://www.allianceforchildhood.net/news/histakes_test_position_statement. htm)

Apple, M. W. (1996). *Cultural politics and education.* New York: Teachers College Press.

Apple, R. W. (2001, January 21). News analysis: In the television age, power by image. *The New York Times.* (Available on-line: http://www. nytimes.com)

Ayers, W. (1993). A teacher ain't nothin' but a hero. In P. B. Joseph & G. E. Burnaford (Eds.), *Images of schoolteachers in twentieth-century America: Paragons, polarities, complexities* (pp. 147–156). New York: St. Martin's Press.

Bakhtin, M. (1984). *Problems of Dostoevsky's poetics* (C. Emerson, Ed. & Trans.). Minneapolis: University of Minnesota Press.

Bakhtin, M. M. (1981). *The dialogic imagination: Four essays* (M. Holquist & C. Emerson, Eds. & Trans.). Austin: University of Texas Press.

Barlow, M., & Robertson, H-J. (1997). Homogenization of education. In J. Mander & E. Goldsmith (Eds.), *The case against the global economy: And for a turn toward the local* (pp. 60–70). San Francisco & Washington, DC: Sierra Club Books.

Barthes, R. (1977). *Image/music/text* (S. Heath, Trans.). New York: Hill and Wang.

Bate, J. (2002, January 4). Ballooning inquiries [Review of the book *Curiosity: A cultural history of early modern inquiry* by B. M. Benedict]. *The Times Literary Supplement,* p. 24.

Baudrillard, J. (1987). *Forget Foucault.* New York: Semiotext(e).

Baudrillard, J. (1995). *Simulacra and simulation* (S. F. Glaser, Trans.). Ann Arbor: University of Michigan Press.

Becker, E. (2002a, July 16). Bush is to propose broad new powers in domestic security. *The New York Times,* pp. A1 & A15.

Becker, E. (2002b, July 17). Yeas and nays for Bush's security wish list. *The New York Times,* p. A14.

Benedict, B. M. (2001). *Curiosity: A cultural history of early modern inquiry.* Chicago: University of Chicago Press.

Benjamin, W. (n.d.). *The work of art in the age of mechanical reproduction.* (Available on-line: http://pixels.filmtv.ucla.edu/community/julian_scaff/benjamin/benjamin1.html)

Bennett, T. (1980). Popular culture: A teaching object. *Screen Education, 34,* 18.

Bennett, W. J. (1988). *Our children and our country: Improving America's schools and affirming the common culture.* New York: Simon and Schuster.

Bennett, W. J. (1994). *The de-valuing of America: The fight for our culture and our children.* New York: Touchstone Books.

Berliner, D. C., & Biddle, B. J. (1995). *The manufactured crisis: Myths, fraud, and the attack on America's public schools.* Reading, MA: Addison-Wesley Publishing.

Best, S. (1994). The commodification of reality and the reality of commodification: Baudrillard, Debord, and postmodern theory. In D. Kellner (Ed.), *Baudrillard: A critical reader* (pp. 41–67). Oxford, UK, & Cambridge, MA: Blackwell.

Boorstin, D. J. (1992). *The image: A guide to pseudo-events in America.* New York: Vintage Books. (Original work published 1961)

Borofsky, R. (Ed.). (2001). When: A conversation about culture [special section]. *American Anthropologist, 103,* 432–446.

Bracken, L. (1997). *Guy Debord: Revolutionary.* Venice, CA: Feral House.

Brooks, R. (Director). (1955). *Blackboard jungle* [film]. United States: MGM-UA.

Broudy, H. S. (1989). *The role of imagery in learning.* Los Angeles: Getty Center for Education in the Arts. (Occasional Paper #1)

Brown, B. (1973). *Marx, Freud, and the critique of everyday life: Toward a permanent cultural revolution.* New York: Monthly Review Press.

Brzezinski, M. (2003, February 23). Fortress America. *The New York Times Magazine,* pp. 38–45, 54, 70, & 75–76.

Bumiller, E., & Sanger, D. E. (2002, June 7). Answer to critics. *The New York Times,* pp. A1 & A19.

Burchell, G., Gordon, C., & Miller, P. (Eds.). (1991). *The Foucault effect: Studies in governmentality.* Chicago: University of Chicago Press.

Bush, G. W. (2001). *No child left behind.* Washington, DC: USGPO. (Available online: http://www.ed.gov/inits/nclb/index.html)

[The] Business Roundtable. (2001). *Assessing and addressing the "testing backlash": Practical advice and current public opinion research for business coalitions and standards advocates.* Washington, DC: Author. (Available on-line: http://www.brtable.org/pdf/525.pdf)

Calvert, C. (2000). *Voyeur nation: Media, privacy, and peering in modern culture.* Boulder, CO: Westview Press.

Carton, E. (1989). Better dead than read: The society of poets. *Tikkun,* 4(6), 64–67.

Casella, R. (1999). The theoretical foundations of cultural studies in education. In S. Tozer (Ed.), *Philosophy of education 1998* (pp. 526–534). Urbana, IL: Philosophy of Education Society/University of Illinois at Urbana-Champaign.

Chabon, M. (2002). *Summerland.* New York: Hyperion.

Clark, K., & Holquist, M. (1984). *Mikhail Bakhtin.* Cambridge, MA: Harvard University Press.

Clavell, J. (Director & Writer). (1967). *To sir, with love* [film]. United States: Columbia Pictures.

Coleman, H. (1987). Teaching spectacles and learning festivals. *ELT Journal, 41,* 97–103.

Corn, D. (2002, January 4). The FBI's black magic? *Alternet.org.* (Available on-line: http://www.alternet.org/print.html?StoryID=12163)

Curran, J. (1991a). Mass media and democracy: A reappraisal. In J. Curran & M. Gurevitch (Eds.), *Mass media and society.* New York: Routledge.

Curran, J. (1991b). Rethinking the media as a public sphere. In P. Dahlgren & C. Sparks (Eds.), *Communication and citizenship.* New York: Routledge.

Dalton, M. (1999). *Hollywood curriculum: Teachers and teaching in the movies.* New York: Peter Lang.

Dao, J. (2002, July 29). Panel urges U.S. to revamp efforts to promote image abroad. *The New York Times.* (Available on-line: http://www.nytimes.com)

Debord, G. (1981). Theory of the *dérive.* In K. Knabb (Ed.), *Situationist international anthology* (pp. 50–54). Berkeley, CA: Bureau of Public Secrets. (Original work published 1958 in *Internationale Situationniste #2*)

Debord, G. (1990). *Comments on the society of the spectacle* (M. Imrie, Trans.). London & New York: Verso. (Original work published 1988)

Debord, G. (1995). *The society of the spectacle* (D. Nicholson-Smith, Trans.). New York: Zone Books. (Original work published 1967)

Debord, G., & Wolman, G. J. (1981). Methods of detournement. In K. Knabb (Ed.), *Situationist international anthology* (pp. 8–14). Berkeley, CA: Bureau of Public Secrets. (Original work published 1956 in *Les Lèvres Nues* #8)

de Certeau, M. (1984). *The practice of everyday life* (S. Rendall, Trans.). Berkeley, CA: University of California Press.

Deconstruct this: Webcams. All me, all the time. (2000, December 15). *The Chronicle Review*, p. B4.

Definitions. (1981). In K. Knabb (Ed.), *Situationist international anthology* (pp. 45–46). Berkeley, CA: Bureau of Public Secrets. (Original work published 1958)

Deily, M-E. P. (2002, August 7). Poll charts impact of good schools. *Education Week*. (Available on-line: http://www.educationweek.org/ew/ew_printstory.cfm?slug=43Penpoll.h21)

DeLillo, D. (1997). *Underworld*. New York: Scribner Paperback Fiction/Simon & Schuster.

Department of Education. (1990). *National goals for education*. Washington, DC: USDOE/USGPO.

Department of Education. (1991). *America 2000: An education strategy sourcebook*. Washington, DC: USDOE/USGPO.

Detournement as Negation and Prelude. (1981). In K. Knabb (Ed.), *Situationist international anthology* (pp. 55–56). Berkeley, CA: Bureau of Public Secrets. (Original work published 1959 in *Internationale Situationniste #3*)

Dewey, J. (1956). *The child and the curriculum/The school and society*. Chicago and London: University of Chicago Press. (Original works published 1902 and 1899)

Dewey, J. (1963). *Experience and education*. New York: Collier. (Original work published 1938)

Dewey, J. (1966). *Democracy and education: An introduction to the philosophy of education*. New York: Macmillan. (Original work published 1916)

Dianda, M., McKeon, D., & Kapinus, B. (n.d.). *A tool for auditing standards-based education*. Washington, DC: National Education Association. (Available on-line: http://www.nea.org)

Doherty, T. (2002). *Teenagers and teenpics: The juvenalization of American movies in the 1950s*. Philadelphia: Temple University Press. (Original work published 1988)

Dowd, M. (2002a, January 20). Black berets rising [op-ed]. *The New York Times,* p. 13.

Dowd, M. (2002b, February 24). Coyote rummy [op-ed]. *The New York Times,* p. 13.

Dreyfuss, R. (2002, March 28). Spying on ourselves. *Rolling Stone* (Issue #892), 31–33, 79.

Dumm, T. L. (1996). *Michel Foucault and the politics of freedom.* Thousand Oaks, CA: Sage.

Dyer, R. (2000). Introduction to film studies. In J. Hill & C. Gibson (Eds.), *Film studies: Critical approaches* (pp. 1–8). Oxford, UK: Oxford University Press.

Edelman, R. (1990). Teachers in the movies. *American Educator: The Professional Journal of the American Federation of Teachers, 7*(3), 26–31.

Egan, J. (2002). *Look at me: A novel.* New York: Anchor.

Eilenberg, L. I. (1975). Dramaturgy and spectacle: A proportion. *Journal of Aesthetic Education, 9*(4), 43–53.

Elkins, J. (2001, November 9). The ivory tower of tearlessness. *The Chronicle Review,* pp. B7–B10.

Emmison, M., & Smith, P. (2000). *Researching the visual.* London: Sage.

Farber, P., Provenzo, Jr., E., & Holm, G. (Eds.). (2000). *Schooling in the light of popular culture.* Albany: State University of New York Press.

Fendrich, L. (2002, January 11). Traces of artistry. *The Chronicle Review,* pp. B12–B14.

Fenstermacher, G. D., & Soltis, J. F. (1998). *Approaches to teaching* (3rd ed.). New York and London: Teachers College Press.

Finn, Jr., C. E., & Petrilli, M. J. (2000). *The state of state standards 2000.* The Thomas B. Fordham Foundation. (Available on-line: http://www.edexcellence.net/library/soss2000/standards%202000.html)

Fischman, G. E. (2001). Reflections about images, visual culture, and educational research. *Educational Researcher, 30*(8), 28–33.

Foucault, M. (1979). *Discipline and punish: The birth of the prison* (A. Sheridan, Trans.). New York: Pantheon. (Original work published 1975)

Foucault, M. (1980). *Power/knowledge: Selected interviews and other writings, 1972–1977* (C. Gordon, Ed.). New York: Pantheon.

Foucault, M. (2000). *Power* (Essential works of Michel Foucault, 1965–1984, volume three; J. D. Faubion, Ed.). New York: The New Press.

Freeland, C. A., & Wartenberg, T. E. (1995). *Philosophy and film.* New York and London: Routledge.

Freire, P. (1970). *Pedagogy of the oppressed.* New York: Continuum.

Fukuyama, F. (2002). *Out posthuman future: Consequences of the bio-technology revolution.* New York: Farrar, Straus & Giroux.

Gabler, N. (2002, August 4). Just like a movie, but it's not. *The New York Times,* Section 4, pp. 1 & 3.

Gallup, A. (2000, October 2). *Education: A vital issue in election 2000.* Princeton, NJ: The Gallup Organization. (Available on-line: http://www. gallup.com/poll/releases/pr001002.asp)

Giroux, H. A. (1994a). *Disturbing pleasures: Learning popular culture.* New York and London: Routledge.

Giroux, H. A. (1994b). Doing cultural studies: Youth and the challenge of pedagogy. *Harvard Education Review, 64,* 278–308.

Giroux, H. A., & [with] Shannon, P. (Eds.). (1997). *Education and cultural studies: Toward a performative practice.* New York and London: Routledge.

Giroux, H. A., & Simon, R. (Eds.). (1989). *Popular culture, schooling and everyday life.* New York: Bergin & Garvey.

Gitlin, T. (2002). *Media unlimited: How the torrent of images and sounds overwhelms our lives.* New York and London: Metropolitan Books.

Gleick, J. (2002). *What just happened: A chronicle from the information frontier.* New York: Pantheon.

Goodheart, A. (2000, September 30). Brand-name auctions, cut-rate connoisseurs. *The New York Times,* p. A27.

Gordon, C. (1980). *Power-knowledge: Selected Interviews & Other Writings, 1972–1977.* New York: Pantheon.

Gore, J. M. (1993). *The struggle for pedagogies: Critical and feminist discourses as regimes of truth.* London and New York: Routledge.

Gore, J. M. (1998). Disciplining bodies: On the continuity of power relations in pedagogy. In T. S. Popkewitz & M. Brennan (Eds.), *Foucault's challenge: Discourse, knowledge, and power in education* (pp. 231–251). New York and London: Teachers College Press.

Gould, S. J., & Eldredge, N. (1977). Punctuated equilibria: The tempo and mode of evolution reconsidered. *Paleobiology, 3,* 115–151.

Hall, S. (1992). What is this "black" in popular culture? In G. Dent (Ed.), *Black popular culture* (p. 22). Seattle: Bay Press.

Haney, W. (2000). The myth of the Texas miracle in education. *Education Policy Analysis Archives, 8*(41). (Available on-line: http://epaa.asu.edu/ epaa/v8n41)

Harper, D. (1998). On the authority of the image: Visual methods at the crossroads. In N. Denzin, N. Lincoln, & Y. Lincoln (Eds.), *Collecting and interpreting qualitative materials* (pp. 110–130). Thousands Oaks, CA: Sage.

Heckerling, A. (Director), & Crowe, C. (Writer). (1982). *Fast times at Ridgemont high* [film/VHS]. United States: MCA/Universal Studios.

Herek, S. (Director). (1995). *Mr. Holland's opus* [film]. United States: Hollywood Pictures/Interscope Communications/PolyGram Filmed Entertainment/Buena Vista Pictures.

Herman, E. S., & Chomsky, N. (1988). *Manufacturing consent: The political economy of the mass media.* New York: Pantheon.

Hill, J., & Gibson, P. C. (Eds.). (2000). *Film studies: Critical approaches.* Oxford, UK: Oxford University Press.

Hiller, A. (Director), & McKinney, W. R. (Writer). (1984). *Teachers* [film/VHS]. United States: MGM.

Hirsch, Jr., E. D. (1987). *Cultural literacy: What every American needs to know.* Boston: Houghton Mifflin.

Hirsch, Jr., E. D. (1996). *The schools we need and why we don't have them.* New York: Doubleday.

Hockney, D. (2001). *Secret knowledge: Rediscovering the lost techniques of the old masters.* New York: Viking.

Hoffman, M. (Director). (2002). *The emperor's club* [film]. United States: Universal Pictures.

Hytten, K. (1999a). Cultural studies in education: What's the point? In S. Tozer (Ed.), *Philosophy of education 1998* (pp. 535–537). Urbana, IL: Philosophy of Education Society/University of Illinois at Urbana-Champaign.

Hytten, K. (1999b). The promise of cultural studies of education. *Educational Theory, 49,* 527–543.

Jackson, P. W. (1990). *Life in classrooms.* New York: Teachers College Press. (Original work published 1968).

James, C. (2001, November 4). Television, like the country, loses its footing. *The New York Times,* Section 2, pp. 1, 26–27.

James, C. (2002, March 13). And now, the 16th minute of fame. *The New York Times,* p. B1.

Jappe, A. (1999). *Guy Debord* (D. Nicholson-Smith, Trans.). Berkeley: University of California Press. (Original work published 1993)

Jay, M. (1994). *Downcast eyes: The denigration of vision in twentieth-century French thought.* Berkeley: University of California Press.

Johnson, J., & [with] Duffett, A. (1999, September 30). *Standards and accountability: Where the public stands: A report from Public Agenda for the 1999 National Education Summit.* New York: Public Agenda.

Jones, J. M. (2001, January 10). *Americans rank education as top priority for the Bush Administration.* Princeton, NJ: The Gallup Organization. (Available on-line: http://www.gallup.com/poll/releases/pr010110.asp)

Keane, J. (1991). *The media and democracy.* Stanford, CA: Stanford University Press.

Kellner, D. (Ed.). (1994a). *Baudrillard: A critical reader.* Oxford, UK, & Cambridge, MA: Blackwell.

Kellner, D. (1994b). *Media culture: Cultural studies, identity and politics between the modern and the postmodern.* London: Routledge.

Kellner, D. (1995). Preface. In P. McLaren, R. Hammer, D. Sholle, & S. Reilly, *Rethinking media literacy: A critical pedagogy of representations* (pp. xiii–xvii). New York: Peter Lang.

Kincheloe, J. L., Steinberg, S., & Weil, D. (Eds.). (2001). *Schooling and standards in the United States: An encyclopedia.* New York: ABC/Clio.

King, R. (2002). *Domino.* New York: Walker & Company. (Original work published 1995)

Klein, S. P., Hamilton, L. S., McCaffrey, D. F., & Stecher, B. M. (2000). *What do test scores in Texas tell us?* Santa Monica, CA: The Rand Corporation. (Available on-line: http://www.rand.org/publications/IP/IP202)

Knabb, K. (Ed. & Trans.). (1981). *Situationist international anthology.* Berkeley, CA: Bureau of Public Secrets.

Kohn, A. (1999). *The schools our children deserve: Moving beyond traditional classrooms and "tougher standards."* Boston: Houghton Mifflin.

Kohn, A. (2000). *The case against standardized testing: Raising the scores, ruining the schools.* Portsmouth, NH: Heinemann.

Lefebvre, H. (1971). *Everyday life in the modern world* (S. Rabinovitch, Trans.). London: Allen Lane/The Penguin Press. (Original work published 1968)

Lefebvre, H. (1992). *Critique of everyday life, volume* I (J. Moore, Trans.). London & New York: Verso. (Original work published 1947)

Leslie, E. (n.d.). *The world as thing and image.* (Available on-line: http://www.militantesthetix.co.uk/opticwb.html)

Levin, H. M. (1998). Educational performance standards and the economy. *Educational Researcher, 27*(4), 4–10.

Lubow, A. (2003, February 16). Architects in theory. *The New York Times Magazine,* 36–41.

Luhmann, N. (2000). *The reality of the mass media* (K. Cross, Trans.). Stanford, CA: Stanford University Press. (Original work published 1996)

McBride, T. (2002, May 31). Curiously average: The way we teach now. *The Chronicle Review,* p. B5.

McGinn, C. (2002, May 5). Machine dreams. *The New York Times Book Review,* p. 11.

McGrath, C. (2003, March 9). Our snoopy pups [The way we live now]. *The New York Times Magazine,* 15–16.

McLaren, P., Hammer, R., Sholle, D., & Reilly, S. S. (1995). *Rethinking media literacy: A critical pedagogy of representations.* New York: Peter Lang.

McLuhan, M. (1994). *Understanding media: The extensions of man.* New York: McGraw-Hill. (Original work published 1964)

McNamee, T. (2002, June 23). The joy of cooking [Review of the book *The fourth star* by L. Brenner]. *The New York Times Book Review,* p. 8.

McNeil, L. M. (2000). *Contradictions of school reform: Educational costs of standardized testing.* New York and London: Routledge.

Maeroff, G. I. (Ed.). (1998). *Imaging education: The media and schools in America.* New York: Teachers College Press.

Maier, P., Smith, M. R., & Keyssar, A. (2002). *Inventing America.* New York: W. W. Norton.

Mander, J., & Goldsmith, E. (Eds.). (1997). *The case against the global economy: And for a turn toward the local.* San Francisco & Washington, DC: Sierra Club Books.

Marcus, G. (1989). *Lipstick traces: A secret history of the twentieth century.* Cambridge, MA: Harvard University Press.

Marcus, G. (1997). *The dustbin of history.* London: Picador. (Original work published 1995)

Mathison, S. (2001). Assessment in social studies: Moving toward authenticity. In E. W. Ross (Ed.), *The social studies curriculum: Purposes, problems, and possibilities* (rev. ed.; pp. 217–234). Albany: SUNY Press.

Mathison, S., & Ross, E. W. (2002, October). The hegemony of account-ability. *Workplace: The Journal for Academic Labor.* (Available on-line: http://www.louisville.edu/journal/workplace/issue5p1/mathison.html)

Matthews, J. H. (1975). Spectacle and poetry: Surrealism in theatre and cinema. *Journal of General Education, 27,* 55–68.

Menéndez, R. (Director). (1987). *Stand and deliver* [film]. United States: American Playhouse/Warner Brothers.

Miller-Kahn, L., & Smith, M. L. (2001, November 30). School choice policies in the political spectacle. *Educational Policy Analysis Archives, 9*(50). Retrieved 2001, December 15 from http://epaa.asu.edu/epaa/v9n50.html.

Mirzoeff, N. (Ed.). (1998). *The visual culture reader.* New York: Rout-ledge.

Mirzoeff, N. (1999). *An introduction to visual culture.* New York: Rout-ledge.

Mitchell, A. (2002, July 28). The perilous search for security at home. *The New York Times.* (Available on-line: http://www.nytimes.com)

Morson, G. S., & Emerson, C. (1990). *Mikhail Bakhtin: Creation of a prosaics.* Stanford, CA: Stanford University Press.

Murphy, M. (2002, October 14). Yes to TUSD board members who have been teachers [letter to the editor]. *Arizona Daily Star,* p. B6.

Nash, G. B., Crabtree, C., & Dunn, R. E. (1997). *History on trial: Culture wars and the teaching of the past.* New York: Knopf.

National Center for Education Statistics (2000, November). *Dropout rates in the United States: 1999.* Washington, DC: US Department of Education/Office of Educational Research and Improvement (Report NCES 2001–022). (Available on-line: http://nces.ed.gov/pubs2001/2001022.pdf)

National Commission on Excellence in Education. (1983). *A nation at risk: The imperative for educational reform.* Washington, DC: USGPO.

Neame, R. (Director). (1969). *The prime of Miss Jean Brodie* [film]. United States: 20th Century Fox.

Nelmes, J. (Ed.). (1999). *An introduction to film studies* (2nd ed.). London and New York: Routledge.

No Child Left Behind. (2001, January 31). *Education Week.* (Available on-line: http://www.edweek.org/ew/ew_printstory.cfm?slug=20bushbox.h2 0)

[The] *No Child Left Behind Act of 2001* [Executive Summary]. (2001, January). (Available on-line: http://www.ed.gov/offices/OESE/esea/exec-summ.html)

Ohanian, S. (1999). *One size fits few: The folly of educational standards.* Portsmouth, NH: Heinemann.

Ohanian, S. (2002). *What happened to recess and why are our children struggling in kindergarten?* New York: McGraw-Hill.

Ollman, B. (2001). *How to take an exam...and remake the world.* Montreal/New York/ London: Black Rose Books.

Olsen, L. (2001, January 31). Few states are now in line with Bush testing plan. *Education Week.* (Available on-line: http://www.edweek.org/ew/ew_printstory.cfm?slug=20test.ht20)

O'Reilly, S. (2002, June/July). Philosophy and the panopticon. *Philosophy Now,* pp. 22–23.

Pedersen, K. (2002, October 14). Labels are unfair [letter to the editor]. *Arizona Daily Star,* p. B6.

Perez, G. (1998). *The material ghost: Films and their medium.* Baltimore, MD, and London: The Johns Hopkins University Press.

Perlman, F. (1969). *The reproduction of everyday life.* (Available on-line: http://www.pipeline.com/~rgibson/repro-daily-life.html)

Peterson, M., Beloin, K., & Gibson, R. (1998). *Whole schooling: Education for a democratic society.* Detroit: Renaissance Community Press. (Available on-line: http://www.coe.wayne.edu/CommunityBuilding/WSPaper.html)

Piper, K. (2002). *Cartographic fictions: Maps, race, and identity.* Piscataway, NJ: Rutgers University Press (cited in "Melange," *The Chronicle Review,* June 21, 2002, B4).

Plant, S. (1992). *The most radical gesture: The Situationist International in a postmodern age.* London & New York: Routledge.

Polan, D. B. (1986). "Above all else to make you see": Cinema and the ideology of spectacle. In J. Arac (Ed.), *Postmodernism and politics* (pp. 55–69). Minneapolis: University of Minnesota Press.

PollingReport.Com. (2002). *Problems and priorities.* (Available on-line: http://www.pollingreport.com/prioriti.htm)

Popham, W. J. (2001). *The truth about testing: An educator's call to action.* Alexandria, VA: Association for Supervision and Curriculum Development.

Popkewitz, T. S, & Brennan, M. (Eds.). (1998). *Foucault's challenge: Discourse, knowledge, and power in education.* New York and London: Teachers College Press.

Prosser, J. (1998). The status of image-based research. In J. Prosser (Ed.), *Image-based research* (pp. 97–113). London: Falmer Press.

Ravitch, D. (1995). *National standards in American education: A citizen's guide.* Washington, DC: Brookings Institution Press.

Ravitch, D. (2000). *Left back: A century of failed school reforms.* New York: Simon & Schuster.

Ravitch, D., & Finn, Jr., C. E. (1987). *What do our 17-year-olds know? A report of the first national assessment of history and literature.* New York: Harper & Row.

Reid, S. A. (2001, August 13). New watchful eyes peer into schools: Video cameras will be on when Atlanta students return to class. *Atlanta Journal-Constitution.* (Available on-line: http://www.accessatlanta.com/ajc/metro/back_to_school/cameras.html)

Reynolds, K. (Director). (1997). *187* [film]. United States: Warner Brothers.

Rich, F. (2000, October 29). The age of the mediathon. *The New York Times Magazine,* pp. 58–65, 84.

Rich, F. (2003, June 15). How 15 minutes became 5 weeks. *The New York Times,* section 2, pp. 1 & 8.

Robelen, E. W. (2001a, January 10). Bush promises swift action on education. *Education Week.* (Available on-line: http://www.edweek.org/ew/ew_printstory.cfm?slug=16prez.h20)

Robelen, E. W. (2001b, January 31). Democrats, GOP agree in principle on federal role. *Education Week.* (Available on-line: http://www.edweek.org/ew/ew_printstory.cfm?slug=20bush.h20)

Rogoff, I. (1998). Studying visual culture. In N. Mirzoeff (Ed.), *The visual culture reader* (pp. 24–26). New York: Routledge.

Roman, L. (1996). Spectacle in the dark: Youth as transgression, display, and repression. *Educational Theory, 38,* 95–109.

Rose, L. C., & Gallup, A. M. (2002). The 34th annual Phi Delta Kappa/Gallup poll of the public's attitude toward the public schools. *Phi Delta Kappan.* (Available on-line: http://www.pdkintl.org/kappan/k0209pol/htm)

Rosen, J. (2000). *The unwanted gaze: The destruction of privacy in America.* New York: Random House.

Ross, E. W. (2000). The spectacle of standards and summits. *Z Magazine, 12*(3), 45–48.

Rothstein, E. (2000, November 18). Turning private and public inside out. *The New York Times*, pp. A21 & A23.

Saad, L. (2002, September 4). *Grade school receives best parent ratings.* The Gallup Organization. (Available on-line: http://www.gallup.com/poll/releases/pr020904.asp)

Sardar, Z., & Van Loon, B. (2000). *Introducing media studies.* New York: Totem Books.

Sassen, S. (2002, September 20). [In] The cutting edge in geography, math, information technologies, criticism [The Short List/The Next Big Thing]. *The Chronicle Review,* p. B4.

Schrag, F. (1995). *Back to basics: Fundamental educational questions reexamined.* Hoboken, NJ: Jossey-Bass.

Schudson, M. (1997). Paper tigers: A sociologist follows cultural studies into the wilderness. *Lingua Franca, 7*(6), 49–56.

Schwartz, J. (2001, February 8). Fighting crime online: Who is in harm's way? *The New York Times*, pp. D1 & D8.

Senese, G., & Page, R. (1995). *Simulation, spectacle, and the ironies of educational reform.* Westport, CT: Bergin & Garvey.

Sholle, D., & Denski, S. (1994). *Media education and the reproduction of culture.* Westport, CT: Bergin & Garvey.

Shulevitz, J. (2001, February 25). The romance of real estate. *The New York Times Book Review*, p. 31.

Sieminski, G. C. (1995, Autumn). The art of naming operations. *Parameters* (US Army War College Quarterly), pp. 81–98. (Available on-line: http://carlisle-www.army.mil/usawc/parameters/1995/sieminsk.htm)

Simpson, G. R. (2001, April 13). Big brother-in-law: If the FBI hopes to get the goods on you, it may ask ChoicePoint. *The Wall Street Journal*, pp. A1 & A6.

Singer, P. (2002, October 11). Navigating the ethics of globalization. *The Chronicle Review*, pp. B7–B10.

Smith, J. N. (Director). (1995). *Dangerous minds* [film]. United States: Buena Vista Pictures.

Smith, S. (2001, August 12). Phenomenon: Sitcom spirituals: American churches are finding inspiration for their Bible study groups from an unexpected source: TV sitcoms. *The New York Times Magazine*, pp. 18 & 20.

Sontag, S. (1977). *On photography*. New York: Farrar, Strauss, & Giroux.

Spectacular Times. (n. d.). Images. (Available on-line: http://www.cat.org.au/spectacular/images.html)

Spring, J. H. (1999). *The intersection of cultures: Multicultural education in the United States and the global economy* (2nd ed.). New York: WCB/McGraw-Hill.

Steinberg, S. (1995). Strategies for media literacy [Shirley Steinberg interviews Rhonda Hammer, Susan Reilly, David Sholle, & Peter McLaren]. In P. McLaren, R. Hammer, D. Sholle, & S. S. Reilly, *Rethinking media literacy: A critical pedagogy of representations* (pp. 225–259). New York: Peter Lang.

Steinberg, S. R., & Kincheloe, J. L. (Eds.). (1997). *Kinderculture: The corporate construction of childhood*. Boulder, CO: Westview Press.

Stiglitz, J. E. (2002). *Globalization and its discontents*. New York: W. W. Norton.

Storey, J. (Ed.). (1994). *Cultural theory and popular culture: A reader*. Hemel Hempstead, UK: Harvester Wheatsheaf.

Storey, J. (Ed.). (1996). *What is cultural studies: A reader*. London: Edward Arnold.

Storey, J. (1998). *An introduction to cultural theory and popular culture* (2nd ed.). Athens: University of Georgia Press.

Stutz, T. (2001, March 23). State warns of massive test failures: Schools told to prepare. *The Dallas Morning News* [DallasNews.com]. (Available on-

line: http://www.dallasnews.com/texas_southwest/319246_1Aexam_23tex.
A.html)

Sussman, E. (Ed.). (1989). *On the passage of a few people through a rather brief moment in time.* Cambridge, MA, & London: The MIT Press.

Swift, P. (2002, February 1). Finding the philosophers' stone in Las Vegas. *The Chronicle Review,* p. B5.

Tester, K. (Ed.). (1994). *The flâneur.* New York: Routledge.

Tseëlon, E. (1994). Fashion and signification in Baudrillard. In D. Kellner (Ed.), *Baudrillard: A critical reader* (pp. 119–132). Oxford, UK, & Cambridge, MA: Blackwell.

Tucker, M. S., & Codding, J. B. (1998). *Standards for our schools: How to set them, measure them, and reach them.* San Francisco: Jossey-Bass.

Tumulty, K. (2002, June 17). Inside Bush's big plan. *Time,* 30–34.

Tyler, P. E. (2002, June 7). Reaction, then action. *The New York Times,* pp. A1 & A18.

Updike, J. (2003, May 15). American icons: Andy Warhol. *Rolling Stone,* p. 112.

Vaneigem, R. (1972). *The revolution of everyday life* (J. Fullerton & P. Sieveking, Trans.). (Original work published 1967). (Available on-line: http://www.subsitu.com/kr/ROEL.htm)

Vaneigem, R. (2002). *The revolution of everyday life* (D. Nicholson-Smith, Trans.). London: Rebel Press. (Original work published 1967)

Vinson, K. D. (1999). National curriculum standards and social studies education: Dewey, Freire, Foucault, and the construction of a radical critique. *Theory and Research in Social Education, 27,* 50–82.

Vinson, K. D. (2001a). Image, authenticity, and the collective good: The problematics of standards-based reform. *Theory and Research in Social Education, 29,* 363–374.

Vinson, K. D. (2001b, April). *Pursuing image: Making sense of popular pedagogical representations.* Poster session presented at the annual meeting of the American Educational Research Association [Culture, Media, and Curriculum SIG], Seattle, WA.

Vinson, K. D. (2001c). Oppression, anti-oppression, and citizenship education. In E. W. Ross (Ed.), *The social studies curriculum: Purposes, problems, and possibilities* (rev. ed.; pp. 57–83). Albany: SUNY Press.

Vinson, K. D. (2002, April). *The end of the panopticon? Baudrillard & Debord—A critique of Foucault's disciplinarity.* Roundtable discussion presented at the annual meeting of the American Educational Research Association [Foucault & Education SIG], New Orleans, LA.

Vinson, K. D., Gibson, R., & Ross, E. W. (2001). *High-stakes testing and standardization: The threat to authenticity.* Burlington, VT: John Dewey Project on Progressive Education/University of Vermont. (Available on-line: http://www.uvm.edu/%7edewey/monographs/ProPer3n2.html)

Vinson, K. D., & Ross, E. W. (2001a). In search of the social studies curriculum: Standardization, diversity, and a conflict of appearances. In W. B. Stanley (Ed.), *Critical issues in social studies research for the 21st century* (pp. 39–71). Greenwich, CT: Information Age Publishing.

Vinson, K. D., & Ross, E. W. (2001b). Social education and standards-based reform: A critique. In J. L. Kincheloe, S. Steinberg, & D. Weil (Eds.), *Schooling and standards in the United States: An encyclopedia* (pp. 909–927). New York: ABC/Clio.

Vinson, K. D., & Ross, E. W. (2001c, March). What we can know and when we can know it: Education reform, testing, and the standardization craze. *Z Magazine,* pp. 34–38.

Vinson, K. D., & Ross, E. W. (2001d, April). *Education and the new disciplinarity: Surveillance, spectacle, and the case of SBER..* Roundtable discussion presented at the annual meeting of the American Educational Research Association [Foucault & Education SIG], Seattle, WA.

Vinson, K. D., & Ross, E. W. (2001e). Education and the new disciplinarity: Surveillance, spectacle, and the case of SBER. *Cultural Logic: Marxist Theory & Practice, 4*(1). (Available on-line: http://eserver.org/clogic/4-1/vinson%26ross.html)

Vinson, K. D., & Ross, E. W. (2003). Controlling images: The power of high-stakes testing. In K. J. Saltman & D. A. Gabbard (Eds.), *Education as enforcement: The militarization and corporatization of schools* (pp. 241–257). New York and London: Routledge.

Wadsworth, D. (1998). Do media shape public perceptions of America's schools. In G. I. Maeroff (Ed.), *Imaging education: The media and schools in America* (pp. 59–68). New York: Teachers College Press.

Waters, M. (2001). *Globalization* (2nd ed.). New York: Routledge.

Weil, D. (in press). Howard Gardner's third way: Toward a post-formal redefinition of educational psychology. *Taboo.*

Weir, P. (Director). (1989). *Dead poets' society.* United States: Touchstone Pictures/Buena Vista Pictures.

Wells, A. S., & Serman, T. W. (1998). Education against all odds: What films teach us about schools. In G. I. Maeroff (Ed.), *Imaging education: The media and schools in America* (pp. 181–194). New York: Teachers College Press.

White, E. (2001). *The flaneur: A stroll through the paradoxes of Paris.* Bloomsbury Publishing Plc.: New York.

Wild, D. (2002, December 26–2003 January 9). Joni Mitchell. *Rolling Stone,* p. 28.

Wolf, R. M. (1998). National standards: Do we need them? *Educational Researcher, 27*(4), 22–25.

Wood, S. (Director). (1939). *Goodbye, Mr. Chips* [film]. United States: MGM.

Xingjian, G. (2000). *Soul mountain* (M. Lee, Trans.). New York: HarperCollins.

Young, I. M. (1992). Five faces of oppression. In T. E. Wartenberg (Ed.), *Rethinking power* (p. 174–195). Albany: SUNY Press.

❊INDEX

-C-

-D-

eXtreme teaching
rigorous texts for troubled times

Joe L. Kincheloe and Danny Weil
General Editors

Books in this series will provide practical ideas on classroom practice for teachers and teacher educators that are grounded in a profound understanding of the social, cultural, political, economic, historical, philosophical, and psychological contexts of education as well as in a keen sense of educational purpose. Within these contextual concerns contributors will address the ferment, uncertainty, and confusion that characterize the troubles of contemporary education. The series will focus specifically on the act of teaching. While the topics addressed may vary, EXtreme Teaching is ultimately a book series that addresses new, rigorous, and contextually informed modes of classroom practice. Authors will bring together a commitment to educational and social justice with a profound understanding of a rearticulation of what constitutes compelling scholarship. The series is based on the insight that the future of progressive educational reform rests at the intersection of socio-educational justice and scholarly rigor. Authors will present their conceptions of this rigorous new pedagogical frontier in an accessible manner that avoids the esoteric language of an "in group." In this context, the series editors will make use of their pedagogical expertise to introduce pedagogical ideas to student, teacher, and professional audiences. In this process, they will explain what they consider the basic concepts of a field of study, developing their own interpretive insights about the domain and how it should develop in the future. Very few progressive texts exist to introduce individuals to rigorous and complex conceptions of pedagogical practice: thus, authors will be expected to use their contextualized interpretive imaginations to introduce readers to a creative and progressive view of pedagogy in the field being analyzed.

For additional information about this series or for the submission of manuscripts, please contact:

Joe L. Kincheloe & Danny Weil
c/o Peter Lang Publishing, Inc.
275 Seventh Avenue, 28th floor
New York, New York 10001

To order other books in this series, please contact our Customer Service Department:
(800) 770-LANG (within the U.S.)
(212) 647-7706 (outside the U.S.)
(212) 647-7707 FAX

Or browse online by series at *www.peterlangusa.com*